THE WORKS OF
KARLHEINZ
STOCKHAUSEN

THE WORKS OF
KARLHEINZ
STOCKHAUSEN

ROBIN
MACONIE

With a Foreword by
Karlheinz Stockhausen

MARION BOYARS
LONDON · BOSTON

Published simultaneously in Great Britain and USA by
Marion Boyars Ltd., 18 Brewer Street, London W1R 4AS
and
Marion Boyars Inc., 99 Main Street, Salem, New Hampshire 03079

Australian and New Zealand distribution by
Thomas C. Lothian, 4–12 Tattersalls Lane, Melbourne, Victoria 3000

© 1976 Oxford University Press
This reprint has been authorised by the Oxford University Press

British Library Cataloguing in Publication Data
Maconie, Robin, The Works of Karlheinz Stockhausen.
1. Stockhausen, Karlheinz
I. Title
785'.092   ML410.S858
ISBN 0–7145–2706–8

Library of Congress Catalog Card Number 79–56837

Printed in Great Britain by
Robert MacLehose and Co. Ltd.
Printers to the University of Glasgow

Foreword
by Karlheinz Stockhausen

ROBIN MACONIE leads the reader through my work like a travel guide. He offers an overall and coherent view. The music is experienced through his eyes and ears, as one who has inhabited this musical world for many years.

Let no one suppose that the composer may be better able to interpret the musical vibrations transmitted through him, than a commentator who immerses himself, body and soul, in this music. All the commentaries that have ever been, and those yet to be written, all the thoughts and dreams and impressions and visions and actions which my music arouses in its hearers, all these, no less, add up to the 'meaning' of this music —something which must always remain largely a mystery, never totally to be comprehended by a single individual. The resonance is different in every person, for each stands on a different rung of the ladder of spiritual self-enhancement.

Knowledge of this music must therefore come via a mind which has thought long and deeply about it. It must be obvious to everyone that each individual must work out his own view of the music he loves, and that a Maconie by his side can only give him a certain amount of help. But there are very few who can manage it with no help at all . . .

Maconie has left many questions open, and these the lover of my music must find out for himself:

Am I a newcomer in musical history, or am I a reincarnation of an earlier composer? Are the superficial parallels between my music and the music of other cultures perhaps grounded in experiences of my earlier lives on this planet?

What are the distinctively *new* vibrations and rhythms in my music, and what laws of the Universe are transmitted in them? To what spiritual planes do the different works, or isolated events from individual works, aspire? To what level of awareness do they bring us?

What are the underlying moods of particular works? Which is the appropriate state of feeling for listening to a given work? Which works are expressly spiritual in tone, that is to say music of praise, prayer, and thanksgiving to God? In which is the spirituality more hidden?

Which works appeal more directly to the physical being, the feelings and sufferings of sensory existence, and which more to the transcendental life of the spirit? Or is a balance of sorts discernible overall between the vibrations and rhythms of the beast and the angel in man?

Which pieces *sing* more than others, which transport us to worlds far removed from our planet? Which works allow us to experience the way of life of much smaller creatures, down to the smallest micro-organism? Which enable us to traverse great distances with the stride and breath of giants, to fly with giant wings?

In which work has the Prince of Satania, Master Lucifer, insinuated himself with his brilliant wit and glittering alchemy? Which works, which parts of works allow us, like a child seeking protection, to cling to God's foot, snug and content in the certain knowledge of complete security?

Where sounds the voice of Prophecy?

Where the voice of Divine Humour?

Kürten, 30 January 1976

Preface

Among living composers Karlheinz Stockhausen is pre-eminent. After an early life of considerable hardship he is now, in a material sense, reasonably secure. A hard-working and prodigiously inventive composer, he is also his own most active publicist, as author, lecturer, conductor, and recording artist and supervisor. Ironically much of the respect he has earned by these efforts is tinged with the sceptical envy usually accorded to self-made men. His music is still little understood, and while his influence is generally acknowledged, his reputation, for one who is undoubted heir to the tradition of Mahler and Schoenberg, remains a prey to rational unbelief and ineffectual enthusiasm.

I have not the slightest doubt that were Stockhausen suddenly to vanish from our midst a great deal of the diffidence with which he is at present regarded would mysteriously vanish, and that we should witness an immediate upsurge of critical interest in the man and his music (though probably the artist-as-prophet more than the musician). But to deny an artist of Stockhausen's stature a measure of sustained critical attention while he is at the height of his powers seems not merely uncharitable but shortsighted too. The composer gains from public interest in his music, and we gain some insight into how the artist's mind works while he is actually working among us (which itself may spur him to greater achievement).

I have attempted to write this book from the viewpoint of a commentator in the future. The difference between present and future critical perspectives is that the former is characteristically an expression of doubt, the latter an affirmation of belief. It seemed only reasonable, for instance, to accept in principle that Stockhausen knows what he is doing, and means what he says. I have also assumed that the pattern of his compositional development is logically continuous, that his earliest pieces were subject to outside influences, and that his later works represent progressive refinements of earlier ideas. My method has been, therefore, first to reconstruct the conditions under which Stockhausen worked, and then to interpret his music as a response, or rather a series of responses, to these changing conditions.

Stockhausen's own writings, which are numerous, I have also interpreted both as studies of interest in themselves and as a parallel account of his creative development. In his early working notes in particular, Stockhausen is apt to turn personal observation or conjecture into general statement couched in more or less scientific terminology;

the result is that the reader looks for consistent criteria and logical progression of argument, instead of consistency of approach and objective in a series of differing situations. Most of his seemingly theoretical writings are in fact reports on the practical implications for music of organizational hypotheses derived from other disciplines. Moreover, the central issue of any one paper almost invariably refers to one or more compositions upon which the composer is working at the time.

If his working notes are over-generalized, his programme notes are rather too specific. When he writes publicly about a work, Stockhausen tends to confine his (and the reader's) attention exclusively to that one work. Of its place in the context of the composer's development, its history or motivation, little is consciously divulged. This perturbed me at first, since it seemed to indicate not that connections between works did not exist, but that he would rather they weren't publicly known. It is a delicate question. Stockhausen's music is an extremely clear barometer of his affections, and at times contextual analysis brings one to a point where to proceed further might appear an invasion of privacy. An obvious instance is the text cycle *From the Seven Days*; in *Kontakte* and *Mikrophonie II* the undercurrents of drama are not so apparent, but are there all the same.

As a general introduction to the composer this book will serve, I trust, tolerably well on its own. The student, however, is recommended to read Stockhausen's texts as primary and mine as commentary, for I have endeavoured to make the two complement each other, by avoiding excessive duplication of either fact or opinion. Mine is not meant as a definitive study. It is rather a speculative view of the whole of Stockhausen's creative development to the present time, intended to allay ordinary suspicions and, it is hoped, stimulate those better qualified than myself into more detailed research. I shall be well satisfied if these aims are achieved.

Acknowledgements

To the composer, to Richard Toop, Jonathan Cott, Joachim Krist, and Robert Slotover, for patient help and advice, many thanks; to Mia Herrmann of Universal Edition, London, to Messrs. Boosey and Hawkes for permission to reproduce music examples from Bartók: Sonata for Two Pianos and Percussion, and the Second Violin Concerto, to Messrs. Robson Books for permission to quote extensively from Jonathan Cott: *Stockhausen: Conversations with the Composer*, my sincere gratitude; finally to John M. Thomson, whose paternal interest and example have been a constant support and inspiration, most hearty thanks.

The examples from Stockhausen's musical works are quoted by permission of Universal Edition, Vienna, and for numbers 30 onwards by permission of Stockhausen-Verlag, 5073 Kürten, West Germany.

Contents

To Shar

Introduction

GREAT composers who are also men of influence are always few in number, and the number seems to remain constant in spite of natural and technological increases in the musical population. 'Creative talent certainly seems to be spreading thinner,' remarked Stravinsky in a mischievous aside, 'if only to support the hypothesis that diffusion is necessarily followed by corresponding loss of density.' Now Stravinsky is gone, and the number of living composers whose progress consistently attracts the professional attention of their contemporaries as well as the admiration of a large public following may be counted on the fingers of one hand. Karlheinz Stockhausen, Pierre Boulez, and Luciano Berio belong to this distinguished group. All three are survivors of a period of radical innovation in music as influential in its field as the Bauhaus in painting and design. The movement was a post-war, European development ('European' in the 'Common Market' as well as the geographical sense), centred on the new music festivals of Darmstadt and Donaueschingen. Its leaders all belonged to the then younger generation, served their apprenticeships together, and for some years applied their skills to solving common problems of musical form-building. The unusual closeness of their association certainly contributed to their early rise to fame, and probably accounts in part for the extraordinary durability of their leadership. They have been a considerable force in music for the best part of twenty years. How much the success of any one of them rests upon individual genius, and how much upon the corporate authority of the group, is a moot point. That they depended upon one another for moral support, and were popularly identified as members of a group rather than as individuals, is certainly true. A shared sense of mission made them noticed; at a time when an older generation of composers was hopefully waiting for recognition (with the war over, and Schoenberg dead, what was to prevent a revival of tonality?) the younger generation alone knew what had to be done, had the courage and the energy to undertake it, and an evangelical conviction of its social importance. This corporate sense of purpose gave them an edge over their sceptical elders, and sustains their authority still over a present new generation of composers who have never experienced, individually or collectively, the intense spiritual excitement of being in at the beginning of a new era in musical history.

This is not to deny the influence of some senior composers on the direction of new developments. The influence of Olivier Messiaen on the young, as composer of the visionary proto-serial *Études de Rythme*, and as teacher (at different times) of both Boulez and Stockhausen, has been profound. Messiaen's concepts of rhythm and form, and to a lesser extent his style of gesture and characteristic opulence of orchestration, have all left their mark on the new music. To his outstanding qualities of aural sensitivity (Messiaen's sound-world is exceedingly animated) and ritual order, Boulez and Stockhausen have added their own exceptional capacity for formal invention and instrumental innovation. More intellectually disciplined than Messiaen's, their music also tends to have greater range and stamina. All the same, many of the younger composers' more startling inventions were prefigured in their teacher's work. To take only two examples, both the formal intricacies of Stockhausen's *Klavierstück XI* and Boulez's strangely elusive tempi compare with features of Messiaen's style of organ writing. There are many more technical similarities.

John Cage is another key figure whose importance to the new music may be said to exceed what his own music has accomplished. Cage's main contribution to the new way of thinking was to shift attention from the musical end-product to the compositional process. This change of emphasis, manifested in a new open-mindedness, a sort of suspension of disbelief towards the musical outcome of a system of choice, enabled composers to work confidently even though they might not have any clear idea what the sound result would be. Cage's example curiously enough restored abstract form to a position of importance by making it unnecessary for form to refer to historical convention or even individual taste. Ironically, his cultivation of indifference, whether we call it a religious impartiality or quasi-scientific detachment, ended by estranging him from music as an art of intervention.

If, then, Messiaen and Cage provided the incentives and theories for the new style of music, it has been the achievement of the Darmstadt group to make those principles work. It was not an easy task. Everything involved in the process of encoding and decoding sound had to be examined anew. Old forms of notation were reinterpreted, and new conventions introduced to make a terminology as 'functional' as possible, reduced to exactly quantified essentials. The young composers took encouragement from the discovery that Webern in his later years had been patiently working towards a similar ideal. But Webern never lost sight of the fact that notation is relative; the younger composers had to learn by trial and error that serial refinements of dynamics, attacks, or durations could not be taken very far before becoming mutually contradictory. Even today the search for an adequate notation has not been satisfactorily concluded, but we may be sure that exposure to the limitations of notation at an early stage of their development gave many young composers a depth of appreciation of the formal and expressive properties of their materials which would not normally be acquired until after a lifetime's experience.

In the sixties their paths began to diverge. While some of their contemporaries have allowed their conspicuous talents to be diverted to political ends, Berio has acquired a reputation for music of sophisticated charm, and Boulez for a glittering and pungent sensuality. Only Stockhausen seems as restless as ever, and his music as unpredictable. The image of an untiring revolutionary is attractively topical, perhaps, and may account for Stockhausen's growing acceptance by enthusiasts of 'progressive rock' music. On the other hand, his bewildering variety of output is all too easily attributed by bemused and sceptical observers to a fundamental instability of character (and his forceful manner, even more unpleasantly, to dictatorial paranoia). But the real difference between the consistency that has emerged in the music of Berio and Boulez, and the consistency we cannot see in Stockhausen, is a difference of spiritual location. Whereas the former pair are essentially instrumental composers who have made sporadic sallies into the electronic field, Stockhausen is basically an electronic composer who makes regular incursions into instrumental music. The ordinary listener and student who is not intimately acquainted with the alien techniques and modes of expression of electronic music is at a loss to understand many of Stockhausen's innovations in the instrumental sphere which arise directly from his synthesis of the two disciplines. In the studio the composer encounters the age-old conflict of expression versus imagination raised to a new peak of intensity. Symptomatic of the conflict is the sense of a discrepancy between what the composer appears to have intended and what (however interesting) he has actually achieved. It is a difficulty Cage tends to sidestep by professing to accept any number of possible interpretations of an extempore work as equally valid; when one is left unsure about even his general intentions (other than to illuminate or divert), the question whether they are—or can ever be—effectively realized remains unanswerable. But with Stockhausen one *is* able to identify particular expressive intentions with some certainty, and as a result more readily notice modifications of the original concept in the final work and deviations in performance. There is evidence, for instance, that the composer's first hopes for his early electronic studies did not materialize; one may query whether, or how, *Zeitmasze* can be made to fulfil the implications of its title ('Different tempi superimposed but distinguishable')—though the question here seems to be one of performance rather than concept; again, I suspect that *Mixtur*'s ring modulators did not turn out to work in quite the way the composer intended.

But whatever the reason for a particular discrepancy, all tend ultimately to refer back to something more fundamental, the problem of translating ideas and techniques learned in the studio into live performance situations. The composer's principal difficulty lies in reconciling a neutral, self-effacing technology with the self-expressive demands of the performing art. The problem is not peculiar to Stockhausen's music but lives in it at a peculiar intensity simply because, working in both fields, the composer draws inspiration from the conflict of techniques, seeking to confront it afresh in every work rather than regarding it as a drawback to be gradually eliminated. Though the area of interaction between studio thought and instrumental practice may be readily identified for a particular work, it would be wrong to judge the work merely on whether it resolved the technical point at issue. Knowing the theoretical situation of a work may help the listener to understand it, but the work is much more than an exposition of theory: it is music as well, after all. On the other hand, one may feel justified in preferring those pieces like *Zyklus, Refrain, Mikrophonie I,* and *Mantra* which are triumphantly successful on both musical and theoretical planes. But more important than success is the palpable presence of the conflict in Stockhausen's œuvre, for it is this opposition of expressive intention and technical limitation that makes the listener pause and consider. Stockhausen is not a composer of empty reassurances, but a philosopher in sound whose role is to rediscover and reformulate questions of perception upon which our survival as sentient beings depends. It takes talent to know what these are, but it takes genius to give them expression.

*   *   *

Karlheinz Stockhausen was born on 22 August 1928 in Mödrath near Cologne. His father was Simon Stockhausen, his mother Gertrud, *née* Stupp. He was the first of three children. Both parents were of country stock, but had risen to positions of respect in the village, though the family was poor. His father taught in a school at the neighbouring village of Reid; the little we know of his mother suggests that she was sensitive and musical. Though he seems to have inherited his father's appetite for study and his mother's musical nature, the child grew up in an atmosphere of constant emotional tension. His mother, a victim of nervous depressions, entered a sanatorium when Karlheinz was only four years old. His father, as a schoolteacher forced to become an active member of the Nazi party, was caught in that terrible conflict between political conviction and private conscience that afflicts all unwilling instruments of militant social reform, as he watched those of his friends who had been in the socialist party before 1933 persecuted and imprisoned by the Gestapo. Karlheinz himself was involved at an early age as party messenger boy for his father.

The family moved to Altenberg, another village on the outskirts of Cologne, when Karlheinz was six. A handsome and gifted child, he began to take piano lessons with the organist of the village church from the time he entered primary school. After four years he won recommendation to a grammar school in Burscheid, where he remained until 1941. From there he proceeded to the Teacher Training College at Xanten, on the lower reaches of the Rhine, a converted monastery and thoroughly Spartan establishment run on military lines. As a boarder at Xanten he lost what little family contact he had hitherto enjoyed. His father had long since volunteered for military service, and his mother was still languishing in hospital. No privacy was allowed in the lonely isolation of Xanten except the privacy of prayer and the privacy of music, to which he now turned. He took lessons in the violin, in the oboe which he played in the college massed orchestra and wind band, and continued his piano lessons, playing piano in the dance band, where he discovered a liking for jazz. Returning home one weekend in 1942 to see his father on leave, he learned that his mother had been put to death as an act of Government policy to relieve pressure on hospital accommodation.

Stockhausen remained at college until October 1944. Still too young for active service, he became a stretcher-bearer attached to a military hospital at Bedburg on the Erft. 'The experience of contact with thousands of seriously wounded and dying soldiers—American, English, German—gave me at an early age a special attitude to death.' He returned to Altenberg. Shortly before the end of the war he saw his father for the last time. Simon Stockhausen returned to the Hungarian front, to be subsequently reported as missing. A comrade later told Karlheinz of seeing his father wounded in action. Stockhausen did not see his father again.

Immediately after the war he took work on a farm. Before long he was working in the evenings as well, as repetiteur for a local amateur operetta society, in order to earn enough to continue his education. He also took lessons in Latin, qualifying in February 1946 for entrance as a senior student at the Grammar School for the Humanities at Bergisch Gladbach. The following year was spent in concentrated study. Stockhausen supported himself by working in the afternoons and evenings as an accompanist for dancing classes and as musical director for the operetta society. In March 1947 he matriculated. Immediately he enrolled for a four-year course at the State Academy of Music *(Musikhochschule)* in Cologne, and for classes in musicology, philosophy, and German studies at Cologne University. At the Hochschule he majored in piano, studying under Hans Otto Schmidt-Neuhaus. The following year, 1948, he took harmony and counterpoint with Hermann Schroeder, the first composer with whom he had close contact, and also a course in school music designed for secondary school music teachers.

It was not until 1950 that he took his first lessons in composition, showing his work to the Swiss composer Frank Martin who had taken a professorship at the Hochschule. They only met a few times, 'four or five' as Stockhausen recalls, but their relationship was friendly. At a distance, judging by a contemporary essay,[1] Martin seems likely to have been a cultivated, undogmatic influence, receptive to if not passionately enthusiastic or particularly knowledgeable about new musical developments. From 1950 date Stockhausen's *Choral*, the *Drei Lieder* for alto voice and orchestra, and the *Chöre für Doris*, settings for unaccompanied choir of verses by Verlaine.

The year 1951 saw the end of his formal apprenticeship and a dramatic change in his personal fortunes. His final year at the Hochschule was devoted largely to composition and analysis of the works of advanced composers, notably the *Sonata for Two Pianos and Percussion* of Béla Bartók, of which he made a characteristically thorough analysis, running to 186 pages, as his final examination thesis. During this time he was still working as a pianist at nights, as a jazz pianist in local bars, and in his final year as accompanist to a touring magician called Adrion ('I improvised on the piano, and distracted the audience at crucial moments').[2] A chance meeting brought him into

---

[1] Frank Martin, *Schönberg and Ourselves*, an essay dating from 1949, first published in *Polyphonie No. 4*, and reprinted in translation in *The Score*, No. 6, May 1952, where it appears alongside Boulez's *Schönberg is Dead*.

[2] Interview, *New Yorker*, 18 January 1964.

contact with Herbert Eimert, and began an association which was to lead, two years later, to Stockhausen's appointment to a position in the electronic music studio of Cologne Radio. Dr. Eimert, then music critic for the newspaper *Kölnische Rundschau*, and also in charge of a late-night series of programmes on contemporary music broadcast by Cologne (North-West, later West German) Radio, was delighted to find in Stockhausen one who shared his enthusiasm for current developments. He invited the young composer to condense his Bartók analysis into a suitable script for broadcasting, and in time Stockhausen became a regular contributor to the evening programmes. Eimert also arranged the first broadcast performance of a Stockhausen work. This was the Sonatine for violin and piano, which he persuaded Wolfgang Marschner, concertmaster of the Radio Symphony orchestra, to record with the composer as pianist. Eimert was also responsible for introducing Stockhausen to the Darmstadt New Music Courses in 1951. He may have had his own reasons for inviting the younger man; one of the items on the lecture programme for 1951 was a seminar, 'Musik und Technik', which he was to conduct together with Robert Beyer and Dr. Werner Meyer-Eppler, two pioneers of synthetic sound production.[3] In addition, Pierre Schaeffer was to give a lecture-demonstration on the activities of his *musique concrète* group.

Stockhausen found much to interest him at Darmstadt. He met Nono, Gottfried Michael Koenig (who later assisted him in the realization of *Kontakte*) and the young Belgian composer Karel Goeyvaerts, with whom he struck up a close friendship. Goeyvaerts had been a student of Messiaen until 1949, before the time of *Mode de Valeurs*, and had since specialized in a study of late Webern scores. He had been attracted by the implications of comprehensive serialism in Webern's handling of pitch, intensity, register, and touch as independent variables, for instance the concentration of material into single notes and the perfect symmetry of Webern's Op. 27 Piano Variations, second movement. But much as he approved of Webern's use of register and time as coordinates of a uniform musical space, Goeyvaerts was struck by the seeming inconsistency between Webern's serialization of pitch and his apparently rudimentary handling of time. His own Sonata for Two Pianos, Op. 1, written in 1950, is an attempt to reconcile the two dimensions. His search for a unified underlying order may have been influenced by Le Corbusier's announcement in 1950 of his celebrated theory of architectural proportion, the 'Modulor'. The Swiss-born architect had found that 'beautiful' and 'functional' forms, both those evolved in nature and those intuitively devised by man, could alike be related to a scale of relationships based on the 'Golden Mean' $[a : b = (a+b) : a]$. Such a 'universal law' for music would in theory provide a series of numerical constants for pitch, time, and other proportions which, consistently applied, would yield results both aesthetically appealing and mathematically harmonious. A

[3] It seems extraordinary, looking back, that Stockhausen could have missed attending the 1950 Darmstadt courses, which included first performances of Schoenberg's *A Survivor from Warsaw*, Varèse's *Ionisation,* and the Op. 1 Canonic Variations of Luigi Nono, and two lectures by Beyer and Meyer-Eppler entitled 'The Sound World of Electronic Music'.

closed system of this kind would tend at first to generate an extremely reticent and static music. On the basis of such purely functional models, however, a composer might eventually progress to forms of greater naturalism and plasticity.

Goeyvaerts called his early works 'static music', and it seems that he, too, regarded them as projections in sound of an ideal formal perfection. Stockhausen was attracted to the monastic austerity of Goeyvaerts' ideas, and though their musical expression did not greatly appeal to him certain of the Belgian composer's formal stratagems did, notably his concept of register-form. In the second movement of the two-piano sonata each repeated pitch is transposed up an octave, reappearing in the lowest available octave when it 'goes over the top'. In this way Goeyvaerts compensates for an intrinsic lack of forward momentum by rotating the music cylindrically about a horizontal pitch-axis. At the same time, he narrows the available pitch range during the movement gradually from just over five to two and a half octaves. In the sonata third movement the process is reversed, the pitch range gradually opening out from two and a half to just over five octaves, and the recurrent pitches transposing downward.

Stockhausen was also impressed by Goeyvaerts' Op. 2 for thirteen instruments, his Op. 3 'for bowed and struck sounds', and Op. 5, an early sine-tone piece. But it was the idea of register-form embodied in the Op. 1 that above all influenced his own pieces up to the first version of *Punkte*, and most clearly *Kreuzspiel* and the *Schlagtrio*.

The most celebrated event of Darmstadt, however, was his encounter with the *Mode de Valeurs et d'Intensités* of Messiaen. Antoine Goléa, the French author and music critic, had come to Darmstadt informally, bringing with him a small collection of the latest French compositions in manuscript and on disc.

This selection included *Le Soleil des Eaux* by Boulez, as recorded by French Radio from a 1950 concert performance conducted by Désormière, and, significantly, the *Quatre Etudes de Rythme* of Messiaen, in the Columbia recording, with the composer himself at the piano. One of these studies in particular, the profoundly radical *Mode de Valeurs et d'Intensités*, had a decisive effect on the young Karlheinz Stockhausen, then an unknown student at Darmstadt . . . I will never forget with what passion he listened over and over again to this study; the outcome of this revelation of a sound world of which he no doubt had an obscure presentiment, was his move to Paris for the scholastic year 1952–3, and his assiduous attendance at Messiaen's classes.[4]

Stockhausen returned to Cologne to prepare for his State examinations to qualify as a secondary school teacher of music. His Bartók thesis was submitted on 1 August and the examination results, announced in mid-October, brought a gratifying pass with distinction. Once through his examinations he returned with renewed energy to composing. A new piece, *Kreuzspiel*, was completed on 4 November and dedicated to Doris Andreae, daughter of a prosperous Hamburg shipbuilder and a fellow student at

[4] A. Goléa, *Rencontres avec Pierre Boulez*, Juilliard, 1958, pp. 77–8. In Stockhausen's opinion, too much importance has been attached to this anecdote.

the Hochschule. Stockhausen completed *Formel* in December. On 29 December he married Doris, and he left for Paris in January.

At this point, where the music takes over, the case history may be thankfully discontinued. The composer's life is his own affair, and it is too easy, when we don't fathom his music, to discover pretexts for our incomprehension in the man's past personal misfortunes. The important fact about Stockhausen's temperament, for instance, is that it is the temperament of a great composer, not, as has sometimes been suggested, an affliction of his upbringing. Nevertheless, we are not obliged tactfully to ignore connections between his present attitudes and past experience which the composer himself brings to our attention. For example, he explains his aversion to music with a continuous periodic beat as a reaction to his experience as a student during the war:

This periodic beat, which makes people march without knowing it . . . I am very sensitive to this because that was exactly the way the Nazis tuned in the whole population with marching music on the radio, and whether it's marching music, pop or even a rock beat, I don't like it.[5]

The influence of jazz is also important. Jazz offered an alternative to the beat regimentation he despised, and the big band sound of swing music has left its mark on his composing affections. One detects without difficulty the affinity between jazz's concept of ensemble relationship and the intuitive sympathy he has laboured to instil in his own performers, but there is more to the jazz influence than a simple question of attitude. In jazz's free, accentual rhythms and intricate combinations of metres, its opposition of latent (frequently cyclical) formal rigidity and surface freedom, underlying continuity and outward elision and fragmentation, we may see elements of his own musical style. Even Stockhausen's serial method may have derived in part from analysis of the rhythmic divisions of time in the jazz classics. The following well-known passage[6] for instance, yields something resembling a duration series:

Jazz also has the happy associations for Stockhausen of his years as a student at the Hochschule, a spirit reflected in the relaxed, often theatrical tone of much of his output, an aspect of his work that the sober German press correctly but disdainfully identifies as 'kabarettisch'.

[5] *Music and Musicians,* May 1971, p. 39.
[6] From 'A String of Pearls' by Jerry Gray arr. Glen Miller.

But the influence of jazz was also a consequence of his practical involvement, as a pianist in the school jazz band at Xanten, later as a working musician in the bars of Cologne, and as the conjuror's accompanist (and accomplice). A composer is more readily influenced by what he hears, less by a music he can only see in score form. Stockhausen was undoubtedly more familiar with contemporary piano music than orchestral or chamber music. Piano music was easier to obtain, and he could play it himself. This accounts, perhaps, for the prominent position keyboard instruments occupy in his music, individually and as orchestral instruments, and the functional importance he frequently attaches to them, whether as a unifying device *(Kontra-Punkte)* or as an instrument of transformation (the Hammond organ in *Mikrophonie II*). The fact, as Karl Wörner puts it, that he was familiar with everything of Schoenberg, Stravinsky, and Bartók that was available in 1950, does not mean that he knew very much. Little was available. During his years as a student in Cologne the Radio Orchestra played very little twentieth-century music of any consequence. Disc recordings were also scarce. The influences we can see clearly in his early pieces are nearly all drawn from the piano literature: the gestural style of Schoenberg's Op. 11, and such features of Bartók's style as the impressionism of No. 3 'Night Music' from the *Out of Doors* suite, and expressive devices (clusters, grace-note figures, parallel harmonies) gleaned from a close study of the *Mikrokosmos* pieces. The sub-Hindemith manner of his first vocal pieces which he quickly abandoned, is attributable to his teacher Hermann Schroeder, though Stockhausen's always happy ear for chord sonority may be a small but important legacy of his study with Frank Martin.[7]

[7] Stockhausen's dependence on the piano as a student may throw some light on his curious casual remark during the Peter Heyworth interview already cited (*Music and Musicians*, May 1971), that 'most orchestral pieces, even up to our own day, have first been written in a piano version and then instrumented afterwards' (op. cit., p. 34).

Chöre für Doris

1950: No. I/11,[1] UE 15135

Three movements after Verlaine for unaccompanied mixed choir.
(Previously known as the 'Chöre nach Verlaine'.)
1. 'Die Nachtigall' SATB (3/8/50).
2. 'Armer junger Hirt' SSAATTBB (n.d.).
3. 'Agnus Dei' SATB (1/8/50).
Duration c. 15 minutes.

To DESCRIBE these as student pieces is to say they exhibit academic priorities: a concern for harmonic and melodic expression without a sense of the role played by rhythm and form in sustaining interest and invention. Characteristic is the reliance on textual cues for rhythm and expression, a style that combines the rhetoric of art song with the rather cramped style of recitative. It ought to be remembered that Bartók was rhythmically and melodically rather dependent on speech patterns: the feminine ending we associate with Bartók's melodies, and which appear here in Stockhausen's, is a Magyar idiom. Stockhausen's harmony in fourths is also a conscious borrowing from Bartók.

One of the immediate effects of attempting to base a musical setting on essentially prosaic features of a poem's recitation, is that many qualities that ought to be intrinsic to melodic shaping and cadence have to be applied externally in the form of 'signpost' instructions. Thus the first few lines of 'Die Nachtigall' (The Nightingale), though set very firmly in regular accents (each syllable stressed separately), carries the instruction to 'declaim in a "floating" manner' with 'a free espressivo between *piano* and *forte*'. This contrast between notation and verbal instruction, sometimes carried to an extreme, is a relatively common symptom in student composition of a dislocation of imagination and technique, but it is interesting that Stockhausen has retained or rediscovered in his mature music an interest in the creative potential of this sort of discrepancy. Some evidence of the discrepancy is to be found in the comparative flexibility of Stockhausen's solo part, which already shows an awareness of the expressive potential of 'irrational' beat subdivisions (sixes and fives). In his dense choral writing he seems to be proceeding from a Lutheran style in the direction of the kind of impressionistic background favoured by Bartók, a tendency underlined by the 'floating' instruction.

[1] The numbering of pieces is Stockhausen's own. The composer comments: 'The way I have numbered the works mainly characterizes the order in which I have conceived and begun the works, not the chronological order as I have finished them.'

At the beginning of 'Die Nachtigall' the writing is dense and constricted, imparting a petitioning urgency to the mood which overrides the imagery and sense of the text. After bar 12, however, the music relaxes, begins to breathe more naturally and to interpret the text. At the indication 'wie zu Beginn', where the opening music is recapitulated, the change in confidence can be easily appreciated. The solo melody rises effortlessly where earlier it strained upward, only to fall:

Note that in both early forms of the phrase, the melody falls to below the starting note; only at the end of the song is the mood sufficiently 'balanced' for its descent to be controlled.

The lyric about a poor shepherd boy who 'has a terror of kisses, as though they were bees', is approached in humorous vein but with an adolescent intensity that leads it to be treated at length and without the light touch of the original:

> Angst hab' ich vor Küssen,
> Als wären sie Bienen.
> Ach! wird man es müssen?
> Angst hab' ich vor Küssen . . .

But even if it is a rather weighty interpretation, Stockhausen's seriousness seems to reflect a growing confidence in his musical prowess. Indeed, 'Armer junge Hirt' is by far the most ambitious setting of the three, making use of variable bars, and frequent changes of tempo and density. This greater technical dexterity, more than any worldly wisdom, is what gives this setting its improved fluency. As with the other songs, the vocal style is recitativo rather than lyric in sympathy, and Stockhausen still tends to rely on 'applied' expression in the form of tempo and intensity fluctuations. Even so, the following example indicates a new suppleness of melody:

um - ar - men und küs - sen

Bartók is still much in evidence, in melodic construction and variation, in the persistence of the feminine ending, the harmony in fourths, the textural thickening of a line by doubling at the third or sixth (a feature noted in Stockhausen's Bartók thesis), and so on. But further features of Stockhausen's own style begin to emerge: a calculated rather than loose episodic construction, for instance, and a personal form of dramatic humour, shown in his division of the choir into dramatis personae in a comic exchange of words, a spirit that also emerges in *Momente* and *Mikrophonie II*.

The third text is again personally relevant: 'Gib uns den Frieden, nicht den Krieg bescher' (Grant us thy peace, nor war on us bestow). An anthem in familiar Protestant church idiom for unaccompanied choir, 'Agnus Dei' expresses an essentially private (unscanned) rite of meditation. An interesting feature is the composer's use of the repeated 'Lamm Gottes' as a structural refrain, and another is the appearance of Bartók's plain up-and-down scales as melodies.

Drei Lieder

1950: No. ¹/10, UE 15154

For alto voice and chamber orchestra: flute, 2 clarinets (in E flat and A), bassoon, trumpet in C (also D), trombone, percussion, xylophone, piano, harpsichord, strings.
1. 'Der Rebell' (Baudelaire).
2. 'Frei' (Stockhausen).
3. 'Der Saitenmann' (Stockhausen).
Duration 17 minutes.

IF A TEXT provides the young composer with a useful basic musical framework, his adoption of a series teaches him at once (1) the value of melodic variation in shape

and rhythm, (2) the relationship of melody (horizontal) and harmony (vertical), and (3) the use and value of certain kinds of *non*-variation, such as note-repetition and ostinato patterns. Serial thinking obliges a composer to use expressive and structural musical devices that the nonserial composer is inclined to ignore, and this may account for the enthusiasm with which total serialism was adopted by young composers at this time. Stockhausen's awareness of variation as an essential element of serial technique is shown on the very first page of 'Der Rebell', in which the same intervallic shape is presented in seven different rhythms:

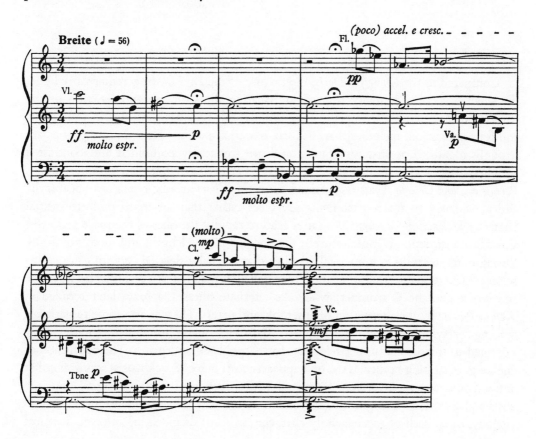

Not only rhythms, but the variation of whole phrases is suggested by the need to maintain interest. Two forms of Stockhausen's trumpet series show the direction in which his scansion was increasingly to tend:

Compared to the *Chöre für Doris*, the texture of the *Drei Lieder* is remarkably light: the small orchestra, in many respects anticipating the structure and function of the *Kontra-Punkte* ensemble, comprises four woodwind, two brass, strings in four parts, and four percussion, including harpsichord as well as piano.[1] These family groups are strongly identified as structural units, and are frequently combined and contrasted antiphonally in ways reminiscent of Stravinsky's *Petrushka* or Bartók's *Music for Strings, Percussion, and Celesta*. Features retained from the *Chöre* are the recitativo vocal style, and a tendency to treat instruments as voices rather than in terms of instrumental character and action—though this latter feature rapidly vanishes as the piece proceeds. Episodic construction is more assured: the unequal phrase lengths and metronomically distinguished tempi (i.e. numerically rather than verbally defined) pointing to a consciously structural ordering of events. 'Der Rebell' is planned as a dialogue between the solo voice and the C trumpet, who take alternate phrases, a form later recalled in *Kontra-Punkte* by the alternation of ensemble and piano. There is also some remarkable writing for xylophone and vigorous use of Bartókian quasi-cluster effects (mysteriously confined to middle and upper registers) for harpsichord and piano. The conclusion of the song, of striking beauty, is the first appearance of one of Stockhausen's most familiar musical images, one invariably associated with a feeling of deep nostalgia—that is, a sustained harmonic background, suspended in time, within or against which a solo melody, often itself of mechancholy character, is heard disappearing into the distance:

[1] Compare Martin's *Petite Symphonie Concertante* for piano, harpsichord, and strings.

'Frei' begins with a little side-drum solo that recalls the 'Game of the Couples' from Bartók's Concerto for Orchestra, and its mood is similarly lively. More smoothly continuous than 'Der Rebell', 'Frei' is also more orchestral in style, and richer in instrumental effects. Here Stockhausen's rhythms, both individually and in combination, begin to assume the complexity and syncopation associated with his later style, and the following piccolo/clarinet combination also displays an emergent melodic angularity:

Stockhausen also uses his orchestra in tutti to a greater extent than formerly, giving the impression that in between composing 'Der Rebell' and 'Frei' the composer made some intensive study of Berg's or Schoenberg's episodic cadences. Section 8, where the voice takes a 3/4 bar against the orchestra's 2/4, in the orchestral glissandi at 13, and the piano waltz fragment 12 bars after 21 are very Bergian in character.[2] Stockhausen's vocal writing is spacious and truly operatic, displaying quite a remarkable leap forward in technique. The extended melisma of the setting 'am süssen Ort' at 13 has extraordinary power:

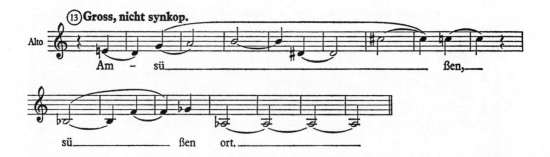

Three more features of this long and remarkable setting deserve mention: Stockhausen's use of clusters in parallel motion for dramatic effect, notably at the climax before 24; the solo roles he assigns to trumpet and trombone, who function as leading voices

---

[2] Stockhausen in fact knew **no** Berg at this stage.

much as they were later to do in *Gruppen*; and further indications of a desire to combine 'free' and 'measured' tempi, of which the ad lib. D trumpet solo at the final cadence is one type and the accentual counter-rhythms of the piano waltz another.

'Der Saitenmann' is a slower, brief setting of a youthfully sentimental poem about 'the musician after the war, to whom nobody listens any more, because they all "kaufen eine neue Welt" (are busy buying a new world); all that remains for him is to listen to his violin, where he hears what nobody has ever heard before—"Das Ungehörte"!' In a relaxed, expressionist setting that still avoids being simply illustrative (a minor exception is the pizzicato accompaniment to the words 'zu hart gezupft'), the most remarkable feature is an extended violin cadenza of Schoenbergian virtuosity, which appears in the score revised for two soloists, presumably on his teacher's advice:

Viewed overall, the *Drei Lieder* display a resourcefulness in the handling of orchestral forces unusual for such an early stage of his development, and like so many of Stockhausen's pieces of this period, actually show his technique growing in confidence as the piece proceeds, from the hesitant motivic serialism of 'Der Rebell' to the mature virtuosity of 'Frei'. The work's unusual instrumentation (the orchestra includes E flat and A but no B flat clarinets, and a C doubling a D trumpet) suggests a model, perhaps the salon orchestra at Xanten or a student orchestra at the Hochschule. Certainly there can no longer be any doubt that Stockhausen's typical preference for a serially-organized small orchestral group including prominent percussion section and piano, is at the root of his composing style: even the three- and four-orchestra ensembles of *Gruppen* and *Carré* are multiples of an orchestra of this modest scale rather than large ensembles subdivided. From the evidence of the motivic writing of 'Der Rebell' one can readily understand why Stockhausen was so powerfully drawn to Messiaen's cellular technique. The score also dispels any lingering supposition that Stockhausen's extension of the serial principle to tempo and phrase-structure was a development subsequent to his Paris period. Some tempo changes in both *Kreuzspiel* and *Kontra-Punkte*, for instance, seem so unrelated to changes in the musical content that one is inclined to assume they had been added as an afterthought. On the evidence of the episodic style of the *Drei Lieder*, and its numerically-differentiated tempi, that particular prejudice may be safely discarded.

Choral

1950: No. ¹/9, UE 15169

For four-part unaccompanied mixed choir
Duration 2 minutes

A FOUR-PART setting of 'Wer uns trug mit Schmerzen in dies Leben' (He who bore us with anguish in this life), *Choral* is in all externals a straightforward exercise in Bach chorale counterpoint—though characteristically Stockhausen has chosen a text with personal resonance. It is chiefly remarkable for a soprano voice that manages to accommodate original, inverted, and retrograde forms of a twelve-note series into the conventional tonic-dominant-tonic phrase construction of a chorale in the key of D.

The subsidiary parts are not serial, but conform to a traditional pattern of stepwise movement (although the result is somewhat chromatic). One notices in all four parts a tendency to rise by leap and fall by degrees, as in 'Die Nachtigall' of the *Chöre*: this would also tend to create an impression of reticence or gloom. But this darkness of mood does not lead, as sometimes in Schoenberg's atonal themes, to a preponderance of diminished intervals. In fact, like Bartók, Stockhausen stabilizes his polyphony in a framework of perfect fourths and fifths. Significantly, it is the soprano voice, whose notes are serially preordained, that seems the most balanced and relaxed in character.

Sonatine

1951: No. I/8, UE 15174

For violin and piano.
Duration 11 minutes.

THOUGH this sonatina is later in date than the *Drei Lieder* of 1950, its style strongly suggests an earlier piece, perhaps begun after 'Der Rebell' but certainly less technically aggressive than the two later settings, the single bar—in the second movement—that at all approaches the final cadenza-like passage of 'Der Saitenmann' being clearly a later addition:

Such exuberance is rare: the mood of *Sonatine* (notwithstanding its serial basis) is generally either pensively Bartók or cautiously Hindemith. The series itself, like those of the *Drei Lieder* and *Choral*, is strongly tonal in implication:

The first movement, 'Lento espressivo', is a short, modestly lyrical study, limited in range (the violin only once soaring as high as a three-line E flat) and curiously undecided between a sober motivic formality and a freer, more rhapsodic style. If the influence of Schoenberg may be detected here, it is less that of his serial violin works

19

(e.g. the Violin Concerto or the Phantasy) than of his Piano Pieces, Opp. 11 and 23: that is, piano works of his atonal period, highly contrapuntal and based on melodic motives. Indeed, the piano octaves and the mood of the final 8 bars of this movement closely resemble the final 12 bars of Schoenberg's Op. 11, No. 1.

With its ostinato piano octaves and parallel sixths and thirds, the second movement, 'Molto moderato', is far from Schoenberg. Stockhausen describes it as 'a very slow boogie-woogie'. Where the piece does innovate is in opposing the violin's six beats per bar to the piano's four. Stockhausen's thickening of parts by the addition of parallel harmonies as the piece approaches its climax is a Bartók mannerism he has used before (compare 'Frei'). The construction of the movement in one continuous sweep is a departure from Stockhausen's usual episodic style. The music looks ponderous, but its effect is hypnotic: 'incredibly meditative—like *Stimmung*'.

The third movement, 'Allegro scherzando', is the longest and liveliest of the three, although the regularity with which germinal motives are developed savours more of the composer's models than of the composer himself. But there are passages of notable originality, such as this episode beginning at bar 37:

—or the dotted rhythms of the penultimate episode, which for all their regularity still look forward to the highly wrought syncopations of *Kontra-Punkte* and *Klavierstück IV*.

Kreuzspiel

1951: No. I/7, UE 13117

For oboe, bass clarinet, piano (and woodblock) and percussion (6 tomtoms, 2 tumbas or congas, 4 suspended cymbals: 3 players).
Duration 10 minutes.
Recorded by members of the London Sinfonietta on DGG 2530 443.

'A HIGH note, a low note, a note in the middle—like the music of a madman,' remarked Webern after hearing an under-rehearsed and unsympathetic performance of one of his pieces.[1] Much the same misunderstanding seems to have greeted the first 'pointillist' scores. The term is exact in the sense that it describes music built out of elemental 'sound-atoms' (as Stockhausen calls them), but it also conveys the impression that such music is intended to sound fragmented and disjointed. Hence the uncanny echo of Webern's complaint in the following earnest description of the new music from an encyclopedia of 1950–3:

There is hardly one among this generation who does not avail himself of the twelve-note method. However, their mentor is not Arnold Schoenberg, but his pupil Anton von Webern. . . . What we hear is only single notes, high and low, first faster, then at a slower rate, and from time to time a glissando or a harmonic tone. These themselves do not constitute the work's meaning, but are merely symbols that we then have to put together to make a whole. This kind of music requires a much more active participation from us as listeners. We experience to a certain extent only the material: the form has to be worked out.[2]

It is a pity that the 'pointillist' label should have so long obscured the necessary feeling for continuity that underlies many of these early scores. Few works of this period, in fact, are truly 'discrete'. Messiaen's *Mode de Valeurs* is one. Boulez's *Structures*, Book 1, is another work in which the intentionally random association of disparate elements is reflected in the composer's choice of instrument—the piano—each note of which has a separate mechanism. But none of Stockhausen's works could be described as simply an aggregate of dissociated particles (though evidently he felt misgivings of the kind about the withdrawn first version of *Punkte*). *Kreuzspiel* and *Kontra-Punkte*, both works for piano with associated instruments rather than democratic

[1] Quoted by Peter Stadlen, 'Serialism Reconsidered', *The Score* No. 22, February 1958.
[2] Friedrich Herzfield, *Musica Nova*, Ullstein Verlag, 1954, p. 264.

ensembles, are designed to mediate between the functional discontinuity of total determinism, and the aurally-desirable ideal of sequential coherence. In these works Stockhausen may be aiming at the effect of a jazz-ensemble 'break', though without jazz's basic framework of repetitive patterns over a regular beat. But to evoke jazz's sense of communal excitement in the traditional concert environment was no easy task. Classically-trained performers were not then used to listening to one another, nor to playing conversationally, adopting the oral culture of the jazz musician while still retaining the articulate skills of manuscript culture.

They did not know what to do, and after the first performance (Darmstadt, 1952) Stockhausen withdrew the score as he withdrew his other 1952 works *Punkte, Schlag-quartett*, and *Spiel. Kreuzspiel* was only revived in 1959 following the successful première of Boulez's two *Improvisations sur Mallarmé* in 1958, works which greatly resemble the earlier Stockhausen piece in instrumentation and mood.

But *Kreuzspiel*'s initial failure may also have been influenced by the political climate of the times, however. The 1952 German audience, living in a time of political uncertainty, looked to new music to revive a spirit of national identity. The festival a Darmstadt had itself been founded with this purpose in mind in 1946; by 1952, however relations between East and West Germany had worsened, with music a weapon in the political struggle.[3] In such an atmosphere it is not surprising that *Kreuzspiel* failed to win popular approval. At a time when young composers were deliberately dissolving nationa differences and bent on discarding political divisions in order to create a new, absolute, and supranational music, the audiences of their respective countries were clamouring for re-establishment of their separate cultural identities and rivalries. The 'new image' he Darmstadt audience was seeking in the heady expressionism of Schoenberg and Berg—one wonders if there was an intended irony in Scherchen's programming of Schoenberg's 'Dance Around the Golden Calf' in 1951—did not comprehend the intimacy of Webern and the young serial composers. Listeners were offended by the cool, personal self-sufficiency of *Kreuzspiel*, and also by its seeming to defer, by its salon-jazz character, to the vulgar influence of the occupying American culture.

Thus the history of *Kreuzspiel* encapsulates the prejudices of relationship that have continued ever since to preoccupy the composer: prejudices against musical conventions of oral cultures, against intimacy, and against political neutrality in music. These pressures may seem unreal nowadays, but it is obvious in his public statements as in his active pursuit of a music beyond even the symbolic constraints of classical literacy, that for Stockhausen these elements of militancy still represent powerful obstacles to the civilizing influence of musical culture.

As in the later *Kontra-Punkte*, in *Kreuzspiel* the piano plays the principal role, with the two melody instruments acting as alternative rather than equivalent voices. The transitions between piano and sustaining wind notes are handled with great delicacy and achieve moments of considerable poignancy of effect, notably in the work's middle

[3] See Current Chronicle, *Musical Quarterly*, 37/4, 1951, p. 590.

section. The roles of the percussion section are (i) supporting the articulation of pulse- and duration-relationships expressed in the pitched instrument parts, and (ii) elaboration of the basic structure by the opposition of secondary rhythmic patterns, which coincide with the principal pattern only at important structural points, generally strongly accented.

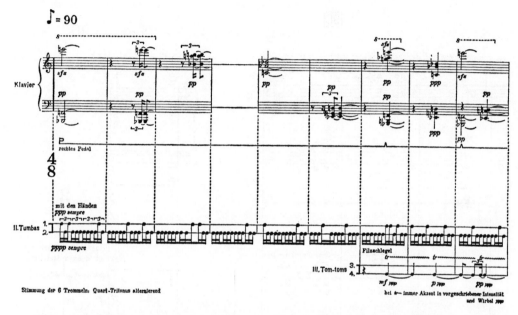

The work falls into three main sections with introduction, link passages, and coda. Part I is anticipated by a 13-bar introduction in which the piano exposes three orders of the series in chord form in phrases of 13, 3, and 10 crotchets' duration respectively.

'Each time notes and noises occur at the same point in time—which happens fairly frequently—the note in some way or another drops out of the series, alters its intensity, transposes into the wrong register or takes a different duration from the one pre-ordained.' (*Texte II*, p. 11.) In the piano's first three statements of the series these inter-actions may be observed altering the original pitch-distribution.

Against this background tumbas (small drums) beat out first the identificatory series 2 8 7 4 11 1 12 3 9 6 5 10, and then the additive duration-series 1 . . . 12 (a touch reminiscent of the Asian practice of identifying the mode of a piece at the beginning of each performance). Each rhythmic series occupies a fundamental duration-unit of 6½ bars' or 13 crotchet beats' duration (in Part III this unit changes to a 4⅓ bar or 13-quaver unit of length). This somewhat naked exposure of the series is modestly concealed behind overlapping contrary rhythmic structures in the tom-toms. Part I proper begins at the tempo-change at bar 14. After two statements of the duration-series on tumbas the woodwind instruments appear (bar 28) and after three further rotations, 19½ bars further on, a woodblock, played by the pianist, signals a serial accelerando taking the music to its Part I mid-point at the end of bar 52 (13 × 4). From this point, Stockhausen remarks, the form is retrograded and inverted, so that at bar 91 (13 × 3 bars further on) the piano parts are again at extreme ends of the keyboard, but with the original pitches transposed (the six highest at the beginning are now lowest, and vice versa).

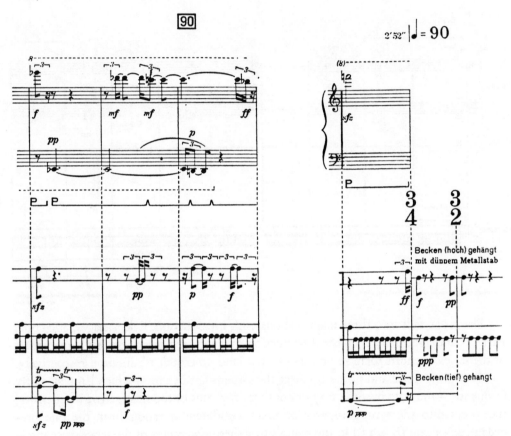

Part II follows without a break. It is introduced by and identified by a new statement of the duration-series, this time played by suspended cymbals. More intensely lyrical than either Part I or Part III, where the interest is created mainly by distributive interaction, here the emphasis is upon assimilation and co-ordination, with the woodwind in contrast to Part I taking the active, linear role, and the piano following. In this section Stockhausen's gift of evoking an atmosphere of quite touching melancholy (throughout his work one finds melody used to convey sentiments of a pathetic sort) is clearly apparent.[4] This section lasts for 3 × 13 bars (to bar 138) and concludes with a short, wistful woodwind exchange similar to a passage that opens the section:

[4] The sudden seizing and sustaining of piano notes by the woodwind is intensely dramatic. Until then the tumbas have as it were been measuring the flow of time in the decay of piano tones, and then suddenly

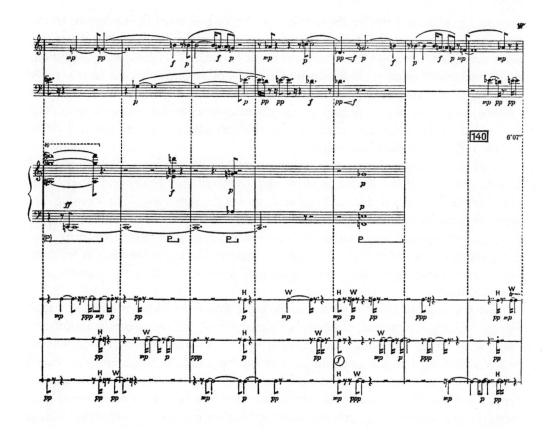

Such writing belies the label 'pointillist'; the serial dynamics, whatever their mathematics, coalesce in a gently nudging accentuation characteristic of 'cool' jazz, say the outwardly nonchalant alto saxophone style of Paul Desmond. One must not interpret the wide dynamic range as expressing extreme emotional instability in the operatic or post-operatic *(Pierrot Lunaire)* sense, but in terms of microphone style, where quite exaggerated variations in perceived loudness (amplitude) occur in a context of conversational evenness of tone, as the instrument or voice approaches and recedes from the microphone in cabaret performance.

A change to compound time, and a return to the tempo of ♪=136 signals the transition to Part III. Again the new section is preceded by an identifying statement of the duration-series, the accents of which make a gradual crescendo. The section itself combines elements of Parts I and II, suggesting virtually limitless possibilities of extension (the technique is used by Berg in his *Kammerkonzert*, and by Bartók). An opening statement of the series (bars 146–50) defines the principal phrase-duration as 13 dotted

the notes are sustained—they 'pass out of time'. The same dramatic interplay arises in the Renaissance voice and lute combination, where the voice selects and sustains single pitches out of a range of ephemeral lute notes. More recently Stravinsky has exploited the juxtaposition of types to powerful effect.

crotchet beats. After a further six rotations of the 13-beat series the mid-point of the piece is reached in bar 176, where it is marked by an encircled tumba-accent. From this point through five more 13-beat orders the music gradually loses complexity, returning to the pitch-distribution of the first section (the final piano pitches are the same as those of bar 14 that begin Part I proper). Over this final chord the tom-toms play a final rallentando-descrescendo statement of the duration-series which, with an extra final beat added for good measure, makes up the sixth unit for this second half of Part III and the 13th unit for the whole section.

Stockhausen acknowledges two influences on the composition of *Kreuzspiel*: of Goeyvaerts' Two-Piano Sonata, Op. 1, and of Messiaen's *Mode de Valeurs*, both encountered for the first time at Darmstadt earlier the same year. The 'crossing' referred to in the title ('Crossplay') is above all that of the registers, though there is also a suggestion of crossing over from piano (non-sustaining) to woodwind (sustaining) and back, and from piano (pitched) to percussion (unpitched). In his handling of registers, however, Stockhausen has Goeyvaerts' notion of systematic register displacement very much in mind.

The influence of *Mode de Valeurs* is more the quality of Messiaen's imagery than the piece's structural appeal, although a comparison of the two pieces is instructive. '*Mode* sounded like "star music", as I called it,' Stockhausen explains. It is vivid, intense, highly articulate; a music combining the immediacy and unpredictability associated with improvisation with the clockwork regularity and consistency of an organized form. *Mode*'s musical structure resembles *Kreuzspiel* in several respects, however. It is based on three interlocking pitch series distinguished by register; it is a form in constant exposition, beginning and ending at arbitrary points in a theoretically much longer permutation stucture; it also exploits dynamics and attacks in a manner anticipating later pointillist music. A feature of Messiaen's usage is that every note in each of the work's three basic modes is also fixed in intensity, duration, and mode of attack. This may be regarded as a compromise between Webern's independent manipulation of the various parameters (Messiaen as well as Goeyvaerts had been deeply impressed by Webern's Op. 27, No. 2), and the fixed palette of timbres characteristic of John Cage's prepared piano, which had caused a stir in the salons of Paris in 1949. The serial durations of *Mode de Valeurs* were Messiaen's own idea, derived from the duration canons of *Canteyodjaya*.

But *Mode* does not breathe (a common failing of works by organist composers), nor does it evolve, and it is against this background uniformity that Stockhausen's innovations can best be judged: *Kreuzspiel*'s wider palette of timbres, deliberate transitions from high to low and back, and introduction of a human scale of gesture and timing in the parts for woodwind (which incidentally anticipate Stockhausen's use of the boy's voice in *Gesang der Jünglinge*). If the suggestion of a relationship between duration and pitch conveyed in Messiaen's association of high with short, low with longer durations, was later on to surface in *Kontakte*, in *Kreuzspiel* these distinctions are firmly ignored.

There remain a number of points worth mentioning which relate to *Kreuzspiel* in itself. The first, a remarkable feature of the work as a whole, is its gentleness and restraint, qualities linking it to *Refrain*, composed in 1959, the year *Kreuzspiel* was revived. Stockhausen instructs his woodwind players to adhere strictly to the indicated loudness (except for an expressive swell at one point), and with the least possible vibrato. This 'plain manner' has since become the rule in 'serious' new music (though it was already a long-accepted convention of cabaret jazz style). The woodwind writing also looks forward to the more elaborate interplay of 'human' and 'absolute' timing in *Zeitmasze*. *Kreuzspiel*'s overall placid serenity throws into dramatic relief the two moments in the piece where expressive (rather than serial) fluctuations of intensity occur: the tumba diminuendo at bar 52, and the unison woodwind poco crescendo at bar 138. Stockhausen's use of the piano as a sustaining instrument for the surrounding percussion (which is why they are raised on platforms) is also of great interest, and in asking the pianist to play woodblock as well, he may be discreetly referring to Cage's *Wonderful Widow of Eighteen Springs* (1942), in which the pianist raps with his fists on various resonant parts of the piano woodwork. In any case, the practice is one Stockhausen has continued to the present day, in *Refrain*, *Kontakte*, and *Mantra*.

Formel

1951: No. ¹/6, UE 15157

Movement for orchestra: 3 oboes, 3 clarinets in A, 3 bassoons, 3 horns, glockenspiel, vibraphone, harp, celesta, piano, 6 violins, 3 cellos, 3 double basses.
Duration 11 minutes

'FORMEL', sometimes listed in catalogues of Stockhausen's works as 'Studie für Orchester', belongs to the same family group of compositions as *Kreuzspiel*, *Spiel*, *Schlagtrio*, and *Punkte*, first version. In all of these works an initial 'gestalt'—a pattern of notes describing fundamental interval and time relationships—is transmuted by degrees into something else. The evolutionary process characteristically depicted in these early pieces can be compared in some respects with a game of chess, in that an initially symmetrical, static arrangement of elements is systematically rearranged, move by move, until a self-governing dynamic situation is created, leading to the eventual dominance of one element or element combination. Two types of displacement can usually be found in these pieces; a note may be dislodged vertically from its original pitch and/or register, and it may also be pushed aside (usually by encounter with another note) from its original position in time. In *Formel*, Stockhausen's last work to be written before his stay in Paris, complete melodic or harmonic units (the latter to be imagined as vertical melodies) are treated in the same way as single 'points' are treated in *Kreuzspiel*. In this way the composer hoped to overcome some of the difficulties inherent in pointillist composition.

This innovation is interesting in two respects. In the first place, the structural units Stockhausen employs are defined by tempo, i.e. instead of a single element of a single serial duration we now have a melody or melodic/harmonic combination defined by the same duration repeated throughout. For example, at bar 58 the basic unit is seven semiquavers, at bar 60 five, at bar 62 four, and at bar 65 three semiquavers' duration. These structural beat patterns are set in opposition to the conducted tempo, and to one another, producing an interplay of 'floating' temporal patterns both reminiscent of jazz (as for instance in the Glenn Miller example cited in an earlier chapter) and anticipating Piano Piece I and *Gruppen*. In the second place, *Formel*'s opposition of groups of instruments also looks forward to *Gruppen*.

The overall time-structure of the work is based on an additive series with the quaver as basic unit. For example, the first 27 bars comprises two statements of the series, 6, 6+5, 6+5+4, . . . 6+5+4+3+2+1, in direct and then reverse order. These major time-units are occupied by subordinate structures defined, as we have already observed, in semiquaver beat values. The theoretical distinction between the two tempo hierarchies is blurred in practice by Stockhausen's use of a highly variable conducted tempo, which is indicated verbally.

The orchestra, composed entirely of pitched instruments (no rhythm section) and ordered in twelves and threes (twelve timbres, twelve woodwind and twelve string instruments each in groups of three), is organized around the vibraphone which (occasionally doubling on glockenspiel) provides the continuous melodic thread stitching the succession of episodes together. Some idea of the vibraphone's unifying role may be gained from the opening ten bars, which also show how Stockhausen uses tempo as a means of liaison:

This first melodic statement of the series strikingly resembles the first statement of the 'mantra' in the work of that name written nearly twenty years later, both as a concentrated statement of basic material, and also in its compression into a limited compass. In fact the vibraphone in *Formel* sticks to this limited alto range throughout, a fact which, whatever its serial necessity, seems to argue an essentially vocal interpretation of the instrument's role. As to why Stockhausen should have chosen the vibraphone as lead instrument, one can surmise that he may have had a cabaret band in the back of his mind.

Formel is a strange piece. It lacks the sparkle of *Kreuzspiel*, and at times its harmonization appears as laboured as parts of the *Chöre für Doris*. It was originally to have been the first movement of *Spiel*, which it resembles in serial essentials and instrumentation. However, when he came to write the two succeeding movements Stockhausen's method has changed to such an extent that he rejected *Formel* as a cul-de-sac in his development, and it was only in 1970 that the movement was first performed. Nevertheless, the score has its interests and attractions. Stockhausen's technique of building linear forms into vertical structures is the same as he was to employ in later electronic works. His instrumental combinations are often strikingly beautiful, for instance the string writing at bar 95, or the piano/celesta/harp/double bass episode at bar 117, which shows the composer typically busy at opposite extremes of register. Over the piano part he

*) Die Klavierstimme ist so notiert, weil ich ein Klavier hatte, in das ich Dämpfer bis oben hin hatte einbauen lassen (in der Erwartung, man würde in Zukunft das Klavier allgemein so konstruieren...).

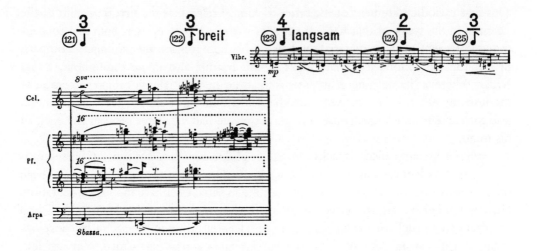

has written a note which at last explains why his early piano writing is so often confined to the upper register:

The piano part is written in this fashion because I used to have a piano in which I had the dampening mechanism extended to the upper extreme (in the expectation that pianos in general might eventually be so constructed . . .).

Paris, 1952

PARIS was the birthplace of the new music, and Paris in 1952, the year of *L'Œuvre du XXe siècle*, was at a peak of creative excitement, with Messiaen, Boulez, and Pierre Schaeffer all producing some of their most abstract and consequential work.[1] The stir created by Cage, a visitor in 1949, was still very much in the air. René Leibowitz and Max Deutsch, pupils of Schoenberg and tireless promoters of the theory and music of

---

[1] The essays, too, are of great creative interest; like those of Kandinsky, Klee and Le Corbusier, they ought to be considered equally with the practical works.

the three Viennese, found themselves in the year of the death of their teacher treated with new public attention and respect.

Some idea of the excitement of the period may be gained from the high level of dissension, from the personal and polemical battles, and from the rivalry that existed between the principal musical factions. Here was Schaeffer holding forth on the revolution in musical consciousness brought on by the tape recorder, there Leibowitz heatedly defending his newly won authority as keeper of the serial keys; between them Messiaen, innocently wreaking havoc among the established as well as the new conventions of musical order, and Boulez, wearing the colours of total predetermination, in the midst of the fracas lashing out at one and all. This euphoric, Pentecostal tumult, occurring at the same time as a noisy popular battle was going on between the defenders of tonal neoclassicism under the banner of Stravinsky and the apostles of 'progressive atonality' (whose standard had no recognizable image but which bore the name of Schoenberg), produced reverberations that are still detectable even today. And though it was the youth, genius, and formidable intellect of Boulez that prevailed in artistic circles while Stockhausen was in Paris, the many unresolved issues that arose during this most fruitful period of conflict presented Stockhausen with a manifold task of reconciliation that has occupied his creative energies ever since.

A special issue of *La Revue musicale* appeared in April 1952 to coincide with the International Festival of the Arts.[2] The issue included two essays of great importance, Pierre Schaeffer's 'L'Objet musical' and Boulez's more celebrated piece 'Eventuellement . . .'. The importance of Schaeffer's contribution is one that we are only now, in the light of Stockhausen's most recent works, able to begin to appreciate.

An advertisement inserted in the selfsame issue by La Maison du Magnétophone invites teachers of music, composers, and music critics respectively to consider the following advantages of possessing a tape recorder:

—to enable your pupils to judge for themselves the quality of their interpretation;
—to note at speed an idea, a musical theme;
—to preserve a very precise recollection of a recording or of a live performance.

These three suggestions pinpoint the decisive areas of innovation in musical consciousness heralded by the tape recorder and pursued by Schaeffer in his researches. The first advantage listed signals a new objectivity towards musical gesture; the second highlights the power of the tape recorder to supersede traditional manuscript, widening the range of contemplatable phenomena to include effects from the most ephemeral to the most complex; and the third identifies the machine as a function of memory, spelling the end of repetition in music.

---

[2] *L'Œuvre du XXe siècle*, numéro spécial no. 212, *La Revue Musicale*, ed. Richard-Masse, Paris, April 1952.

From Pierre Schaeffer: *Introduction à la Musique Concrète* (1949): Musical applications
of tape montage.

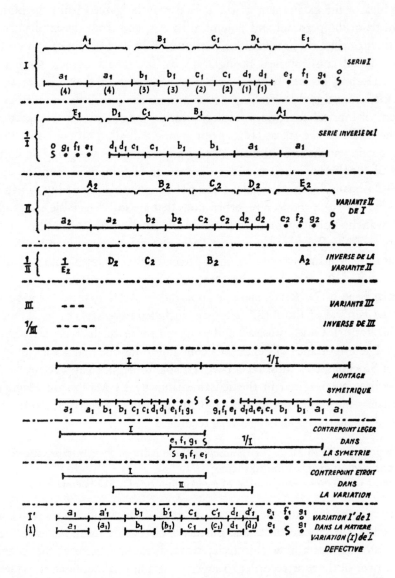

Schaeffer's own ultimate inability to bridge the gap between the new perception
and the new musical discipline does not diminish the importance of his first theoretical
propositions. Already in 1949 the essay *Introduction à la Musique Concrète*[3] shows him

[3] *Polyphonie No. 6*, 'La Musique Mecanisée', ed. Richard-Masse, Paris, 1950. Schaeffer's essay is dated
December 1949.

thinking in terms of serial modular construction, i.e. the permutation of note-groups as distinct from note-series. The diagram reproduced from this essay presents a prototype of the kind of structural organization Stockhausen was to follow both in his instrumental and his electronic works. One notices in particular the concepts of (1) variation by substitution of related material ('related' here meaning 'of similar constitution': that is, range of timbres, loudness, gestural character, resonance—those qualities distinct from musical or thematic content that identify two isolated fragments of tape-recorded music as originating from the same source-context); (2) variation by *omission*: the new tension experienced between sound and silence, between the presence and absence of a signal, a concept also utilized by Boulez; and (3) hints at the concept of *time-* (as distinct from mere *order-*) reversal. Something resembling each of these concepts was already acknowledged in the instrumental music of the period: cellular construction (itself inspired by the episodic construction of film), the elided music of Webern, and the concept of tempo as external to musical content (as the flow of a stream is external to objects floating upon it), were all part of the currency of advanced French music at that time. However the tape recorder offered an image and an impetus to these hitherto independent and idiosyncratic elements, expressed them with a new vividness and coherence, and suggested far-reaching new lines of development in both the instrumental and electronic fields.

Some of these lines of development are pursued in Schaeffer's 1952 essay, though many of the suggestions are not Schaeffer's own, but his pupils' (Stockhausen included). Building on the machine-revealed distinction between form and content, on the new technical criteria of sound-relationship, and on the machine's capacity to seize and replicate transient phenomena, Schaeffer explores and defines some of the new properties of musical articulation. He examines a sound such as might be made by lightly strumming a few strings of the piano with one finger. According to the way it is played—with the nail or flesh of the finger, gently or abruptly, lightly or heavily, etc.— the resulting sound may seem more or less like music or like a noise: thus even at the pre-recording stage one reckons with a scale of possible effects ranging from pure musical sound to indeterminate noise, a scale related to the 'manner of self-preparation' adopted by the performer. 'Having recorded the sound, we are at liberty to modify it mechanically, for example reproducing it at a higher or lower pitch, repeating it in a rhythmic pattern, and so on.'[4] But one might also, he continues, modify the internal structure of the prototype 'complex note', and create a family of related objects varying from the original in intensity or conciseness, in internal distribution, or in dynamic envelope:

[4] Schaeffer, op. cit.

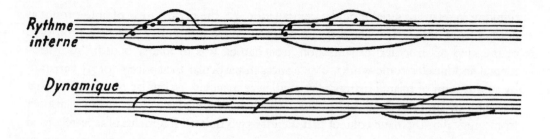

Schaeffer is thus led to the important observation that such a succession, 'by transformation of the intrinsic form . . . constitutes a series, a sort of anti-melody'. In turn, the notion of a melody may be enlarged to include other types of evolution than movement in pitch:

A series of the same sound-objects, identical one with another, but at different intensities, could in fact be taken not as a series, but as a *dynamic melody*. A precedent may be recognized in ordinary music: the repetition of a particular note in crescendo, diminuendo, or with sforzando accents [e.g. Stravinsky's *Augures Printaniers* from *The Rite of Spring*].

By correlating changes in timbre with melodic change in pitch one should be able to realize Schoenbergian *Klangfarbenmelodie*. Such an experiment would show that 'such melodies are obtained by virtue of the close fusion of the three parameters of musical variation: arithmetical variations of pitch, intensity and timbre not considered here as separate elements within a duration, but as inflections (of a subtle, not to say refined order), of all these parameters in union'.

As if transported, the Paris group's collective imagination flies from one original insight to another. One may transform an original complex note into an endless and homogeneous, enriched super-note, the vertical thickness of which may be modified at will, the upper extreme independently of the lower (op. cit., p. 72) (cf. *Kontakte*, 22′ 17, 7″–22′ 30, 4″). Electroacoustic equipment also furnishes a means of realizing a polyphony that is not subject to the constraints of a common beat-structure. 'One has only to let run at different speeds three turntables carrying the same theme on disc, to obtain a three-voiced fugue transposed in tempo with exact conformity to pitch, and impossible by any conventional standard of notation or execution.'

To the unprejudiced ear this last example may seem unredeemably banal; even so, it foreshadows the three-layer tempo structure of *Gruppen*, the experiments with tape loops that led to *Solo*, the concept of interplay of live music and its recorded image(s) that recurs in a whole host of works of the fifties, by among others Varèse, Pousseur, Maderna, and Berio. Indeed, it even anticipates the fugato passages of *Kontakte* itself (e.g. at 12′ 21, 5″, or the notoriously difficult marimbaphone 'cadenza' at 14′ 31, 8″). But without pausing for breath Schaeffer leaps to the astonishing prophecy 'one sees that a new "Well-Tempered Clavier" could be written from the starting-point of the correspondence of duration as a function of pitch'—a remark that encompasses in a single phrase nearly ten years of Stockhausen's subsequent theoretical development, including the Piano Pieces, *Gruppen* (the essay '. . . how time passes . . .'), and culminating in the *Kontakte* essay 'The Concept of Unity in Musical Time'.

Stockhausen's attitude to Boulez's ideas emerges in the following note from *Bearings 1952/53*:

Always the same search and research: the *power to transform*: its action as time: as music. Thus no repetition, no development, no contrast. Those devices all assume the existence of *Gestalten* —themes, motives, objects—that are repeated, varied, developed, contrasted; dissected, elaborated, expanded, contracted, modulated, transposed, inverted or turned back to front. All that has been given up since the first purely pointillistic works. . . . No Neo. . . ! What then? Counter-Points: a series offering the most comprehensive and meaningful potential for change and renewal—without foreseeable limit. One never hears the same thing twice [*sic*]. Still, one is always aware of an unchanging and underlying constancy of flow permeating the whole. A latent power, that holds together related proportions: a structure. Not the same *Gestalten* in a changing light. Rather: different *Gestalten* in the same light, that penetrates everything.[5]

The last remark distinguishes Stockhausen's thought from Boulez's insistence on pure manuscript transformations (rhythmic cells); it also shows his instinctive feeling for the numen of music as distinct from its bare material aspect—a spirituality also alien to Boulez's agnostic literalism.

Schaeffer's enthusiasm is shared by Boulez, whose own contribution, 'Eventuellement . . .', is prefaced by the remark, 'Rarely has there been a time of such sheer exaltation in the history of music'. But whereas Schaeffer's attention is concentrated upon what one actually *hears* with the new equipment, and on the formal possibilities suggested by the new mode of listening and the manipulative potential offered by recording devices and accessories, Boulez's essay shows him to be more concerned with *l'écriture*: with solving the problem of total serial predetermination in notational terms. This idea he pursues with infectious vigour and wit, drawing on the examples of Debussy, Webern, Schoenberg, Stravinsky, Messiaen, and Cage with casual ease and authority. This degree of familiarity with the great names of contemporary music gives Boulez a certain advantage in debate; his eagerness to promote total serialism also sets him apart from, or even at loggerheads with Schaeffer. What is interesting about the essay where Stockhausen is concerned, however, is (1) the ease and thoroughness of Boulez's theory, and (2) his view of the electronic medium as an ideal instrument for the realization of abstract formal concepts: as a mirror of theory, that is, and not as a tool. One was now able to conceive a perfect structure of relationships, and then to turn to the tape recorder, sound-generator, etc., to obtain a 'print-out'. This view, which had

---

[5] 'Orientierung 1952/53', *Texte, I*, p. 37. Stockhausen's evocation of latent uniformity of motion may be interpreted as a philosophical reduction of his experience of recording media: of the constant speed of tape movement, for instance, or constant level of radio emission, opposed to the notion of temporal continuity embodied in the musical artefact.

enormous vogue among theorists and became the electronic *idée reçue* of critics and anthologists, much as the computer is regarded today, was directly opposed to Schaeffer's view. Since he is concerned with intellectual organization first and with sound second, as a function not of organization but of *instrumentation*, Boulez is able to propose the dissection and reordering of a recorded sound without reference to whether the resulting variants would indeed display recognizable properties of coherence and quality (Exx. XVI, XVII).[6] His proposal to this effect would seem incomprehensible to Schaeffer; the identity between the original and its 'variants' would be entirely a visual relationship.

Boulez also examines the question of serial tempi:

To include the whole register from bass to treble, we are obliged to transpose these twelve sounds at 6 different speeds (i.e. 6 octaves) . . . Organizing the tessitura and speeds in this way implies the use of a multiple of the smallest value, a series $t_1, t_2, \ldots, t_{12}$; speeds increasing continuously in a geometric progression of 2; since the octave serves as base, the durations will diminish in inverse proportion.[7]

Boulez also introduces the possibility of generating variable densities of harmonic material from simple basic resources: the principle of 'multiplication'. This too is a theoretical discovery of great practical usefulness, since it enables pointillist material to be expanded and shaped in otherwise forbidden ways (and incidentally reconciles the abstract world of Webern with the more opulent and variegated effects of Debussy). And he describes the composition of serial relationships between instrumental groups with reference to *Polyphonie X* (though the work is not named)—a procedure already employed by Stockhausen in his own way, in *Formel*.

Messiaen, whose course in Analysis and Aesthetics at the Conservatoire centres on a specific topic each year, chose fortunately to concentrate his attention on 'rhythm' for the year in which Stockhausen attended his classes. Stockhausen recalls (in *Texte II*, p. 144) 'rhythmic analyses of all Mozart's piano concerti, the rhythm of Gregorian chant, Indian rhythm; analyses of Debussy's, Webern's and Stravinsky's music, and of Messiaen's own works (from the original sketches to the final score)'. In Gregorian chant he encountered a style of notation that implies intuitive rather than chronometric quantification; a notation that includes signs for a variety of note-groups as well as single pitches; and an art of melodic invention based upon different juxtapositions of these unit gestures, which he saw applied to contemporary practice in Messiaen's *Neumes Rythmiques*. Neumata-like forms are also hinted at in the notation of *Zyklus*, and in his sketches for the manipulation and variation of electronic material in *Kontakte*.[8]

---

[6] The examples in Roman numerals refer to Boulez's own article, which is also reproduced in *Rélévés d'Apprenti*, du Seuil, 1966.

[7] *La Revue musicale,* op. cit., p. 134. In '. . . how time passes . . .' Stockhausen dismisses Boulez's theory as an over-simplification.

[8] See Helmut Kirchmeyer, *Zur Entstehungs- und Problemgeschichte der 'Kontakte' von Karlheinz Stockhausen*, p. 40 (included with recording Wergo 60009), 1963.

The 'magic syllables' of Messiaen's *Harawi* seem to foreshadow the 'magic names' of *Stimmung*; the isorhythms and duration-scale canons of *Cantéyodjayâ* figure in *Kontra-Punkte*. And since this was also the era of the *Messe de la Pentecôte* and the *Livre d'Orgue*, Stockhausen was also exposed to the inspiring influence of Messiaen's organ music, the vivid style of which articulates new modes of perception of musical time, a concept of music in which instrumental resonance plays a major part, involving moreover the composition and manipulation of timbre. In the *Livre d'Orgue,* for instance, Messiaen claims to have emancipated mixture stops for the first time, using them as melody stops in their own right. As a result the listener is confronted with a music in which sub-tractive analysis of timbre plays as vital a part as additive synthesis. Messiaen's extremely plain permutational forms in the *Livre* are also of considerable interest. No. I 'Reprises par Interversion', for instance, uses the kind of modified repetition Stockhausen recommends to be used in *Spiral*:

(a) The structure is built up of three 'personnage rythmiques', *pratâpacekhara, gajajhampa,* and *sârasa*, which appear in the first statement of *Reprises* in the following order:

123	132	231	213	321	312
PGS	PSG	GSP	GPS	SGP	SPG

(b) The six statements of *gajajhampa* are developed as follows:

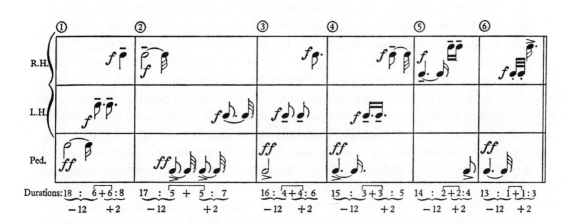

Strangely enough, the new dialectic of organ music corresponds in principle and in significant detail with that proposed for and afterwards adopted by electronic music, e.g. in the much closer relationship between sound-complexity and sound-duration, and in the desire to integrate the organization of timbre into the structural work-plan of a piece. Organ music also conveys the same sense of objective dislocation described by Schaeffer for tape recorded sounds. In its cathedral role one encounters the concept of instrumentation and performance tailored to a specific environment: music, that is, as a function of architecture, coming indirectly to the listener from an invisible and distant source. Music in church ritual is one element of a total sensory experience involving the contrasts of darkness and light, flesh and stone, movement and stillness. The energy with which Stockhausen has pursued the idea of a complete sound environment, in the distribution of loudspeakers in his electronic works, and of players in *Ensemble*, not to mention the *Hinab-Hinauf* project and *Musik für ein Haus*, is doubtless due as much to the powerful impression made on him by the religious environment as to the Wagnerian idiosyncrasy frequently attributed to him. An instance of the secular listener's imperviousness to the emotional—and thus artistic—significance of such factors in music as resonance, direction, and spatial distribution, is Karl Wörner's nonchalant observation concerning *Gruppen*, that 'fundamentally, Stockhausen's work is based on the idea of space music in the sense of sixteenth-century polychoral writing. . . . However he was led to polychoral procedures not by any sensuous delight in sumptuous sonorities, but by technical aspects of the craft of composition'.[9]

Wörner's assumption that strict formal control is incompatible with 'a sensuous delight in sumptuous sonorities' is as untrue of Stockhausen as it is of the Venetian polychoral masters—but who, listening to *Gruppen*, could take such an observation seriously? It is, on the contrary, *always* the case that the sounds of music appear most fresh and exciting when their formal relationships have been most clearly determined. In traditional church music, where neither the notation system, nor the instrumentation, nor the functional circumstance preconditions the shape and character of musical utterance, there exists a possibility—a need even—to organize music in a purely abstract manner, and the natural tendency of such music is to reconcile extremes of intellectual organization and sensory extravagance. So it is in the case of Messiaen's organ music: the notation does not imply a beat, the instrument does not imply a breath, the function does not imply a dance, the environment does not imply competition for attention, nor any limit to attention time. Such music can only be held together either by intelligence or by a sublime sense of occasion. Talents of this sort are rare and unrecognized today because the combination of circumstances is rare, because doctrine has replaced celebration in the spirit of music, because composers are teachers today and not priests, and because concerts have evolved into performer-focused entertainments or lectures. What electronic and concrete music has done has been to restore musical consciousness suddenly and totally to that ancient level of mystery.[10] An early, frequent objection

[9] *Musical Quarterly*, Vol. XLV, 1954, p. 237.

[10] The difference between a Stockhausen and a Cage is between a celebrant and a participant: Cage's art, like Duchamp's 'ready-mades', is essentially submissive; an art dependent upon social convention—as all good wit is—but also sharing the current values of social convention, which today is secular and ephemeral ('corrupt'). The religious attitude creates a more suitable environment for contemplation, and

raised against tape music was that it eliminated the performer. So it did: worse still, it suddenly exposed the purpose-built auditorium, its fixed seating, sloping floor, unique focus of attention, sealed enclosure, and characterless acoustic, in all its specialist nakedness. Music could no longer remain a spectator sport relying on the motions and postures of performers on a stage. Audiences would have to learn to listen again. Composers were no less subject to the terror and shame of self-discovery inflicted by the electronic medium than were its most vociferous critics. Even those who worked with Schaeffer, and to some extent Schaeffer himself, were uncertain how to cope with the idea of a music for ears alone. As Boulez acidly observed, most of the Paris group's composing efforts seemed to rely upon witty juxtapositions of cliché effects; although this produced a lively sideline in humorous collage, it could not aspire to serious formal research. And unfortunately their uncertainty blinded the Club d'Essai to the importance of Stockhausen's investigations as an apprentice at the ORTF studio.

I made hundreds of analyses of instrumentally produced sounds, European and exotic, in the musique concrète studio, and made tape recordings of exotic sounds in the Musée de l'Homme in Paris. There was a large sine-wave generator in a basement studio of the PTT, which I used to produce the first synthetic sound-spectra by superimposing sine tones. The work was infinitely arduous; as there was no tape-recorder in the studio I had to copy each sine tone on to disc and then re-copy it from one disc to another. This first 'composition' by electronic means was witnessed by the French scientist Abraham Moles, who thought me quite mad at the time. . . . These earliest sound-compositions using sine tones resulted from intensive correspondence between Goeyvaerts, who was living in Antwerp, and myself in Paris (it was only a question of individual sounds, not yet of 'music' in any sense). We wanted absolutely pure, controllable sounds without the subjective emotional influence of interpreters.[11]

What was the point of wanting to be able to produce 'pure, controllable sounds'? It was this: that only when it could be shown that such sounds could be synthetically produced would the serialization of timbre be a practical proposition. The attraction of being able to synthesize timbres was twofold: to satisfy an abstract ideal of total musical formation, and to be able to generate a range of previously unheard and practically unimaginable sounds, with the eventual possibility of mediating between conventional instrumental sound and artificial timbres.

With equipment so obviously unsuited to his purpose, it is not surprising that Stockhausen had little success in his efforts. In a letter to Eimert late in the year he despairingly confesses that 'the possibility of realizing a Klangatom is quite beyond me'.[12] But he was also affected by Schaeffer's incredulity and mistrust.

---

a higher-than-average probability of sudden revelation, than ordinary life affords: not merely a translation of the commonplace (as in Pop Art) but a transformation of it into a new reality. Cage refuses to engage to this extent. As a result, his 'delight' is more dependent on intellectual than sensory stimuli.

[11] 'The Origins of Electronic Music', *Musical Times*, July 1971, pp. 649–50.

[12] Herbert Eimert, 'So begann der Elektronische Musik', *Melos*, 1972/1. The reference is not to Stockhausen's *Konkrete Etüde* (q.v.), but to an earlier attempt.

In a quarrel that seems rather pointless, Pierre Schaeffer reproaches Stockhausen for preferring electric sound to sound of natural origin. . . . 'Before all electric music (he has said) I recoil, mindful of the fact that my father was a violinist and my mother a *chanteuse*. We are craftsmen. My violin, my voice, I recapture in all this hardware of wood and metal, and in the sound of my "revolving clarions". I want to achieve direct contact with the matter of sound, without electrons getting in the way.'[13]

He had not grasped the fact that the recorded image of a natural sound was as artificially 'electric' as any synthetically produced complex of tones.

Etüde

1952: No. ¹/₅

Musique concrète.
Duration unknown.

T HE concrete study *Etüde* was composed in Paris in December 1952, using tape-recorded piano notes from which the onset and decay were cut, leaving mid-section wave forms of reasonably stable composition and fairly constant amplitude. These were re-recorded on disc at 78 r.p.m., and transferred in the final assembly to a master disc. The recopying from disc to disc gave the final recording a prominent underlying 'rumble', but Stockhausen liked it all the same, and the rumble returns transmogrified in the deep bass thundering passages of *Kontakte* (e.g. section X).[1]

The disc, which was deposited with the Groupe de Recherches Musicales in Paris, is unfortunately now lost. The score and manuscript sketches, mislaid for many years, came to light recently in Stockhausen's papers (together with plans for the abortive study referred to in his letter to Eimert).[2]

Etüde is a study in the organization and order-permutation of six basic sounds. The score shows a fundamental time-unit represented as 216 cm., a tape measurement

[13] Claude Samuel, *Panorama de l'Art Musical Contemporain*, Gallimard, 1958, p. 626. The quotation from Schaeffer is taken from Schaeffer's *A la Recherche d'une Musique Concrète*.

[1] The sound of the needle spinning to the centre of a 78 r.p.m. record and stopping, is also evoked at the end of *Kontakte*, in the circular movement of brushes on the snare-drum surface.

[2] See page 39.

corresponding to about three seconds' duration. Stockhausen's serial application of durations (defined in centimetres) and his distribution and rotation of the basic sounds, closely resemble the compositional processes of the first set of piano pieces, in particular Piece I.

Spiel für Orchester

1952, revised 1973: No. ¹/4

Two movements for orchestra: 3 oboes, 3 clarinets in A, 3 bassoons, double bassoon, 3 horns, glockenspiel, vibraphone, celesta, electric organ, piano, strings (6.6.0.6.6.). Two groups of percussion (7–9 players):

Percussion I: small Indian bell, small triangle, 2 suspended cymbals (high and low), 2 tom-toms, wood block, 2 temple blocks, hi-hat, African pod rattles, small snare drum, tenor ratchet, 2 antique cymbals, 2 tamtams, 1 pedal timpanum.

Percussion II: 5 cinelli (tuned small cymbals,) 4 suspended cymbals (2 high 2 low), hi-hat, 1 large sizzle-cymbal, 3 tom-toms, 1 pedal timpanum.

1. 'Paris 11. III. 52'.
2. 'Paris 4. V. 52'.
Duration c. 16 minutes.

'SPIEL für Orchester' was to have been a three-movement work with *Formel* as first movement, but having completed the two additional movements Stockhausen became dissatisfied with what he felt to be *Formel*'s stylistic inconsistency, and the earlier piece was dropped before the first performance of *Spiel* at Donaueschingen in 1952. These inconsistencies are instrumental and procedural. Stockhausen added considerably to the percussion sections of the second and third pieces, and though the revised instrumentation alone would be sufficient to indicate a change of orientation (scope in Stockhausen being synonymous with function), differences in internal organization—in instrumental sub-grouping as well as timing—reveal a change of tactics only reconcilable with *Formel* in the unflattering terms of a 'before and after' comparison.

These changes may be directly attributed to his move to Paris and introduction to the world of *musique concrète*. As much may be inferred from a reading of *Spiel*'s additional instrumentation, which supplements *Formel*'s orchestra with two massive groups of mainly unpitched percussion. The piece's extraordinary range of attack instruments reflects two things: Stockhausen's systematic study of instrumental timbre through the recording and dissection of a wide variety of individual sounds; and his discovery through this study that most musical sounds could be separated into 'attack' and 'decay' components, and that the personalities and distinctive timbres of wind and percussion instruments chiefly reside in the initial attack. These revelations suggest an entirely new categorization of musical instruments according to purely acoustic criteria; throw light on previously unrecognized affinities between instruments of different families; and—most important at the time—suggest the possibility of creating new timbres by transplantation of attacks to different resonances.

The importance of this last possibility was that it gave credibility to Messiaen's intuitive serialization of attacks in *Mode de Valeurs*; it now seemed physically possible to manipulate attacks independently of pitch-resonances and to produce, either deliberately or by structured coincidence, an entirely new range of musical sounds. This, then, was a way forward from Webern.

The new way of hearing implies new types of serial predetermination, in particular the formation of instrumental sub-groups within the orchestra to function as 'collective timbres', with independent time-structures. Stockhausen was never happy with the simple arithmetic of Messiaen's duration scale; while it had accuracy as a measure, it lacked nuance. In *Spiel* he therefore organizes the enlarged orchestra into four subgroups, each combining 'attack' and 'resonance' instruments, and assigns a different but closely related duration-scale to each:

$(\eighthnote = 1)$												
I	$11\frac{2}{3}$	$10\frac{1}{2}$	$9\frac{1}{3}$	9	$7\frac{2}{3}$	$6\frac{1}{2}$	$5\frac{1}{3}$	5	$3\frac{2}{3}$	$2\frac{1}{2}$	$1\frac{1}{3}$	1
II	$11\frac{1}{2}$	$10\frac{1}{2}$	10	$8\frac{2}{3}$	$7\frac{1}{2}$	$6\frac{1}{3}$	6	$4\frac{2}{3}$	$3\frac{1}{2}$	$2\frac{1}{3}$	2	$\frac{2}{3}$
III	$11\frac{1}{3}$	11	$9\frac{2}{3}$	$8\frac{1}{2}$	$7\frac{1}{3}$	7	$5\frac{2}{3}$	$4\frac{1}{2}$	$3\frac{1}{2}$	3	$2\frac{2}{3}$	$\frac{1}{2}$
IV	12	$10\frac{2}{3}$	$9\frac{1}{2}$	$8\frac{1}{3}$	8	$6\frac{2}{3}$	$5\frac{1}{2}$	$4\frac{1}{3}$	4	$2\frac{2}{3}$	$2\frac{1}{2}$	$\frac{1}{3}$

These durations include a greater or lesser proportion of 'rest' corresponding to the attack sign with which each is associated. Characteristically Stockhausen associates longer durations with portato and soft dynamics, and shorter with progressively louder dynamics and more abrupt attacks.

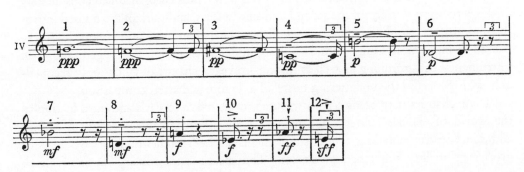

When four separate structures based on interlocking duration series are combined, two advantages are gained. A more stable beat pattern is statistically assured,[1] and the higher note density increases the probable incidence of spontaneous attack and resonance combinations, and melodic or rhythmic associations. *Spiel* is therefore more efficient on two counts: richer and more flexible than *musique concrète* in its investigation of attack and resonance, and better integrated (i.e. sounding less erratic and fragmented) than music using simpler additive duration series. All the advantages claimed exclusively for the tape-recorder, in fact, Stockhausen simply and effectively transcribed into ordinary notation.

Piece I, of 100 bars, dated 'Paris 11.III.52', depicts a gradual formation of melodic chains from atomistic serial 'points'. As in *Formel*, the guiding instrument in this process of synthesis is the vibraphone; glockenspiel and piano provide a continuous alternating background pulsation of two-note serial intervals at high and low extremes of pitch. Gradually the initially sparse instrumentation is added to, and one by one the newcoming instruments converge on the vibraphone's growing cell-motif. The 'feel' of the piece seems very similar to Schoenberg's Op. 16, 'Péripétie': the same ostinato ringing background, sense of suspended time, sudden mysterious night-time disturbances and brief flurries of sound. The first complete statement of the series comes at bar 42. (see p. 44). Shortly afterward, in bar 49, a vibraphone statement of the series as two-note intervals triggers off a grand percussion tutti, reviewing their 'attack' series in their differing periodicities. But the mood relaxes from here on, as though the previously repressed melodic impulse were suddenly released; the music becomes increasingly tranquil and sustained and finally resolves in a calm blend of sonorities.

Piece II, of 114 bars, dated 'Paris 4.V.52', develops in a reciprocal way from Piece I, and depicts the synthesis of point-formations as a process of condensation from a resonant background of sustained metallic percussion sounds. Gradually elements pass from this amorphous complex reverberation to wind and string instruments; the distribution reaches a maximum at bar 56, marked by a resoundingly clear note struck on the glass (a favoured sound of *musique concrète* composers).[2] (See p. 45). From this peak the music gradually declines to its end, wind and strings sinking back into the original background of percussion resonance.

In a perceptive if generally sceptical review of the first performance, the critic R.-A. Mooser observed:

Thirty or so traditional instruments . . . provide a resonant background, sometimes scarcely audible, upon which the percussive elements in turn project their particular vibrations, at irregular intervals and in very free rhythmic patterns. . . . One is forcibly reminded of the primitive orchestras dreamed up by the inhabitants of darkest Africa.[3]

[1] It was precisely this regularity of flow which Stockhausen later criticized in '. . . how time passes . . .' (*Die Reihe* III, pp. 12–15).

[2] At the première the glass was struck so hard that it shattered, causing an uproar which stopped the performance.

[3] R.-A. Mooser, *Panorama de la Musique Contemporaine*, ed. René Kister, 1955.

It is certainly interesting to find Stockhausen at such an early stage in his career resorting to the sustained effects of what is generally assumed to be a much later meditative style. In this connection, perhaps with reference to his subsequent withdrawal of the score, we may consider two fragments from his writings of the period:

Pre-formed material cannot be organized, only arranged.[4]

and

The inherent instantaneity of through-organized music, the fact that it does not 'develop', can only induce a state of meditative listening. Attention becomes fixed in the music, having no need to consider what goes before or what follows in order to perceive the actual, present event (the individual sound). Certainly it is assumed that the individual event is already complete in itself, satisfying at once all the order-criteria specific to the whole work—thus, absolute and incontrovertible.[5]

In 1973 *Spiel* was revised for publication. In the first movement Stockhausen's changes are minimal, simply rationalizations of serially 'necessary' but technically impracticable rhythms or dynamics, with some skeletal re-orchestration. In the second movement these same revisions persist, coupled after the half-way point with an 'incrustation' of the points into melodies (though only sparingly) which also, curiously enough, brings the end of the piece much nearer to *Formel*. The percussion instrumentation has been considerably revised.

[4] 'Situation des Handwerks', Paris, 1952 (*Texte I*, p. 19).
[5] Stockhausen, op. cit., p. 21.

Schlagtrio

1952, rescored 1973: No. ${}^{\mathrm{I}}/3$, UE 15943

Originally known as 'Schlagquartett für Klavier und 3 × 2 Pauken'.
For piano and 2 × 3 timpani.
'Paris, den 1. Juni 1952'.
Duration c. 11 minutes.

STOCKHAUSEN'S commentary on *Schlagquartett*[1] ('Percussion Quartet'), written in a letter to Dr. Herbert Hübner—and reproduced in *Texte II*—is the earliest intimation we have of a conception of music as audible moments of transition between states inaccessible to hearing; an affirmation of some philosophic weight born of his experience of pointillist music, the 'points' of which, he observed, seem to resemble points of reference (nerve endings, or electrical contacts) seen as a two-dimensional cross-section of a continuously evolving three-dimensional form. 'Two entities emerge from a region beyond the physically describable and perceivable, into one bounded in space and time. They are diametrically opposed ('als Pole aufeinander bezogen')'.[2]

Schlagtrio is a more deeply reasoned exposition of the dualistic ideology expressed in *Kreuzspiel*. The encounter of Stockhausen's two entities, also called 'voices', may be likened to the appearance and passing of two express trains headed in opposite directions on parallel lines: first the two engines meet, then the two first carriages, and so on; by the meeting of the two last carriages the engines are already retiring from one another at speed. For all that the pattern of encounter is remarkably stable: its formation is perfectly symmetrical in relation to a central point of balance which does not move. Stockhausen has captured this image of dynamic symmetry in terms of a multi-dimensional convergence of pitch, duration, and dynamic series, a movement from extremes of pitch to the middle register, from widely differing durations to scarcely distinguishable median values, and from maximum dynamic contrast to mezzoforte and mezzopiano.

Two superimposed note structures, the two 'voices' referred to by the composer, jockey for position at extremes of the piano keyboard and then, by a process of encounter and displacement, make their way towards the middle register. The work is divided into twelve sections representing successive stages of this process.

[1] As it was then.
[2] *Texte II*, p. 13.

47

Each voice manifests a twofold possibility of existence. . . . Either (a) it may hold to its original identity, that is, to the tonality laid down for it in the twelve notes of the chromatic scale. Or, (b) it may be temporarily obscured by a passing phase of change. This means that besides the chromatic system of pitches there must also be an alternative system of pitch coordinates in which the original tonality cannot be expressed. They must therefore be pitches which cannot be mistaken for notes of the sounding voice; but by the same token, in which a frequency deviating from the original specification may be located. . . . The two possibilities (a) and (b) alternate during the course of the work. . . . Both voices . . . set off on their appropriately polarized courses in the two extreme octaves and move alternately from the chromatic realm to the deviant pitch-spaces.

The alternative 'contrary pitch region' is represented by the six timpani, tuned to a fixed whole-tone scale a quarter-tone flat relative to the piano, so that each instrumental pitch may 'refer' to successive pairs of adjacent semitones without actually coinciding with any of the twelve chromatic pitches. Each of the six timpani corresponds to one of Stockhausen's six 'piano-octave' divisions of the keyboard.

Schlagtrio

Piano series

Tuning of the 6 timpani, in pairs.

$\natural$ = quarter tone flat
$\natural\flat$ = three-quarter tone flat

Stockhausen chose timpani (which are not in this case pedal instruments) for their flexibility of timbre and high resonance capability—not, as might appear on the surface, for added rhythmic interest. The range of attacks specified for timpani are evenly matched to those of the piano, giving the latter a range and versatility of colouring that clearly opens the way to the later piano pieces.

Piano:

V	secco, staccatissimo, no Ped.
•	staccato $+ \frac{1}{2}$ Ped.　⌒ [sustaining]
ı	as • but stressed: ⸚
⸱⸱	staccato + pedal: released almost at once
—	portato senza Ped.
∩	attack senza Ped., release with Ped.
⌒ ⸨⸩—	Precede with Ped., staccatissimo attack, ped. resonance
↑	'Normal': 'as far as possible without sustaining pedal.'

Note: When several different attack indications occur simultaneously or in close opposition, the rhythmic polyphony must predominate (pedal notes yield to notes without pedal; rests prevail over pedal indications).

Timpani:	V	with 1 (felt stick; *simultaneously* dampened with the other hand
	.	with 1 stick; at the edge
	ı	with 1 stick; in the middle (midway between skin edge and centre)
	≟	with 2 sticks: at the edge
	–	1 stick at edge, 1 at the centre simultaneously
	∩	with 2 sticks; in the middle (midway between edge and centre)
	⌒	with 2 sticks in the middle, then tremolo *pppp* until next note
	ſ	with wooden part of stick, or hard felt

Note: Rests signify total dampening of skin vibration with the hand.

"Schlagquartet"

♩= 80-100

Klavier

Pauken I.

II.

At the central point of greatest coincidence—corresponding to the instant when our two trains are met length to length—each twelve-note statement is unfolded to its greatest extent. Here, says Stockhausen, 'a third voice comes into existence'. This third voice is the revealed total reciprocity of the two series, which only at this point represent all the possible stages of development in complete symmetry one with another, also piano with timpani.

Schlagtrio is probably the work to consider alongside Stockhausen's *Etüde*, the lost study in dissected and rearranged piano tones. If so, then like *Spiel* it may be 'read' as an instrumental model of an essentially studio concept; all the same a tangible link with the Bartók of the *Sonata for Two Pianos and Percussion* ought not to be overlooked. But the piece is probably most immediately interesting as a prototype of the symmetrical evolutionary process more familiar in works of recent date: *Pole für 2*, of course, and *Mantra*.

Punkte[1]

1952: unpublished, withdrawn

For orchestra.
Flute, 2 oboes, 3 clarinets (E flat, B flat, bass), 3 saxophones (sopr. doubling alto, bar.,
bass or bass sarrusaphone); 2 bassoons, horn, cornet in B flat, trumpet in C, trombone;
12 bongos tuned B flat – a¹ (3 players), 2 pianos, harp I, harp II (muted); strings 2.0.2.1.1.
Duration c. 8½ minutes.

'P UNKTE' was composed immediately before *Kontra-Punkte*, the first version of
which also dates from 1952. The similarity in their names is intentional; when Stockhausen finished *Punkte*, and decided that he wasn't satisfied with it as a compositional
stratagem, he began again with the 'points' of *Punkte* at the beginning of *Kontra-Punkte*,
gradually transforming them into group-formations ('counter-points').

Little apart from the underlying point structure relates *Punkte* in the original version
to its later recomposition of 1962. The first version is shorter in duration, and for an
orchestra of considerably smaller dimensions. Its orchestral palette is richer than *Spiel*
and unusual in specifying exclusively instruments of definite (equal tempered) pitch,
including a scale of chromatically tuned bongos, which, however, he later decided to
remove.

The music itself differs from *Spiel* in having less to do with the juxtaposition of
attack and resonance instruments, and more with the gradual transformation of pitch
orders by semitonal and register displacement in the manner of *Kreuzspiel* within a
strict, seemingly logarithmic time structure. But this process does not lead as in *Spiel I*
or *Kontra-Punkte* to the germination of linked themes—musical molecular chains—nor
to the unification of timbre depicted, for example, in *Kontra-Punkte*'s reduction of
instrumental diversity into one highly inflected sonority. The compositional process
seems to have allowed only compression or rarefaction of density, and though the
bongos were possibly intended originally to weld the ensemble into a single vast percussion instrument (in '. . . how time passes . . .' Stockhausen expresses a wish for a
duration keyboard by which 'one depresses a key, and this releases a mechanism which
measures a defined length of the note; and one determines the pitch . . . by the variable
pressure of the key') it is clear from his subsequent elimination of the percussion section
that he must have had second thoughts. Dissatisfaction with this aspect of the work may

---

[1] For *Punkte* (1952–62: No. 1/2) see p. 155.

have persuaded him to turn to tempo modulation as a more reliable means of imposing shape and a sense of direction on outwardly amorphous point structures. Both *Kontra-Punkte* and *Punkte 1962* employ scales of tempi, whereas *Punkte* first version is mapped out according to a regular MM=112 grid.

Kontra-Punkte

1952-3: No. 1, UE 12207, revised version UE 12218

For 10 instruments: flute, clarinet, bass clarinet, bassoon, trumpet, trombone, piano, harp, violin, cello.
Duration c. 12 minutes.
Recorded by Pierre Boulez (conductor) on Vega C30 A66; by Bruno Maderna (conductor) on RCA Victrola (London) VICS 1239 and RCA Italiana (Rome) SLD-61005(3) (same recording); and by members of the London Sinfonietta on DGG (De. 2530 443). All recordings are of the revised version.

STRAVINSKY was impressed by *Kontra-Punkte*; indeed in *Movements* for piano and orchestra the piano functions as serial co-ordinator of the orchestral figurations in very much the same way as in the work of his younger contemporary. But for many others not gifted with a composer's insight *Kontra-Punkte* was the first, and for many years one of the only pieces from which one could attempt to read the personality of a young composer about whom little was known except his talent for exciting controversy. It has taken Stockhausen nearly twenty years to live down that first popular image of ferocious intellectualism created and sustained by critics who did not like the music they heard, could not fathom the composer's programme notes, and when the scores became available, found little there to persuade them to adopt a less hostile attitude.

The music *was* difficult, to play as well as 'hear', and Stockhausen's own explanations often *were* (perhaps deliberately) obscure in terminology and reticent in information (in the case of *Kontra-Punkte*, presupposing the reader's intimate acquaintance with the compositional principles of the unpublished and withdrawn *Punkte 1952*, for instance).

The pity is that the confusion surrounding *Kontra-Punkte* unjustly alienated the composer from public affection for so long, and buried the charms of a delightful piece in a verbal thicket. Even today I wonder how many well-disposed English-speaking readers will be able to follow the latest authorized translation of the composer's original programme note:

Kontra-Punkte for ten instruments originated from the idea of resolving the antitheses of a many-faceted musical world of individual notes and temporal relationships to the point where a situation is reached in which only the homogeneous and the immutable is audible.[1]

It seems to me that Stockhausen is trying to combine two statements in one in his original note. The first is a general statement of fact, that in pointillist music contrasts tend to cancel one another out until no contrast carries weight any more.[2] The second is a statement of intent concerning *Kontra-Punkte* in particular, the idea of expressing this levelling-out of response in instrumental terms as an audible progression from maximum 'scatter' to maximum coherence, both counteracting the falling-off of attention, and turning an intrinsic perceptual drawback of pointillist music to positive compositional advantage.[3]

The work is in one movement. Six different timbres are employed: flute—bassoon, clarinet—bass clarinet, trumpet—trombone, piano, harp, violin—violoncello (three characteristically differing types of wind instrument, in pairs, and three types of stringed instrument with struck, plucked, and bowed strings respectively). These six timbres are resolved into one, that of the piano (struck strings). One by one the trumpet, trombone, bassoon, violin, bass clarinet, harp, cello, and flute drop out. Six different loudness levels (*ppp*—*sfz*) likewise reduce one by one to *pp*. Great differences between very short and long durations are gradually eliminated, leaving closely related middle values (semiquaver, triplet semiquaver, dotted semiquaver, quint semiquaver, etc.). Out of the opposition between vertical and horizontal tone-relationships emerges a two-voice, monochrome counterpoint.[4]

At the same time as it represents a systematic impoverishment of timbre resources, *Kontra-Punkte* also depicts an increase in flexibility and coherence of musical expression. It is this, I would suggest, that is the real 'counter-action' implied by the title of the piece. In a subsequent programme note for a Cologne Muzik der Zeit concert in 1962 (also reproduced in *Texte II*, p. 20) Stockhausen does in fact describe the formula of *Kontra-Punkte* as a transformation of 'punctual' material into 'groups'.

[1] Wörner, op. cit. (Faber, 1973), p. 31. (For the text in German, see *Texte II*, p. 20.)

[2] See *Texte I*, p. 230: 'The problem is to avoid taking element-independence ('Vereinzelung') so far that through the requirement of constant alteration all the elements lose their differentiation—in the larger view, reducing to one level—that such a kind of organisation easily degenerates into structural uniformity, i.e. falls back into divisiveness and repetitiveness.'

[3] The idea of gradually revealing a condition of 'unchanging One-ness' ('ein Einheitliches, Unverändertes') also suggests by its choice of terminology a process of making audible the 'latent unity' of pointillist music (see Stockhausen's definition of aims in *Bearings: 1952/53*, p. 35).

[4] *Texte II*, pp. 20–1.

As this view of its programme suggests, the piece presents a transition from an abstract, conceptual order that is essentially static, to an audibly organized dynamic continuum; effectively a reconciliation of Webernian *klangfarben* technique with the post-Schoenbergian thematicism represented by Boulez's second Piano Sonata. Sections of more or less dissociated 'points' alternate with sections of a more assertive melodic counterpoint, the latter increasingly assigned to the piano part as the piece progresses. These sections are also defined by variations in tempo, a fundamental pulsation of MM=120, with which the more cohesive elements of the music are associated, alternating with six other tempi, which together make up an incomplete tempo scale, perhaps calculated to correspond to the frequency-relationships of the following interval-succession:

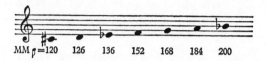

The missing chromatic values in the scale may be accounted for by substitution of another duration (e.g. in the above spelling, 'F sharp' would correspond to a dotted semiquaver in the tempo 'quaver=120'). Stockhausen's bar-unit of a dotted crotchet is particularly suited to serial combinations,[5] not only recalling Boulez's and Messiaen's mode of 12 duration-values reached by addition from demi-semiquaver to dotted crotchet, but also suggesting the possibility of subdivision from one to one-twelfth of a bar (in fact the piece employs all equal subdivisions of the bar-length from 1/1 to 1/2 except 1/8 and 1/11):

*Not used in *Kontra-Punkte*

Even if the serial relationships of frequency (pitch), metre, and duration are not as explicit as, say, Boulez's *Structures Ia*, it is clear that at the same time as he is reacting against the tendency towards monotony inherent in pointillist music, Stockhausen is also moving towards the theory of metrical transposition that governs the composition of *Gruppen*.

[5] Cf. Messiaen's use of the unit in *Turangalîla*, and Schoenberg's in Op. 16, No. 1. The earlier works do not use serial durations, of course, but adopt the basic unit of time best suited for the co-ordination of complex rhythms (additive in Messiaen, divisive in Schoenberg).

The general structure of *Kontra-Punkte* suggests that it was originally planned as two (possibly with scope for more) sections each of 12 units of 22 bars. The 22-bar subdivision is clearly indicated in the first half of the piece, in which the basic tempo is alternated with each of the other tempi in ascending order, making intervallic pairs that are mostly of 22 bars' duration:

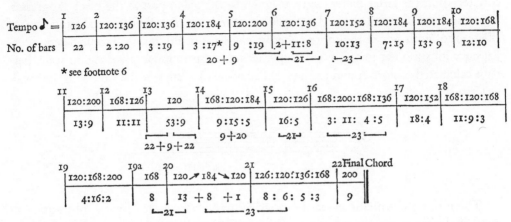

* see footnote 6

The 22-bar unit is too obvious and persistent to be an accident, and it seems likely that having completed the first twelve sections Stockhausen had the impulse to modify this structural regularity, which may account for the greater complexity of the second half as well as for the deviations of part 1. The number 22 is itself significant from a serial point of view, both as the sum of the series (1, 2, . . . 6)+1, and (in terms of 66 quaver pulses) as the sum of the series 1, 2, . . . 11,—that is, a complete series 1–12 *minus* the maximum value.[7]

Again, from a consideration of the layout of the first twelve sections, it seems possible that Stockhausen's Haydn-like idea of discarding the instruments one by one to leave only the piano, may itself have developed out of an original plan simply to bring the disparate counterpoint of structures into a coherent time-continuum. There are three reasons for such a supposition: one, that most of the instruments do not disappear until the second half; two, that the pattern of ensemble-reduction bears no obvious relationship to the basic structure; and three, because the pivotal thirteenth section, though dominated by the piano, nevertheless suggests a resolution in the direction of ensemble rhythmic unanimity rather than the tendency towards a single tone-colour.[8]

[6] In the earlier published version, the metronome change occurs at bar 92 (cf. bar 87 in the later) making section 4 3:22 and 5 4:19 bars (25, 23). This suggests the alternative symmetries (22–22–3–22–22/ 23–21–23) bars.

[7] Stockhausen is not yet employing the Fibonacci series, but is still working with additive duration values.

[8] Though the idea of discarding instruments may have come at a later stage in the composition, it was always a feature of the music, from the very first (unpublished) version of 1952.

Apart from the paradoxes of the piece's construction, however, two features of the music stand out. The first is the sustained originality and vigour of Stockhausen's piano writing in particular; the second is a comparative lack, unexpected in a work of such virtuosity, of true metrical counterpoint. With few exceptions, the unit subdivision of a given bar is the same for all parts, that is, if one instrument has to count 5 or 7 in the time of 6, other entries during that bar will also conform to that subdivision. Thus the 'counter-points' tend to be accentual in the French manner, rather than combinations of metres in the style of the three Viennese masters (and later, of *Gruppen*). In this connection it should be noticed that Stockhausen's use of barring for co-ordination in *Punkte 1952*, *Kontra-Punkte*, and *Kreuzspiel*, contrasts with the phrasing barring of *Formel* and *Klavierstücke I–IV*. Only at the end of the piece at the second climax where the piano in a controlled accelerando and ritardando 'reviews' the six tempi MM=120–184 and back (a nice touch)—do we find a completely assured *metrical* two-part counterpoint, rotating all the combinations of bar-subdivisions from 1 to 6. One may contrast Stockhausen's progression from static accentual polyphony to dynamic rhythmic counterpoint, with the precisely opposite development in Stravinsky's *Rite of Spring*, from the static metrical complexity of the piece's early 'dawn chorus' (which Stravinsky himself came to prefer) to the dynamic accentual continuum of 'The Sacrifice'.

Perhaps surprisingly, the piano writing connects more easily with the styles of Piano Pieces VII and VIII than with Pieces I–IV. There is the sound and feel, if not the substance, of Messiaen's isorhythmic procedure in the piano-dominant midsection of the piece; and though the permutational repetitions of the final bars call to mind the serial echo-effects of Boulez's *Structure Ia*, the contrapuntal style of the piece at this point is quite different (compared with the obviously imitative Piece IV, for instance).[9]

Comparison of the two published versions (both dated 1953 and bearing the catalogue number UE 12207—subsequently changed to UE 12218), shows mainly corrections of a minor nature. For example, the harp B natural in bar 8 becomes a G; in bar 20 the piano acquires a missing E natural; in bar 94 the cello *f cresc.* becomes a *p cresc.*; a fermata is added to bar 117, bass clefs are replaced in bars 118 and 530, missing pitches appear as new grace notes in the bass clarinet at bars 162–3; a slur between cello and harp appears in bar 239, *rit. . . . tempo* in bar 127 and again at bar 399; and in bar 437 the harp is given a newly emphatic final note. These alterations are in the nature of simple rehearsal and engraving corrections. More serious compositional revisions include the re-allocation of the trombone low D in bar 18, to harp and bass clarinet; the added left-hand figure to the piano part in bar 310, the change from *col legno* to 'c.l. Haar und Saiten' ('with wood and hair'—i.e. with the bow held sideways) throughout; the recomposed flute-clarinet combination of bar 23 (see below); and overall raising of soft harp dynamics.

The most dramatic rewriting occurs in bars 88–89, where a dense ornamental tremolo effect, similar to but more elaborate than the effect at bar 109, is replaced by two bars of highly-charged, 'speeded-up' material, a hail of points that resembles in context the similar accelerated interpolation at 16′ 33.6″ of *Kontakte*. So much more complex is this passage than anything else in the score, as a result of the considerable technical progress Stockhausen had made in the intervening months through working on *Studie I* and *Klavierstück I*,—that retrospective alterations to the score almost become necessary to

---

[9] No doubt Stockhausen's play on the F–B flat interval in the final bars will be taken as a dominant-tonic reference, though what interests me is the resolution implied by the ultimate high B, which like the last notes of Pieces II and III seems to have been held in reserve for the purpose.

ensure stylistic unity. This may account for the change of rhythm in the flute-clarinet combination at bar 23:

Original version

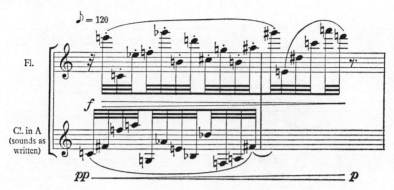

Revised version

—when the larger similar combination at bars 181–93 is left unchanged in its original equal pulsation. Stockhausen's tendency towards more sophisticated combinations as the piece progresses also provokes a doubt as to whether it has to do with his compositional scheme or whether he is simply becoming bolder as he writes. Certainly the 'cloud-burst' effect of the re-composed bars 88–89 seems inconceivable before *Studie I* (see overleaf):

Original version

Revised version

Pitches: | 2 4 5 3 6 1 | 5 6 1 4 2 3 | 5 1 2 6 3 4 | 3 5 6 4 1 2

Attacks: | 3 4 5 2 5 1 | 5 5 1 4 2 3 | 5 1 2 6 3 2 | 3 5 4 4 1 2

Intensities: ($pp = 1, p = 2, \ldots sfz = 6$)

| 5 4 2 4 5 6 | 5 6 6 4 5 4 | 2 6 5 4 4 6 | 6 6 5 5 6 6
   6 6 6 6 6   4 1   5 6 6   5   6 1 5 5   4 4 1 4   5
    3 5 5 4   3 2   3   5   4   5 6 4   5 2 $\frac{6}{3}$ 6
    5 4   3   6 5   6   3   2   3   5 2 3
     3   2   2 3   6   6   3 4
     1   4   3

Incidence of Intensities: (per unit of 6 pulses)

        pp – 1   *mf* – 4
         p – 2   *f* – 5
       mp – 3   *sfz* – 6

Klavierstücke I-IV

1952-3: No. 2, UE 12251

Piano solo.
Duration c. 8 minutes.
Recorded by Aloys Kontarsky on CBS 32 210008 (New York), S77209 (Paris),
72591–2 (London), (2-record set).

PIANO pieces I–IV were written immediately after Stockhausen's arrival in Paris, as a birthday present for Doris his wife. Piece III was written first, and Piece I, the most complicated, last. The collection marks a further stage in Stockhausen's evolution from 'point' to 'group' composition, and in many ways may be regarded as a sketchbook for his later electronic studies.

Piece III

Piece III, deceptively simple in appearance, is as hard to analyse as it is to perform. Its pitch organization is based on three abutting groups of four adjacent pitches: D–F, F–G sharp, and G sharp to B, an arrangement leaving C and C sharp as 'free radicals'. The order and octave transposition of pitches within each four-note unit is serially varied; occasionally at first, more frequently as the piece progresses, notes from adjacent groups are interchanged (the D in group 1 anticipates group 3, for instance, and the B flat and F in groups 5 and 6 have been exchanged). At bar 8, which begins with a 'wild' D flat, the substitution process becomes more difficult to follow, but it eventually leads to a merging of pitches into the compass of a tritone G–C sharp. The final sequence of seven pitches, measuring in semitones from the C sharp of bar 13, forms the interval series 3 5 6 1 4 2, but this seems to have little bearing on the intervallic construction elsewhere.

The piece's organization of durations is easier to grasp. Here the grouping is in threes, either successive or superimposed. The first six durations form the sequence

It divides into two groups of three. What should be noticed is not the visual, absolute value of each duration but its relationship to others within the group. The first group of three consists of a note followed by a gap, then two equal values, and the second is an unbroken succession, the first short, the second long, and the third of medium duration. We may express it this way:

In bar 2 the sequence is changed as follows:

Then follows a sequence of combinations of three unequal durations, which develop the linear relationship of the second part of the original motif in various orders and superimpositions. Five permutations of the three-note group are presented in succession, bringing us to the half-way point of bar 8. To help matters they are reproduced pictorially, the durations being expressed as lines of unequal length:

Then follows another variant of the linear sequence, from the F in bar 8 to the G sharp of bar 10. Here Stockhausen transposes the break from the first to the second subgroup:

The final G sharp of this group is shortened and overlapped with a further statement of the second motif, which completes the bar:

Another linear group follows (bar 11), accentuated at the second beat by superimposition of a 'harmonic' motif, and overlapping (but not this time combined) with yet another at the end (bar 12):

A final statement of the linear series ends the piece, this time accentuated at the first beat by a harmonic combination representing the *first* linear subset, i.e. a note with a pause and two even notes:

The final linear series begins at the C sharp and is as follows:

The dynamics of Piece III are not intended to delineate melodic or contrapuntal structures, but do have an effect on the apparent durations of individual notes. For instance, in bar 5 the dynamics are graded according to note-duration, whereas in bars 3–4 the reverse is the case, the longest note of the group being the softest, and the shortest, the loudest. This, and the composer's attitude to duration, his 'cutting' and superimposition techniques, and his use of *time*—(as distinct from mere *order*—) reversal, interestingly foreshadow Stockhausen's later organization of tape-recorded sounds. It is important, therefore, that the purpose behind Stockhausen's unequal durations should be clearly understood and expressed. The performer must pay particular attention to the ends of notes, their liaison, overlapping, and release. For obvious reasons no sustaining pedal should be used, but it may help performance to keep in mind the characteristically sustained quality of the organ (though the organ cannot produce the dynamic variation required).

Pieces II and IV are more expansive, and in terms of phrasing and structure, which is harmonic in II and contrapuntal in IV, more accessible. Piece II is also composed of note-clusters: this time groups of usually three notes of adjacent pitch, which gives an analysis the appearance of having been copied from one of those scholastic advertisements for Webern. Again, however, the work is not twelve-note in the classical sense, but permutational. In fact, Stockhausen quite deliberately omits the note B flat until the very last chord, so as to end on the proverbial 'note of surprise'. One observes as before the composer's interest in asymmetric patterns of durations, and his use of 'forward' and 'reverse' combinations. Bar 3 in reverse, for example, or the reverse of bar 22, do not look in the least out of character:

Piece II

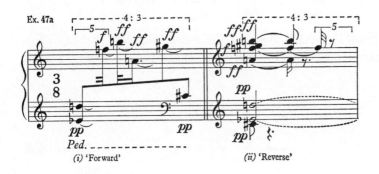

(i) 'Forward'   (ii) 'Reverse'

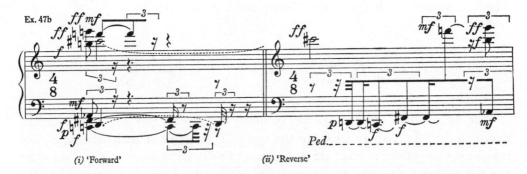

(i) 'Forward'   (ii) 'Reverse'

The main problem with Piece II, as with all four pieces, is one of counting. Here the question resolves itself into threes, which makes the piece less difficult than it appears at first sight. The basic 'pulse' is a quaver unit; the first page may be counted as follows:

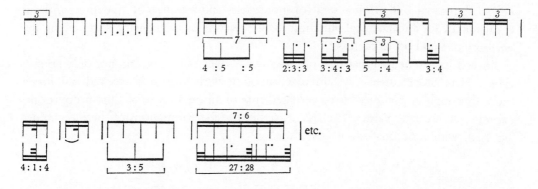

I like to think of Piece IV as Stockhausen's comment on Boulez's *Structures,* which it resembles in its sense of line and momentum, its clearly-notated counterpoints, and its use of dynamics to identify individual voices. Of the four pieces, this one seems most to have a rhythmic life of its own, helped by a frequent and engaging use of hocketing. However the piece does differ from Boulez in the crucial aspect of duration control. Whereas Boulez's rhythmic combinations tend to reduce to a common pulsation, Stockhausen builds on a vast range of subtly differentiated basic units.[1] This has the

Piece IV

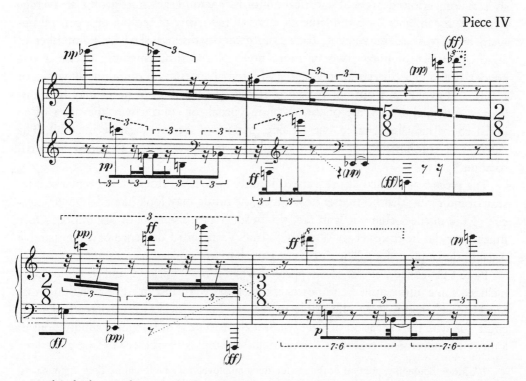

[1] This rhythmic richness results from the progressive *shortening* of fundamental durations by serial fractions.

effect of preserving an original sense of spontaneity and freshness of invention, without the tendency for a mechanical pulsation to take over. This spontaneity is something the performer should try to preserve.

Piece I has excited a great deal of controversy over the years, and not only among critics. Here Stockhausen's system of composing with groups is worked out much more thoroughly. The piece is constructed first of all on a series of time proportions, expressed in crotchet values, 1, 2, 3, . . . 6. Six order-permutations of these six values are used, with occasional slight deviations:

$$5\ 2\ 3\ \mathbf{1}\ 4\ 6 \parallel 3\ 6\ 5\ 4\ 2\ \mathbf{1} \parallel 2\ 6\ 4\ 1\ 3\ 5 \parallel 4\ 1\ 6\ \mathbf{2}\ 5\ 3$$

$$6\ 5\ 1\ 4\ 3\ 2 \parallel 3\ 5\ \overline{(\mathbf{1})\ 1\ 4\ \overset{\frown}{2}\ 4} +$$

In the first group, 1 is actually 1½ (a 3/8 bar); in group 4, 2 is actually slightly less (two bars adding to a 7/16 bar); in group 6, a crotchet rest is transferred from the final 6 value to come between values 5 and 1, leaving the last bar as a 4 plus a rest of indeterminate length. These rotations of six durations are 'groups of groups', since each serial unit of length is subdivided and occupied by a differently characterized group of pitches. What distinguishes Stockhausen's groups from his pointillist style is that emphasis is laid on various degrees of statistical uniformity within each note group, an average dynamic, for instance, or a fundamental internal regularity of tempo, or a general upward or downward movement. Each note group is distinguished by its number of attacks, number of notes (two or more notes played simultaneously count as one attack), their range, direction and degree of internal contrast (in duration, dynamic, or pitch), and evolution from horizontal to vertical (a succession of notes may be transformed into a chord by use of the sustaining pedal, or contrariwise the notes of an initial chord may be released one by one, making a sort of negative melody). The choice and combination of *tendencies* within a group is also determined by serial rotation.[2]

The piece was written at great speed in only two days, Stockhausen remarked, by way of indicating that no matter how much the music may look like a laboured exercise of the intellect alone, it is in fact the product of a moment of inspiration. Only much later did he discover in Webern's Piano Variations I evidence of a comparable organizational procedure. The discovery gave him great pleasure.

Piece I provoked a storm of disapproval when it first appeared, and its critics (who included some distinguished composers and pianists) were all agreed on one thing, that Stockhausen's tempi were impossible to realize. The criticisms must have had some effect, for with the exception of *Gruppen* Stockhausen's use of fractional subdivisions of a metre has never since recaptured the matchless complexity of Piece I's first page:

[2] A more thorough exposition of the serial criteria employed may be found in *Texte I*, pp. 62–74, which covers (though by no means exhaustively) the first 14 bars, comprising the first two orders of six durations.

Piece I

*) Das Tempo jedes Stückes wird vom kleinsten zu spielenden Zeitwert bestimmt: So schnell, wie möglich. Wenn dieses Tempo ermittelt und metronomisch fixiert ist, können alle komplizierteren Zeitproportionen in Klammern (⌐----- ⌐-----⌐) durch Tempowechsel ersetzt werden.

The tempo of each piece, determined by the smallest note-value, is "As fast as possible." When the player has found this tempo and determined it metronomically, all the more complicated time-proportions under the brackets (⌐----- ⌐-----⌐) can be replaced by changes of tempo.

However, a proper case against Stockhausen's chosen system of notating time values has yet to be made out. There is an important difference between changing the tempo from group to group, expressed in a change of metronomic value, and changing the internal frequency from group to group against a constant background pulsation. In the former case there is simply a change in the field of reference; in the latter, a change in the *density* of events. The distinction is not academic: in order to feel degrees of compression or rarefaction between groups there must be a sense of constant measure to which they may be referred, and if the time proportions among groups are to be respected the piece must be counted according to its time signatures. ·

This can be done quite easily if the performer times the piece in the manner of a dramatic recitative. Verbal mnemonics may be invented for the more complex subdivisions (spoken advertising is rich in examples), and the speed and inflection of the pattern within a measured unit of time will also help the performer to realize the expressive intensity of the passage in question.

Elektronische Studie I

1953: No. 3/*1*

Electronic music.
Duration 9 minutes 30 seconds.
Realized in the electronic studio of North West German Radio, Cologne; on DGG LP 16133 (mono).
Stockhausen's analysis, including a score of the first thirteen seconds of music, is reproduced in Texte II, *pp. 22–36. There is no complete score.*

D RAWN back to Cologne by the prospect of better equipment and sustained encouragement, Stockhausen applied himself afresh to the problem of tone-colour synthesis that had defeated him in Paris. In his notes of the period can be found the following optimistic basic propositions:

How then is the necessary harmonization of material structure [timbre] and work structure [form] to be achieved? How does one gain an entry to the microtonal world of sound phenomena? Instrumental notes, all 'natural' sound events, are already more or less complex waveforms, preconditioned 'by Nature', and we must always remember that this pre-conditioning limits our scope [i.e. for intervention] in turn.

The wave-constitution of instrumental notes and the most diverse noises are amenable to analysis with the aid of electro-acoustic apparatus: is it then possible to reverse the process, and thus to synthesize wave-forms according to analytic data? To do so one would either have to take and combine simple waves into various forms, or else have a very dense band of frequencies at one's disposal, from which the various wave-forms could be extracted with the aid of filters.[1]

Every existing sound, every noise is a mixture (we call it a spectrum) of sine tones. The number, interval, and loudness relationships of the sine tones in combination give each spectrum its individuality. They define the tone colour.[2]

These remarks of Stockhausen reflect the prevailing opinion among acousticians. It was generally held that Fourier's theory that every tone or noise could be expressed as an aggregate of sine tones, meant that any type of complex wave might be synthesized artificially by piling up layers of frequencies.[3] Fourier analysis had certain known drawbacks. One was that it could identify as a component frequency what was simply a difference tone produced by the interaction of two other components, a second, that it did not specify the phase-relationship, or 'in-stepness' of the constituent tones. As long as the theory was only used for analysis, these drawbacks did not really matter much, but as soon as interest turned to synthesis their importance became crucial, for until the inter-relationships of the superimposed 'partials' could be exactly controlled, the resulting timbre quality could not be predicted with certainty.

Until the experiment had been tried, however, it was easy for composers to hope that differences in the phase relationship of partials would not greatly affect the tone quality. How much Stockhausen learned from his experiences in synthesizing the two electronic studies may be gauged from his subsequent essay *The Composition of Sound*, in which he remarks: '*Every note mixture* may thus be considered in either of two ways: as a *composition of sine tones*, or of "*coloured noises*". The sine tone itself may in this sense be regarded as the smallest stratum of "white noise", or as an extremely narrowly filtered "coloured noise".'[4]

Studie II is a composition of note mixtures, and note mixtures are not based on overtone relationship. In *Studie II* the frequencies from which the mixtures are composed are taken from a scale of constant interval $25\sqrt{5}$. The second technique may be regarded as an attempt to reach the degree of fusion not obtained by direct signal-to-tape recording in *Studie I* by using the basic material to excite an echo-plate or common

---

[1] *Texte I*, pp. 37/38.

[2] 'Entstehung der Elektronischen Musik', *Texte I*, p. 42.

[3] See Helmholtz, *On The Sensations of Tone*, Dover, 1954, p. 34b.

[4] *Texte I*, p. 53.

volume of air in an echo-chamber. In other words, by giving the partials an opportunity to interact before recording, he may have hoped that they would fuse together.
Nevertheless, most of the time the listener is able to hear that the complex material is
built up of separate pitches. So Stockhausen had to concede not only that the use of pure
waves did not automatically guarantee their fusion into unified timbres, but also that
even when a single vibrating body was simultaneously excited by several pure tones,
it did not make them blend together much more effectively; the conclusion to be
drawn from both *Studie I* and *Studie II* being that the perception of timbre could not
be assumed to be merely a physiological phenomenon, a fusion in the ear rather than
in the vibrations themselves.

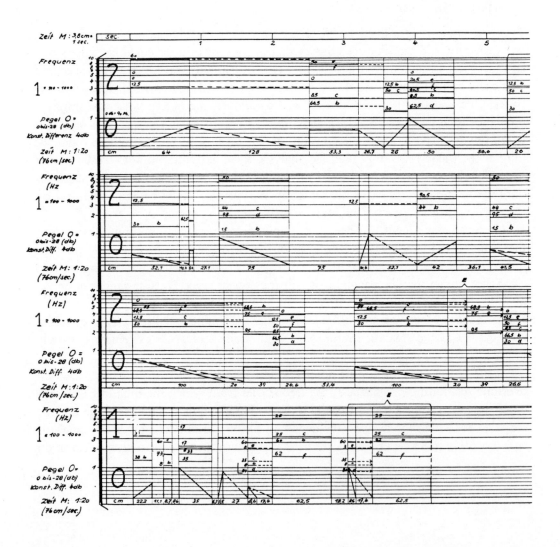

In a splendid passage written in this same period Stockhausen observed:

We are all more or less treading on ice, and as long as this is the case, the organization systems being put forward represent guiderails to prevent the composer from faltering. And one has to face the fact that there are as many systems as there are grains of sand, systems that can be dreamed up and set in motion as easily as clockwork. Their number is probably infinite, but certainly only a very few of them are acceptable systems, compatible with their means of expression, and applicable without self-contradiction to all the dimensions of music. Of these, still fewer are so perfectly prefigured that they yield beautiful and interesting music. This last is naturally difficult to be precise about, since one has only the music to go by. But just as we find Mozart's music beautiful and interesting without feeling the need to justify our opinion,— just as we can identify our sense of 'the beautiful' and 'the interesting' with that shared by a vast number of people,—so one is free to pass an opinion on the concepts and systems that the composer selects as being 'beautiful' and 'interesting'. From making up one's mind over this, one may judge directly whether the composer is more than just a good craftsman—and the evaluation will stand independent of the actual state of the craft.[5]

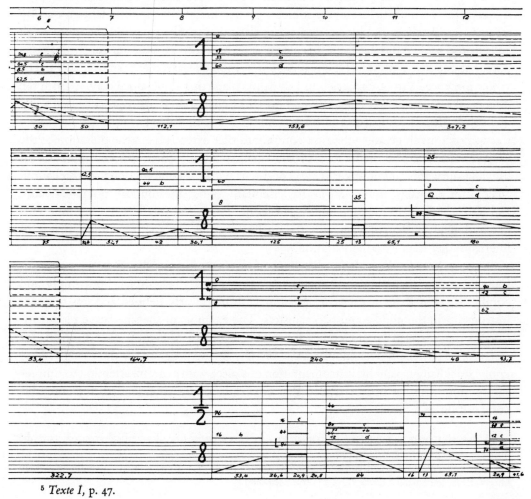

[5] *Texte I*, p. 47.

For the period, this is unusually candid. In complete contrast to the proselytizing manner of Eimert or Schaeffer, and without a hint of Boulez's acrimony, Stockhausen asks the listener to consider electronic music in the same spirit as he would any other music; not to refuse to have an opinion about it because he does not understand its theoretical basis, nor to accept it merely because the arguments spoken in its favour sound impressive. Clearly, besides the personal aspect—that in spite of not having realized a major theoretical ambition in these pieces he nevertheless feels that they are valid works of music—Stockhausen is aware even at this time of the danger that verbal argument may overtake the production of music as the main means of self-justification of studio composers, and that the public in turn may be led to rely upon the apparent authoritativeness of composers' statements about their works, as a guide to the value of the music itself.

Like his later *Refrain*,[6] *Studie I* gives an immediate impression of inhabiting the treble register, an effect created by the relative clarity of tones in the middle and upper frequencies. It is a gentle, transparent piece, given a meditative, slightly tentative air by frequent small echoes and by a sound-vocabulary that seemingly ranges between small bells in the middle distance and low drum reverberations at close range, the latter so pure that one may almost feel them as decompression effects rather than hear them. The whole piece seems to be displayed on a dynamic plane that slopes up and away from the listener like a de Chirico perspective. This effect corresponds with Stockhausen's frequently-expressed comparison of sound and light, i.e. that what we perceive is only a fraction of a much greater vibration continuum that extends from the pulsation of the Universe itself to the oscillations of the smallest atomic particles. The sensation of listening outwards and upwards is also consistent with the contemporary 'constellation' analogy of pointillist music. *Studie I* is essentially static: the musical 'points' advance and retreat, appear to move in and out of focus. This is less an effect of the music's inherent dynamism than of changes in the quality of aural response, an illusion, that is, of internal rather than external variation.

It seems less of a coincidence that since *Studie I* Stockhausen has shown a particular fondness for high ringing instruments like crotala and glockenspiel, both singly and combined (as in *Refrain, Kontakte, Mantra*) with less clearly defined and less resonant instruments in the middle and bass registers. The example of the sine-wave pitch continuum may explain his preference for wooden-topped tom-toms over timpani, for instance, or cow-bells over tubular bells, or why he has little use for the triangle. Certainly Stockhausen plans his instrumentation of a piece with a careful attention to timbre-transposition: he has in fact argued that copyright ought to extend to the ensemble composition of a piece.[7]

---

[6] 'In each tone-group one tone predominates . . . This *strongest tone* of a vertical group dictates the duration of its group.' *Texte II*, p. 32.

[7] 'The specific choice and constitution of instrumentation of a given work . . . ought to remain unrepeatable, uncopiable.' *Texte II*, p. 131 (on *Momente*).

Elektronische Studie II

1954: No. 3/*ii*, UE 12466

Electronic music.
Duration 3 minutes.
Realized in the electronic studio of North West German Radio; on DGG LP 16133
(mono).

'Studie II', a single-track 'mono' piece in contrast to the multi-layer composition of *Studie I*, is conceived in rather different terms, the result of Stockhausen's studies with Meyer-Eppler at Bonn University. For all the valuable experience he gained from the earlier piece, he may have been puzzled, not to say disappointed, at having had only qualified success in fusing synthetic partials into coherent, unified tone-colours. Whether or not Meyer-Eppler was able to identify the source of the problem as phase-relationship is difficult to know for certain. In his essay 'Statistic and Psychologic Problems of Sound' *(Die Reihe I)* Meyer-Eppler refers to the 'triple pitch level quality', also known as the 'Schouten effect', by which it may be shown that a recorded instrumental note deprived of its fundamental (i.e. its written, played pitch) by means of a band-stop filter, will continue to sound at that same frequency as a result of the interaction of the remaining higher partials, the 'chroma'. Not only does the chroma reinforce the basic pitch, but it also endows it with a characteristic colour and texture: the scraping sound of the violin, the reedy quality of the oboe, the 'breathy' quality of the flute, and so on. Without the chroma, the fundamental tone is remarkably bland and uninteresting.

Since isolating the chroma involves splitting up a musical note into its 'pure' harmonic components, it is almost certainly one of the scientific starting-points of Stockhausen's compositional procedure in *Studie I*. Significantly, however, Meyer-Eppler makes no reference in his essay to the criterion of phase relationship. It is possible that he didn't realize how important a factor it was in timbre-synthesis: his main preoccupation in this particular essay was the relationship of unpredictable performance factors with the known physical characteristics of musical instruments in the production of aesthetically pleasing musical sounds. Or he may not have known what was the matter, since on the question of the timbre of instruments with 'gliding formants', such as the clarinet, he remarks that 'examination of spectra of this type has been limited to the period in which one has been able to work with electric sound generators'.[1] Or he may simply have chosen to overlook the problem because equipment and techniques then available could not reach the necessary accuracy.

The uncertainty arises because after the delicacy and precision of *Studie I* the technique devised by Stockhausen for the generation of the sound-mixtures of *Studie II* seems much less sophisticated, indeed one in which there is absolutely no possibility of obtaining a unified timbre.[2] The technique used is mechanical rather than scientific. Sine tones are again employed, but instead of being combined in complexes of one to six 'partials', sets each of five pitches are generated, which in principle represent artificial chromata of varying band-widths. The idea that the constituent frequencies of these complexes might interact to give the illusion of non-existent fundamental tones is attractive, but Stockhausen's method of synthesis does not give this possibility a chance. The sine-tone elements were recorded separately, constant tape lengths of each tone were joined end to end, and the resulting ascending 'arpeggio' was made into a tape-loop and re-recorded indirectly from an echo-chamber, from which the composite reverberation alone was extracted for use.

It is highly probable that Stockhausen was forced into this comparatively crude method by an inadequacy or insufficiency of equipment (five oscillators would have been needed, and an oscilloscope as well, for the production of perfectly-tuned timbres in this case). But the question is academic because his subsequent composition of the resulting tone-mixtures into *Studie II* was clearly determined by the quality of sound actually produced rather than what he may have hoped to obtain in theory. In changing his objective and method, Stockhausen also changed his attitude to his material. What the listener hears is a vocabulary of homogeneous note-mixtures of varying size and density, ranging from approximately semitonal clusters to aggregations of near-fourths. Both the way these are notated, and the comparison made, in the Introduction to the score, between the notation and a sample spectrogram of part of the music,[3] suggest that the material was being manipulated as *formants* instead of as *chromata*. Formants are distinctive areas of peak resonance in a reverberating body. They result from the shape of the resonator, and are perceived as regions of constant reinforcement of instrumental or vocal sound. Whereas the chroma of a musical note varies as the fundamental pitch varies, the formants of the instrument by which it is played do not: thus the notes of a scale played on the violin will sound more consistent than a recording of the lowest note of the same scale transposed through the appropriate degrees. Similarly, if one were to sing the vowel [a] up and down the scale, the pitch will change but the identity of the vowel, resulting from the shape of the mouth, will remain much the same.

---

[1] Op. cit., *Die Reihe I*, p. 60.

[2] Recent attention to the homogeneous string sound created by certain dance orchestras suggests that the reverberation technique used in *Studie II* may have been proposed by a professional sound technician.

[3] Nr.3 *Studie II*, facing page viii.

Seen from the composer's viewpoint, the difference between characterizing a timbre according to its partial frequencies, and according to its resonant quality, could seem rather pedantic, especially if one is considering individual, fixed resonators like bells, cymbals, drums, and woodblocks—precisely the kinds of resonators Stockhausen spent time in analysing in Paris. Imagine trying to define the spectrum of the vowel [a] from a single example sung at low pitch. Without being able to examine the vowel as sung at a series of pitches, it is impossible to tell which characteristic features of the spectral analysis refer to the *pitch*, which to the *vowel*, and which to peculiar features of the resonant aperture (mouth and nasal cavity of the singer). One could thus be easily led to suppose that all three are equally variable attributes of pitch-resonance, although two of them are in fact relatively stable.

The formant, then, is an inflection given to a sound by the resonating surface, and is not a property of excitation of the sound. But if a student were to ask for a definition of the two principal formants of the vowel [a] for example, *for the purpose of synthesizing the vowel electronically*, he would be told that they were two bands of frequencies, the one centred on 720 Hz, the other centred on 1,300 Hz. The definition would thus imply positive sound-content rather than simple boundary values. And if the same student were to ask about the structure of sound vibration within each formant, he would be told that providing the prescribed frequency bands were of the correct width, position, and intensity, any homogeneous sound would do as basic material. Some famous 'Vocoder' experiments conducted by the Bell Telephone Laboratories in the United States, using a complicated transformation process involving considerable degradation of the original speech signal, had shown how continuous speech patterns could be imposed upon background noises of various kinds, such as the sound of a jet plane, a train, or an automobile. But at the same time it was also widely believed by phoneticians that human speech could be depicted in reality as a train of mutually independent phonemes, corresponding to written consonants and vowels. Experiments were being conducted in both the synthesis of separate consonants and vowels, and their assembly into coherent words and phrases.

In devising the material and form of *Studie II*, Stockhausen may well have been influenced by contemporary experiments in the synthesis of speech patterns. This would explain his shift of attention from the fusion of pure tones into a complex wave form, to the envelope characteristics of inflection and liaison that are responsible for expressive continuity: for movement, that is, and the expression of feeling. In these respects *Studie II* undoubtedly succeeds, a feat all the more remarkable when one considers the imperfect understanding of speech processes that obtained at the time among scientists accredited in the field.

The piece's greater sense of movement is aided by Stockhausen's choice of denser sound material, and incidentally by the homogenizing effect of the reverberation process which adds a slight but audible tremor to each tone mixture, apparent in the upper register as a faint liquid gurgling and in the lower as an effect like a sympathetic rattling

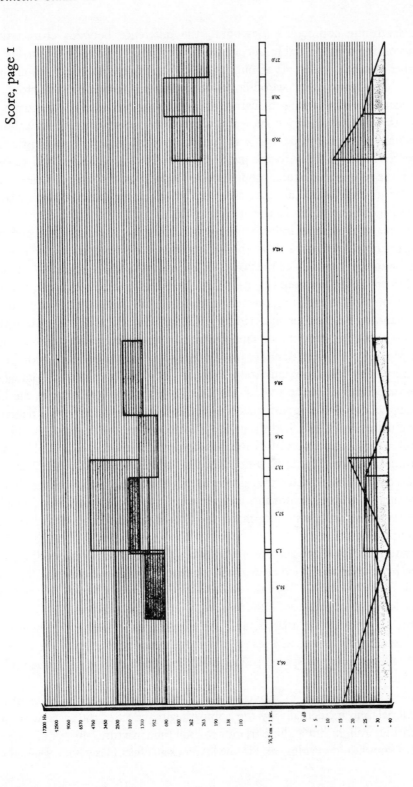

Score, page 1

of snares. *Studie II* explores the area of aural response between consciousness of the external shape and awareness of the inner structure of sound (which may be likened to listening first to the 'tone of voice' and then to the 'sense' of heard speech). The relevant factor as shown by *Studie II* is *duration*: the longer the interval between changes, the more the complexes sound harmonic, while when changes are rapid, the more one attends to the suggested inflection pattern. Thus the continuous succession of 5 'blocks' at the end of page 1 and beginning of page 2 may resemble a Debussyan parallel chord progression (cf. the woodwind introduction to *Le Martyre de Saint-Sébastien*, in which a static chord is pushed about as if by an external force), whereas by contrast the complex central group on page 12 of the score has much more of a syllabic character.

Page 12, central complex

A rising intensity seems to assist, and a falling intensity to retard momentum, though this effect may also be altered by the duration and complexity of a particular event. Interestingly, one perceives the inner structure and separate entries of a cumulative aggregation of rising intensity more easily than one 'hears' what happens with a complex of diminishing intensity whose several components successively vanish (compare for example the rising complex on page 11 with the falling complex on page 9). Vertical aggregations of blocks which overlap tend to sound 'choric' whereas those that do not (e.g. the final complex on page 16) sound both more 'noisy' *and*, ironically, more like genuine timbres.

Page 16, final complex

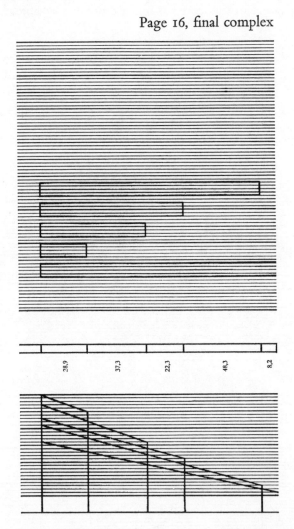

Element separation in time, such as in the sequence of pages 13 to 15, perhaps not quite so unexpectedly, makes for an impression of jazz-like percussive energy and excitement.

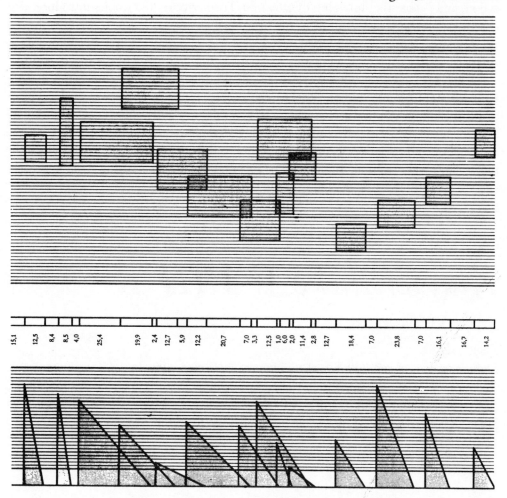

These short sounds are among the most spontaneously allusive of the piece. The final 'drum-roll' effect, a characteristic Stockhausen surprise ending, is also very impressive.

These two electronic studies provide us with coherent and perfect images of the passive and active aspects of musical response, *Studie I* expressing the 'visionary' or contemplative mode and *Studie II* the 'gestural' or participational mode. Association of the former with sounds of clear pitch, and the latter with indeterminate pitch but decisive articulation, enables the listener to analyse his own reactions to music with more certainty, and the composer to plan both his instrumentation of a piece and his manipulation of these two areas of human response with security and subtlety. In Stockhausen's subsequent works we may see *Refrain* and *Zyklus* as an instrumental pair matching these two electronic studies. The studies also demonstrate the close relationship between perceived time and timbre, and the difference between *momentum*, or continuity of action, and *liaison*, the sustaining of attention. Furthermore, the studies introduce new criteria of precision and contrast in the instrumental sphere: *Studie II* for instance is a prototype of those musical forms, determined in external features but aleatoric in detail, of which *Gruppen* is a great early example and *Fresco* one of the more recent.

When one considers what was being said and done by his contemporaries in both the Paris and Cologne studios, Stockhausen's achievement in these two works appears as a contribution to musical knowledge of great dignity and value. These qualities are directly attributable to his choice of purely discipline-orientated objectives, to the imagination and integrity of his methods, and to the care and patience with which the works have been realized. Both stand as splendid vindications of the serial approach, and are models of artistic discipline at the highest level.

Klavierstücke V-VIII

1954-5, VI revised 1961; No. 4, UE 13675a, b, c, d

Piano solo.
Durations: V c. 6 minutes; VI c. 26 minutes; VIII c. 7 minutes; VIII c. 2 minutes.
Recorded by Aloys Kontarsky on CBS 32 210008 (New York), S 77209 (Paris),
72591-2 (London), Klavierstück VI (1955 version) by David Tudor on Vega C30
A278, Klavierstück VIII *by David Burge on Vox STGBY 637.*

LIKE the first set of piano pieces, numbers V to VIII are studies, but unlike the former set, which are essays in abstract formal organization, these are essays in the more tangible aspects of performance: sonority, timing, and association. The difference in emphasis reflects not a change of mind but a change of ear: the new ways of perceiving sounds and sound-relationships which he had discovered through electronic music and his studies of acoustics.

If after 18 months of work devoted exclusively to electronic compositions, I now find myself working at piano pieces, it is because in the most strongly structured compositions I have encountered important musical phenomena which are non-quantifiable. They are no less real, recognizable, conceivable, or palpable for that. These things I am better able—at the moment anyway—to clarify with the help of an instrument and interpreter, than in the field of electronic composition. Above all it has to do with the provision of a new sense of time in music, whereby the infinitely subtle 'irrational' nuances, and stresses, and delays made by a good interpreter are often truer to the piece's intended effect than measurement by centimetres. Such statistical form criteria will give us a completely new, hitherto unknown[1] style of relationship between sound that is 'of the instrument' and sound that is 'of *playing* the instrument'.[2]

Piece V is in six sections, identified by tempo: MM=80–90–71–113·5–101–63·5; the tempi belong to the same 'tempo-octave' series, MM=60–120, that is to be found in *Gruppen* and the revised *Punkte*. These tempo norms correspond more to intensities than to speeds. There is little regularity in the musical accidence: one perceives tempo-changes less in terms of material density than in differences in the quality and speed of phrasing, pedalling, touch, and *posture*. These degrees or moods are cut into by small-note anacruses which, like a singer's breath-taking, occupy gaps in the general continuity without appearing to interrupt it. However the anacruses are not for that reason to be thought of as liaisons, nor are they ornamental disturbances after the manner of arpeggios or mordents, taking their time from the antecedent measure; rather, they dramatize the hiatus between up- and down-beat, between ebb and flow, like a seabird coming to rest on the crest of a wave. Stockhausen's frequent notation of an accelerando or a ritardando during a sustained note or chord may put the performer in mind of the apocryphal story of Webern marking a rest with a crescendo; both ideas do in fact make the same kind of sense, even if they seem to elude logical explanation: the stress implied affects the performance of what follows even if there is no sound to correspond to the actual sign.

Within each principal section there are no bar-lines. Stockhausen's more flexible timing is thus generically related to the elaborate, expressive distortions of classical and nineteenth-century slow movements, and those of such twentieth-century rarities as Stravinsky's 1924 Piano Sonata and Bartók's *Out of Doors* suite:

Bartók

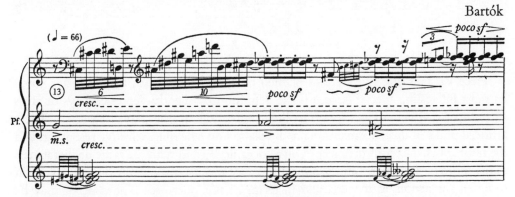

(Note the coexistence of local and general crescendi.)

[1] Stockhausen's word 'unbekannt' carries the German implication of 'not known because not formulated according to known laws'. These aspects of performance were recognized, of course, but only as localized deviations.

[2] *Texte II*, p. 43.

Apart from the compression and distension of time suggested by performer gesture, Piece V phrases principally by pedal, leaving the hands conveniently free to attend to touch-differentiation (as in *Zeitmasze*, heavy notes have a slightly adhesive quality like agogic accents or downbeats: the small notes are contrastingly light and up-beat in effect, played as if the keys are hot to the touch).

Whereas the direction 'As fast as possible' may galvanize the performer of Pieces I–IV into a condition of extreme stage-fright (which itself is no more than a painfully heightened awareness of time), the reference-tempi of Piece V act simply as measures against which individual time dilations or compressions may be gauged:

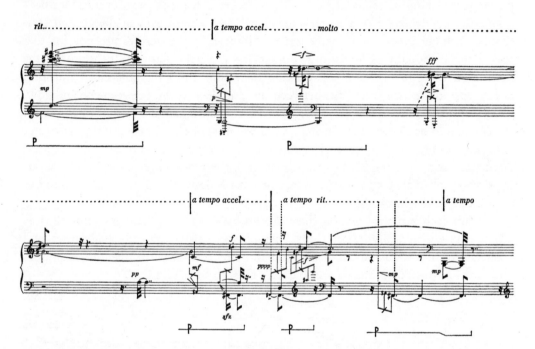

Piece VII falls into five sections defined by tempo (MM=40; 63·5; 57; 71; 50·5). Its most interesting special feature is the definition by silently-depressed keys of areas of resonance which are set in sympathetic vibration by the played material. These artificial peaks or quasi-formants make the piano into a flexible, selective resonator, and the resonant character of the piece evolves organically and with the same deliberateness as the more positive notes and groups. One may thus hear the work on two levels: in terms of the action, as it were, and in terms of the 'aperture'. The concept may be likened to the change in tone-colour made available by the wa-wa mute on a trumpet or trombone; the experience to some extent corresponds to the changes of resonance one hears in walking through a succession of rooms of different sizes and acoustic characters. In Piece V the pedals are primarily for phrasing, assisted only occasionally by artificial resonance (e.g. page 4). In Piece VII their roles are reversed, with artificial resonance leading and pedals helping out. The una corda pedal is also used, but only to provide further tone-colour (*sforzato una corda*, for example) and not to 'dampen' the sound. Stockhausen also employs a scale of pauses differentiated not by shape but by the duration of rests (demisemi- to dotted-quaver) over which they occur:

Piece VII

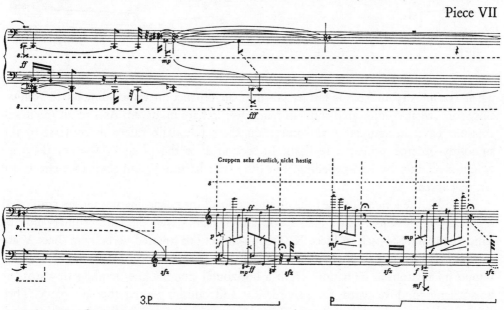

By far the most intriguing section of Piece VII is the fourth episode, MM=71, where a fast, articulate beginning progressively disperses into shifting bass resonances, which themselves become more and more attenuated—the whole up to this point rather resembling a tape-recorded music gradually being slowed down. Suddenly, when time and motion are almost at a stand-still, rapid grace-note groups appear in the high register, as if descending from an ultrasonic region (in studio tape recording a normally ultrasonic frequency laid down by the electrical current input becomes audible when a recording is played back at greatly reduced speed). A similar passage is also to be found in *Kontakte* at 19' 31, 5″.

The brief Piece VIII, in two sections (MM=90, 80), is principally organized around a scale of dynamics. Each of the major formal units makes a selection of six adjacent values from a basic scale of 10 dynamics. Different dynamics within a chosen selection define the internal structure; the average dynamic value distinguishes one group from the next. Major structural divisions are indicated by long notes; internal subdivisions, as in Piece V, by grace-note anacruses. Whereas those of Piece V are linear series of one to six notes, the interruptions of Piece VIII are composed of successions of chords of one to six-note thickness, which also vary in intensity.[3]

[3] The grace-note dynamics in Piece VIII are selected from different areas of the dynamic range than the contexts in which they occur.

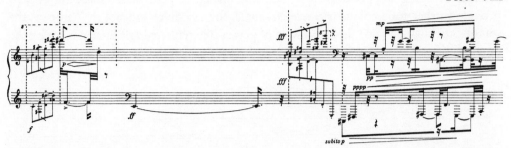

Their complexity makes 'as fast as possible' an instruction rather difficult to follow, since somewhat complicated shifts of hand position are involved. As a result the interruptions have an aggressive and uncertain character, deliberately in contrast to the smoothly-ordered principal sections. In section 2 of the piece (MM=80) they are coloured slightly by half-pedalling, but otherwise harmonic and resonance effects are entirely absent.

Piece VI, the longest of the four, draws upon all the co-ordinating modes employed separately in the three other pieces, and anticipates as well the extraordinary flux of time that manifests itself in Piece X. Tempo-inflections notated verbally in Piece V are depicted in Piece VI on a separate 13-line stave. This method of notation reproduces tempo fluctuations as deviations from a horizontal straight line, tending upwards for an accelerando, downwards for a ritardando, and vanishing altogether at a pause. Thus the 'mood' connotation of tempo in Piece V is graphically depicted as a mood-intensity gradient in Piece VI, with the further suggestion of a metabolic relationship of pitch and tempo—like the correspondence in speech between an increase in excitement and an attendance rise both in the pitch and the speed of utterance. (Contrast this 'normal' relationship with the operatic convention of balancing a rise in pitch and intensity—as at a climax—with a *broadening* of tempo.)

We may describe the time envelope of Piece VI, therefore, as 'conditional tempo'. Reproducing tempo in this fashion offers several advantages, the most obvious being that a line is able to describe much more subtle nuances of timing than may be achieved by the use of mere words. Also important is the fact that the performer may see at a glance the relationship of the nuance in its local context to the tempo of the piece as a whole.

Grace-note groups have a new function in Piece VI, partly as a result of the re-establishment in the tempo-line of an essentially external and (to all appearances) rigid system of time-modulation. They function here not to heighten or anticipate as much as to blur events at the principal level. This fusion of ephemeral and continuous time produces effects of iridescent beauty and variety. As in Piece VIII, 'passive' non-articulated sympathetic resonances provide a subharmonic system of phrasing; here they contrast with the 'active'—and similarly mute—performer preconditioning offered by the tempo-line.

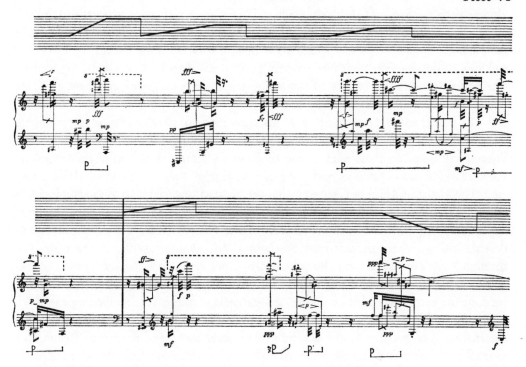

Though initially stimulated by his discovery of the intangibles in vocal liaison through his work with Meyer-Eppler and on *Studie II*, Stockhausen's interest in the stage-presence factors of performance attracted the enthusiasm and practical assistance of the American pianist David Tudor, whom he encountered at the time and to whom the cycle Pieces V–VIII is dedicated.[4]

Tudor also renewed Stockhausen's acquaintance with Cage's *Music of Changes*, in which the relationship between chronometric time and performer action (the notation is distributed spatially, not metrically in time)—produces an effect of reactive spontaneity, like hearing only one side of an animated telephone conversation. In his notes to the performer, Cage remarks: 'Accelerandos and ritards are to be associated with the rhythmic structure, rather than with the sounds that happen in it'[5] and he also makes careful and imaginative use of pedal effects (including 'pedal-sustaining-overtones'), silently-depressed keys, and tone clusters.[6] But the Cage pieces in turn derive much of their characteristic physical sensibility from the example of Boulez, in

---

[4] See *Music and Musicians*, August 1972, pp. 24–5. Tudor's comments in this article frequently refer to earlier versions of the pieces, often very different from the published scores.

[5] *Music of Changes*, Peters Edition.

[6] Stockhausen was eschewing note clusters at this stage. They first appear in the piano part of *Gruppen* and in Piece XI. But he would have known of Bartók's use of clusters (in *Mikrokosmos* and 'Night Music', bar 39).

particular the latter's Second Piano Sonata, which Cage had got to know through visiting Paris in 1950, and Boulez's reciprocal New York visit shortly afterward. So the *Music of Changes* in effect acted as a catalyst between Stockhausen and the French tradition, which in turn helps to explain why Boulez took such an interest in Piece XI, and why to the observer their piano works in the mid-fifties have so much in common. The advantage to Stockhausen of reviewing the French temperament through Cage was the American composer's intuitive grasp of the French style of rhetoric. In Pieces IV and VIII Stockhausen seems to draw on his knowledge of Boulez's scores, reproducing the wide leaps and contrasts and contrapuntal complexities of *Structures* and the Second Sonata, but ignoring their relationship to Boulez's tempi, which in characteristically French fashion are notated as *modes of performance* (e.g. *Vif, Très Modéré, Assez Large,* etc.). The virtue of *Music of Changes* is that the notated material is so obviously incidental to the dynamic of performance that one cannot help noticing how much the piece depends upon performer sensibility, even in the case of material so expressly uninflected, and with an instrument as mechanical and discontinuous, as the piano. So through Cage's example and the practical demonstration offered by Tudor, Stockhausen came to see beyond the written notes to their relationship with the temperament of the composer. This new kind of awareness accounts for the baffling ease with which he is able to move from one style to another while remaining faithful to the external signs of each: why the notation, instrumentation, and timing of *Refrain,* for example, make such coherent sense and yet are so different from those of *Zyklus,* written at the same time.

From this viewpoint one may interpret Pieces V–VIII as a set of dialogues between Boulezian precision (that is, notational precision subject to tempo-temperamental variation) and Stockhausen's own natural impulsiveness (represented by notational uncertainty combined with a rigidity of approach) a clash of personalities seen in its simplest form in the confrontation between mensural notation and grace-notes. This idea of dialogue leads to some intriguing questions over Stockhausen's tempi. Where he indicates a metronomic value, as in Pieces V, VII, and VIII, is it a temperament (French) or a measure (German)?[7] Where he omits both tempo and metronomic indications, as in Pieces I–IV, is the performer expected consciously to bring his sensibility to bear, or should he strive to be as accurate as possible? In Piece VI the tempo-line indicates with the greatest precision modulations of sensibility of a subtlety associated with dramatic soliloquy; on the other hand the scale of six relative tempi of Piece XI resumes an essentially French orientation to performer timing.

These pieces, let us remember, are studies, and it is in the nature of a study to be private and meditative, a performer-centred exercise in performance. But the technical discoveries involved in their mastery is matched or rewarded by aural revelations of a sudden, profound beauty, of which section 4 of Piece VII is an outstanding example—

[7] The tempi are certainly measures, in that they refer to a structured scale of tempi originally planned for the whole cycle, but how they appear to function in performance is another matter (as Piece I shows).

which elevate the pieces from the merely virtuosic to the lyric plane. And though their compass is wide, their scale is the magr•ication of intimacy: they relate to the privacy of Schoenberg's Op. 11, No. 1, not to the public world of the Op. 11, No. 3; to the spirit of Dowland's lute pieces, not of his songs.

Zeitmasze

1955–6: No. 5, UE 12697

For five woodwind: oboe, flute, cor anglais, clarinet, bassoon.
Duration c. 14 minutes.
Recorded by Robert Craft (conductor) on Philips A 01 488L/CBS Odyssey 32 160 154 (same recording); by Pierre Boulez (conductor) on Vega C 30 A 139; by Heinz Holliger (cor anglais) with members of the Danzi Quintett: Koen van Slogteren (oboe), Frans Vester (flute), Piet Honingh (clarinet), Brian Pollard (bassoon) on Philips 6500 261; and by Members of the London Sinfonietta: Janet Craxton (oboe), Sebastian Bell (flute), Robin Miller (cor anglais), Anthony Pay (clarinet), William Waterhouse (bassoon) on DGG 2530 443.

PITCH and time, whether they may be physically related or musically relatable, are Stockhausen's constant preoccupation between 1952 and 1959. His efforts at reconciling the two principal dimensions of serial form are set out in the celebrated essay '. . . how time passes . . .' published in *Die Reihe 3*. As a sequence of speculations on the nature of time the essay is difficult to follow or digest. As an exposition of text-book acoustics it has been severely criticized. But Stockhausen's essay is concerned less with the wider implications of his theorizing (though he was sensitive to them) than with solving practical questions of compositional efficiency, and these are easier for the reader to grasp.

There were several loosely connected reasons why he should wish to integrate the two systems of measurement. The first was Goeyvaerts' argument against the incompatibility of pitch- and duration-series. The former is based on a logarithmic progression (the tempered scale), the latter is commonly arithmetic (e.g. the serial aggregations of demisemiquaver values favoured by Messiaen and Boulez). But to those composers who aimed at musical forms of architectural purity, the inconsistency amounted to measuring height and length with different rules. Another reason, however, arose out of this very attitude to music. Stockhausen was becoming impatient with the lack of movement in pointillist music, and also its obliteration of depth and scale. It was star music without recognizable constellations, or follow-the-dot pictures without guiding numbers. Le Corbusier had related the proportions of his Modulor to human dimensions: if the measurement of musical time could likewise be geared to natural rhythms a palpable continuity might be generated. But the most pressing reason for reconciling scales of pitch and time was scientific. Stockhausen was fascinated by the electronically demonstrable continuum between frequencies perceived as rhythm (e.g. sine waves of up to 20 cycles per second) and higher frequencies which are audible as pitch. This 'official' sanction of serial necessity seemed to him of mystical significance.

From his own experience in instrumental and electronic composition, as well as from observation of scientific investigations in related fields, the inadequacy of a theory of form by spontaneous association of juxtaposed particles was becoming increasingly obvious. Pointillist music refused to flow, juxtaposed 'attacks' and 'resonances', whether joined on tape or orchestrally superimposed (as in *Spiel*) hung uneasily together, and mixtures of sine waves failed to jell into the confidently-predicted 'new, unheard-of timbres'. Comparable experiments in speech synthesis, involving splicing tape-recorded individual syllables together, had produced only caricatures of spoken language in successions of disconnected grunts. In each case theory had neglected a vital connecting ingredient. The musical 'points' needed an underlying rhythm, the attacks and resonances did not combine because their resonant characteristics were incompatible, the sine-wave mixtures did not coalesce because their partials were out of phase, the synthetic words missed the transitional sounds between syllables which are as important as the syllables themselves.

These discoveries were made in piecemeal fashion, and their implications were not always fully recognized at the time. But they spelt an end to the euphoria in which the new musical age had got under way, and effectively sounded the death knell of pointillism as a technique. Disappointed, composers were forced to come to terms with an acoustic reality beyond the powers of their ideal abstract systems to define. Gradually it dawned that organization depended not only on functional distinctions but also on functional interrelationships, and that a workable system of composition would have to take account of aspects of sound production and liaison that had previously been ignored. These factors were physical (instrument construction, reverberation), physiological (breathing, bowing, etc.), and psychological (the connecting function of rhythm, narrative continuity of a sung text, etc.).

Many of these conclusions were philosophically unacceptable. It was not easy to abandon a pointillist system in which all elements were seen as democratically equal, in favour of reimposed hierarchies, especially beat regularity. There was no going back to the old forms, as Schoenberg and Webern had done: Boulez had seen to that. What then? Stockhausen immersed himself in study with Meyer-Eppler, who was investigating the statistical bases of perceptual association.

One by one, scores were written in which statistical processes became very important. I started doing this in 1954, highly influenced by my teacher Meyer-Eppler who was teaching communication science at the University of Bonn where aleatoric processes in statistics, primarily in mathematics but also in sociology and physics, played a strong role.

In the seminars at that time, we were making artificial texts by cutting up newspapers into one-, two-, three-syllable units, sometimes going to the extreme and cutting up individual letters. We'd shuffle them like cards, make new artificial texts, and then study the degree of redundancy. Naturally, the more you cut down a given text, the less redundant would be the result of the new chance-produced text.

The Heisenberg Uncertainty Principle is based on this hypothetical behaviour of components of the atom. That was the main thing in the air at the end of the forties and beginning of the fifties. We worked with micro theories in communication science; Shannon was very important as a mathematician—Markoff, too. And I simply transposed everything I learned into the field of music and for the first time composed sounds which have statistical characteristics in the given field with defined limits. The elements could move, and later on this was also expressed in the scores. In the beginning I used the deterministic notation for indeterminate textures—I didn't know how to notate it.[1]

Paradoxically, the pointillist method, which to its users symbolized an ideal of democratic freedom and individual self-determination, had been interpreted by its critics as symbolic of totalitarian repression. It was ironic, therefore, that the introduction of statistical models, intended to strengthen and humanize serial form, should be taken as a sign of the system's deterioration. The study of redundancy to which Stockhausen refers may be understood in its widest sense as a study of the norms of register, intensity, tempo, ratio of long to short vowels, or hard to soft consonants, etc., which make the sound of speech flow naturally, reinforcing the intended logical continuity of ideas expressed.

Long before he began his studies with Meyer-Eppler, however, Stockhausen had begun instinctively to employ statistical procedures in musical form. Already in *Formel*, back in December 1951, we see him articulating the duration-structure (or macro-structure, as opposed to the pitch- or micro-structure) of a piece by assigning a different pulsation to each basic unit duration. It was then thought functionally necessary to distinguish the absolute time-scale of the whole work, in *Formel* based on a unit quaver, from the relative tempi of sub-sections, which in the same work pulsate in multiples of a semiquaver. In this early example the distinction does not amount to very much, and subsequently in Piano Piece I Stockhausen chooses tempo divisions so inconsistent with the structural duration series and with each other that no performer could possibly mistake the tempo of a given subsection for the time-scale of the work as a whole. At this stage however Stockhausen's distinctions are still mainly intellectual: differences more visible than audible, in a temporal context ('as fast as possible') conceived as independent of the notated events themselves. They could perhaps be likened to the different scales of measurement employed to distinguish planes of distance in a perspective

[1] Cott, *Stockhausen: Conversations*, Robson, pp. 67–8.

drawing. It was only through practical experience of Piece I and subsequent piano works that Stockhausen, assisted by David Tudor, came to see these time-scales as relative intensities, and to appreciate the close relationship between gestural unity and structural unification.

Once the idea of relative tempi was accepted, it was an obvious step to relate tempo serially to pitch. This in turn suggested several important lines of development, all designed to close the gap between pitch and time. In Piece I the flow of time is constant and tempo a variable. In Pieces V–VIII he reverses the situation, making tempo serially constant, as opposed to grace-note figurations which are absolute in principle ('as fast as possible') but in practice expressively variable, since their speed is related to their playability. These pieces explore the ambiguities of timing and tempo, of gestural unity and metrical coherence. Another line of development was suggested by the possibility of relating structural durations (as well as substructual tempi) to a basic pitch series. This suggested not only a music proportioned in tempi, with a rhythmic structure corresponding to serial pitch-relationships, but also proportional time-divisions within each structural tempo, corresponding to the partial frequencies of different timbres. This idea he pursued in *Gruppen*. A third possibility lay in inflecting both gestural and metronomic tempi to such an extent (by accelerandi and ritardandi) that additive 'macro-structural' duration values merged with divisive 'micro-structural' tempi. A piece composed of several independently varying temporal layers (or 'tracks') would thus be able to move back and forth between synchronized periodicity and a polyphonic flux of tempi only perceivable statistically.[2]

This last alternative is explored first in *Zeitmasze*, then in the electronic piece *Gesang der Jünglinge*. In *Zeitmasze*, 'a very simple piece for woodwind', Stockhausen returns to a vocal, breath-controlled style of utterance. The relationship of its woodwind to the piano of Pieces V–VIII is the same relationship we observe between the woodwind and piano of *Kreuzspiel*. The two instrumental types embody different attitudes to co-ordination and continuity of pointillist material. Keyboards are essentially discrete-pitch instruments which the composer and performer contrive to make sound continuous; voices and woodwinds on the other hand are essentially inflecting instruments which have to be practised in accurate intonation and precise rhythmic articulation. Continuity in keyboard music is thus an effect of psychological momentum outwardly expressed in visible actions. With woodwind, however, gestural continuity and pitch liaison are interrelated: a legato passage actually connects successive pitches by audible transients. It is this flexibility of woodwind instruments, their power of articulating continuous processes of change, that makes *Zeitmasze* so fascinating a

---

[2] Schillinger remarks (Vol. I, Chap. 14 'Rhythms of variable velocities'): 'The rhythm of variable velocities presents a fascinating field for study and exploration. The very thought that various rhythmic groups may speed up and slow down at various rates, appearing and disappearing, is overwhelming. . . . The idea stimulates one's imagination towards the complex harmony of the universe, where different celestial bodies (comets, stars, planets, satellites) coexist in harmony of variable velocities.' (p. 95.)

study. Transitions of intensity or tempo are far less exactly quantifiable than fluctuations of pitch. Our awareness of crescendo or diminuendo, accelerando or ritardando, derives from an evaluation of what music is doing over a period of time, not what it 'is' at a given moment. Classical notation is accordingly not designed to express these subtle degrees of change quantitatively.

It is of course with tempo relationships that *Zeitmasze* is above all concerned. The piece explores a two-dimensional surface, ranging between tempo-conformity to tempo-diversity along one co-ordinate, and between metrical regularity and rhythmic irregularity along the other. The range of combinations is enormously wide, e.g. parts may be synchronized metronomically, but pointillistically scattered, or at another extreme each may be metrically regular but independently accelerating, retarding or stable in tempo.

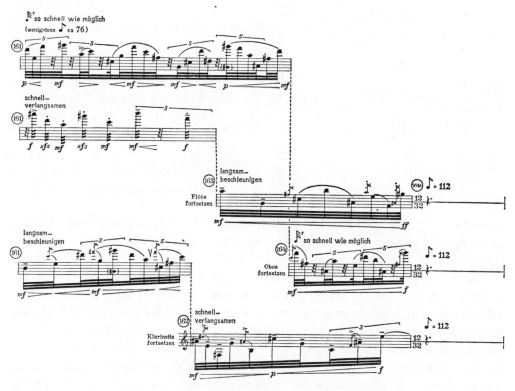

Five different measures of time are employed, successively and in combination: (1) an 'absolute' scale of metronomic tempi (MM=60–120) corresponding to an octave chromatic scale of pitch frequencies; (2) the subjective maximum 'as fast as possible'; (3) the subjective ritardando from 'very fast' slowing down to 'about a quarter' of the starting speed; (4) the subjective accelerando beginning from the same 'quarter of [maximum] speed' to 'as fast as possible'; and (5) the subjective minimum 'as slow as possible'.

The five instrumental parts of *Zeitmasze* may be likened to five tracks of taped music which may in mixing be independently varied in speed, sometimes aligned to a common ad hoc pulsation, at other times individually fading into, out of, or across an

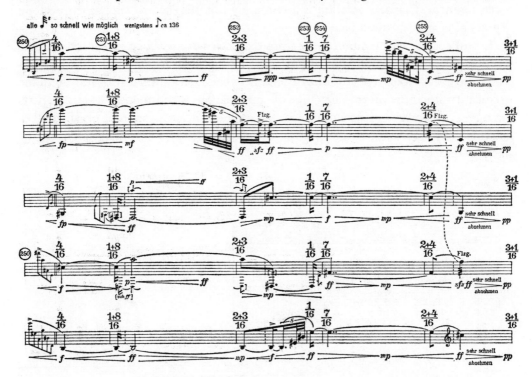

imaginary tempo of reference. The piece is articulated in a fundamentally similar way to the impulse passages of *Gesang der Jünglinge*, and explores a similar range of tempo-frequencies (limited in *Gesang* to up to 20 impulses per second). Stockhausen draws attention, however, to important distinctions between the two sound-sources. No technician, he remarks, would be able to cope with *Zeitmasze*'s subjective tempi, not recognizing their dependence on human and instrumental limitations. The same distinction applies between keyboard and woodwind. There are others. Slowing down or speeding up impulse material does not give the same results. If pre-recorded impulses are altered in speed, their durations automatically shorten or lengthen, and the tone quality changes. If alternatively the impulse frequency is manually altered during recording, what one hears is less like a change of tempo than a change of density of points within a uniform time-field. Tempo is the product of a balance between articulation and pitch: a ratio of notes—their pitches, dynamics, and density—to performer and instrument response. It is a human measure of intensity of action, therefore, not a mechanical concept: a quality of performance, not of notation.

Early recordings of *Zeitmasze* tend to make the listener wonder whether the tempo-interactions so seductively realized on paper could in fact be translated into sound. All too often one misses the vital element of breath control upon which the perception of temporal continuity depends. This applies to passages of sparsely scattered 'points', as much as to continuous chains of notes. The quality of a note varies with the size of a performer's breath, and according to its position within the breath, early notes appearing to 'push', later notes to 'lean'. When a passage of points separated by rests is played in the ordinary fashion, with frequent and arbitrary taking of breaths, continuity collapses. Only when the same breath is held to the end of a passage is continuity retained, with the rests perceived as measured interruptions. Schoenberg was well aware of the relationship of temporal and gestural unity when he urged Zemlinsky not to make cuts in a projected performance of his *Pelleas und Melisande*: 'It will not take so long to play, but it *will not really be shorter*! A work that has been shortened may well give the impression of being an excessively long work (because of the exposition) that is too short in various places (where it has been cut).'[3]

Similarly in *Zeitmasze* a note that is indicated as short may very well be intended to give the impression of a long note (because of its quality of delivery) that appears only for a short period (the notated duration). Recent performances directed by the composer himself have remedied matters. Stockhausen now insists that as far as possible the breathing of the ensemble must be co-ordinated, and this leads to much stronger feelings of continuity, both individually and collectively. Performers also adopt stylized playing attitudes which mirror the tempo-movements within the music; in particular no movement is allowed during rests between notes that belong to the same breath- and tempo-span. The result of these changes is that performers now give a firm, almost adhesive quality to their notes, whether long or short; the music no longer sounds merely intellectual and aimless, but exuberant, quick, and jazz-like; an experience of startling physicality and balletic intricacy of movement.

Gesang der Jünglinge

1955–6: No. 8

Electronic music.
Duration 13 minutes.
Realized in the electronic music studio of North West German Radio, Cologne, on LP 16133 (mono), 138811 (stereo), and 138811 (new stereo version, 1968). No published score. An analysis of the work may be found in Stockhausen, Texte II, pp. 58–68, and a sample page of a study score (abandoned before completion) in Texte III, p. 239.

[3] Schoenberg, *Letters*, Faber, 1964.

'GESANG der Jünglinge' is Stockhausen's first work since the early vocal pieces to carry an explicit extra-musical message. With his talent for choosing personally appropriate texts, the story of the three young men in the fiery furnace (Daniel 3) may be interpreted as a parable of the three young composers—Boulez, Nono, and himself— in the fires of critical and public incomprehension.[1] And the comparison holds good at a deeper level, since the ordeal is also an act of spiritual purification. The fire, with its power to burn or make clean, is also the new music.

This programmatic message is linked notwithstanding to a more scholarly interest. As *Zeitmasze* had been inspired by speech continuity, so *Gesang* takes as its point of departure analysed speech sounds, their quality and liaison, imitating them electronically.

Up to this time our basic material has consisted solely of sine tones. In the new composition, a sung text is combined with electronic sound. Sung phonemes are structurally more differentiated than any [synthetic] sounds hitherto composed. A quite natural bond of association between the given phonemes and the composed electronic sounds is intended.

This can only be done when the sung text is 'objectified' by artificial treatment and thereby brought within the range of electronic sounds.[2]

When one takes a length of tape-recorded speech and cuts it into progressively shorter sections, strange things seem to happen to the recorded sounds. With longer segments one attends to the sense of the spoken words, hearing the cuts as interruptions of a continuous flow. But as the size of the segments decreases, fewer transitional elements are clearly audible, and the listener increasingly perceives the recorded sounds as stable individual tone- and noise-spectra, frequently of surprising purity. Such experiments probably suggested to Stockhausen the possibility of synthesizing artificial speech sounds which could be made either to gravitate toward 'real' recorded speech or to dissociate into independent compositional elements.

Since all the categories of electronic sound used in *Gesang* are related to phonemic elements from the recorded text (recorded as sung fragments, not as a sung continuity), they do not relate to a common serial base as do the various tone-mixtures of the previous two studies. Both electronic and vocal elements are classified according to scales of comprehensibility, another departure from the composer's usual practice.

There are eleven such categories of element. They are (1) sine tones; (2) sine tones fluctuating periodically in pitch; (3) sine tones fluctuating randomly ('statistically') in pitch; (4) sine tones fluctuating in amplitude, periodically; or (5) statistically; (6) sine tones fluctuating periodically or (7) statistically in both pitch and amplitude; (8) filtered 'white noise' (known as 'coloured noise') of constant density or (9) statistically varying density; and (10) streams of impulses of constant or (11) statistically varying periodicity.

---

[1] All the same, one notices that there is only *one* boy's voice in the piece.
[2] 'Aktuelles', *Texte II*, p. 51.

'These elemental forms,' Stockhausen adds, 'are controlled in all parameters and may be freely adapted to the exigencies of manual production.' In contrast to his earlier studies Stockhausen defines his materials as evolving in time, not as static quantities. They are sounds with a known inner life, not just events to be ordered into movement.

Of special interest is his synthesis of statistical impulse complexes.

Let me describe how we've gone about making a sound texture of twenty seconds' duration. I sat in the studio with two collaborators. Two of us were handling knobs: with one hand, one of us controlled the levels and, with the other hand, the speed of pulses from a pulse generator which were fed into an electric filter; a second musician had a knob for the levels and another for the frequency of the filter; and the third one would manipulate a potentiometer to draw the envelope—the shape of the whole event—and also record it. I drew curves—for example: up-down, up-down up-down up-down, up, which had to be followed with the movement of a knob (let's say for loudness) for the twenty-second duration. And during these twenty seconds, another musician had to move the knob for the frequency of the pulses from four to sixteen pulses per second in an irregular curve that I'd drawn on the paper. And the third musician had to move the knob for the frequency of the filter following a third curve.

So, everyone had a paper on which different curves were drawn. We said, 'Three, two, one, zero', started a stopwatch . . . we'd all do our curves, . . . and this resulted in an aleatoric layer of individual pulses which, in general, speeded up statistically. But you could never at a certain moment say, '*This* pulse will now come with *that* pitch'. This was impossible to determine. Then we'd make a second, third, fourth, fifth layer—the number of layers was also determined—and I'd synchronize them all together and obtain a new sound.[3]

Complex procedures giving unpredictable results are difficult to notate in retrospect, which is a principal reason why the projected realization score has had to be shelved. But without doubt the impulse-generated material is *Gesang*'s most memorable feature, giving the work an articulateness at times reminiscent of the extravagant flourishes of classical keyboard music (not for nothing is J. S. Bach the most celebrated present-day composer for synthesizer).

The vocal text, the 'Song of Praise of the Three Youths', is taken from the Apocrypha to the Book of Daniel, Chapter 3. Words and phrases were selected as required from a number of recognized translations. The recurring phrase 'Praise the Lord' ('Preiset/Lobet/Jubelt den (dem) Herrn') acts as a textual refrain throughout, and also as a key to the electronic transformations of the sung material: whenever the sung text becomes momentarily intelligible, the words are in praise of God. Thus the text resolves acoustically in the same direction as it tends spiritually.

The 'Song of the Youths'— is composed in six wholly connected textures. This formal arrangement may be detected in that in each of the longer textures 'preist' or 'jubelt' in association with the words 'den Herrn' is clearly audible. In this fashion continuity is assured over long passages of time.

In the first texture (after 10.5″) 'jubelt' is dimly audible in the background.

[3] Cott, *Stockhausen: Conversations*, pp. 71–2.

In the second texture (beginning from 1' 10"), first of all 'dem Herren jubelt' is heard in chorus (at 1' 08.5") and soon afterward (at 1' 58.5") 'preiset den Herren' sung by solo voice in closeup.

In the third texture (from 2' 52") a solo voice sings 'preiset den Herrn'.

In the fourth texture (from 5' 15.5") several voices sing 'den Herrn preiset' in chords (a second time at 5' 46.5").

In the fifth texture (from 6' 22"), 'Herrn preiset' rings out many-voiced from the far distance (at 7' 20.5"), then 'preiset den Herrn' (at 7' 51").

In the sixth texture (from 8' 40") a solo voice sings in great melodic sweeps 'jubelt dem Herrn' (at 8' 42"), 'preist' (at 8' 51"), then (at 10' 50") 'ju————belt'.[4]

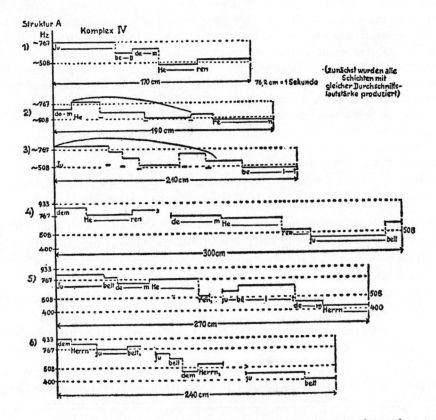

Soon after *Gesang der Jünglinge* had acquired a reputation it was put about that since the work incorporates a boy's recorded voice it qualified as *musique concrète*. Since 1952 the prestige of the Paris school had diminished as that of Cologne had steadily been growing, and one suspects that the label represents an attempt either to transfer some of the credit for Stockhausen's achievement or alternatively to reduce the work in public eyes to the level of a Parisian caprice. But whatever the motive behind the label (and it has tended to stick), it is positively misleading. The manner in which Stock-

[4] *Texte II*, p. 59.

hausen integrates vocal sound into the electronic fabric of the piece would never have been sanctioned by the school of Schaeffer ('*mon* violon, *ma* voix'), even if its members had been technically well enough informed to understand what he was doing. The qualities of intelligence and workmanship, that made Schaeffer so keen to claim the work in retrospect as *musique concrète*, elevate *Gesang* to an altogether higher plane.

Stockhausen's treatment of the voice should also be distinguished from the analytic approach favoured by other composers of electronic music, such as Berio in *Omaggio a Joyce* or Eimert in *Epitaph für Aikichi Kuboyama*. In these works originally continuous speech is progressively pulverized and more or less arbitrarily dispersed into an electronic flux. This technique has since become something of a cliché, since a sentimental association between the textual fragmentation and a portrayal of physical or mental breakdown is frequently implied.

Gesang also innovates on the level of sound reproduction. Though in the world of the cinema considerable advances in multi-channel sound projection had already been made, *Gesang* is the first major work of concert music to take practical advantage of the formal possibilities of stereophony. Stockhausen's original scheme (outlined in the essay 'Actualia', in *Die Reihe I*) called for six-channel reproduction with speakers surrounding the audience. This was eventually reduced to five channels, the speakers distributed in a panoramic arch across the stage. Ironically even this modest exercise in stereophony was criticized early on as a distracting gimmick alien to the true nature of loudspeakers, that being to speak 'with one voice' directly and unambiguously to an audience.

Whereas *Studie I* gives the impression of sounds radiating outward, and *Studie II* introduces a keyboard-like freedom of movement, *Gesang der Jünglinge*, in many respects Stockhausen's most perfectly contained electronic work (in the sense of satisfactorily resolving the composer's original intentions), is consciously directed in both time and pitch towards the middle register occupied by the boy's voice. This aural tension in both horizontal and vertical dimensions is previously found only in some instrumental works, *Kreuzspiel* for instance. The point is significant because in his later electronic works Stockhausen progressively changes the locus of attention from the centre to the extremes of the audible pitch spectrum, and the implied point of view of the listener from marginal or external (listeners *to*) to central (listeners *within*). Here the focus on the boy's voice naturally draws attention to the 'message' content of the text, which (however appropriate the text may be) tends to obscure awareness of the purely formal relationships of the electronic sounds. It did not inhibit audiences, nevertheless, from instinctively recognizing the potency and authority of Stockhausen's handling of the medium.

Klavierstück XI

1956: No. 7, UE 12654a, b

Piano solo (1 page, 93 × 53 cm), UE 12654b with clip-on frame.
Duration c. 14 minutes.
Recorded by Aloys Kontarsky on CBS 32 210008 (New York), S 77209 (Paris),
72591–2 (London) (two-record set). Also by Marie-Françoise Bucquet on Philips 6500
101, 'Tresors Classiques'.

Piano Piece XI (says Stockhausen) is nothing but a sound in which certain partials—components—are behaving statistically. There are nineteen components, and their order can be changed at random, except that once you choose a connection from one element to the next, the following element is always influenced by the previous one. . . . As soon as I compose a [synthetic] noise, for example—a single sound which is nonperiodic, within certain limits—then the wave structure of this sound is aleatoric. If I make a whole piece similar to the ways in which this sound is organised, then naturally the individual components of this piece could also be exchanged, permutated, without changing its basic quality.[1]

PIECE XI is more closely related to *Gruppen* than to Pieces V–VIII. The gap in numbering arises because the piece is based on the serial orders originally calculated for the eleventh of a projected cycle of 21 piano pieces, and because the numerical order is also serial in implication. Its closer affinity with *Gruppen* is twofold. First, like the three-orchestra piece, Piece XI's time structure is based on a magnification of the vibration characteristics of a single sound (in *Gruppen*, a series of sounds). Second, the relationship between fixed and random time-structures in Piece XI neatly inverts Stockhausen's order of formal priorities in the orchestral work. Each 'group' in *Gruppen* translates the underlying pitch of a single note into an underlying tempo, and the harmonic or partial frequencies of the same note, corresponding to its timbre, are expressed as metrical subdivisions of the fundamental pulsation. The same relationship of partials to fundamental frequency relates the tempi of segments of Piece XI to the mean tempo selected by the performer for the performance as a whole. A musical sound in nature does not begin to vibrate over all of its harmonic spectrum at the same time or at the same amplitude, however. In the evolution of a naturally overtone-rich sound certain partials will emerge more strongly than others; some early, some late, some rising to a peak and abruptly falling away, others rising more slowly and persisting longer. Furthermore, the balance and sequence of partials is never quite the

---

[1] Cott, *Stockhausen: Conversations*, p. 70.

same twice: sounds that we hear as similar vary considerably in their inner structure, not only from instrument to instrument and from one player to the next, but even from moment to moment. The fine detail of timbre may even be effected by environmental factors such as the amount of reverberation of an auditorium and the temperature of the air.

In *Gruppen* the variable evolution of 'partial frequencies' in a group is composed; in Piece XI the sequence and 'frequency ratio' (relative tempi) of sections is left free. This freedom is theoretically permissible because the piano piece's structure is modelled upon the evolution of a complex wave-form of unspecified pitch, a 'noise' (e.g. a magnified tam-tam note), whereas *Gruppen*'s note-groups correspond to fixed (synthetic or real) pitches and timbres. The piano piece's six tempi constitute in effect a constant formant structure for the whole work, a stable 'timbre', as it were; the fact that these tempi are associated with passages of varying density can therefore mean simply that at times certain formants are more pronounced than others.

Piece XI is composed in nineteen sections of varying length and complexity. In purely notational terms, these sections are proportioned according to a Fibonacci series. They are liberally intercut, however, by pauses of different sizes, and also by passages of grace-notes which move at tangential speeds to the prevailing tempo. The nineteen sections are distributed over one large page of stiff paper in such a way that spontaneous visual associations may not arise. A player starts by letting his eye wander at random over the page. He begins the piece by playing the first group on which his eye settles, at a speed, dynamic, and touch of his own choice. At the end of the group he reads symbols specifying the tempo, dynamic, and touch of whatever group he may chance to play next (indications for touch and dynamic are absolute, those for tempo correspond to a subjective scale). Certain groups provide for octave or two-octave transposition of right or left-hand parts in the event of a repetition; when a group is encountered for the third time one version of the piece may be considered over.

The work has excited a great deal of controversy, and has been studied and criticized, sometimes severely, by a number of distinguished composers, among them Boulez, Stravinsky, and Cage. These criticisms centre on two issues: one, the piece's random order of sequence, the other (a more technical argument) its fidelity to serial principles of proportion and liaison.

The first objection is based on the notion that a piece of music is organized only if it follows a fixed, supposedly logical, order of sequence. To this one need only reply that there are perfectly acceptable forms of classical music (such as variation-form) in which the notion of consequence is much reduced, if not entirely suppressed. (This is not of course to imply that Piece XI is the same as a set of variations.)

The second objection, to Piece XI's random changes of scale, arises from a misinterpretation of the structural function of the nineteen segments. This objection reflects an 'architectural' interpretation of the piece's form.

I talked at great length about it with Stockhausen, conceded Boulez. I think personally that he goes too far in his Klavierstück XI. I would say that the manner in which he hands over the reins to the performer merely produces a new sort of automatism, one which, for all its apparent opening the gates to freedom, has only really let in an element of risk that seems to me absolutely inimical to the integrity of the work. The performer proceeds as it were haphazardly, by chance glances that are no more than chance—or glancing—blows; all that happens is the transformation in duration, timbre and intensity of already predetermined sound- and rhythm-structures, which themselves remain unchanged. I well realise that the principle at work is simply a development of variation-form; nevertheless I do not believe, particularly in the case of duration, that it is possible for any rhythmic structure whatever to adapt to any tempo whatever and still retain its formal identity. I want to stress that the chance element, whether Stockhausen wishes it or no, is what seems to me to be the operative factor in any given interpretation of his work.[2]

In his first book on the Modulor, Le Corbusier describes a game called the 'Panel Exercise'. The 'panels' are flat rectangular shapes based on the Modulor scale of proportions; the 'exercise' consists of arranging selections of these shapes into larger rectangles whose outer dimensions are also harmoniously proportioned. 'The "Panel Exercise",' remarked Le Corbusier, 'has the satisfying effect of showing that in the very heart of this impeccable geometry—which some might think *implacable*—the personality has complete freedom of action.'[3] Now if one compares the structure and

---

[2] Goléa, *Rencontres avec Pierre Boulez*, Julliard, 1958, p. 229.
[3] *The Modulor*, Faber, 1954, p. 96.

freedom of Le Corbusier's exercise with the structure and freedom of Piece XI (for the Modulor is not very different from a Fibonacci series of proportions), one is bound to end by voicing precisely the same objections as Boulez makes in the quotation above. For the point of the game of modular permutation is that every imaginable arrangement of the standard pieces is by predetermination harmonious; 'balanced' because the juxtaposition of elements proportioned to a Fibonacci series is bound to generate overlapping interior symmetries, and 'integrated' because smaller elements combine to form larger elements in the same series. However, for this to happen (1) the elements must adhere strictly to the prescribed dimensions, and (2) they must be fitted together without gaps. Piece XI satisfies neither supposed requirement. The durations of individual groups are freely variable (the six degrees of tempo not themselves corresponding to a Fibonacci series), and the temporal continuity necessary to perception of proportional durations is, as we have seen, frequently broken and distorted. Since Piece XI does not conform to the rules of modular permutation, Boulez appears to be arguing, how can its structure possibly hang together? By what possible precedent could it be argued that this is a valid system of musical construction?

One might also observe that Stockhausen's own comparison of Piece XI with the evolution of a complex wave does not altogether explain the work's curious system of liaison. Fortunately we do not have to look very far for an acceptable precedent, however. There is a piece in Messiaen's *Livre d'Orgue*, the fourth, called 'Chants d'Oiseaux'. It acts as an interlude in the sequence of seven pieces, an escape from the post-*Mode de Valeurs* serial rigours of the other six into the composer's private world of birdsong. In 'Chants d'Oiseaux' six identifiable structures (birdsongs and link material) are rotated. Each has its own subjective tempo. The structures vary in length, and repetitions of the same structure may also vary. At the end of each structure there is a pause for a notated change of registration. These changes affect the dynamic and timbre of the succeeding structure, and may in some cases cause the written notes for right or left hand (which play on separate manuals) to be transposed up or down one or more octaves.

Messiaen: 'Chants d'Oiseaux'

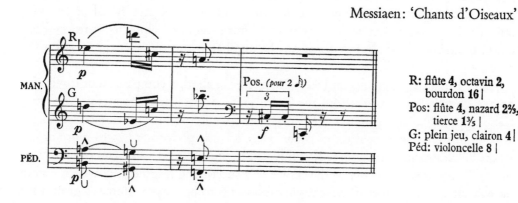

R: flûte 4, octavin 2, bourdon 16 |
Pos: flûte 4, nazard 2⅔, tierce 1⅗ |
G: plein jeu, clairon 4 |
Péd: violoncelle 8 |

If, then, Piece XI is unacceptable as theory, it may quite safely be regarded as a systematic and imaginative application of principles of organ music to music designed for piano. The sequence of events in 'Chants d'Oiseaux', though written in fixed order, was designed to give an impression of randomness, chance encounters with birdsong in the course of a walk through the forest—one of Messiaen's favourite images. In such a piece time is not felt as measure, but as place: each event is a self-contained moment of awareness, and its duration expresses the intensity of awareness. So, too, perhaps, with Piece XI.

Leaving aside the question of origin, Piece XI is an object lesson in notation, clearly distinguishing the permutatable constants of tempo, duration, dynamic, and timbre (touch), from the relatively fixed local deviations of accelerando, ritardando, pauses, and accents. The function of secondary grace-note formations is also interesting, though we have seen the device already in operation in Pieces V–VIII, in view of the permutatable time-proportions of Piece XI. Since the grace-notes are always played 'as fast as possible' they act as a constant foil to the arbitrarily changing tempi of the main structures. They also incidentally act as useful guides to the sequence of groups in performance, since their own tempi remain relatively constant. They also allow the performer considerable freedom of action, in contrast to the rigidly calculated contrasts of the passages written in large notes. Thus a certain reciprocity is reached between the demands of abstract form on the one hand, and ductile expression on the other.

Since Boulez's comments on Piece XI have been aired, a comparison of it with his own 'Constellation-Miroir' (from the Third Piano Sonata) may be useful. The latter is also composed of a large number of unequal fragments of music distributed seemingly at random over one large sheet of paper. Here too the performer begins more or less where he pleases and then proceeds as directed by signs placed at the end of each fragment. These signs relate only to the choice of a succeeding fragment, however, and in no way affect the manner in which what follows is to be played. Boulez's groups are totally determined, and he limits the choice of sequence to a few calculated orders. Boulez presupposes a uniform time-flow, into which events are fitted; Stockhausen implies an underlying dynamic of expectation, and his events define their own time-spaces. Whereas the events of Piece XI create a heightened sense of actuality, those of 'Constellation-Miroir' (alternating passages of 'points', printed in green, with 'blocs', printed in red) convey above all a sensation of transience, as when two simultaneous scenes are intercut in a film, so that the viewer is never sure which is 'in the present' and which 'flashback'.

Boulez: 'Constellation-Miroir'

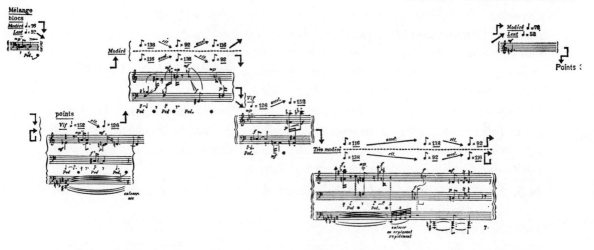

Boulez's treatment of duration as a structural constant, and tempo as the subjective variable (inflected within metronomically-defined limits) corresponds closely to Le Corbusier's fine distinction between size and scale. Stockhausen by contrast clearly regards tempo in Piece XI as the primary structural specification, and duration as merely its passive expression. Time for Boulez is 'time within which'; for Stockhausen it is 'time taken'. In dynamics as well Boulez sticks to *a priori* absolute specifications, while Stockhausen's are dependent on performer action and not answerable exclusively to theory.

These differences ultimately refer beyond individual temperament to the composers' respective traditions. On one side, a French tradition with its priorities firmly in the realm of ideas, its emphasis on notation, and its fastidious regard for purely literal distinctions (such as the sequence of chords in *Blocs I*, the first *fff*, the second *fff sforzato*, the third *ff marcato*, and all *molto staccato*). On the other side, a German tradition of music as sensation, expressed in Stockhausen's primary concern with material matters, sounds produced and manipulated, *things heard* (e.g. 'groups' as against 'structures'). The two complement one another exactly.

Gruppen

1955-7: No. 6, UE 13673

For three orchestras:

Orchestra I: Flute (also piccolo), flute in G, oboe, cor anglais, clarinet, bassoon, 2 horns (high-low), 2 trumpets, 2 trombones, tuba; marimbaphone, glockenspiel, 5 cowbells, tamtam, 3 cymbals, 2 wood drums, 4 tomtoms, snare drum, tambourine (4 players); keyboard glockenspiel (or celesta), harp; strings 10.2.4.2.

Orchestra II: 2 Flutes (1 also piccolo), oboe, piccolo clarinet, alto saxophone (also clarinet), baritone saxophone, bassoon; 3 horns (high-low-high), 2 trumpets, trombone, bass trombone; vibraphone, 14 tubular bells, 4 cowbells, tamtam, 3 cymbals, 2 wood drums, 4 tomtoms, snare drum, tambourine, ratchet, 2 triangles (high, low) (4 players); piano (without cover), electric guitar; strings 8.4.2.2.

Orchestra III: Flute (also piccolo), oboe, cor anglais, clarinet, bass clarinet, bassoon; 3 horns (high, low, high), 2 trumpets, 2 trombones, contrabass trombone (or tuba); xylorimba, 4 cowbells, tamtam, 3 cymbals, 2 wood drums, 4 tomtoms, snare drum, tambourine (4 players); celesta, harp; strings 8.4.2.2.

N.B. Cowbells, tamtams and cymbals, wood drums, tomtoms in each orchestra are selected from regular pitch-scales.

Duration 25 minutes.

Recorded by the WDR orchestra, conducted by K. Stockhausen, Bruno Maderna, Michael Gielen on DGG ST 137002.

'GRUPPEN' introduced a new grandeur of scale to the serial music of the fifties. It was Stockhausen's longest and most ambitious work to date, its size an assertion that he at least was no longer content to be classified as a 'post-Webern' miniaturist. The work is in one continuous movement, and is immediately distinguished in being composed for three orchestras under separate conductors. The music of *Gruppen* is Stockhausen's most elaborate translation of pitch vibrations into complex rhythms, and sums up a period of concentrated research into the relationship of serial pitch and time which had also generated Piano Pieces V–VIII, *Zeitmasze*, *Gesang der Jünglinge*, and Piano Piece XI. *Gruppen* derives less from these works, however, than from *Formel* and Piano Piece I. In both of these much earlier pieces the interior structure is articulated by changes of metre. This device suggested further possibilities of serial integration and control, but their precise formulation took many years to evolve. In essence *Gruppen* translates a pitch series into a tempo series, and the timbres, durations, and modes of attack associated with these pitches into metrical aggregations of corresponding shape.

Pitch is translated as the conducted tempo of a group, the tempi of *Gruppen* being organized in a logarithmic progression expressing the same proportions as a tempered, chromatic scale. Stockhausen had used such tempo scales before. In his essay '. . . how time passes . . .' he describes how a sequence of structural durations may be derived from a basic note series. The octave register of each original note determines whether its corresponding duration appears as a breve, semibreve, minim, crotchet value, etc. (high notes being shorter, low notes longer), and its place in the chromatic scale determines its metronomic value. This procedure yields a series of basic durations, but no tempi (which imply repetitions of the same duration). Stockhausen saw that he could economize in metronome changes by altering some of the time signatures in his series where the change between adjacent durations expressed a simple ratio. For example, a $\frac{2}{2}$ bar at MM=60 followed by another $\frac{2}{2}$ bar at MM=80 could be written more simply as a $\frac{2}{2}$ bar followed by a $\frac{3}{4}$ bar in the same tempo of MM=60. Pursuing the implications of proportional relationship in the sequence as a whole, he realized that each metronomic degree stood in a known harmonic ratio to every other, and that the numerical equivalent of these ratios could be expressed as tempi:

The proportion 2:10 means that the duration of a first phase is two-tenths of the duration of a second fundamental-phase, i.e. five times as short. But it also means that two phases of a second duration are equal to ten phases of a first. We can therefore reverse the proportions (10:2/3:4, etc.), because now we refer not to the duration-relationships of the single fundamental durations, but to the relationships between the numbers of fundamental durations in each group.[1]

Stockhausen's drawing of the resulting tempo-ratios at this point in the essay so closely resembles a series of diagrams in Helmholtz[2] that one is driven to speculate over the possible influence of the great nineteenth-century acoustician on his deliberations. As it happens, several of Helmholtz's observations in the context of the said diagrams are curiously apt:

Alterations of pitch in melodies take place by intervals, and not by continuous transitions. The psychological reason of this fact would seem to be the same as that which led to rhythmic subdivision periodically repeated. All melodies are motions within extremes of pitch. . . . Every motion is an expression of the power which produces it, and we instinctively measure the motive force by the amount of motion which it produces. . . . How long and how often can we sit and look at the waves rolling in to shore! Their rhythmic motion, perpetually varied in detail, produces a peculiar feeling of pleasant repose or weariness, and the impression of a mighty orderly life, finely linked together. . . . But the motion of tone surpasses all motion of corporeal masses in the delicacy and ease with which it can receive and imitate the most varied descriptions of expression. Hence it arrogates to itself by right the representation of states of mind, which the other arts can only indirectly touch. . . .

Melodic motion is change of pitch in time. To measure it perfectly, the length of time

[1] *Die Reihe* I, p. 14/ *Texte* I, p. 119.
[2] *On the Sensations of Tone*, Dover, 1954, pp. 264–5.

elapsed, and the distance between the pitches, must be measurable. This is possible for immediate audition only on condition that the alterations both in time and pitch should proceed by regular and determinate degrees. . . . The musical scale is as it were the divided rod, by which we measure progression in pitch, as rhythm measures progression in time. Hence the analogy between the scale of tones and rhythm naturally occurred to theoreticians of ancient as well as modern times.[3]

Helmholtz not only endorses the principle of equivalence of pitch and time, but even describes motion in music and nature in statistical terms. Stockhausen could hardly have asked for a more impressive testimonial for *Gruppen*.

From a number of possible alternatives, Stockhausen chose a rhythmic structure leading to frequent overlapping of different tempi.

I originally wanted to write a normal orchestra piece, but when I started composing several time layers I had to superimpose several metronomic tempi, and it was impossible to find a solution by which one conductor would be able to lead the three sections of a large orchestra in different tempi. So I finally concluded that the only way was to split the diverse time layers and put each group in a separate place.[4]

This division of the orchestra into three led to further imaginative flights of a less systematic nature. But before these could be contemplated, the work's detailed inner structure had to be worked out, and for this Stockhausen drew on his studies of phonetics and timbre. Each 'group' in *Gruppen* is composed, in Helmholtz's words, as 'a motion within extremes of pitch'. To each fundamental duration of the basic rhythmic structure he assigned a pitch interval according to an interval series ranging upward in size from 0, or unison (corresponding to the spectrum band-width of a single filtered frequency). Instead of 'points', then, *Gruppen* is a structure of essentially rectangular 'fields' similar to the rectangles of *Studie II*. Each field is composed vertically of intervallic strata, as in the electronic work, the number and density of layers varying with the height of the field; in time it is also divided into layers of harmonically related metrical frequencies. Only in the rhythmic sense do the fields correspond to timbres; as pitch aggregations they belong to the note-mixture, quasi-formant class of the *Studie II* complexes.

Each group-field is thus composed as an area of characteristic resolving power upon which an image of musical movement might be 'exposed' as a photographic image is exposed on a half-tone screen for printing. Continuously evolving images are articulated in terms of the preordained pitch and rhythm co-ordinates like those animated signs which work by programmed illumination of a grid of tiny lights.

The three orchestras are of roughly equal size and in each the following instrumental families are represented: woodwind, brass, plucked, and bowed strings; each of these four families is further subdivided into a 'sound' group, playing exactly determined pitches, and a 'noise' group, playing approximately determined pitches. For the transition from sound to controlled

[3] Helmholtz, op. cit., pp. 250–3.
[4] Cott, *Stockhausen: Conversations*, pp. 200–1.

noise within each instrumental family there is a selection of many percussion instruments of metal, wood and membrane. With instruments such as the piano, the celesta, tubular bells and cowbells, sound and noise can be combined in a single instrument.[5]

Stockhausen may originally have intended the flow of points within each group to correspond to the vibration structure of particular types of musical sound. 'Points' of short duration (staccati, pizzicati, quickly damped percussion notes, etc.) are one typical category. Sounds of this kind are generally of rapid onset, building to a peak of intensity in which the upper partials (which define the attack and to a great extent characterize the timbre of the sound) are strongly and simultaneously audible. After passing its peak, a short sound by definition rapidly attentuates of its own accord, or is quickly suppressed. In general, the sharper the attack, the more rapid the onset and

[5] Wörner, op. cit., p. 162 (*Texte I*, p. 155).

richer the overtone spectrum of the resulting note (though this also depends on the material by which the sound is set in motion, hard substances—plectrum, wood—producing a rich sound more easily than soft—finger, felt). Higher partials speak more rapidly than lower, consuming less energy, and it is sometimes the case that a short note is extinguished before the fundamental has time to establish itself, as in the case of a rapidly stopped cymbal crash. A *Gruppen*-like pattern of articulation based on the evolution of a short sharp sound would therefore be composed as a dense complex of higher 'partial frequencies' with the fundamental audible, if at all, as a regular dynamic fluctuation. An example of this type is to be found in Orchestra I, group 1 (page 109).

A note of abrupt attack, but allowed to reverberate, settles into a more or less coherent periodic vibration, gradually diminishing in intensity as the initial impact is converted into sound and used up. A 'group' of this kind would be complex and 'statistical' at first, then gradually resolving into a coherent rhythm made up of relatively simple metres. An example is the Orchestra III ritardando from 113 to 115, part of which is illustrated below:

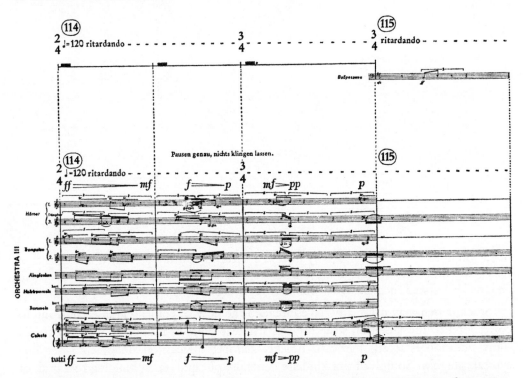

A third type of evolution is the note which builds up very slowly to a peak of intensity, an onset associated with woodwind, string harmonics, and organ with swell pedal (or indeed, with many instrumental sounds taped and played back in reverse). Rhythmic passages structured according to this type belong to a well-known category of ostinato writing which builds increasingly complex aggregations over a simple underlying pulse. Much of Stravinsky's *Rite of Spring* is composed in this fashion. Patterns of this type are infrequent in *Gruppen*, understandably in view of the composer's aversion to incessant periodicity. The synchronized build-up of brass 'points' in the three orchestras at 118, leading to a climax of chord exchanges from orchestra to orchestra at 119, may be understood as a magnified image of an accelerating tremolo (with hard beaters) on tamtam, ending with the instrument swinging alone back and forth, casting its resonances first one way, then another:

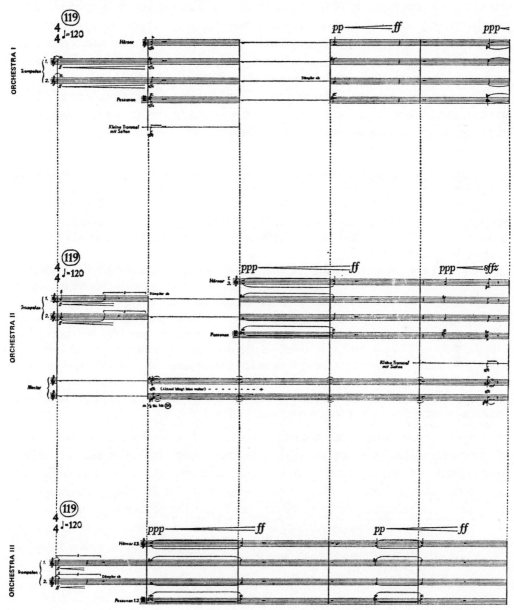

A fourth type of note structure is produced when a sound is prolonged by constant friction or renewed attacks, as in the case of a drum roll or bowed string tone. Such sounds, once established, retain a measure of statistical complexity within audible limits. Many groups in *Gruppen* conform to this type.

These observations arise simply as an extension of Stockhausen's structural method. The composer himself does not reveal whether the inner structures of groups are meant to resemble the onset and decay of specific natural sounds. It is all the same interesting that *Gruppen*'s groups nearly all belong to the first and last categories mentioned: short sounds abruptly suppressed, or long sounds prolonged by continuous agitation. For these sounds correspond, curiously enough, to the 'points' and sustained wind or bowed sounds which are the principal elements of *Spiel* and *Punkte 1952* (they also conform to the short and long note mixtures of *Studie II*).

It is nevertheless true that the sound patterns of *Gruppen* do not so much define the work's form as 'occupy' it, and whether or not he may have started by relating the shapes of groups to natural sound processes, Stockhausen eventually began to indulge his fantasy a little more freely.

Whole envelopes of rhythmic blocks are exact lines of mountains that I saw in Paspels in Switzerland right in front of my little window. Many of the time spectra, which are represented by superimpositions of different rhythmic layers—of different speeds in each layer—their envelope which describes the increase and decrease of the number of layers, their shape, so to speak, the shape of the time field, are the curves of the mountain's contour which I saw when I looked out the window.[6]

Once I had the idea of separating the three groups—each consists of thirty-six or thirty-seven musicians—I began to think in terms of alterations of sound movements: triangular rotation . . . with accelerando-ritardando; then alternations between two groups; and moments when one group would add only short sound events to the continuous alternation of the other two groups. I also thought in terms of moving timbres: there's one spot [119, see above] that led to something I hadn't expected myself—a chord is moving from orchestra to orchestra with almost exactly the same instruments (horns and trombones) and what changes isn't the pitches but rather the sound in space. Each orchestra, one after another, makes a crescendo and a decrescendo; at the moment when one starts fading out, the next orchestra begins to fade in, producing these very strong waves of revolving timbres.[7]

Are the groups comparable with the flourishes of classical music, such as trills, arpeggios, turns, etc.? Yes and no. Their 'incidental' nature is similar, and they relate to an expressively inflected overall tempo in much the same way as ornamental figurations to the pliant pulsation of classical slow movement. But Stockhausen's groups are not entirely subordinate to the form, having taken on a life of their own in the course of composition; at times the discrepancy between the moving patterns of notes and the static rhythm of a group is unusually pronounced. To equate groups with ornaments is to end by reducing *Gruppen* to mere decoration.

[6] Cott, op. cit., p. 141.
[7] Cott, op. cit., pp. 200–1.

Berg: 'Marsch'

Out of the impersonal system arises a personal imagery: in *Gruppen*, impressions and reflections of natural movement, leaves disturbed by wind, patterns of rainfall, sunlight dancing on the waves. Visible manifestations of invisible forces whose laws we know better today than two centuries ago, the statistical events captured in Stockhausen's groups are no longer symbols of disorder as they were then. 'It is always a question of functionally directed sound, rather than of sound effects,' says the composer, and the function—the motivation—is musical as well as representational. He had made careful analyses of statistical patterning in the music of Debussy, and of multiple tempi in the Concerto for Nine Instruments of Webern, in the years preceding *Gruppen*'s composition, and these studies have their place in its genealogy. So too has Berg, whose Three Orchestral Pieces not only employs orchestral forces similar to *Gruppen* but also incorporates a number of model 'groups', for example in the opening bars of 'Praeludium', and in bars 25, 36–7, and 136–142 of 'Marsch'. For Berg the group has a cadential function, surging upward to meet on a unifying downbeat, or spreading outward from an initial attack.

All this is consistent with Stockhausen's often-repeated aim of delving deeper and deeper into the micro-structure of musical vibrations, and ultimately reinforces a listener's first impression that *Gruppen* is pointillist music in spirit. The work began in 1955 as a project of very specific aims: (1) to pursue and regulate the composition of multiple tempo-structures stimulated by Piano Piece I; (2) to invent a functional notation for time corresponding to the tempered scale of pitch; (3) to discover a means of injecting flexibility and continuity into serial music which did not infringe existing serial principles; and (4) to write a work of major length with unlimited possibilities of continuation. Out of this mixture of formal and personal incentives came the system of group composition, and out of the system a new delicacy of imagery, plasticity of movement, and the rediscovery of musical space. By any standard *Gruppen* is a formidable achievement. That it was completed by a composer in his twenty-eighth year is truly astonishing.

Zyklus

1959: No. 9, UE 13186

For solo percussionist.
Small drum, 4 tomtoms, 2 African wood drums, guero; triangle, Indian bells, 4 cowbells,
2 suspended cymbals, hi-hat, gong with centre dome, vibraphone, marimbaphone.
Duration 10–16 minutes.
Recorded by Christoph Caskel on Mainstream 5003 (formerly Time Records, Series
2000-58001); by Christoph Caskel and Max Neuhaus on Wergo 60010, Heliodor
2549061 (2 versions); by Max Neuhaus on Columbia MS 7139; by Sylvio Gualda on
Erato GU STU 70603; and by Yasunori Yamaguchi on CBS Sony, SONC 16012-J
(Japan).

This is what I do in music. I go into the deepest possible layer of the individual sound. . . . In *Kontakte,* I composed every sound from individual pulses which I spliced on tape. I made loops of one rhythm with individual electric pulses that I recorded on tape with a duration of one second, for example, and sped the rhythms up a thousand times . . . so that in the evening I had [a sound of] about 1,000 cycles per second. And one cycle of the 1,000 cycles per second was my original rhythm.[1]

'ZYKLUS' for solo percussionist was composed at the time Stockhausen was deeply involved in the preliminary work for *Kontakte,* and incorporates many of his most interesting discoveries concerning the relationship between the inner structure of a complex wave-form, synthesized as rhythm, and its perceived character as timbre when the original rhythm is looped back on itself and accelerated until it becomes audible as pitch. *Zyklus,* which means 'cycle', is conceived as a single immensely distended pulsation of a note of indescribable richness. All of its structural levels are governed by symmetrical undulations of compression and rarefaction, like the fluctuating density of air molecules which conveys a sound from its source to the ear. The basic, 'skeleton' cycle of *Zyklus* is modelled on a tape-loop impulse structure originally synthesized for *Kontakte* on 4 June 1958 (see p. 138). In this structure five monotone layers of electronic impulses, serially differentiated in pitch (60, 84, 105, 160, and 200 Hz respectively) and 'out of phase' with one another in that each layer reaches its maximum density at a different point in the cycle, are spliced together into a single tape loop. The resulting train of impulses is completely regular, with only changes of pitch distinguishing the five layers. This style of hand-made pulse-code modulation was a

[1] Cott, op. cit., p. 76.

more efficient way of combining several vibrations into one envelope than the alternative of recording each layer individually and then mixing them on to a master, which would have required six tape recorders precisely synchronized to a degree unattainable at the time. Nevertheless the desired precision cost so much in preparation time by the cut-and-stick method of assembly, that Stockhausen soon abandoned this method of synthesis in favour of speedier, more automated procedures. One can easily imagine him considering the possibility of saving time by using a live instrumentalist to produce the basic envelope patterns on conventional instruments. A percussionist would be ideal for the purpose, since the sounds he produces are closest to impulses, and the range of percussion instruments available offer an enormous range of sound types, from precise to indeterminate pitch, and from sharp to indistinct attack.

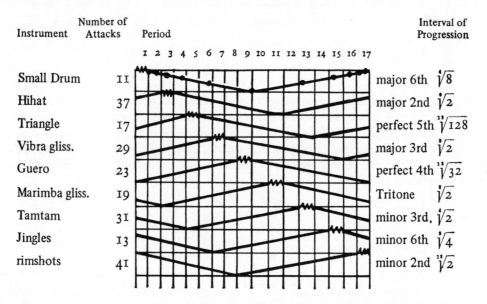

Instrument	Number of Attacks	Period		Interval of Progression
Small Drum	11			major 6th $\sqrt{8}$
Hihat	37			major 2nd $\sqrt{2}$
Triangle	17			perfect 5th $\sqrt{128}$
Vibra gliss.	29			major 3rd $\sqrt{2}$
Guero	23			perfect 4th $\sqrt{32}$
Marimba gliss.	19			Tritone $\sqrt{2}$
Tamtam	31			minor 3rd, $\sqrt{2}$
Jingles	13			minor 6th $\sqrt{4}$
rimshots	41			minor 2nd $\sqrt{2}$

Zyklus is basically a structure of nine layers of instrumental impulses. Each layer is assigned to a different instrument, and each contains a different number of pulses (attacks). The overlapping cycles of ritardando and accelerando are contained in a structure of 17 periods of equal length, drawn to scale and marked to facilitate reading in units of constant duration, 30 per period. The score consists of sixteen pages, spirally bound so that a performer may begin at any point and read straight through back to the point from which he started. The score may be read either way up, i.e. 'forward' or 'reverse' (even the pitch-cycles for vibraphone and marimbaphone are calculatedly symmetrical). Fifteen of the seventeen periods are printed one to a page; the remaining two periods, which Stockhausen in his *Texte II* analysis (pp. 74–100) numbers 17 and 1 in the cycle, occupy the final page, which is divided in two laterally by a double black line.

The skeletal structure of impulses is fixed for the entire work. Each layer consists of a logarithmically measured accelerando over 8 periods, a maximum in which the instrument dominates—and in which the number and distribution of attacks is free—of 1 period, followed by a further 8 periods of measured ritardando. Each layer reaches its maximum intensity at a different point in the cycle: the side drum during period 1, the hi-hat (pedal cymbals) during period 3, triangle in period 5, and so on, successive maxima occurring in the following odd-numbered periods.

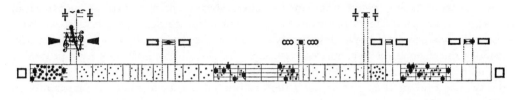

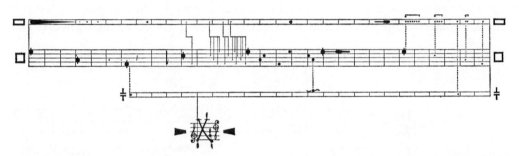

The number of attacks (not counting periods of maximum density) varies with each layer according to an inconstant progression of prime numbers from 11 through to 41. This means that though the oscillation from high to low is the same for all layers the density of attacks in all layers is not homogeneous throughout, as in the *Kontakte* prototype, but subtly fluctuating.

Over this skeletal structure Stockhausen has composed a second cycle of points and groups which oscillate between complete determinism (i.e. structural conformity with the basic point-complex) and various degrees of indeterminacy (statistical scatter of secondary elements within defined limits). It is as though the composer, having determined the ideal composition of his unaccelerated rhythm-timbre, then decided to incorporate certain characteristics of the sound as reverberated by a single resonating body (e.g. an echo plate). These are, notably, harmonic interference between the constituent partials, and cyclic distortion of the pitch-structure caused by periodic stretching of the resonating surface (e.g. metal or skin) as a result of being struck. Stockhausen's alternate blurring and focusing of the principal structure is beautifully controlled, and oscillates at twice its frequency, peaking at the fifth and thirteenth periods, with corresponding nodes of 'no interference' at first, ninth, and seventeenth periods.

In one important sense, however, the structure evolves non-symmetrically. This is in its progression from the pointillistic precise notation of period 1 to the *Gruppen*-like (or *Gesang-* or *Zeitmasze*-like) notation of statistical 'field-complexes' of period 17. The beauty of this aspect of the form is that it gives *Zyklus* a sense of direction; Stockhausen's genius is revealed in the imperceptible merging of the two extremes at the crossover point between periods 17 and 1.

Thus one gains the impression of moving in a circle, always tending towards greater freedom (clockwise), or greater fixity (anticlockwise), in which nevertheless at the critical meeting-point the two extremes embrace inseparably. . . . To close open form by bending it in a circle, embody the static in the dynamic, endlessness in the pursuit of a goal—not by a process of excluding or destroying one or the other, nor wishing to create a third reality by synthesis of the two: instead an attempt to abolish the dualism and reconcile tendencies apparently so divergent and contrary.[2]

Stockhausen compares the indeterminacy of *Zyklus* with that of Piano Piece XI, and indeed the degree of formal 'scatter' available to the performer—as distinct from the progression from fixed to statistical notation laid down by the composer—is limited to the selection and/or distribution of subsidiary points or groups within fixed divisions

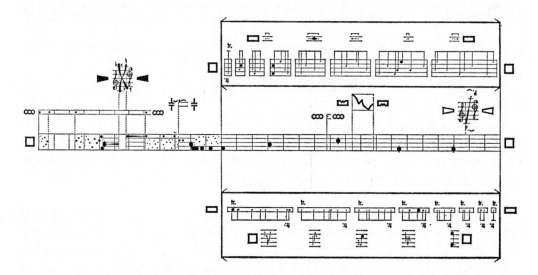

of the time-structure. These follow a cycle of fluctuating range of choice, with the greatest number and differentiation of options available at the two peaks, where the interference of subsidiary with primary levels is also greatest. The compositional rules regulating the size and relationship of subsidiary to primary elements, for instance the influence of the Fibonacci series 1, 2, 3, 5, 8, 13 on subsidiary orders, may be compared with those regulating the grace-note constellations of Piece VI or of 'Nebennoten'

[2] *Texte II*, p. 73.

(auxiliary notes) to the 'Zentralklänge' (central sounds) of *Plus-Minus*. In the preceding example the player chooses either the upper or lower bracketed system to play concurrently with the central primary structure. All subsidiary elements are drawn to scale and retain their written time proportions when incorporated into the principal structure.

Seen from a distance, the range of cyclic structures interwoven in *Zyklus* might suggest the ultimate disintegration by mutual interference of any fundamental periodicity. Or it might be more carefully argued that a dynamic cycle is not equivalent to a pitch cycle or density cycle, if the composer intends them, as he almost certainly does, to correspond to component partial vibrations of a single complex tone. Stockhausen answers these criticisms in detail in his essay, 'The Concept of Unity in Musical Time',[3] and more succinctly in the following words:

The secret of timbre composition lies in the production of very specific cycles of rhythmic changes. At first it's not so important what these changes are because you speed them up to such an extent that the resulting timbre is a newly perceived unity. It has a certain timbre characteristic, and you don't consciously analyse how it's composed in its micro-structure, you *can* no longer analyse the original components once such a sound is obtained, since the same timbre can be obtained in many different ways. . . . All the parameters become interchangeable . . . Very early on I made some experiments, splicing electric pulses . . . in different rhythms and speeding up these rhythms in periodic sequences. . . . I could also achieve the same result simply by taking a sustained tone and changing its dynamic curve. . . . It became very clear to me that certain aspects of time composition can lead us to the same results. It's just a matter of attaining something the quickest way, and it shows that these parameters are only theoretical parameters that make a certain method of sound production composition possible.[4]

At the level of a straightforward piece for percussion, which is a level more congenial to the ordinary listener, *Zyklus* has a great deal of interest to offer. It is Stockhausen's first piece for percussion alone, and also his first to break clear of pitch-dominated serialism. It is pleasant to interpret the piece in this light as a friendly tribute to Varèse, whom he had grown to admire, and whose love of percussion was coupled with an intense mistrust of the equal-tempered scale, but the idea for such a piece as *Zyklus* had clearly been germinating in his mind for many years. In *Punkte 1952* he had attempted unsuccessfully to harness the dynamic momentum generated by bongos to impart a sense of movement to a static point structure. In the essay '. . . how time passes . . .' he twice calls for the invention of instruments in which the size, shape, colour, and intensity of notes is regulated by pressure. From his researches with Tudor and Meyer-Eppler, he had become acutely conscious of the relationship between structural and gestural coherence. *Zyklus* thus represents a point of convergence of these preoccupations from his past and the particular problems of electronic timbre-synthesis upon which his mind was engaged at the time.

[3] *Perspectives of New Music*, I/2, 1963.
[4] Cott, op. cit., pp. 86–8.

Stockhausen's new notation for *Zyklus* is an innovation of great interest, made possible by his limitation of the piece to 'attack' structures and instruments, producing sounds which, once initiated, cannot be modified (in contrast to the woodwinds of *Zeitmasze*, for instance). This restriction allows a scale of note-sizes to be used, size corresponding to loudness, a clarity impossible if the breadth of a note were also to indicate its duration.[5] The notation further allows the various stages of indeterminacy in the timing and internal structure of musical events to be depicted with extraordinary elegance. (Pianists struggling to grasp the difference between action-time and chrono-metric time in the Pieces V–XI would be well advised to consult the notations for tom-toms.) Functional precision distinguishes Stockhausen's notation from the derivative note-forms of Haubenstock-Ramati (*Liaisons*, etc.), François Bayle *(Points Critiques)* and other minor exponents of 'musikalische Grafik'. It also explains why Stockhausen himself has since made only limited use of the new note-forms.

Zyklus is the first of three pieces dating from this period—the others are *Carré* and *Kontakte*—expressing the idea of enclosure put forward in his essay 'Music in Space'.[6] Here, of course, only the performer is enclosed in a circle of instruments, whereas in the other two works the audience is surrounded. Such a concept is essentially meditative, for all *Zyklus*'s intensity of activity;[7] there may yet come a time when, thanks to quadraphonic recording, we may hear its cyclic movement of sound from the still point of focus of the performer.

Carré

1959–60: No. 10, UE 14815 I–IV

For four orchestras and four choirs:

---

[5] Cf. Cardew, 'Notation—Interpretation, etc.', *Tempo* 58: 'there can be no indeterminacy in the notation itself . . . but only in the rules for its interpretation (as in Cage's piano concerto [·] means soft or short)'.

[6] *Die Reihe*, V.

[7] *Zyklus* seems aware of jazz, as does *Refrain*, and one should not dismiss the influence of his renewed contact with jazz during his 1958 tour of the United States. But *Zyklus* is not designed as a vehicle for mere technical display: its 'freedoms' are tightly circumscribed, and allow none of the self-indulgence expected of jazz and improvisatory 'serious' music.

Orchestra I: Flute (also flute in G), oboe, tenor saxophone, bass clarinet, D trumpet, high horn, bass trumpet, bass trombone; choir 2.2.2.2; piano, percussion (2 tomtoms, bongo, 3 cowbells, snare drum, bass drum, Indian bells, suspended cymbal, hi-hat, gong, tamtam): 2 players, strings 4.2.2.0.

Orchestra II: Flute, cor anglais, clarinet, bassoon, C trumpet, high horn, low horn, tenor trombone; choir 2.2.2.2; vibraphone, percussion (2 tomtoms, bongo, 3 cowbells, snare drum, Indian bells, suspended cymbal, hi-hat, gong, tamtam): 2 players, strings 4.2.2.0.

Orchestra III: Oboe, clarinet, baritone saxophone, bassoon, C trumpet, low horn, alto trombone, bass tuba; choir 2.2.2.2; amplified cymbalom, percussion (2 tomtoms, bongo, 3 cowbells, snare drum, bass drum, Indian bells, suspended cymbal, hi-hat, gong, tamtam): 2 players, strings 4.2.2.0.

Orchestra IV: Flute, clarinet in A, alto saxophone, bassoon, C trumpet, high horn, low horn, tenor trombone; choir 2.2.2.2; harp, percussion (2 tomtoms, bongo, 3 cowbells, snare drum, Indian bells, suspended cymbal, hi-hat, gong, tamtam); 2 players, strings 4.2.2.0.

Recorded by the choir and orchestra of North German Radio, conducted by Mauricio Kagel, K. Stockhausen, Andrzej Markowski, Michael Gielen, on DGG ST 137002.

IN VIEW of their juxtaposition on record and outward similarities of design (multiple orchestras, sounds moving in space, etc.) the listener is easily drawn to the conclusion that *Carré* ('Square') continues a line of development initiated by *Gruppen*. This is not so: *Carré* is no 'son of . . .', it is something else. Only the most tenuous link unites the two scores, fig. 119 of *Gruppen*, that unexpected development in the earlier piece where 'a chord is moving from orchestra to orchestra . . . and what changes isn't the pitches but rather the sound in space'.[1] In all important respects the two scores are fundamentally different.

Stravinsky was impressed by *Carré*, 'although it will no doubt be discovered that my admiration extends only to superficialities'.[2] He also preferred it to *Gruppen*. In several respects *Carré* is indeed recognizably nearer to the Stravinskian temperament than *Gruppen*: in its greater precision and timing of utterance, for instance, its sparer, clearer sounds and more economical scoring. But whereas *Gruppen*'s characteristic element is the point, *Carré*'s is the line; the earlier work is dynamic, co-ordinated by gesture, whereas *Carré* is reflective and slow-moving, a study in intonation. Both works investigate timbre, but *Gruppen*'s approach is abstract and synthetic whereas *Carré*'s is concrete and analytic. And in the final analysis the sounds of *Gruppen* in themselves

[1] See p. 112.
[2] *Themes and Episodes*, Knopf, 1966, p. 12.

are static phenomena disturbed by external forces; the sounds in *Carré* are continuous, and they move of their own accord.

Carré takes the interior fluctuations of a continuous reverberation as its point of departure; no longer the dynamic of onset or attack, but the dynamics of response, partial interaction, and decay of complex resonances. Gone is the desire to construct rhythmic equivalents of ideal timbres in their constituent frequencies. Instead we find— at the surface anyway—a simpler attention to rich single sounds or sound combinations which by analogy with the speeded-up impulse complexes of *Kontakte* could be construed as having highly organized interior rhythms. Such sounds, many of them mechanical in origin, make up a fair proportion of our day-to-day listening. Many of these sounds are made by machines in motion, so the sounds themselves move, and we hear their movements reflected in changes of pitch, dynamic, and focus (phasing, Doppler effects, etc.) which form no part of their vibration structures but are indications relative to the individual listener of the distance, speed, and direction of their movement in space.

Carré is thus much more directly representational in its choice of material than any previous Stockhausen work.

In *Carré* a new experience of time came into my music because of a very specific, personal experience. I was flying every day for two or three hours over America from one city to the next over a period of six weeks, and my whole time feeling was reversed after about two weeks. I had the feeling that I was visiting the earth and living in the plane. There were just very tiny changes of bluish colour and always this harmonic spectrum of the engine noise.

At that time, in 1958, most of the planes were propeller planes, and I was always leaning my ear—I *love* to fly, I must say—against the window, like listening with earphones directly to the inner vibrations. And though a physicist would have said that the engine sound doesn't change, it changed all the time because I was listening to all the partials within the spectrum. It was a fantastically beautiful experience. . . . I made sketches for *Carré* during that time, and thought I was already very brave in going far beyond the time of memory, which is the crucial time between eight- and sixteen-second-long events. When you go beyond them you lose orientation. You don't recall exactly if it was fourteen or eighteen seconds, whereas you'd never make that mistake below that realm of memory.[3]

The instrumentation of *Carré* marks a change from *Gruppen*, and looks back to the lighter combinations of Stockhausen's earliest orchestral compositions. *Gruppen*'s orchestral forces amounted in sum to a traditionally-balanced ensemble, with the heavy string sections that suggest, as in Mahler or Berg, an underlying melodic emphasis. In *Carré* however the string sections are greatly reduced, corresponding with the composer's shift of attention from gestural inflection to resonance, and the sound is closer as a result to chamber music. There are no double basses: each of the four orchestras has only four violins, two violas, and two cellos. In this way the strings are displayed as a 'colour' rather than as a 'force'. Other colours disposed with careful asymmetry among the orchestras are woodwind and brass choirs; each orchestra has

[3] Cott, op. cit., p. 31.

furthermore a small mixed choir of voices which mediate between string and wind timbres. The vocal parts, elaborated from his treatment of the boy's voice in *Gesang*, are composed of mimetic consonant and vowel combinations—including occasional recognizable names and ejaculations—chosen according to desired percussion and resonance criteria. A large percussion section, including chromatic scales of tuned drums and cowbells, plays 'consonants' to the harmonic instruments' 'vowels'. Both attack and resonance characteristics are brought together in the four equal-tempered percussion instruments, each of which acts as a focus for its particular ensemble: the piano (felt-struck string), cimbalom (stick-struck string), harp (plucked string), and vibraphone (struck metal).

The detailed working-out of *Carré* was undertaken by the English composer Cornelius Cardew, working under the composer's supervision.[4] By his own account Cardew worked for most of the time with only the haziest notion of what Stockhausen intended the work to express. Stockhausen himself was engaged full-time in other projects, chiefly *Kontakte*. Cardew's uncertainty was probably all to the good in preventing creative conflicts from arising, but in one respect his collaboration has left an audible mark.

The eight percussionists were my greatest worry, since I have but little penchant for the sounds. In the rough score, I sketched their parts vaguely, simply, mechanically and minimally, assuring myself that Karlheinz would brush them up when he came to correct the final score. This he never did, or only in a very few cases, and so the percussion parts retained their simplicity, and were finally completely appropriate and unobtrusive almost all the time (they play incessantly).[5]

First impressions on listening to the music are of extraordinary slowness, and an emphatic, deliberate discontinuity. In view of the strong feeling for liaison so characteristic of Stockhausen's other works—even *Refrain*—the sense of temporal dislocation is immediate and disturbing. *Carré* has Piano Piece XI's feeling of exploration and encounter, but the feeling is intensified by the combination of long durations, and sudden vivid changes, into a non-sequentiality of response similar to film, where successive scenes are understood to represent events not necessarily contiguous in space or time. Here in *Carré* 'time does not pass, only we pass', in Stravinsky's powerful phrase, and we feel our passing the more strongly in having to wait, time and again, for the expected change. To add to the listener's apprehension, as well as to dramatize the suspension of continuity, Stockhausen frequently cuts episodes off into periods of silence. (Whole sections of the piece can also be left out: the recorded version of *Carré* is quite severely 'edited'.) These silences are not the straightforward breaks and preparatory pauses to be found in Piece XI, but are palpable voids. One can neither anticipate them, nor, because the cuts have been so artfully timed, can one remember where or

---

[4] See Cardew: 'Report on Stockhausen's "Carré" ' (in two parts), *Musical Times,* Oct.–Nov. 1961.
[5] Cardew, op. cit.

how they came about.[6] The mind reacts without fully engaging, proceeding as it were by a series of tentative 'contacts'. It may be a touch, an alarm, or a sudden transformation, but in each case the process of adjustment to the new situation is constantly harried by uncertainty over what in fact one is adjusting to. Thus the sudden cut-off leaves the listener in a sort of vacuum. What has not been clearly experienced cannot be clearly recollected. Silence thus becomes a more than usually tangible element in the musical fabric, comparable with 'white space' in advertising, or the shaped and calculated voids of sculpture.

These elements all combine to give the work a special monumentality.[7] And because silence is as plastic and tangible an element as sound, space too becomes palpable, and one begins to recognize in the music the experience of being conveyed; of flying, or of being driven somewhere by car. Most of the events and transformations we hear in *Carré* may be related to sounds associated with being conveyed.

Music which has a beat can be mentally 'paced', but music which is airborne—or at least 'off the ground'—obliges the listener to measure his progress in time by other means. We listen as comfortably sitting passengers. Sounds pass by in a flash, or they overtake in slow motion, and these external events encroach upon long, sustained constant tones, which signify both our motionlessness *and* our being moved—sounds representing, that is, the whine of a motor. All these images appear in *Carré*, and the same indirect associations between disparate elements may be heard to apply: the relationship of a sustained pitch (moving at constant speed) to the intensity of inner activity of opposing (overtaking) blocks of sound, or to the sharpness and 'speed' of staccato chords (sounds moving in an opposite direction), or to the relationship between distance and rate of change.

Another consequence of this altered frame of reference, apart from the loss of physical correlates of gesture and effort, is the necessary inclusion of statistical phenomena into the perceived structure of events. Many of these go unrecognized in ordinary life because we look ahead further than we can hear. Events that, blindfolded, we would hear as random, such as the staccato incidence of passing vehicles, become useful markers of the passage of time when we can see and anticipate their arrival. Nevertheless, the basic situation is by nature unstable: one hopes for a smoothly continuous passage, but expects otherwise. So it is that parts of *Carré*, like detours, may be bypassed at will; so too the timing of events is elastic, like Piece VI (durations being determined by consensus among the four conductors on a latent speed of passage).

Part of the listener's uncertainty in listening to *Carré* may be due to cross-currents between the orchestral work and *Kontakte*, the composition of which was giving

[6] It is a well-known effect of film editing that the innocent viewer is hardly ever able to recall the exact point at which a jump-cut is made, presumably because adjustment to the new situation obliterates all recollection of the final state of the previous image. A similar effect seems to operate here.

[7] One thinks too of the monumentality of American art of the time, of Barnett Newman and Robert Motherwell, for instance, whose works Stockhausen encountered during his 1958 visit to the United States.

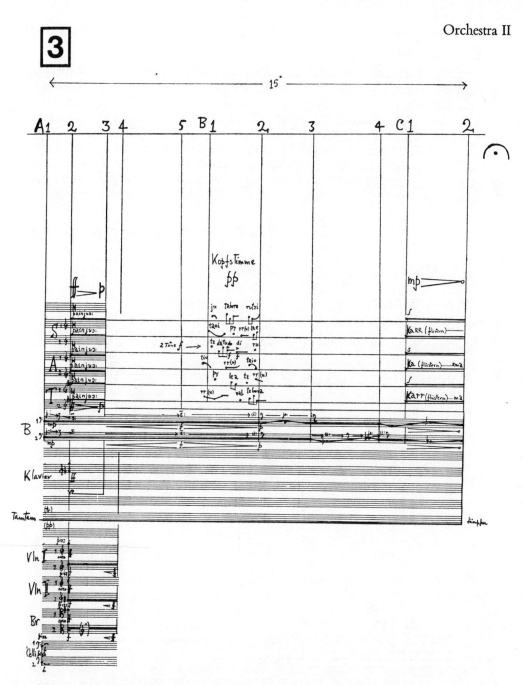

Stockhausen considerable trouble. The four-orchestra layout of *Carré* bears a fairly close resemblance to the original quadratic disposition of the electronic work, which Stockhausen conceived for four players, each also controlling one track of a four-channel tape of electronic sounds. In this original conception the players were intended

Carré

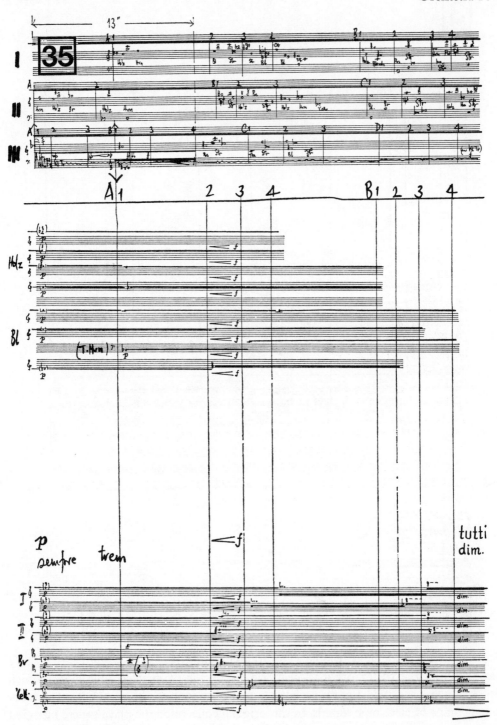

to 'conduct' the tape-recorded sound in its movement through space. By altering the loudness levels of channels in carefully co-ordinated ways, disturbing the balance between them, sounds can be made to appear to move in the direction of the loudest speaker. This would have amounted to a simple manual realization of the kinds of stereophonic effect made popular by the earliest demonstration records.[8] If we translate the same concept into the terms of four orchestras and conductors, we are faced with the interesting possibility that Stockhausen may have intended the four conductors to manipulate the sound of their respective orchestras in much the same way, casting the music back and forth across the auditorium, to use his own analogy, like tennis players (Debussy's *Jeux*, which he had analysed many years before for its 'statistical' content, must have made an unusually deep impression on him). This would account for the predominantly static character of the music, as for parts of *Kontakte* (section III, for instance), not so much as a calculated monumentality, but as material designed to be modulated dynamically more or less freely in the course of performance, so as to create an impression of waves of music surging across space, instead of simply passing around the periphery. In this light, *Carré* could be interpreted as a much more dynamic piece than it has become, a dynamism dependent however on unscripted inflections to be imposed on the written music by the conductors.

The resemblance becomes even more striking when we consider the inserts in *Carré* and their relationship to Stockhausen's development of a recording turntable designed to enable the sounds of *Kontakte* to rotate automatically from speaker to speaker around the auditorium. Stockhausen's first experiences of this new technique for electronic music inspired him to try out the same effects in *Carré*.

On the eve of my return to England, Karlheinz sprang the idea of the 'insertions' (episodes outside the general run of the piece—at this stage they had very little in common with what they eventually became) which were to delay the completion of even the rough score until March 1960, when I finished the last page (containing 3,000-odd notes) of the last insertion (comprising ten or so such pages) in a sun-filled library in Amsterdam.[9]

These insertions, shown in the score by an X following the rehearsal number, are passages in which the four conductors suddenly break into strict time, and the sounds, staccato chords at 32X and 63X, but often extremely dense statistical masses, begin to circle around the auditorium, flashing in regular succession from one orchestra to the next. The listener welcomes these seething complexes—the first of which seems to rise up like a swarm of bees—with relief after the uncertainty which has gone before, and feels transported in a kind of ecstasy, cut loose from the physical ties of place and gravity.

The important point about the insertions, so memorable in themselves, is that they embody a completely different concept of sound movement in space. Just as in *Kontakte* automatic rotation of the electronic material was brought in as a substitute for manual,

[8] See p. 144.
[9] Cardew, op. cit.

crosswise movement, so in the *Carré* inserts Stockhausen takes the burden of moving the orchestral sounds away from the conductors and leaves them simply to co-ordinate

Orchestra III

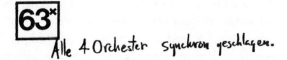

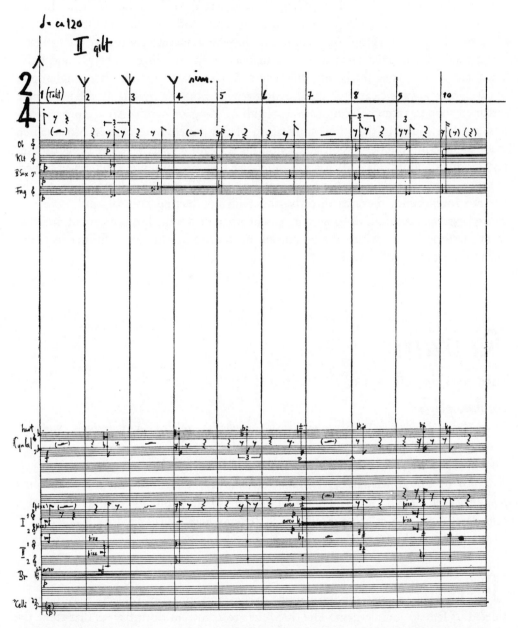

their respective entries and exits. And the combination of loss of physical control over
the sounds' movements, and the substitution of circular, enveloping movements for

straight-line movements—i.e. an enclosed for an open space—changes the character of the music from active to passive, and its mood from playful to reflective.

Ligeti and Penderecki were both deeply influenced by the textures of *Carré*, and it is interesting to observe that similar effects in their own works are associated with meditative or ritualistic subjects (*Atmosphères*, *Threnody*, etc.) to the point of cliché. Boulez as well seems to have been impressed by the insertions, and one can point to passages in *Pli selon Pli*, especially 'Don' and 'Tombeau', in which staccato chords are set against a background of sustained resonance in a manner very reminiscent of 32X and 63X. There are, all the same, intriguing differences. Stockhausen's tenuti, often single notes but if chords always clearly defined, contrast with Boulez's invariably indeterminate sustained sounds, often continuous tremolandi of gong or cymbal. A reciprocal contrast may be found in their instrumentation of the punctuating chords. Stockhausen tends to superimpose percussion attacks on his staccato chords whereas Boulez leaves his woodwind chords clear. What this difference seems to imply is a difference of perspective, aural certainly, perhaps also intellectual. Whereas Boulez focuses on the staccato foreground, the area directly under his conducting control, and leaves the background as a continuous hazy blur, Stockhausen draws the listener's attention away from the foreground, which the percussion makes too bright and indistinct to grasp, out to the clear sound-horizon.

Refrain

1959: No. 11, UE 13187

For three players.
Piano (also woodblocks), vibraphone (also cowbells), celesta (also antique cymbals), celesta preferably amplified.
Duration 8–9 minutes; 11–12 minutes when celesta amplified.
Recorded by Aloys Kontarsky, Bernhard Kontarsky, Christoph Caskel (celesta not amplified) on Time Series 2000/Mainstream 5003. Also by Aloys Kontarsky, Christoph Caskel, Karlheinz Stockhausen (celesta amplified), on Vox Candide CE 31022 (New York) STGBY 638 (London).

'REFRAIN' is contemporary with *Zyklus*, and in many respects may be considered its female complement. The title refers to recurrent disturbances that ruffle the ringing tranquillity of the music. These are engraved on a transparent strip, which is movable on its axis; thus the music may be disturbed at any number of places from those intersected by the strip leaning to the left to those affected by leaning the strip to the right-hand extreme of the system curvature. The score is read as a single page, from left to right, top to bottom, in the ordinary way. Although the angle and distribution of notes on the strip change according to whether it leans one way or the other, vertically-ranged notes are always simultaneous. Thus a line on the strip may be interpreted variously as a slow glissando (near-horizontal) or as a cluster (vertical) depending on how the strip is positioned. The curvature of the score results from the practical problem posed by the strip, and was not devised merely for effect, although it is visually very attractive. The notation refers not to counting, but to loudness and listening: dots and lines are graded according to intensity, and chord changes are regulated by the time taken for a principal note (cued as a line) to die away to the indicated final intensity.

The piece is scored for piano, celesta, and vibraphone: tempered, keyboard instruments inhabiting Stockhausen's beloved middle to high range of frequencies. For most of the time they play as a single instrument, producing unisons of fragile intensity and clarity, varied by careful adjustments of balance, pitch-sharing and inflection (this last with the help of auxiliary chimes and occasional voiced attacks). The resulting high, measured tintinnabulation suggests exotic ritual, but the piece is not ritualistic in intention, nor is it directly inspired by Asian models. In fact, the three strains of influence that converge upon *Refrain* are American performance style, French sonority, and German structure.

Cage is the unwitting source of the work's sense of timing. Introducing his *Music of Changes IV* to a radio audience in 1957, Stockhausen remarked how Tudor, who was playing the piece, would 'wait almost motionless, letting the last sound before a pause die away very gently', before making his next move 'with unbelievable rapidity'.[1] Cage is also in evidence as the originator of proportional notation, though the sound-orientated *tapered* lines of *Refrain* are a significant innovation of Stockhausen's own.[2] The sound and instrumentation of jazz, in particular of the Modern Jazz Quartet, may also be detected. Visiting New York's Birdland (a jazz nightspot) in 1958 with John Lewis, the group's pianist, Stockhausen was much impressed by what he saw: 'I learned a great deal, above all, from their instrumentation and technique, . . . also the way they played, their gestures, their level of sympathy'.[3]

[1] *Texte II*, p. 148. In the same context Stockhausen remarks 'Frequently in this score the pianist is asked to follow *simultaneously* so many different instructions in a given measure of time that he is obliged to leave out particular actions, and thus to play less than the music indicates'. Perhaps Cage sowed the seed of the selective options in *Zyklus* as well.

[2] See '. . . how time passes. . . .', p. 33. 'He (Cage) makes *all* proportions less distinct than ever before (logically enough, he is in fact not at all interested in proportional time-relationships, and the result is a continual disorientation in time, as a result of which the duration of a time-lapse is felt unusually strongly.'

[3] *Texte II,* p. 232. Stockhausen adds: 'They [the musicians] were exceptionally friendly and *sympathisch*. Yet it struck me how hopelessly divided their world was from mine; whereas I had already come across the names of one or two among them and could relate them to particular kinds of jazz music that I had previously heard, it was obvious from their expressions and conversation, that they hadn't the slightest idea of what was going on in music apart from their own.'

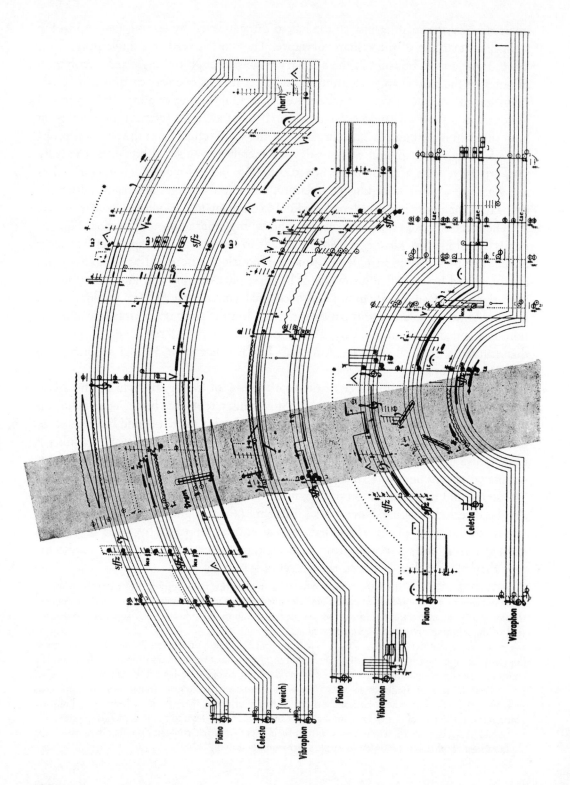

This last quality is what links *Refrain* with jazz rather than with Boulez's *Une dentelle s'abolit* (also 1958), with which it otherwise has a great deal in common. Considered as sonority, the piece is certainly 'very French', calling to mind Messiaen's 'sons impalpables du rêve'—the sentiment, of course, not the piano prelude. But whereas Boulez's concern in *Une dentelle* is primarily with the position and initial quality of his ringing sounds, *Refrain* requires sustained attention to the subsequent resonance, and to the quality of liaison of adjacent events. Thus one is meant to hear Boulez's resonance as reminiscence, and Stockhausen's as anticipation. In practice the distinction between 'waiting' and 'expectation'—between a mood of stasis, that is, and one of high tension—may amount to little, but it expresses nevertheless a fundamental difference between the French 'vertical' and German 'horizontal' attitudes to time and continuity, thus between theories of organization by loose association (Boulez) and tight adhesion (Stockhausen).

Like *Zyklus*, *Refrain* is also a summing-up of past theory: not pointillism in this case, but *Klangfarbensynthese*, the composition of new tone colours. Again the earlier idea is reinterpreted in its own terms by an elegant artifice of instrumentation. The problem of timbre-fusion is attacked in much the same way as the problem of colour reproduction in printing: by superimposition of several separate images in layers of primary colour, and relying on the uncertainty of sensory discrimination to create an illusion of intermediate shades and tints. Just as one is not expected to peer at a colour reproduction through a magnifying glass, so one should be wary in recording, or amplifying *Refrain* for performance, not to differentiate the instruments and thereby hinder the blend of sonorities.

The phonetic content of the piece, comprising not only the voiced attacks but also the woodblocks, cowbells, and crotala (which correspond to pure 'k', 'g' and 't' consonants respectively), refer as in *Gesang*, *Carré*, and *Momente* to his studies with Meyer-Eppler. Here they introduce a discreet tactile emphasis, and also serve conveniently to obscure the primary instrumental attacks, since it is there that the audible individuality of the struck sound chiefly resides (the resonances themselves are much simpler wave forms and thus less easy to distinguish). Since the piece was first written Stockhausen has made some changes to the style of vocal articulation. Though the 'clicks' (alveolar rather than velar) continue to present no difficulty, the consonant-vowel combinations proved not to merge sufficiently with the instrumental sound, principally because the abrupt cut-off of each syllable created an audible discontinuity not altogether bridged by instrumental sympathetic resonance. For this reason in the second recording of the work the vocal interjections are made to trail away rapidly downwards after the initial attack, and are now voiced in the higher and purer 'head tone'.[4] A second change in performance practice has resulted from the natural imbalance of the three instruments. Since the celesta is much weaker than piano or vibraphone, Stockhausen now balances

[4] The idea of a falling inflection is compared by the composer to the call-style of the Noh percussionists, but it is curiously similar to Schoenberg's prescription for *Sprechgesang* in *Pierrot Lunaire*.

the ensemble electronically, and the problem here is to place the microphones so that resonance may be amplified without making attacks unduly prominent. In this respect the recorded version of 1968 should be taken as the standard for future live perform- ances.[5] As a result of amplification the dynamic range of the piece, and with it the scale of durations, have become magnified to such a degree that ensemble pauses have had to be doubled in length. The entire piece now lasts around 11½ minutes compared to its original approximate duration of 8 minutes.

Like *Zyklus*, *Refrain* is a parable of time: of the experience of time as an expression of mortality, and a reconciliation with the transitory nature of human existence. Mor- tality is not signified by the decay of the sustained sounds, since they do not really decay, but merely fade from hearing. The image of man is in the *Refrain* itself, in the sudden disturbance in the order of things, the brief melody and tiny suggestion of momentum that appears without warning and vanishes without trace.

Kontakte

1959–60: No. 12, Realization score UE 13678

Electronic music.
Duration 34 minutes 30 seconds.
Electronic realization by WDR, Cologne; on DGG 138811.

Kontakte

1959–60: No. 12^{1}/2, Performance score UE 12426

For electronic sounds, piano and percussion.
The percussionist plays:
2 African wood drums, marimbaphone, 3 tomtoms with plywood playing surfaces, 1 guero fixed to a stand, 1 hanging rattle of suspended bamboo claves, 2 woodblocks, 4 cowbells, chromatic scale of 13 single antique cymbals, fixed to a board; upended cymbal, hi–hat, small tamtam, Indian bells, 1 bongo, 3 or 4 tomtoms, 1 suspended bongo containing a handful of dried beans (used as a rattle), snare drum.
Between percussionist and pianist, and played by both, stand:

[5] See *Texte III*, pp. 25–7.

1 Large tamtam, 1 gong with centre dome.
The pianist also plays the following percussion instruments:
1 Suspended bamboo rattle, 2 woodblocks, 4 cowbells, 3 single antique cymbals (fixed to a board), 1 suspended cymbal, 1 hi-hat, Indian bells, 1 bongo.
Duration 34 minutes 30 seconds.
Recorded by David Tudor (piano), Christoph Caskel (percussion), K. Stockhausen (sound balance) on Wergo 60009. Also by Aloys Kontarsky (piano), Christoph Caskel (percussion), K. Stockhausen (sound balance) on Vox Candide CE 31022 (New York), STGBY 638 (London).

A COMPOSER'S first period is usually marked by technical innovation and consistency of vision, for the simple reason that the first problem he has to face is not what to say, but how to say it well. It is in the process of finding a satisfactory mode of self-expression that the apprentice acquires the vocabulary and sense of form that at a later stage may themselves inspire him to more practical exercises. But a point is finally reached where that first imaginative impulse is within reach of his technical competence. This point marks the end of his first period, since the composer's work must inevitably undergo a change. He may choose to rest on his laurels, letting technique take charge over invention, or he may after reflection, seek out new imaginative goals. Either way, the decision signifies a crisis in that the sense of achievement is accompanied by disillusionment about the nature and value of the original objective. *Kontakte* crowns Stockhausen's ten-year engagement with numerical serialism, and its uncertainties, philosophical as well as practical, are those attending the realization that pointillism is only, after all, one of many modes of musical organization.

The piece took over two years to complete, from early 1958 to mid-1960, a period during which Stockhausen was increasingly attentive to recent developments in American music, to the composers Cage, Brown, and Feldman, to musicians like Tudor, and to jazz. American influences in the scale and style of musical utterance, and in notation and timing, are clearly evident in the instrumental works of this time. These changes of emphasis are outward signs of a profound emotional upheaval of which *Kontakte*, by virtue of its long gestation, is both focus and record. But the delay was not simply due to difficulties of mental adjustment; it is accounted for at least in part by the fact that the Cologne studio was having to be shared with Ligeti and Kagel over this period, for the production of *Artikulation* and *Transición I* respectively.

One is bound to consider *Kontakte* on two distinct levels: first as theory, and only after that as a finished work of music.

The realization score's detailed prescription of the synthesis procedure is as important to our understanding of the work as the two performance versions of the music, for electronic sounds alone and for electronic tape with instruments. Only rarely does a suggestion of conflict surface in the music itself, which by and large radiates the confidence of a newly-acquired technical virtuosity. It is when one begins to read between the lines of the realization score, and senses the day-to-day struggle involved in the making of the electronic sound material, that the anguish and the drama become apparent.

At the outset Stockhausen's approach to the synthesis of electronic material shows little change from the direct craftsmanship of his earlier electronic studies, in which the equipment serves primarily to make theory audible. This time the problem which had to be solved was the synthesis of new timbres as wave forms in constant evolution, that is, as single lines of varying amplitude. This contrasts with the vertical harmonic combinations of his earlier electronic works. In the first process detailed in the realization score, a train of ten short impulses varying in amplitude and duration (but not in pitch) is put together according to a symmetrical series:

20.2.58

Duration:	5	1	4	2	3	8	7	9	6	10
Amplitude:	1	5	2	4	3	8	9	7	10	6

This is the familiar type of series based on expanding-interval and mirror symmetries, used by Nono in *Incontri* (of similar title), and also resembling the series prescribed for *Schlagtrio*. The impulse pattern illustrated represents one cycle of a wave form. Made into a tape loop, it is accelerated until a single note of characteristic timbre is heard. This use of discrete impulses may seem an odd way of synthesizing a continuous wave, but Stockhausen's method is similar to the process evolved by Bell Telephone Laboratories in the United States for synthesizing speech using a voice as matrix and another recognizable noise as material. This process also transforms the original continuous speech input into a stream of impulses of varying density and amplitude. Stockhausen had already noticed in composing *Gesang* that an impulse generator could not only impose a rhythm upon sine-wave material but also had a tendency to influence its timbre. So we may surmise that Stockhausen may have originally intended to use impulses as a means of transforming percussive, unpitched sound ('pure rhythm') into continuous timbres ('pure sonority'). Not only does the tape-loop make it theoretically possible to derive tone colour from a series, but it also unexpectedly draws together time and pitch, two separate dimensions of human auditory perception, into a single electronic frequency spectrum.

The process outlined in the second entry, dated 25.2.58 in the realization score, makes one significant alteration: the amplitude of impulses is constant. This may be in response to the discovery that the softer-sounding components of the first series of impulses tended to vanish under acceleration. But if it is a reaction, the change also suggests a significant shift of approach. Firstly, amplitude is removed from the list of independent variables. The dynamic of an event, considered as a separate 'parameter' in pointillist music, is now accepted as the indirect product of pitch, timbre and duration structures interacting. It marks the first step away from intellectual precision, towards acoustic and technological reality. Technological, since constant signal strength is a built-in criterion of the electronic equipment Stockhausen was using. In discarding amplitude, the composer discards inflection, and thus feeling, and the deeper repercussions of doing so relate to subjecting purely expressive criteria to mechanical constraints on the one hand, and discarding abstract speculating *in* sound in favour of natural speculation *about* it, on the other.

In the experiment dated 29.5.58 the composer seems to have made a completely fresh start. Both in his theoretical approach and in reverting to sine-wave material he looks back to *Studie II*, constructing a sort of contracting tremolo by alternating a basic pitch with three higher 'partials' in descending sequence:

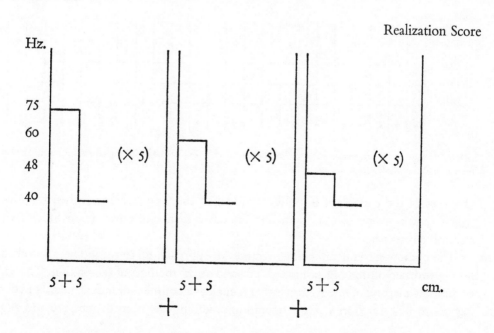

These pitches are related to serial tempi (40–48–60–75). The method of synthesizing complex tones is obviously based on *Studie II*, except that no reverberation is employed, and each interval cycle is repeated 5 times, presumably to make individual pitches more clearly discernible. Also like *Studie II*, but in contrast with the two previous experiments, each pitch is cut to a uniform 5 cm tape length. Stockhausen may have been interested to find out whether this constant fundamental duration would be translated by acceleration into an underlying pedal tone. This does not seem to have happened. The resulting complex, unaccelerated, sounds as follows:

[pitches approximate]

and may be heard in transposed form punctuating section XIIB of the score.

The entries dated 2.6.58 and 4.6.58 present a number of combinations of the two previous methods. Theoretical necessity accounts for this as much as practical interest; since they represent two quite distinct kinds of serial convention they would presumably have to be reconciled somehow in order ultimately to justify the piece as theoretically consistent. Several compromises are attempted, with an emphasis always on the unifying qualities of symmetry (regularity of wave form) and sonority (the production of 'energized' timbres). But the last example, in which five pitch-cycles of independently varying density are incorporated into a single stream of impulses, breaks new ground:

Realization Score

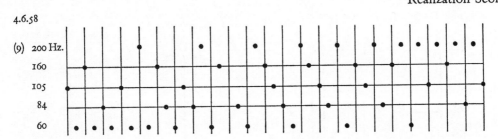

Each dot represents a 5 cm. section of tape. The aggregate 47 × 5 = 235 cm. was copied twice, joined 'forward' to 'reverse', and the whole recopied.

One sees in the pattern of impulses a model of the form scheme chosen for *Zyklus*, which may now be seen as 'spin-off', in more than one sense, from Stockhausen's electronic researches.

The composer's craftsmanlike directness of approach up to this point is matched by his dependence on the old-fashioned 'cut-and-stick' method of fabrication. The virtue of this new method of integration is that it enables a complex of independently evolving partials to be created in a single operation, avoiding the need to measure and align a combination of separately recorded tracks. The procedure bears comparison with the time-sharing principle of pulse-code modulation, which Milton Babbitt has also incorporated into his serial method.[1] But the advantage of superior co-ordination could only be won at the cost of greatly increased preparation time. The process would have to be speeded up. Automation was a possible but not a practical alternative: the studio did not possess suitable equipment, nor was Stockhausen himself temperamentally disposed in favour of such a solution.

The time question was eventually solved by a mechanical innovation which also had the effect of precipitating the theoretical crisis. Stockhausen suddenly discovered that by changing the order of the three heads in a tape recorder from the normal order of 'erase-record-playback' to the succession 'playback-erase-record', it became possible to superimpose layer upon layer of material on a single tape loop automatically, modifying the aggregate continuously as required at the same time. Having invented the 'copy head' as the new arrangement came to be called, Stockhausen found himself forced to rethink his entire compositional procedure, for in eliminating the need to 'cut and stick', the new device also called into question the fragmented numerical serialism of electronic music, and of instrumental 'pointillist' music as well, opening up in its place possibilities of timbre synthesis on an undreamed-of scale of richness and subtlety. Lack of experience, and pressure of time, both of which had hitherto justified the composer's dependence on serial consistency (by limiting his freedom of choice), no longer applied. He could now speculate and sample at will, and the new freedom to experiment brought an attendant obligation to make and select from a range of possible sound combinations where before he had been obliged to make do with one. And there were no rules for this exercise of taste. Thus the concept of a closed, theoretically integrated and essentially speculative system of composition had to be abandoned in favour of an open, subjective, series-orientated but practically inexhaustible range of choices, governed in the last resort by an intuitive awareness of the 'good sound'.

Before long we see 'naturalism' emerging as a favoured criterion. Synthetic sounds begin to be given names, like 'bell-like' or 'skin-like'. Imitation of instrumental timbres is not itself a new idea, but most of the resemblances with which *Kontakte* makes play—the categories of 'wood', 'metallic', 'skin' sounds—are similarities based on direct experience of simple sine-wave and impulse effects and do not require either analytic skill or complicated synthetic processes. The snare-drum effect at the conclusion of *Studie II* is typical. It may fairly be described as a chance discovery, even though the fact that it may be precisely accounted for is a tribute to Stockhausen's systematic approach. A crotala-like sound may be produced by reverberating a short and intense pure tone of high pitch; an unreverberated sine tone in the middle register gives a reasonable approximation of a marimbaphone. Stockhausen almost certainly knew of these resemblances from his early tape experiments.

If the idea of connecting electronic and instrumental music is not new, then, the

[1] See Babbitt, 'Twelve-tone Rhythmic Structure and the Electronic Medium', *Perspectives* I/1, 1962.

notion of authenticity probably is. The copy head certainly did suggest a much closer imitation of the evolution of instrumental resonance. Some painstaking research in this field was in fact undertaken by Gottfried Michael Koenig, Stockhausen's assistant at the time. But again, time proved a major obstacle, since the effort involved in analysing comparatively simple instrumental sounds could only delay further an already frustratingly long preparation time. Koenig's patient investigations may not have made *Kontakte*'s synthetic timbres very much more accurate or 'resemblant', but certainly helped to make them richer and more seductive.

In his experiments of 4.7.58 Stockhausen varies the speed, and thereby the pitch and density, of impulse aggregates within fixed filter and reverberation characteristics: the effect corresponds to altering the transmission speed of recorded speech without affecting its vowel quality. From this point on the technical processes become increasingly elaborate and the quality of sound input less and less precisely defined. Stockhausen's exactly-prescribed but piecemeal sound constructions of the experiments up to 4.7.58 are succeeded by processes for generating continuous inflected sounds within more flexible limits. In effect he now looks to his instrumentation to provide a range of possibilities from which to choose. As if coming to terms with a new orchestral instrument, the composer's concern is now simply to set a wind in motion, as it were, and to find the 'right sound'—most pleasing and most natural—by trial and error.

Though Stockhausen's synthetic procedure had radically changed, the essential form-scheme of *Kontakte* remained much the same, and contradictions arise between the form and material. *Kontakte*'s overall structure, as shown in Stockhausen's earliest sketches, is closed, permutational, and ordered in *sixes* for each parameter (compared with the five-unit series of the first experiments). The inconsistency between the work's strict form and the free range of serial orders ultimately employed in synthesizing the sound material is immediately obvious, even though this fundamental rigidity of form probably gives *Kontakte* its aura of confidence and articulate precision. Another inconsistency is suggested by the narrow range of electronic sound-families from which the work is composed, which suggests an arbitrary serial limitation of basic materials, rather than an exhaustive investigation of potentially usable combinations.[2]

The piece begins and ends with cyclic gestures, on gong and snare drum respectively, which suggest, perhaps unintentionally, the actions of starting and stopping a 78 r.p.m. gramophone record. After a short hiatus, the music opens with a vigorous résumé of some of the principal types of electronic sound, ranging from the dense flux of section IB to the comically nasal exclamation of ID and the solitary complex tone of IF. This initial burst of energy gradually peters out in both electronic and instrumental parts, and leads via a short passage of droning electronic sounds with built-in Doppler effects, which sound like distant propeller aeroplanes, to section III. *Kontakte* was originally to have begun here. Section III's sound-world is static and contemplative,

[2] One gets the impression from the realization score that Stockhausen may have originally planned a series of 12 'sound-families', each comprising 12 variants of a basic prescription.

like *Refrain*, but the electronic sounds have an inner life which makes them appear to issue outward in straight lines from a central source, like beams of light from a lighthouse. The instrumental parts here are also spare and austere. After some four minutes of rather awesome music, section IV abruptly cuts in with a second dynamic interlude similar in kind to the passage IB–IF but shorter and more concentrated. Section V reverts to the 'Doppler effects' of section II, beginning with a sound rather like an electric motor starting. This time, however, the long continuous transitions one hears in II are dissected into shorter moments and reshuffled. These lines of sound eventually converge into a single note which then divides again, a symbolic gesture of 'contact' which recurs later in more elaborate forms. In VB the solitary tones of III are overlaid on the continuous transitions of II; again the music moves by increasingly rapid changes to a point where the two elements seem about to merge into a single tone colour. Here there is another sudden cut to a further anticipatory passage, this time descending in pitch to the point of confluence to which the previous passage seemed to be rising, that is, the deep, loud 'close-up' complex at VI through or within which staccato saxophone-like melodic fragments can be heard. Unexpectedly, this intimidating foreground sound is succeeded by an even louder, deeper, and 'closer' growl at VIIA, which recedes quickly enough to merge into a gently animated series of exchanges between the instruments and their electronic mirror-opposites. Four such 'sparring' episodes introduce the first major fugato at VIIF, a short-lived episode brusquely interrupted by buzzing signals. A series of musical gear-changes leads to a passage of more agitated and less sharply focused counterpoint at VIIID, which rapidly fades to leave only the high, tinsely rattle of a greatly accelerated sound complex. After a passage of ornamental figuration of a kind already familiar in Piano Piece V, a further fugato begins between the marimba and its electronic counterpart. This is played out against an accelerando which introduces a feeling of urgency and anticipation. At IXB the music returns to ornamental figurations, this time more aggressive in character and in a lower register. It is followed by a rapid succession of short episodes depicting different aspects of accelerated frequency, namely high bell-like pitches (IXD), a sensation of great speed (IXE) and of great interior or textural energy (IXF), to the passage made famous by Stockhausen's own analysis of it in his essay 'The Concept of Unity in

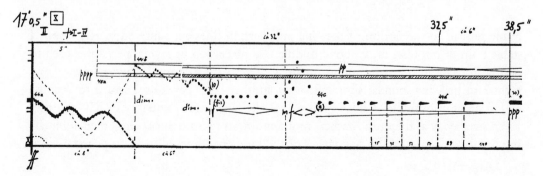

Electronic Music'.[3] Here a train of impulses is transformed before our ears from a continuous whine into a rapid up-and-down glissando that declerates into separately perceptible impulses. A melodic figure briefly appears, and then finally the repeating note
settles into a tolling reverberation on E below middle C. In this good-humoured and
brilliant transformation may be found the essence of Stockhausen's 'contact' concept:
the descent of music from the intangible into the perceivable. Contact is made in that
final drop to the note E, where the electronic tone is joined first by the piano, then the
marimbaphone. The electronic pitch itself passes into a timeless, resonant limbo out of
which emerge low frequencies of an intensity so great that the listener feels rather than
hears them; the ultimate contact, one may suppose, but also closing the cycle of rhythm
(impulses)—tone—rhythm (low frequency vibration).

This deep, continuous background is crossed at sporadic intervals by brilliant ornamental gestures. Gradually a melancholy mood settles on the piece, reflected in the
complicated, sometimes angry transformations which follow in section XI. Here the

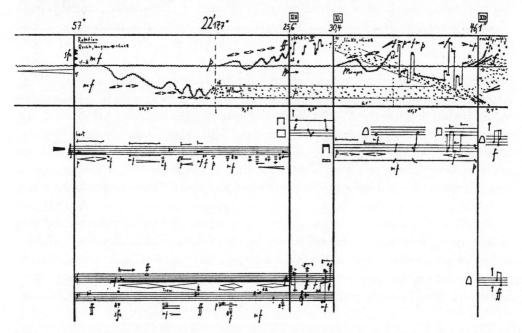

music returns to the notion of meeting and parting lines encountered in VA. From a
stable train of impulses on F above middle C a succession of layers 'peels off', each to
be transformed into a basic sound-category. The first layer moves away upward and
turns into bell-like sounds; simultaneously another layer bears downward to become
an indistinct drumming. A third spins off to take on a wooden quality in XIC. Further
layers peel away as the music gathers momentum, its texture thickening, then attenuating to allow deep, metallic resonances of the kind encountered in III to penetrate into

[3] *Perspectives*, I/2, 1963.

the foreground. Section XIIA, in which both instrumentalists cross to the gong and tamtam at centre stage, marks a high point of Stockhausen's original plan. In this and the subsequent section static complexes again predominate. The effect is heavy and mannered, however, and the passage is one of the rare occasions in *Kontakte* in which the composer seems conspicuously uneasy. The music remains overbearing in spite of

Bartók: Violin Concerto No. 2

attempts to introduce elements of contrast in between major outbursts. Relief comes with the explosive disintegration at XIIIC; this is followed by another low-pitch ornamental exchange structurally similar to those of VIIIF and IXB but texturally more varied. Once again the music accelerates in pitch and speed, and it reaches a peak of elevation and tension at XIV, where Stockhausen simulates a progressive 'switching off' of electronic frequencies from low to high. This image signals a return to the earlier feeling of melancholy, and the echoing melodic fragments heard through the electronic haze at this point have all the plaintiveness of the boy's voice in *Gesang*.

From this point the listener senses the end of the piece approaching, but the mood remains strangely exalted. The electronic sounds seem to lose their grip, breaking off and floating separately away. The instrumental parts become high-pitched, sustained, and generally tranquil. Sudden rushes of sound descend from the stratospheric turbulence to alight on the snare drum and take off again, and the work ends on a note of heavenward withdrawal.

It ends, yes: but the piece remains incomplete. 'He would probably still be working on *Kontakte* today had he not brought it to a finish with a decision as to a definite performance date. . . . The present finish seems to him very much like a dummy ending.'[4]

Stockhausen's misgivings are not difficult to understand. Ending a permutational

[4] Wörner, p. 110.

form is nearly always a matter of taste, not design. While the listener may be satisfied with a sensation of completion, the composer knows that though a series of permutations may eventually be exhausted, it does not automatically resolve. The ending's essential arbitrariness has to be disguised; *Kontra-Punkte* for instance sounds and looks dramatically complete even though there is scope in theory for a great deal more. But Stockhausen's doubts over *Kontakte* seem more like an expression of frustration at not having adequate time either to prepare or fully to explore the potential of his musical material. A sense of the gulf between what is theoretically possible and what is actually achieved is implicit in the studio situation and is already observable in the formal uncertainties of *Zyklus* and *Carré*.

But *Kontakte* is unfinished—'imperfect'—in a different sense as well.

Kontakte in its first version was not only a combination of fixed parts of instruments and tape, but the instrumentalists were to react freely during the performance in handling also individually the fading in and out of one channel per player of a multiple tape recording. Then I started to rehearse this and it was a real disaster. The musicians did not know what to do. From that moment on I began to fix entirely the parts of the players and I also did not want to change the tape any more.[5]

His original plan was to have four instrumentalists, three percussion and one piano, who would extemporize in imitation of the tape, without a written score. Each would also regulate the dynamic level of one of the four electronic channels. According to Kirchmeyer[6] Stockhausen 'had a very clear mental image of a musical tennis match, with the players serving and returning balls of sound one to another'. Such a concept goes some way to explain the sense of inertia one feels at sections III and XIIA; it is easy to imagine how splendidly these long sounds would respond to being bounced from one set of speakers to another. That he had not originally planned to write out the instrumental parts in full may also account for the unexpectedly derivative quality of *Kontakte*'s instrumental writing.

Perhaps the most surprising of these revelations, however, is the thought that Stockhausen was considering at such an early date the principles of performer participation usually associated with the reactive imitation style of *Prozession*, *Kurzwellen*, and other pieces of the late sixties. The kinds of imitation that are spelt out in detail in the instrumental parts for *Kontakte* may thus be understood as blueprints for the exchanges obliquely prescribed in these 'meta-musical' plus-minus scores.

Stockhausen's personal dissatisfaction, let us remember, does not seriously reflect on the quality of the final outcome. *Kontakte* is superb music which depicts the interaction of the timeless and the actual, and of the potential with the real, with clarity and wit. In the final analysis, furthermore, the music does relate to earlier composers. Those parts of the score in which continuous transitions predominate, i.e. the less rigidly

[5] Stockhausen to the author, 1972.

[6] Kirchmeyer, *Zur Entstehungs und Problemgeschichte der 'Kontakte' von Karlheinz Stockhausen*, sleeve essay, Wergo 60009.

defined episodes, composed later, seem unconsciously to recall the gestural world of Bartók. The ghost of Bartók's Sonata for two Pianos and Percussion can frequently be detected in Stockhausen's scoring, but the music's emotional world seems to relate especially closely to Bartók's Second Violin Concerto. One may point to overall resemblances in construction (linking short, contrasted episodes), and technique (the fundamental oscillation between lows and highs, parallel and independent motion, collage-type polyphony, etc.). But there are specific resemblances as well. For example, one may compare *Kontakte* at section XI with the solo wavy impulse-like tremolando around the same note F at bar 165 of the third movement. The transition from impulses to bell-like tones at XIB of *Kontakte* seems like a distant echo of bars 284 and 126 of the concerto's first and third movements respectively. The fragmentation effect at XIF makes the same sort of gesture as Bartók's pre-cadential *poco rubato* in bar 379 of the concerto first movement; further on, in *Kontakte*'s section XIV the timing and character of Stockhausen's plaintive melody recall the melancholy theme of Bartók's second-movement *molto tranquillo*:

Bartók

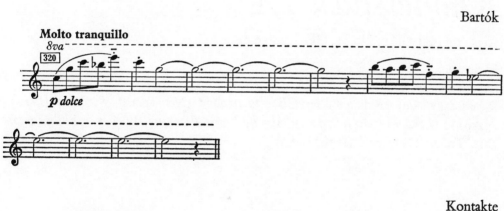

Kontakte

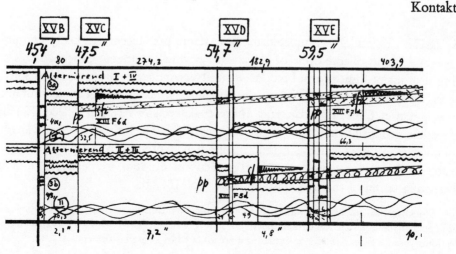

Finally, Stockhausen's idea of a coda loosely assembled from shards and 'offcuts' of earlier material, heard clearly at the end of *Kontakte* but also found for example in section V's fragmentation of previous section II material, is a familiar Bartók feature, the characteristic last-movement pot-pourri of earlier themes. Even the detail of *Kontakte* is constantly throwing up vague hints like the tantalizing glissando at XIIIC, resembling the dramatic slide and dénouement at bar 279 of the concerto. But as I have said, it is the 'deviant', less precisely prefigured electronic material which is most suggestive of earlier influence, and the measure of influence seems in proportion to the degree of free choice admitted during the realization process.[7]

Klavierstück IX

1954, revised 1961: No. 4, UE 13675e

Piano solo.
Duration c. 10 minutes.
Recorded by Aloys Kontarsky on CBS 32 210008 (New York), S 77209 (Paris), 172591–2 (London) (two-record set). Also by Marie-Françoise Bucquet on Philips 6500 101, 'Tresors Classiques' (Paris).

PIECES IX and X, completed in 1961, reinterpret pieces originally composed in 1954, and round off the cycle of eleven pieces which represent Stockhausen's earliest project of major dimensions. Like *Punkte* in its second state, the revised versions apply to originally austere pointillist exercises procedures which were discovered but not fully investigated in *Carré*, *Kontakte*, and *Momente*—especially *Kontakte*. Piece IX falls into 33 sections grouped by tempo into two main episodes. The ratio of 8:3 seems an obvious holdover from Stockhausen's original plan: it is expressed in the proportions of the major to the minor episodes, 24 and 9 sections' duration respectively, and in the alternating tempi of the first episode, MM 160/MM 60.

[7] Stockhausen is emphatic that these are no more than coincidental resemblances. But they may help the listener all the same, and it is curious that in both *Prozession* and *Third Region of Hymnen with Orchestra*, electronic passages from *Kontakte* or similar to it are imitated by string instruments.

The first episode emphasizes *measure*. It develops out of two basic elements, repetition (the famous repeated chord), and the sustaining and ornamentation of a chord: active and passive prolongation respectively. These two types of treatment intercut, overlap, and finally merge, creating an effect of a fundamentally simple 'pointillist' structure subjected to various kinds of simulated electronic transformation. This is most immediately obvious in the 'feedback' reverberation process suggested by the piece's lengthy introduction, but there are other things, such as the gradual addition of pedal reverberation on page 3 ('allmählich ganz niederdrücken'), or the manner in which his initial chord gradually dislocates as if right and left hands were tape tracks moving slowly out of synchronization, or in general the relationship of duration to attack. All of these are imitations of electronic processes. On page 5, for instance, chords in sequence are graded dynamically and juxtaposed as though they were snippets of pre-recorded tape.

Few legato markings are in evidence, but the piece is obviously tightly edited, right down to measurement of pauses in seconds (a measured pause is not the same as a rest). Durations are organized according to a Fibonacci series (1, 2, 3, 5, 8, 13 . . .) which is probably a 1961 innovation. The evanescence of piano sonority is brought out by both 'feedback' and pedal effects; however, a strange tension arises out of the contrast between instrumental reverberation time and the composer's use of a greatly extended scale of duration values. The listener's reaction to a seemingly artificial distension of musical time is paradoxically a sense of heightened expectation, the same feeling already anticipated in *Refrain* and shortly after rationalized as 'Moment-form'.

Strict measurement of time yields to ornamental uncertainty in the second, smaller section which begins at the change to MM=120 on page 6. Linear and monophonic rather than chordal in character, the episode is also more relaxed, in fact more continuously flowing, though in no particular direction. Stockhausen's distribution of ornament calls to mind Boulez's constellations of motives within a fermata, such as we find in the Mallarmé Improvisations of 1958; but the procedure also looks forward to Piece X's extraordinary suppleness of gesture. In sum, then, a rigid, mechanical, vertical organization gives way to a music that is flexible, horizontal in emphasis and *intuitively* timed; a transition that in view of the composer's subsequent development seems highly prophetic: a triumph of lyricism over structure.

Instrumental imitation of electronic distortion effects becomes increasingly important to Stockhausen's musical imagery during the sixties (and this is in addition to his introduction of 'live' ring-modulated sound). But the combined tape-loop and feedback image of Piece IX's opening repeated chord still cannot obscure a debt to Bartók. The vertical combination is a compound of the cadential repetition of the slow movement of Bartók's Sonata for Two Pianos and Percussion, and its treatment may be compared with the opening of 'Ostinato' from the same composer's *Mikrokosmos VI*:

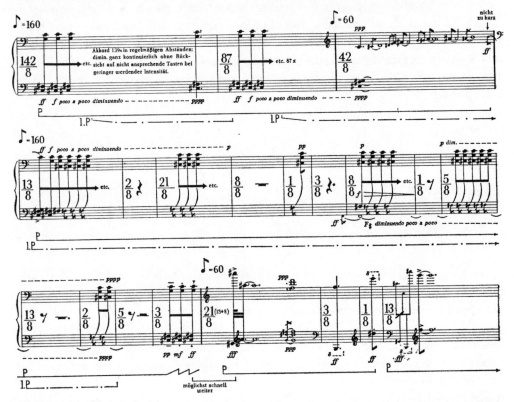

Bartók: 'Ostinato'

The tempo is not Bartók's, however, and seems to have profounder reference. The repeated chord is Stockhausen's image of *dis*order; at the given tempo it carries an echo of marching feet.

Klavierstück X

1954, revised 1961: No. 4, UE 13675

Piano solo.
Duration c. 23 minutes.
Recorded by Frederic Rzewski on Wergo 600 10/Heliodor Wergo 2549016/HÖR ZU
SHZW 90 3 BL. Also by Aloys Kontarsky on CBS 21 31 0008 (New York), S 77209
(Paris), 72591–2 (London) (two-record set).

Piece X unites the filigree intricacy of Debussy (e.g. 'Voiles', bar 41, or 'Feu d'Artifice' bars 43–5) with the energy and intensity of impulse-generated electronic sound. The work is densely and delicately wrought, and carries an expressive charge in striking contrast to his normally articulate but emotionally detached style; among the composer's instrumental works *Zyklus* is perhaps closest to it in terms of sheer physical impact. This new outspokenness is revealed most obviously in Stockhausen's boldly rhetorical employment of note-clusters, which before *Kontakte* had made only discreet appearances in his piano writing. As in *Punkte 1952/62*, the successions of clusters create an effect of shifting surfaces of sound (repetition considered as a sustaining, not an accentual device). They represent an important addition to the piano's expressive vocabulary and are so subtly manipulated as to persuade the listener into an awareness of the piece's strangely heightened eloquence.

The appearance of tremolo and glissando clusters in Piece X may have something to do with similar usages in the electronic part of *Kontakte*. Both devices appear late in

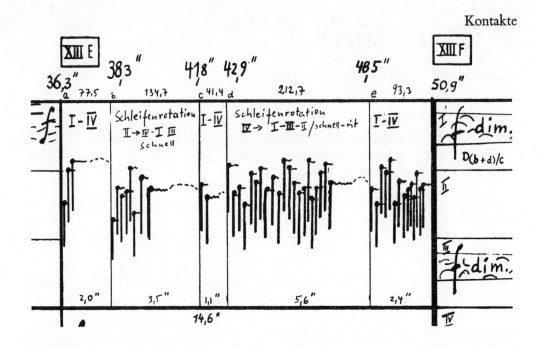

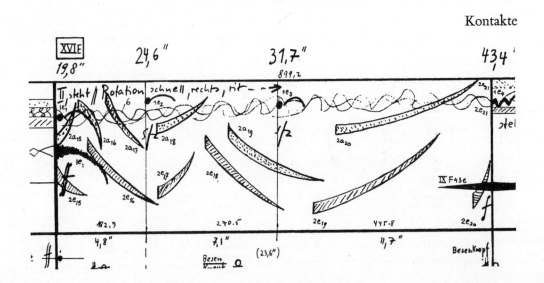

the electronic score; the 'cluster', or vertically-extended 'point', complicated to synthesize and therefore difficult to investigate in an electronic context, and the glissando (its tapered shape indicating not a narrowing of width, but a diminuendo) associated in *Kontakte* with feelings of floating and withdrawal:

Sliding intervals also appear in the Bartók Sonata for Two Pianos and Percussion:

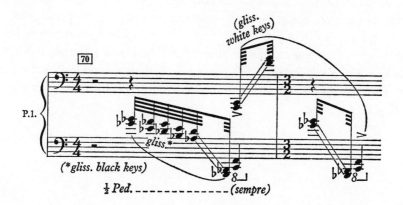

A new 'radiophonic' element, found in *Kontakte* but used here with a special overtone of pathos, is the device of the high repeated 'Morse' tone. Used in Piece X as a kind of short-wave signal, it conjures up the same feelings of solitariness in an electronic maelstrom that one senses in the coda-like melodic fragments of *Gesang* and *Kontakte*. Similar signals occur in his music throughout the sixties, and become part of the fabric of *Mantra*.

Silence is another important element. If Piece IX's introduction is a test of the listener's stamina, then the sudden blackouts of Piece X (during which, Roger Smalley has observed, the music may be imagined as continuing as it were 'underground') counsel the listener to patience. The silences speak with all the urgency of a lost connection, and do not signify arrested motion or suspension of action, but breakdowns of perception.

Piece X

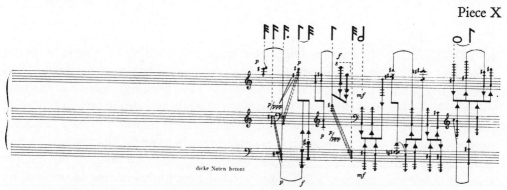

The kind of touch indicated for Piece X—light, quick, and consistent for all pitches in all dynamics—combines the sound quality of an electronic organ with the action of a clavichord. In the field of radio background musical effects the electronic organ cluster is a cliché device for suggesting dreams, darkness, and terror. Tone-homogeneity within the cluster is important. It enables the listener to hear Piece X not only as a form in constant evolution in the ordinary sense, but also as a sonority in constant exposition, the sonority in question being the total resonant capacity of the piano itself. Such a way of hearing leads us directly to the concept of music as derivation exposed in *Mikrophonie I* and latent in *Momente*. Uniformity of timbre is not a feature of the modern grand piano, but it was a feature of the fortepiano, which raises the interesting possibility that Piece X may have more in common with Beethovenian sensibility than might at first be apparent.

Originale

1961: No. 12²/3

Musical theatre with 'Kontakte'.
Duration 1 hour 34 minutes.
Text published in Stockhausen: Texte Band II, *pp. 107–29. The music is* Kontakte, *for electronic sounds, piano, and percussion.*

STOCKHAUSEN describes *Originale* as 'musikalisches Theater', that is, as theatre in musical terms. Critical opinion has ranged from well-intentioned perplexity (Karl Wörner) to cynically dismissive (Stuckenschmidt). The prevailing opinion at the time seems to have been that this was Stockhausen's 'happening', and it was said to be an imitation of Cage's *Theater Piece 1960* which had attracted notoriety in New York the previous year. But with hindsight it is possible to see how useful an exercise *Originale* must have been to the composer after his long struggle with *Kontakte*. At the simplest level, *Originale* is a gesture of relief, a technical and emotional release. In terms of his musical evolution it may be seen as a study in the kind of productive collaboration he was increasingly to undertake with musicians. In this sense he is returning to the roots of creativity, to inspired play: the title signifies new beginning as well as novelty.

He had, of course, composed with an assistant before: with Cardew in the composition of *Carré*. And in *Zyklus* also the boundary between 'forming' and 'performing' is deliberately blurred. *Originale*'s more radical approach seems to arise, however, from his difficulties with *Kontakte*, when he found his players unable to invent spontaneously for themselves from what they heard on tape. *Originale* is partly designed to acquaint the composer with the techniques of a related art in which such collaboration is taken for granted, namely theatre, and partly to accustom his musicians to the new style of participation.

In *Klavierstück XI* and *Zyklus* the performer's freedom to interfere with the musical structure is more or less restricted to re-arranging the order of sequence of a music constructed in sections and already defined in detail. External shape is therefore the major variable, predetermined in the case of *Zyklus*, ideally spontaneous in the case of the piano piece. In *Carré*, on the other hand, the overall structure is predetermined (though it may be cut in performance) and it is the detail which is affected by collaboration with an assistant. Although one is readily aware of the performer's role in shaping the first two pieces, the element of collaboration is very difficult to gauge in those works which end up as more or less fixed scores. Not only does selecting a particular option to be committed to tape or conventional notation tend to deprive the music of its intentionally elusive character, it can also involve, as in both *Carré* and *Kontakte*, considerable expenditure of effort and time. *Originale* may thus be seen as a preliminary essay in the instantaneous realization (not 'improvisation': the two musicians have to be capable of playing *Kontakte*, after all) of a predetermined structure of events themselves depicted only in outline. Stockhausen's approach is typically exuberant. In contrast to the fairly austere confrontation of a few players in Cage's *Theater Piece*, or Kagel's jokey and essentially literary effort *Sur Scène*, Stockhausen opts for richness of aural effect and a high degree of visual activity. This is itself one of a number of compensating safeguards appropriate to a first attempt in a new medium. The 'improvising' in most cases is simply role-playing: the actors act, the technician makes recordings, the street singer sings what he is used to singing, while the newspaper seller, a part written for a well-known local identity, simply comes in on cue to play her idiosyncratic self, just as she would in a coffee house or bar. Only a few participants are entrusted with actual invention on stage. Stockhausen's simplicity of characterization and readiness to respond to performer 'feedback' while maintaining strict overall control, all set *Originale* apart from anything modishly *laissez-faire*.

Both Cage's and Stockhausen's theatrical exercises ultimately refer, deliberately or intuitively, to well-known conventions of recorded theatre: film, television, and radio. In each work the dramatic impulse is created not so much by action or word as by the situations suggested by the presence of various types of recording media: the tape recorder, the cameras (still and film), the newspaper, and their attendant operators. All of these intrude on the privacy of participants (audience included) and exert, as instruments of memory, a powerful influence on the perceptions. As with his music, then, our understanding of the composer's intentions depends entirely on whether we are able to see his work in a media context and to respond appropriately.

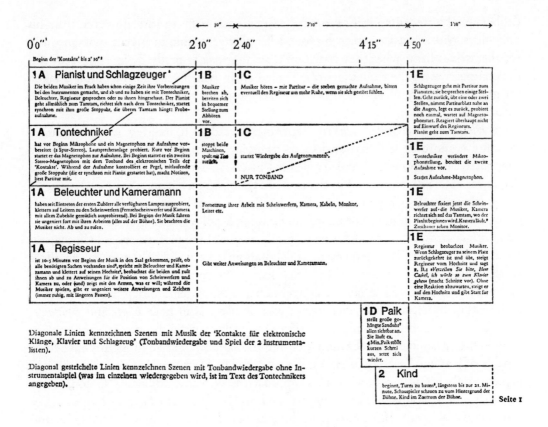

Diagonale Linien kennzeichnen Szenen mit Musik der 'Kontakte für elektronische Klänge, Klavier und Schlagzeug' (Tonbandwiedergabe und Spiel der 2 Instrumentalisten).

Diagonal gestrichelte Linien kennzeichnen Szenen mit Tonbandwiedergabe ohne Instrumentalspiel (was im einzelnen wiedergegeben wird, ist im Text des Tontechnikers angegeben).

In *Originale*'s opening scene, for instance, two musicians begin to perform *Kontakte*, they are recorded by a sound technician (translating the performance situation from continuous 'present' into 'future perfect'), and the recording session is simultaneously filmed by a director and cameraman ('future imperfect': a performance 'in action', 'in the making'). Time is telescoped; expectation and reminiscence meet around a kernel of actuality, which is the musical performance. In its turn, the music of *Kontakte* expresses the same temporal paradox in reverse, since it too juxtaposes actuality—the live performance—with an electronic music expressing a technical process completed in the past but as music equally belonging to past, present, and future.[1]

One of the characters in *Originale* is a child. In the script it plays with blocks, 'building them into towers', but it also acts as a silent observer of what the adults are up to. It is difficult not to interpret the recurrent child image in Stockhausen's work (previously encountered in *Gesang der Jünglinge*, later in 'Oben und Unten' from the *Aus den Sieben Tagen* texts) as personifying the composer himself.

[1] In later performances this interpenetration of tenses was further complicated by the addition of delayed-action replay circuits, somewhat in the manner of *Solo*.

Originale's imitation of the studio process, and its open exposure in telescoped 'real-time' of the complicated succession of activities that go into the making of a synthetic time-continuum, makes an interesting contrast with *Kontakte*'s concealed process of speculation, collaboration, and adjustment. And it underlines the composer's new attention to 'realistic' sounds and sound images, and the contrast between these and the artificial order-system. However, the combination of a strong formal prescription and openness of expectation just as strongly recalls the spirit of his earliest serial pieces.

Punkte 1952/62[1]

No. 1/2, UE 13844, 13844a (1964), 13844c (1966)

for orchestra:
3 Flutes (all doubling piccolo, 3rd also doubling flute in G), 3 oboes (1st doubling oboe d'amore, 3rd doubling cor anglais), 3 clarinets (E flat, B flat, bass), 3 bassoons (3rd doubling double bassoon); 3 horns, 3 trumpets, 2 trombones, 1 tuba; tubular bells, glockenspiel, vibraphone, marimbaphone, 2 pedal timpani (3 players); 2 harps, 2 pianos (2nd also celesta); strings 8.8.8.6.4 ('all solistic').
Duration 22 minutes.

UNTIL *Trans* was composed in 1971, *Punkte* in its 1962 revision was the only piece of Stockhausen's for a single orchestra of symphonic dimensions which did not involve electronic intervention of any kind. No revision of the original was undertaken in the ten years separating the two versions, and though the pitch material of the original is embedded in the 1962 version, the published version is effectively a new composition of the sixties.

The 1962 recomposition is primarily concerned with the linking together of predetermined tonal 'constellations' into tractable lines and textures. The revision begins with the instrumentation: a larger orchestra, especially in the brass and string sections. Stockhausen's percussion section is also bigger, but is still restricted to instruments of equal temperament. The music itself is complex, scintillating, and very densely written (and it is worth noting that the composer's subsequent revisions add more material than they take away). The original point-structure has been fleshed out into masses of

[1] For *Punkte* (1952) see page 51.

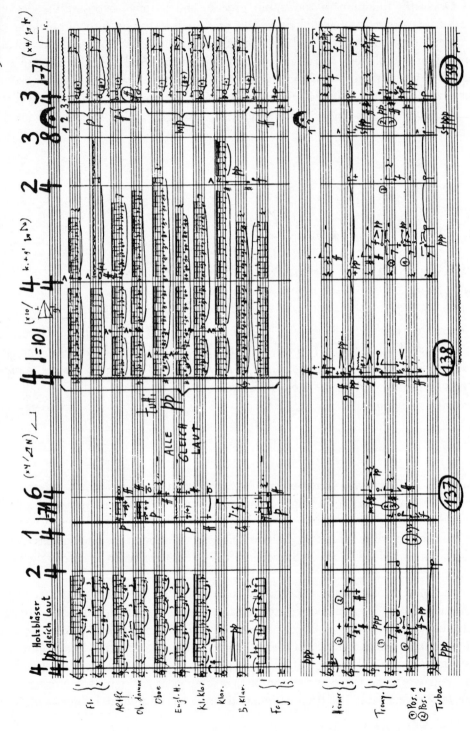

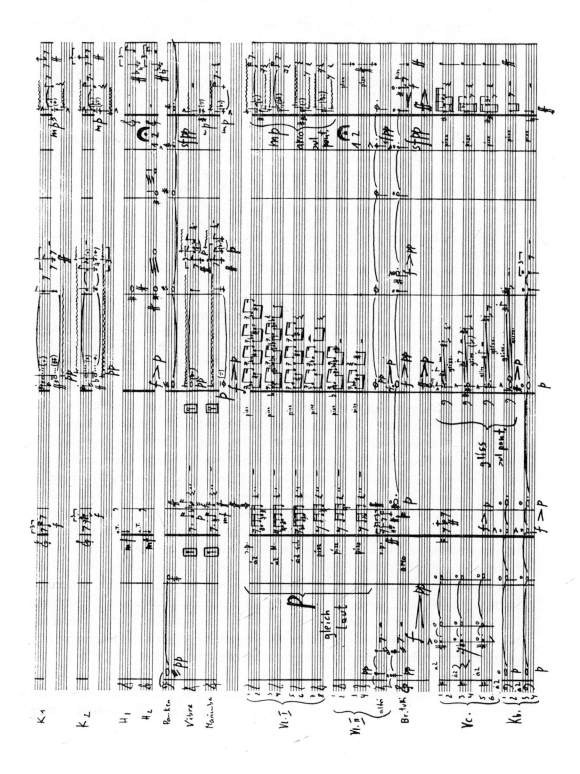

sound that, particularly in the writing for strings, produce effects of palpitating lushness, a quality of sensuality far removed from the aesceticism of the earlier version.

Though the relationships of the new shapes and textures to the underlying structure suggest ornamental accretions around a basic theme, the shapes themselves are determined by subsidiary serial orders not unlike his treatment of electronic note-complexes in *Kontakte*.

In the new version the 'points' of the title are rarely simple note-points. To distinguish the original points I used four formal types: a point expands upwards, or it expands downwards [making a triangular shape in time]; or a vertical note-aggregation narrows upward or downward to a point. Both expanding and narrowing types have characteristic textures (sostenuto, tremolo—repeating on the same note or notes—, trill; staccato, portato, legato; glissandi, chromatic melodies, etc.), also characteristic timbres, intensities, and relative speeds.

The intervallic limits and tempi within which these transformations occur remain constant for set durations and so link up to form larger structures.

During composition so many layers of sound sometimes accumulated that the mass of sound became too great for the available space. (Why must we always imagine music simply as note-structures in empty space, instead of beginning from a homogeneously filled acoustical space and *carving out music*, revealing musical figures and forms with an eraser?)

So I composed negative forms as well, to correspond with the positive forms mentioned above; holes, pauses, cavities of various shapes and sizes, sharply or vaguely defined. At a further stage of composition I changed these back and forth: shaping leftover areas in one case, or making an empty space resound in another.[1]

The compositional problem confronted in *Punkte 1962* is the same problem that faced the composer of *Kontakte*: having defined his material, he must discover ways of composing it into an audibly coherent unity. The sense of continuity perceived in *Studie II* arises from the association of basically similar, though intrinsically inert, vertical complexes. *Gesang der Jünglinge* is held together by a combination of polyphonic complexity and sheer rapidity of articulation, the latter leading to a harpsichord-like quality of animation. In *Kontakte* however, texture itself comes under serial control instead of arising spontaneously in the realization process, and it is tempting to draw a parallel between the often forced association of events in the electronic work and *Punkte 1962*'s organization of textures. For in spite of its richness and inner fluidity the 1962 version remains, like *Kontakte*, essentially an episodic construction. Recurrent dissatisfaction with this aspect of the piece is indicated by Stockhausen's further revisions of 1964 and 1966, which show the same increasing tendency away from fixed note-structures in the direction of more elusive qualities of musical relationship, that we see in his other instrumental and electronic works of the sixties.

Stockhausen's treatment of line and texture in *Punkte 1962* is reminiscent of Berg. Both his modulation of melodic weight by addition and subtraction of unison instruments, and his manipulation of two-dimensional shapes, are foreshadowed in Berg's

[1] *Texte III*, p. 12.

Berg: 'Marsch'

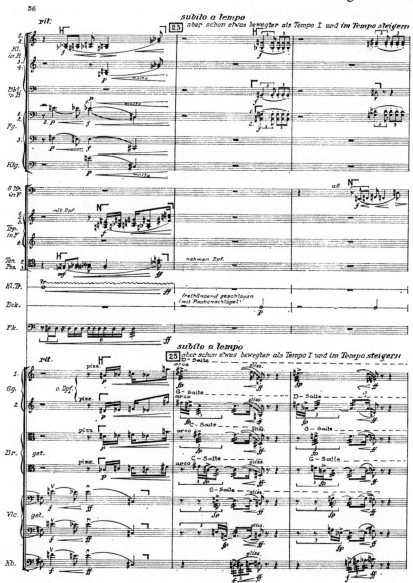

Three Orchestral Pieces, in the violins of 'Reigen', bars 17–20, and in 'Marsch', bars 25 and 36–7, respectively. A comparison of the two works suggests that *Punkte 1962* is less flexible in time control, though in Berg this very suppleness tends to distract the listener's attention from the many novelties of the earlier work.

The 1964 version makes some alterations of a minor sort for greater ease of performance, such as the transposition of the high trumpet trills at fig. 27 and trumpet and horn parts at 35 to a more comfortable level, and the reshuffling of woodwinds at 139.

To these may be added adjustments mainly of string dynamics for better balance and/or accentuation (curiously, these changes seem to occur mostly in the section from 79 to 115). Stockhausen also removes a Ligeti-like introductory page 'o' which, though related in pitch to the falling F–E cadence at the end of the piece, has little in common structurally with page 1. The most interesting changes, however, concern timing: a liberal introduction of general pauses, and the raising of the overall tempo. 'All tempi can be taken one degree higher',—that is, MM=60 at MM=63·5; 63·5 at 67·5 and so on up the tempo scale. The pauses, in many cases heightened by a simulated feedback repetition of material, seem designed by contrast to rupture the continuity, and to provide points of orientation for both performer and listener. The pauses thus function cadentially—which is interesting in that the musical shapes too are cadential in implication, and also because interruption is a device frequently used by Boulez. The same may be said of the way in which Stockhausen varies his cyclically repeated material (which we may also see as the germ of an idea for *Solo*). Though Stockhausen's building-up and peeling-off of layers of sound in successive stages of repetition of a phrase is anticipated in *Kontakte*, the combination of a long fermata with an aleatoric reshuffling of parts is a device very dear to Boulez (though he in turn has adapted it from Berg, notably the coda of Berg's *Kammerkonzert*).

1964 version

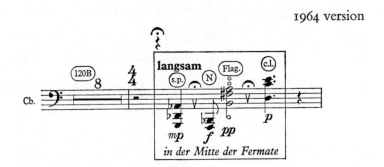

In the latest revision of 1966, however, Stockhausen has removed all but a few of the pauses, and retains only the feedback repetitions at 66 and 114. In place of the passages of feedback with alterations, he introduces into some of the remaining fermatas focal harmonic or melodic elements, e.g. the string accents at 51 and 71, the trumpet signal at 58 and woodwind interruptions at 129. Harp and piano parts are also reinforced, harp bisbigliandi in many instances being rewritten as measured tremolandi. Background sustained harmonies are added in brass and woodwind parts, restoring a certain amount of brass material previously removed in 1964, especially in the final pages from 133 to the end.

Perhaps the most remarkable innovation, however, is Stockhausen's filling-out of remaining 'points' into melodic lines, and his addition of a considerable amount of new, continuous melodic material.

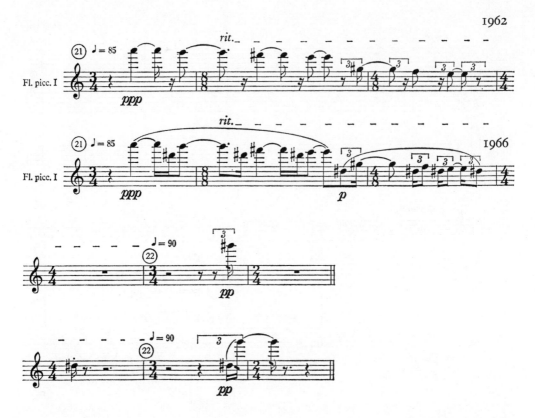

We see this in the first six pages of woodwind, and again at 20, 92, and 123; in the strings at 8, 26, 30, 35, and 48; and in piano and harps at 4, 15, 48, 54, and 58. The 1966 version reverts, in fact, to the 1962 concept of a generally uniform musical flow, assisted by the new material and improved instrumental and dynamic balance, but retaining enough of the 1964 pauses to clarify and aerate the structure, at the same time treating the pauses in a stylistically more appropriate fashion.

Thus the work has swung from post-Webern to post-Berg, from the pole of abstract purity to the opposite pole (or rather, equator) of undisguised expressionist expansiveness. To some the change may come as a disappointment—one remembers Stravinsky's complaint, 'Already they are saying "la série chez Berg est plus cachée" '—but in Stockhausen's own terms the shift of allegiance is further evidence of his growing awareness of organic form.

Momente

1961-64: No. 13, Realization score UE 13816

For soprano solo, 4 choir groups, and 13 instrumentalists.
Each of 4 choir groups 4S, 4A, 4T, 4B or 3S, 3A, 3T, 3B; 4 trumpets, 4 trombones, 2 electronic organs (e.g. 1 Hammond or Lesley organ, 1 Lowrey organ); large and small tamtams, vibraphone, 3 tomtoms, 5 suspended cymbals, 5 antique cymbals (tuned f″–c‴), kidney-shaped drum, 3 tambourines (3 players).
In addition the choir members play percussion instruments: Choir I tuned cardboard tube drums, Choir II claves scaled in pitch, Choir III plastic shot-rattles, Choir IV metal tube claves scaled in pitch.
Duration 80 minutes.

No. 12^{1}/2, 'Cologne version', UE 15151

Performance version of the above.
Duration 80 minutes.

1965: 'Donaueschingen version'

Recorded by Martina Arroyo (soprano), WDR choir; choirmaster Herbert Schernus, members of the WDR Orchestra, conducted by the composer, on Wergo 60024/Nonesuch 71157.
Duration 61 minutes.

1972: 'Europa version' (also known as the 'Bonn version')

Choir and orchestra as above, except that 3 tomtoms replaced by 1 snare drum and 2 additional kidney drums. Stage arrangement revised.
Additional music composed 1969–1972.
Duration c. 90 minutes.
Recorded by Gloria Davy, soprano, Cologne Radio Chorus (chorus master: Herbert Schernus), soloists from the chorus (Rita Fischer, soprano; André Peysang, tenor; Werner Engelhardt, baritone; Arno Reinhardt, bass); Harald Bojé, Roger Smalley (organs); members of Ensemble Musique Vivante, Paris, conducted by the composer. DGG (in preparation).

'MOMENTE' for soprano solo, four choirs, and thirteen instrumentalists, is Stockhausen's first major vocal work since the early *Chöre für Doris* of 1950, and only his second major work, after *Gesang der Jünglinge*, in which the voice and text play an overtly programmatic role. Cantata-like in scale, it is operatic in scope, treating the subject of love in a vast and demanding stream-of-consciousness soliloquy of considerable emotional and stylistic range, from coolly spiritual aria to sensual and highly-charged recitative. When Stockhausen writes for solo voice we may be sure that he has something highly personal to divulge, and the fact that he does so explicitly with voice and text is a further indication that he feels in control of his situation. This is what makes *Momente* so much more interesting to consider as a self-portrait, instead of simply another of the many large-scale works for female voice and orchestra (call it the genre Cathy Berberian) which appeared at the turn of the sixties, marking a change-over from the austere radicalism of the fifties to the more outgoing sensibility of the new decade. Evidence of a developing self-awareness is found when we compare *Momente* not with Boulez's *Pli selon Pli*, then, nor with Berio's *Epifanie*, but with the electronic *Gesang der Jünglinge* of six years before. The earlier image of boyish innocence changes to one of feminine, even feline experience, and *Gesang*'s message of faith and self-mortification yields to a celebration, albeit still biblical in spirit, of sensual delight. The composer's altered outlook may be likened to his switch of interest, noted in *Kontakte*, from abstract to natural forms, from the ideal, that is, to the real.

Momente's literary antecedents are the stream-of-consciousness novel and its dramatic analogue, the radio play. The text is meditative in character and episodic in structure. It thus differs from conventional stage drama in depending neither upon action nor upon chronological sequence for its effect. Events recollected order themselves by association, not by temporal sequence, and the pattern of association, which may vary, derives its coherence from values attributed to them in isolation, not from a general pattern they may collectively reveal. These events are the 'moments' of *Momente*. It is the same sense of the word that Eliot has in mind when in *The Dry Salvages* (lines 206–7) he speaks of

'. . . the unattended
Moment, the moment in and out of time'

Stockhausen's delicate structure of associations expresses a new set of principles of musical form, compatible with serial thought, answering a need, for a long time widely felt by composers, to break free from an alien (because illusory) causality in both electronic and instrumental music. Stockhausen recognized the need in the randomized sequence of *Klavierstück XI*, and the problem continued to harass him in *Carré* and *Kontakte*. In *Momente* he proposes a remedy, and the laws of moment-form, based on perceptual rather than numerical association, are what give the work its special didactic importance.

Though perfectly suited to his chosen literary form, the music of *Momente* poses problems of adjustment to both performer and listener. The main difficulty is identifying Stockhausen's dramatic convention. One does not readily recognize that the work is a stage version of a non-visual narrative form normally encountered on radio. Nor is it easy to grasp the inherent drama of a situation where no linking action is proposed to connect the depicted succession of emotional states. In its original concept, *Momente* is ritually symmetrical and totally static as a stage work; the solo soprano is on a raised dais in the centre, silhouetted against a huge tam-tam, with Hammond and Lowrey organs and two sets of percussion grouped at her feet, and the four choirs, each one supported by a trumpet and trombone duo, distributed in a semicircle around the platform periphery.

The tight cluster of singer and instruments in the centre of Stockhausen's early sketch, and the suggestion of empty space between the central group and outlying choirs and instruments, is significant. The work resembles a scaled-down version of *Carré*, with electronic organs substituting for strings, and the whole transferred to a single stage so as to be manageable by a single conductor. And it is also dramatically a sequel to *Carré*, if one imagines the listener-composer at the centre of the vocal and instrumental turmoil of the earlier work deciding to stand up and talk back, seize control of the flow of events and channel them towards a higher order. Much of *Momente*'s dramatic effect hinges on the suggestion of open confrontation between the composer and his public detractors.

The reaction to my music in Germany is as violently hostile as ever. Last year, for example, when I conducted my *Momente* in Cologne, the audience made so much noise I just gave up—stopped the performance. After about five minutes, I started again, and went through to the end, although they were yelling so that even *I* couldn't hear anything. At home, it is always that way.[1]

---

[1] *New Yorker* interview, 18 January 1964.

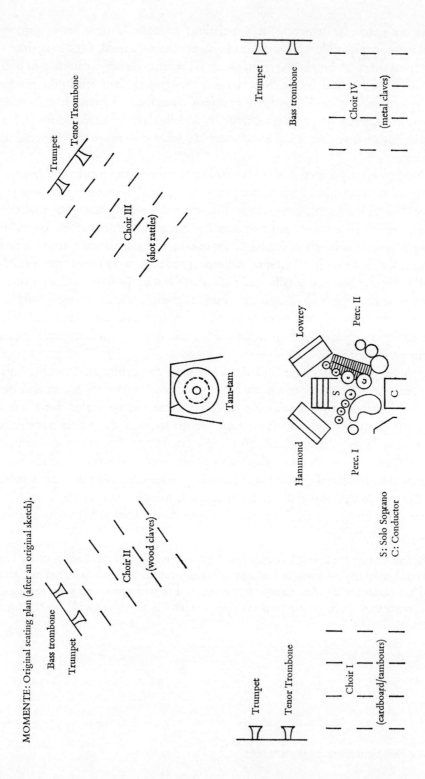

MOMENTE: Original seating plan (after an original sketch).

Trumpet
Tenor Trombone

Choir III
(shot rattles)

Trumpet
Bass trombone

Choir IV
(metal claves)

Bass trombone
Trumpet

Choir II
(wood claves)

Tam-tam

Lowrey

Perc: II

Hammond

Perc: I

S

C

S: Solo Soprano
C: Conductor

Trumpet
Tenor Trombone

Choir I
(cardboard/tambours)

The public reaction was not unexpected. Stockhausen pre-empts audience hostility by incorporating elements of disturbance into the music for choir, adding interjection, hissing, clapping, stamping, finger-snapping, and rudimentary percussion parts to their conventional repertoire of effects. In addition, audience participation is an unstated but essential element in the musical fabric.

Momente's form is Stockhausen's first to be governed systematically by affective rather than purely numerical criteria. The structure has three principal lattices, issuing respectively from the elements K, M, and D (*Klang, Melodie,* and *Dauer*²), which qualify the musical context as orientated towards timbre (homophony), melody (monody or heterophony), or duration (polyphony). K music tends to resolve, M music to evolve, D music to sustain, broadly speaking. From these categories, which refer to what we hear synthetically, not to what analysis may reveal, Stockhausen evolved a Mendelian family tree of relationships in which these types are paired in progressively subtler combinations:³

Linking the main K, M, and D structures are i-moments (amorphous or indeterminate) which neutralize these distinctions and act as bridges between the work and the public, between musical order and audience disorder. At first the structure appears open and hierarchical, but in practical terms the system closes back on itself, the subtle distinctions of the highest-level D-moments merging imperceptibly with the i-moment flux. (It is

² The same letters are also said to signify K(arlheinz), M(ary Bauermeister), and D(oris Stockhausen). *Momente* is dedicated to Mary Bauermeister.

³ The 3 × 7 basic structure of *Momente,* curiously enough, recreates the outward form of Schoenberg's *Pierrot Lunaire.* Though Stockhausen disclaims the suggestion of a conscious connection between the two works, it is strangely concidental that, like Schoenberg, he marks his creative coming-of-age (at the time, *Momente* was Stockhausen's acknowledged Op. 21) with a work for female voice and chamber ensemble in 21 parts.

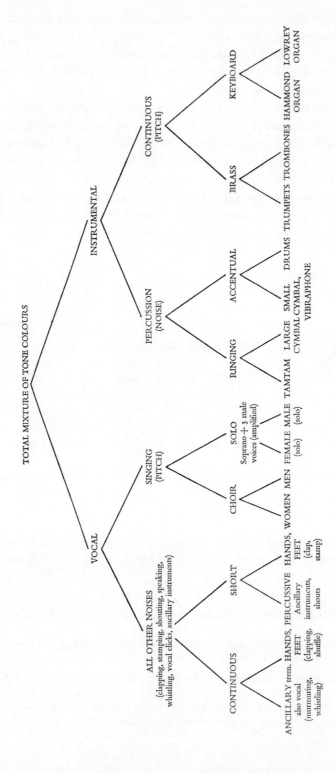

Tonal hierarchy of 'Momente' (after composer's sketch, reproduced in *Ein Schlussel fur 'Momente'*, ed. Boczowski, Kassel).

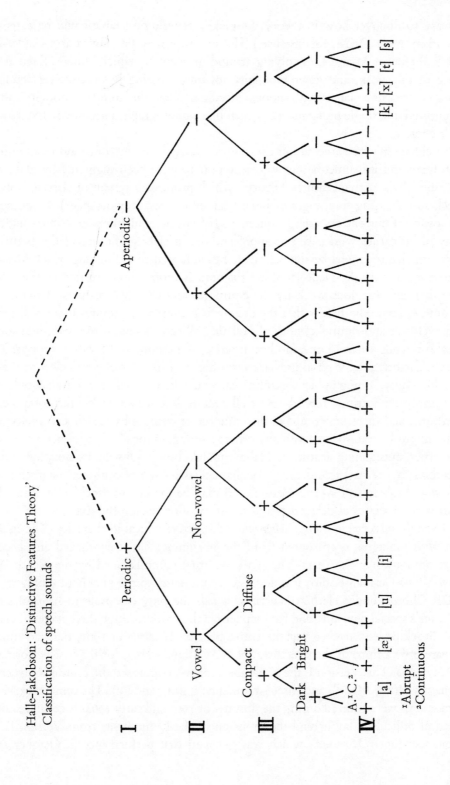

Halle-Jakobson: 'Distinctive Features Theory'
Classification of speech sounds

not easy to discover how in theory the piece's genealogical table could be extended beyond moment DKM, for instance.) The structure may be viewed as a Calder-like mobile, branches M and D revolving around moment K, which remains fixed at the centre of the work, and lesser moments not only rotating but themselves acting as minor centres, like planets with moons. Needless to say, this complex mobility cannot be captured in a single performance, which like a photograph is necessarily fixed in the order chosen.

Stockhausen's instrumentation expresses a similar hierarchy of sound relationships. Both form and instrumentation systems appear to have been suggested by Halle and Jakobson's 'Distinctive Features Theory', which proposes a system of classification for speech sounds using five stages of binary definition (see previous page). Stockhausen was aware of current research in phonetics, of course, and phonetic criteria underlie many of his earlier works. But to appreciate the special significance of this particular theory one has to emphasize the radical alteration in structural thinking which *Momente* represents; in fact, the Halle-Jakobson diagram is more closely related to the piece's form than any previous work by the composer himself. Two features of the theory are outstanding. The first is that the system is inclusive and sound-orientated, rather than exclusive and symbolic, not only relating all speech sounds to a common source but also relating them to one another in terms of a common derivation process. That process, furthermore, is serial in character, offering a new set of parameters to replace the old, faulty, typographic variables. An equivalent system for music would not only imply the intrinsic relatedness of all sounds, but would enable the composer to determine, and therefore compose, the sequence of changes by which any one type of sound might be transformed into any other: a solfeggio for *Klangfarbenmelodie*, no less. The other outstanding feature is Halle and Jakobson's plus-minus notation, which resembles to a remarkable degree Stockhausen's later use of arithmetic signs for *Prozession* and subsequent works. Here indeed may be the key to Stockhausen's involvement with processes of derivation and transformation during the sixties.

Though universal in theme, *Momente* is distinctively local in character. The association with Cologne, deep-rooted from the beginning, has strengthened and become more obvious over the years. The work was first commissioned by the North West (now West) German Radio; it is addressed, in a sense, to the people of Cologne; the WDR Chorus, under Herbert Schernus, is still the only ensemble to have mastered *Momente*'s special demands, and has shepherded the work through three stages of evolution. Stockhausen sketched out the entire plan of *Momente* in 1961, but had time to prepare only a third of the structure, about 25 minutes long, for the first performance in May 1962. This Version I, the 'Cologne version', comprised the central K-structure, moments M(m), MK(d), and three i-moments: i, i(m), and i(d). The remaining M and D moments were realized during the summer of 1963 and early 1964. A combination of practical difficulties lay behind the omission of the D moments from Version II, the 'Donaueschingen *Momente*', which was given its first performance in October 1965.

This 61-minute version was subsequently released as a record. Not until 1969, with the prospect of a further series of performances in view, did Stockhausen compose moment i(k), and corrections to the 90-minute Version III (the 'Europa version'), were still in hand in 1972 up to the première in December.

MOMENTE : Formschema der " Bonner Version 1972"

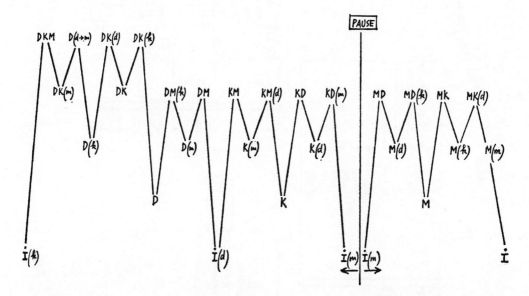

Progress has not always been easy. From the very beginning Stockhausen has had to cope with objections from his performers. At one point in the score, for instance, he had asked the choirs to take a deep audible breath, and since this could have put severe strain on the singers, it was, after representations, changed to a less hazardous gesture. There were grumbles from the choirs at the non-union work they were being asked to do, like clapping, stamping, making 'prrr' noises, and playing wood claves, metal-tube claves, tuned cardboard tambours, or tubular plastic shot-rattles. It was hard work for everybody to adjust to Stockhausen's timing and notation, both more radically new than anything they had previously encountered, including *Carré*. With patience these foreseeable problems were eventually resolved. One compositional complication, however, passed unrecognized and has not been resolved. At an early stage in the composition Stockhausen decided to intercut adjacent moments one with another in the form of inserted quotations, either anticipating the moment to come, or echoing the moment just passed. One's curiosity is aroused over the inserts for a number of reasons. In several important respects the idea of adding inserts seems to conflict with the basic principle of moment-form, that of modular transposability. The procedure for adding inserts, furthermore, is uncharacteristically makeshift in appearance and

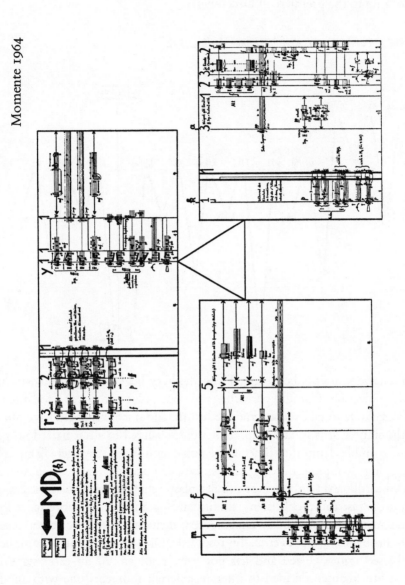

clumsy to operate. Together these two objections create an impression that Stockhausen is suddenly back-tracking on the profounder implications of his new invention. He was never one to be content with a simple juxtaposition of moments. One can imagine him weighing the temptation to connect adjacent moments against the need to preserve their structural independence, and succumbing to the feeling that by adding inserts he would in fact be tightening the structure, improving the continuity, adding variety and contrast, and thereby creating an immediacy to compensate for what spontaneity might otherwise be lost in having to immobilize the structure of events for performance.[4]

But Stockhausen succeeds at out-Mallarméing *Pli selon Pli* only at considerable cost to the work's clarity and intelligibility of design. A score which without inserts could have been re-ordered from one performance to the next by a simple reshuffling of pages, was turned with them into a major exercise in collage. Neither in *Mixtur* nor in *Mikrophonie I*, two subsequent pieces in which the order of moments may be varied, do such pagination problems arise.

More serious criticism could be made of the effect of inserts on the audible structure. The problem here is of presenting the music in such a way that inserts may be distinguished from the moments they resemble. In its present form listeners coming fresh to the work have virtually no way of knowing whether a sudden change in the music signals a transition in the principal structure, or a shift from 'actuality' to 'prediction' or 'memory'. A case could be made for detaching the inserts from the main context either by having them played by a spatially separated ensemble of reduced dimensions, or by having them played back pre-recorded over loudspeakers. One thinks for comparison of *Mikrophonie II*'s 'windows' into taped fragments of *Carré* and *Momente*, or of the distinction central to *Solo* between live sound and tape-loop 'memory' transfigurations.

Stockhausen exposed his private self to public scrutiny in *Momente* as he had never done before, and it is fair to assume that part of his motivation for so obscuring his original intentions may have been as an emotional barricade against more wounding attacks on his personal integrity. Subsequent developments reinforce this hypothesis to a certain extent. When Stockhausen returned to work on Version III of *Momente* in 1969, he was at a peak of popular esteem, having received governmental approval of his ambitious plan for West Germany's spherical music pavilion for Expo '70. It is clear from the new version's changed disposition of players on stage, as well as in his new textual and musical material, that his feelings towards the work have radically altered.

[4] Or he may have been reading Schillinger again (Vol. II, Chap. 8, 'General Theory of Directional Units'): 'The only authentic element of melodic figuration is the *auxiliary unit* [passing note]. The latter is not bound to bear any relation to Σ, or to any substructure of it . . . Chromatic passing units are always to be regarded as elements (to be inserted *a posteriori*) of chromatic variation, applicable to any type of harmonic progression.'

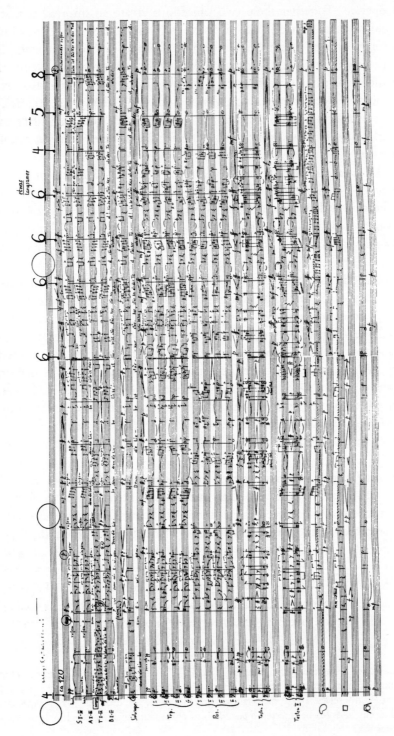

'Europa version' 1972

Page from moment i(k)

The difference is most obvious in moment i(k), written in 1969, with which Version III begins. Strictly speaking, i(k) ought to be transferable to the middle or end of the work like the other i moments, but this could only be done with i(k) by reversing the action and music, and changing the text (as Stravinsky reverses the music of welcome, 'Euntes in mundum', for the final benediction and dismissal 'Illi autem profecti' in *Canticum Sacrum*). The music is given a totally different character in i(k). It is warm, public, theatrical, 'involved'; 'Come on in!' cries the soprano solo, and over loud, sustained E naturals at extremes of the organ compass, accompanied by concerted, triple-time drumming by the two percussionists—certainly the nearest Stockhausen has come to pop music—in troops the choir, each member singing individually on a small group of notes, among them the trumpets and trombonists, also sporadically sounding fragments of a fanfare-like character. The processional is one that could have been devised by Fellini. The choirs move down the aisles and take up their positions on the stage, singing and playing all the while. Only when they are all in place does Stockhausen as conductor make a sudden and unobtrusive appearance on stage from the front row, bring the music to a climax, and follow on into the piece proper. This new introduction has action, is relaxed, engaging, and though musically a suspension, linear and continuous in implication. It is in complete contrast, therefore, to the original music, with which it makes an uneasy partnership. The texts of i(k) and the D-moments are also more continuous, intelligible, and public in tone. The choirs, whose part in the narrative was at first anonymous and incidental, are now given a more positive dramatic role. Identifiable characters emerge from the male ranks: a tenor as 'Lover', a baritone (affecting the Louis Armstrong growl also encountered in *Mikrophonie II*) as 'Questioner', and a bass in the character of a local (Cologne) barfly. These characterizations weaken the static, reflective quality of the earlier music, and draw the listener's attention away from the soprano, once the persona around whom all the events revolved, now something between a high priestess and a carnival personality. These changes are reflected in the staging. The great tamtam, which used to face the audience, presenting (as in *Kontakte*) an image of heliocentricity, is now turned on edge; the percussionists, previously shielding the soprano against the verbal assaults of the choirs, are now banished to the stage periphery. The improvement in Stockhausen's relations with the public is something we may all applaud, but it seems a pity that in adapting *Momente* to suit his more conciliatory mood he has turned the work, musically and dramatically, against itself.

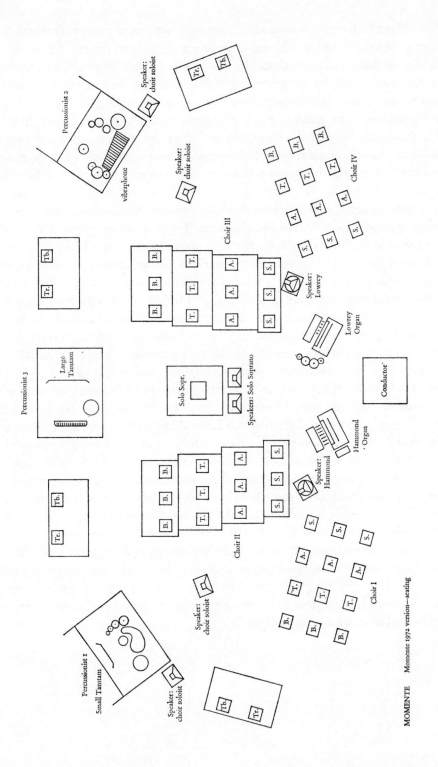

MOMENTE   Momente 1972 version—seating

Plus-Minus

1963: No. 14, UE 13993

2 × 7 pages for working out.
Instrumentation unspecified.
Duration unlimited.

'PLUS-MINUS' is a composition in which the essential processes are expressed symbolically, allowing an interpreter to decide, within limits, what musical form the piece may take. Originally devised as an exercise for the first composition class of the 'Cologne New Music Courses' in 1963, *Plus-Minus* consists of seven pages representing form-schemes, and another seven pages of musical material. For each form page one page of notes is chosen, and one alone. The forms and note reservoirs are designed to allow two or more form-schemes to run concurrently as interacting layers in a composite structure.[1] The symbol pages are not meant to be played from, but to serve as guidelines for a conventionally-notated score which must be composed and written out in advance.

Each form-scheme consists of a series of 53 frames, representing successive stages of musical development. Their order of sequence is fixed (reading left to right, top to bottom) and not to be confused with Haubenstock-Ramati's look-alike mobile pieces, in which the order of events is relatively free. Each frame or moment contains a standard structural formula built up around a principal 'central sound' ('Zentralklang') and an ancillary group of 'Nebennoten' which stand in somewhat ornamental relation to it. The central sounds define the form, while the ancillary notes define the central sound (compare the functions of small and large notes in the first half of Piano Piece VI). Black 'Akzidentien'—triangular, lozenge-shaped or round symbols, signifying respectively short, medium, and long durations—govern the shape and complexity of subsidiary formations. (A question mark in place of an 'Akzident' may be interpreted as either short, medium, or long.) There are seven typical combinations of 'Akzidentien' and 'Zentralklang'. The interpreter assigns one of seven note-groups marked with a Roman numeral on his chosen note page, to the central sound of each of the seven types. The 'Nebennoten', symbolized by a quaver stem and associated Arabic numeral, take the correspondingly numbered note-group from the second system on

---

[1] In his essay 'Musik und Graphik' (*Texte I*, p. 176), Stockhausen refers to a poem by Hans G. Helms, the 8 pages of which present 8 different 'planes' of a 3-dimensional lecture: one may read 'through' as well as across the page. A similar thought seems to have inspired *Plus-Minus*.

Symbol page (for explanation see text)

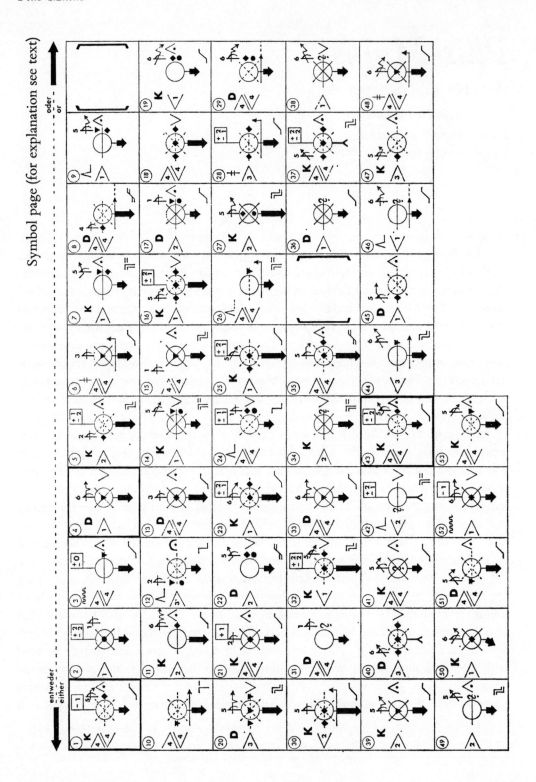

the note page. Thus, whenever the same symbolic figuration recurs, the same central sound recurs, though the note content of its ancillary figure may change. The relative tempo of an ancillary figure is indicated by a stroke through the quaver sign. 'Akzidentien and Nebennoten are to be composed as the attacks, onset transients, and decays of the Zentralklänge (according to position)' (*Instructions*, note 26).

We now come to the processes which give *Plus-Minus* its name. These involve, first of all, successive expansions or contractions of the seven basic Akzidentien-Zentralklang combinations, by repetition or removal of either Akzidentien or Zentralklang or both. Changes of this kind are indicated in square flags which appear from time to time over the circular Zentralklang symbol. A number in a flag, prefixed by a plus sign, means that each time that particular structural formula recurs, the symbol appropriate to either or both constituents is reduplicated the indicated number of times.[2] A number in a flag prefixed by a minus sign means that when the same formula comes round again *either* it will be reduced, in whole or in part, by the number of repeats indicated (assuming it is being reduced from a previously expanded state), *or*, if the formula is not large enough to contain the indicated reduction, the affected element reduces to an empty space of corresponding duration, or double, treble, etc., for minus quantities below zero. So that these negative values may be clearly heard, the interpreter introduces continuous bands of sound, one for filling negative spaces left by the central sounds, another to do the same for the Akzidentien. These negative bands, which should sound in complete contrast to the positive figurations, may be interpreted in various ways. When the value of a part reduces to 0, a negative band may play continuously, with further minus quantities, -1, -2, etc., expressed as an appropriate number of silences or 'holes' interrupting the negative band. Alternatively, a zero-value part may be interpreted as a silence of the appropriate duration, with further minus quantities represented by a negative band subject in turn to progressive modifications analogous to the positive transformations. Ancillary notes, 'Nebennoten', do not however appear in negative areas.

It follows that in the course of the piece the symbol content of each formula type will wax and wane by a sort of cell-division process affecting Akzidentien and Zentralklang independently. Each page of symbols begins with a different formula, and ends with the same formula repeated, thus enabling the interpreter to measure its transformation over an extended period. The maximum increase in either direction is 13-fold. When *both* Akzidentien and Zentralklang in a given type reach plus 13 times their original symbolic value, the formula reverts to its original condition, but is henceforth interpreted in a completely new way, having transcended its former identity, as it were, and become a new unity. A given type which declines to minus 13 in both Akzidentien and Zentralklang 'dies' and never returns; its notated recurrence is ignored and not even marked by silence or negative bands.

[2] That a symbol is repeated does not necessarily mean that the music simply repeats. Though its note content may remain the same, the order of notes may be permutated (see *Instructions*, note 16).

Sample note page

The second main transformation process, indicated by numbered crescendo or decrescendo signs, regulates transpositions in pitch, dynamic, or absolute duration, of Akzidentien and Zentralklang. It refers therefore to the musical content of a formula, not to its symbolic value. On each page of note material, both reservoirs of material have one note as a common point of reference. The other pitches are derived from this starting-point by intervallic displacement. The size and order of interval aggregations is calculated on the basis of a Fibonacci series: 1, 2, 3, 5, 8, . . ., or a multiple of the series, expressed in semitones. An interval may be open or filled (a cluster). The Zentralklang intervallic models, numbered in Roman numerals, express a constant proportional framework. The Nebennoten reservoirs, indicated by Arabic numerals, articulate these intervallic proportions in a number of ways. Some consist of various combinations of Zentralklang intervals, expressed as two-note groups, i.e. aggregate interval sizes. Others resume individual pitches of the Zentralklang structures, expanding them into intervals by a constant amount (e.g. the note sheet marked 'Akzent G flat') or serially (the page of 'clusters'). Each of the seven basic structure-types is fixed, therefore, in two dimensions: in time, by the a priori relationship of Akzidentien to Zentralklang, and in pitch by a constant reference note and subtended interval-structure. The pitch-content of a structure-type may change during the course of the piece, but since the rules governing pitch-transposition protect both the reference note and the inner proportions, its identity is effectively preserved.

Additional signs of more or less explicit nature determine the rhythmic regularity, accentuation, reverberation, and muting of an event, whether it leads into the following event or is separated from it, and by how much. Cross-hatching of the circular Zentralklang symbol defines its sound quality as hard or soft, clear or indistinct. When a number of form-scheme pages is to be realized in succession, events from one page may be inserted into a previous or succeeding page. Only those events framed in a thick black line may appear on another page, and only after they have been composed out in full. Arrows, with or without numbers, at the top of the form-scheme page indicate in which direction and how many events are to be inserted on other pages. Empty frames are found on every page for the insertion of such 'foreign' material.

In the event that several layers are to be combined simultaneously, each should be clearly differentiated from the rest both in characteristic sound and also in its forms of expressing the Zentralklänge, Akzidentien, and Nebennoten. Heavy arrows pointing downward from the Zentralklänge regulate the co-ordination between layers, and symbols at the bottom right-hand corner of each frame explain what to do should one or more pitches of the event coincide by accident with those of another layer, or how its pitch content or overall dynamic may be brought into line with another layer or layers. By and large, however, the relationship of layers in polyphonic versions is more a matter of co-ordination in time than of integration of material, certain pages showing a pronounced antecedent or consequent character (angled arrows) by comparison with the others. This reliance on synchronization as a major integrating factor distinguishes *Plus–Minus* from *Prozession* and *Kurzwellen*, in which direct imitation plays a much greater role.

Plus–Minus is something like a game, progressing by moves according to rules, and leading to the promotion or annihilation of material as these rules interact. It is a game for composers based on the intrinsic tension between form and content, fixed process and variable expression, which Stockhausen came face to face with in the composition of *Carré* and *Kontakte*, and which was still bothering him. The problem was that the series could generate a reservoir of allowable note combinations, but to all intents and purposes was static and homogeneous; to form music a completely different set of numerical criteria had to be imposed on the note material. And the two systems did not really relate. The discrepancy between the two sets of principles is characteristic of electronic music, and the aspiring composer-performer of *Plus–Minus* would do well to consider the division of functions outlined in the realization score of *Kontakte*, if he wishes to understand, let alone solve, *Plus–Minus*'s apparent contradictions.

'For many years I had worked on the idea of writing a piece having such powers of metamorphosis that I might come across it one day and hardly recognize it as my own, until a further encounter assured me of its authenticity.'[3] In 1964 Frederick Rzewski and Cornelius Cardew each prepared one page of *Plus–Minus* for a joint performance on two pianos. Both decided to use an accessory instrument for the negative-band material. Rzewski chose a cluster played on the harmonium; Cardew opted for transistor radio 'static'. Stockhausen, who had not been consulted in advance, was astonished at the result:

When I heard the tape of the Cardew–Rzewski version of *Plus–Minus* for the first time, I was, in a truly unselfish sense, fascinated by it . . . Sounds and sound combinations that, while recognizing their use by other composers, I had personally avoided (prepared piano and radio music), where now being brought by performers into my music, and in exact accordance with the functional sound requirements laid down in the score. The result is of a highly poetic quality, reached as a result of the way *Plus–Minus* is constructed: when such a result is obtained, detailed considerations of sound and material become unimportant. I now find myself listening more adventurously, *discovering* a music summoned forth from me: feeling myself an instrument in the service of a profound and intangible power, experiencable only in music, in the poetry of sounds.[4]

[3] *Texte III*, p. 40.
[4] *Texte III*, p. 43.

Mikrophonie I

1964: No. 15, Realization score UE 15138

For tamtam, 2 microphones, 2 filters, and potentiometers: 6 players.
Duration 20 minutes minimum.

No. 15¹/2, 'Brussels version', UE 15139

Performance score based on the recorded version.
Duration 29 minutes.
Recorded by Aloys Kontarsky, Alfred Alings (tamtam); Johannes G. Fritsch, Harald Bojé (tamtam, microphones); K. Stockhausen, Hugh Davies, Jaap Spek (filters and potentiometers), on CBS 32 11 0044 (New York), S 77230 (Paris), 72647 (London).

'MIKROPHONIE I', completed in 1965, is described by Stockhausen as 'a personal breakthrough'. The work uses only one source of sound, a large tamtam. From it is drawn the entire range of sounds from which the music is composed. These are more or less conventionally notated for timing and pitch, but tone quality is indicated verbally, as 'trumpeting', 'whirring', 'grating', 'scraping', and so on; defined, this is, in terms of their appearance to the ear. The manner of extracting these sound qualities from the tamtam is left to the two players who activate the instrument to decide. What makes the work so special is that each sound and gesture in the work is acoustically related; the listener may perceive the elements simultaneously on two levels: as distinctive local events, and as parts of a resonant image of the whole, the tamtam itself.

Alongside the two tamtam players, who stand one on each side of the instrument, stand microphone operators who monitor the sounds produced stethoscopically with hand-held microphones. The sounds they pick up are relayed to separate variable-bandwidth filters operated by two more players seated in the auditorium. They then pass, filtered and amplified electronically, to separate speakers located at either side of the stage. The tamtam itself, edge-on to the audience, is situated towards the centre back of the stage.

The work is composed in 'moments', thirty-three in all, played alternately by each group of three performers (tamtam-microphone-filter). The sequence of moments is determined according to a fixed scheme of relationships which determines three relationships for every connection between two structures. For example, a structure may be followed by one that is *similar* to it, and whose relationship remains *constant*, and that *supports* it; or a structure may be followed by one that is *contrary* to it and *increasingly destroys* it; or by one that is *different* and becomes *decreasingly neutral*, etc. According to these criteria, the musicians choose the order of the structures, which are themselves composed in respect to these same characteristics. Although the relationships (between structures) composed into the 'connection scheme' remain fixed for all versions (in order to guarantee a strong and directional form), the *order* of structures may vary considerably from version to version.[1]

The relationships to which Stockhausen's note refers are symbolized as follows:

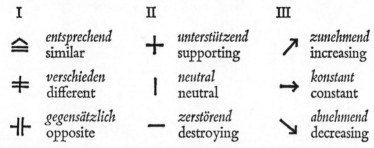

Note: Each liaison is defined by a combination of one of each of the three categories.

A quick comparison with *Momente* shows the new form-scheme to be once again stressing liaison and progression; but Stockhausen's attention to the totality of relationships shows a more specific sense of overall direction than *Zyklus* or *Momente*, and greater definition than *Plus-Minus*.

The sounds, or sound qualities, from which *Mikrophonie I* is composed, fall into the following loose categories (the materials referred to are those employed in the original performance):

(i) 'Voice' sounds, such as those produced by rubbing cardboard tubes against the surface of the tamtam; sounds in which the resonant cavity of the tube imparts a vocal quality to the tamtam reverberation;

(ii) 'Room' sounds: general resonance, as when the instrument is struck gently with a large, soft mallet;

(iii) Percussion effects: where the instrument is struck repeatedly by sticks, metal or plastic rods;

(iv) Texture effects, such as scraping, brushing, or crackling sounds, where the material used to produce the effect is more readily perceived than the musical quality of the sounds themselves; and

(vi) Filter modifications of sound, sometimes also perceived as pitch changes. Filters with a discontinuous sweep are employed, i.e. instead of a smooth transition,

[1] Sleeve note to CBS recording.

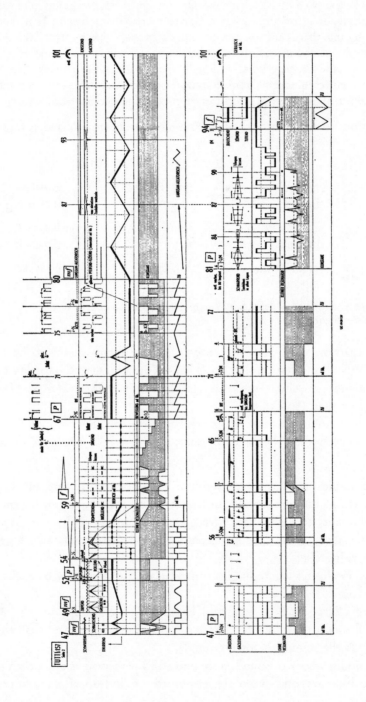

one hears

Introducing the work to his composition class in 1964, Stockhausen explained that he did not want to describe how the different types of sound were to be produced, but to distinguish them by name. He wished 'to search for the micro-structure of a wave' and he was also determined to make use of the microphone as a musical instrument. The work represented a breakthrough for him in allowing the continuous, reactive modification of sound to be composed and performed live (instead of the comparatively messy and time-wasting matter of recording and subsequent processing). He divided the musical process of *Mikrophonie I* into three stages, (1) excitation, (2) microphones, and (3) filters. Originally he thought of composing three independent structures for these three stages, but later he abandoned the idea.

The work tends, as it unfolds, to move from 'identical' sound-events to contrasts; in the centre events sound 'similar' and at the finish, 'opposite'. In one moment only, 'Tutti 157', both groups of players come together in a passage in which, Stockhausen says, '*all* moment-types are heard at once and in succession'. This idea of a central core —something like an extremely concentrated action replay—is reminiscent of moment 16′ 33,6″ in *Kontakte*, or the high-speed résumé near the end of *Mantra* (the 'Tutti' of *Mixtur* is quite another matter, however).

Two strains of ritual converge in *Mikrophonie I*. They are the French church tradition passed on by Messiaen both in the formal aspect and by imitation of his church organ technique, and the colour and sensibility of Oriental music, which the French have always found fascinating. In matters of detail some surprising coincidences appear between music of the church and *Mikrophonie I*, for instance a latent tendency in organ music for changes of register to underline the form (an influence already observed in Piano Piece XI). Frequently the sound itself resembles the swinging resonance of a great bell. The device of identifying the quality of a sound *by name* is also standard organ practice.

Of more general interest in the comparison with church music is the functional relationship obtaining in the latter between the musical signal and the resonating space: I am referring not merely to the blurring effect of church acoustics and the special resonance-conscious timing adopted by renaissance church composers, but also the spatial forms designed to take advantage of these effects. *Mikrophonie I* illustrates

[2] Problems created by the filters are recounted by Hugh Davies in 'Working with Stockhausen', *Composer* 27, London, 1968.

the environmental aspect in its absorption of individual events into the acoustic of the tamtam, and the formal aspect by the antiphonal arrangement of tamtam and speakers (significantly, the tamtam was almost hidden in darkness in early performances, producing an effect of disorientation similar to that experienced in a church where the sources of sound are frequently invisible). Perhaps the oddest correspondence of all, however, is Messiaen's claim for the *Livre d'Orgue*, that 'he was the first composer to use mixture-stops on the organ as melody stops in their own right' compared with Stockhausen's stated intention in *Mikrophonie I* 'to explore the micro-structure of a wave', for notwithstanding the difference in terminology, their musical intentions are fundamentally the same. As for Oriental influences, the tamtam itself is the most obviously exotic element, but it should also be noted that Messiaen's cellular forms, to which Stockhausen's 'moments' bear a family resemblance, owe a good deal in theory (if less in fact) to alleged principles of Indian and Japanese music.

We may also compare some of the procedures of *Mikrophonie I* with practices of *musique concrète*, bearing in mind the divergent approaches of Cologne and Paris during the fifties. In contrast to electronic music, *musique concrète* customarily worked from complex source material, laying great stress on the recording process, whereas electronic music prided itself on working from simple tones and attended more to sound redistribution. Much of the Paris research had to do with the phenomenon of resonance, in which a large duralumin plate played a major part. None of these facts is particularly extraordinary in itself, but all share the significant characteristic of being fundamental to *musique concrète* and virtually ignored in electronic music. To find all three playing substantial roles in *Mikrophonie I* is therefore to sense a perhaps nostalgic reversion to French practice. The material of Stockhausen's piece is complex, the microphone gains new status, and the sound-source employed is a large metal resonator.

Between 1964 and 1966 Stockhausen broadcast a series of programmes for the WDR under the general title, 'Do you know the music that can only be heard over a loudspeaker?' One of the pieces played in the first programme of the 1964 series was Pierre Henry's concrete study *Tam Tam IV*. Stockhausen introduced the work in these words:

We hear now the composition *Tam Tam IV* of 1950, by Pierre Henry, for many years one of Schaeffer's closest associates. I understand by the title that for this piece Henry recorded sounds of a tamtam on tape and then proceeded to work on the taped material; a tamtam is a very noise-rich and resonant metal percussion instrument, which according to the size and material of beater produces a sound of greater or lesser depth and complexity. If however one transposes such a sound very high (from a recording), as at the beginning of the following work, its entire character changes beyond recognition. It is thus clear that quite new sounds are obtainable through the transformation of natural (let us rather say, 'familiar') sounds.[3]

It is in relation to electronic music, though, that *Mikrophonie I* begins to show its

[3] *Texte III*, p. 244.

sophistication. As we have seen, electronic music up to this time had been plagued by inbred technical difficulties: lack of flow, lack of direct 'feed-back' control, lack of integration, lack of resources for the continuous modification of sound, and the impossibility of knowing precisely in advance how a given complex process may sound. *Mikrophonie I* solves these problems triumphantly. Noises are transformable into pitched sounds in a continuous process; different structures are superposable without interference or co-ordination problems; on-the-spot adjustments of all kinds are possible; more strongly differentiated textures can be obtained; transformations of pitch *without* corresponding alteration of timbre are easily effected; stronger liaisons of gesture with gesture and structure with structure are also possible, without the composer having to fall back on the echo-plate for a veneer of continuity; a much greater subtlety of gesture is possible (one is able to *practise*); and above all, there is a guaranteed family inter-relationship of all sounds in the piece. If nothing more, *Mikrophonie I* passes judgement on the classical fragmented approach to music synthesis, Stockhausen's own works included.

One may also discover a vocal influence in the work. As a *process* of sound-articulation, *Mikrophonie I* closely resembles the mechanics of speech. Taking the tamtam as representing the vocal cavity, the filters as 'lips' (modifying the aperture), a comparison may be made between the voice's continuous modulation of a characteristic resonance, injecting percussive consonants at points of transition, and *Mikrophonie I*'s process of excitation, amplification, and filtering. Stockhausen's music has frequently profited from the composer's formal training in phonetics, but such a close imitation of a natural process of articulation is highly unusual.

The peculiar genius of the work is that without any sacrifice of variety or potential for expressive manipulation, the music of *Mikrophonie I* is derived entirely out of a single complex vibrating body. Not only is the piece integrated in theory, it is also acoustically integrated in fact. For the first time a perceptual equivalent to totally-organized structure has been found, and it is particularly significant that this has been achieved by very simple means.

Mixtur

1964: No. 16, UE 14261

For 5 orchestra groups, 4 ring modulators and sine-wave generators.
Orchestra groups: Woodwind, brass, percussion, pizzicato (half the string complement and harp), arco strings.

Number of instruments unspecified. A typical formation may consist of 3 flutes, 3 oboes, 3 clarinets (3rd doubling bass clarinet), 3 bassoons (3rd doubling double bassoon), 5 horns; 3 trumpets, 3 trombones, tuba; 3 percussion players, each with 1 suspended cymbal and 1 tamtam, all with contact microphones; harp, strings 12.12.10.8.6; microphones, 4 sine-wave generators, 4 ring modulators and 7 loudspeakers.
Duration 28 minutes.

1967: No. 16^{I}/2, UE 13847

For 5 orchestra groups, 4 ring modulators and sine-wave generators.
Arrangement for small ensemble; Flute/piccolo, oboe, clarinet (doubling E flat, bass clarinet), bassoon/double bassoon, 2 horns (1 high, 1 low); trumpet, trombone; strings 4.4.4.2.2. Everything else as in version above, but no harp.
Duration c. 28 minutes.
Recorded by the Ensemble Hudba Dneska, conducted by Ladislav Kupkovič, a WDR recording, on DGG ST 643546.

'MIXTUR' is the first work in a new genre confronting live instrumental sound with its electronically refracted image. It is composed in 20 short episodes or 'moments'. Each moment has a name and is largely confined to one characteristic gesture or musical image. Much of the specially simplified notation, which varies graphically according to the expressive requirements of the moment, is designed to produce textural effects with a minimum of rehearsal and fuss. These textures are given shape and direction by electronic ring modulation. The orchestra, which is large, is divided into five groups by timbre: woodwind, brass, pizzicato strings, arco strings, and percussion. The first four groups are each linked by microphone to a scaled sine-wave generator and ring modulator. The percussion section, three sets each of a suspended large cymbal and a tamtam, is amplified via contact microphone but not ring modulated. The orchestra thus consists of a central body of metallic resonance and four satellite groups of distinctive timbre that may be transformed by degrees into something not unlike metallic resonance. The arrangement suggests a music in which one instrumental colour is transformed into another instrumental colour via an intermediate stage of neutral modulation. Stockhausen saw the possibility of producing instantaneously continuous scales of timbre which had taken him so long to synthesize in the studio for *Kontakte*.

Though the instrument and pitch composition of each moment is serially determined, its essential shape is sketched out with pictorial directness and simplicity. 'I wrote the score fairly rapidly and without interruption in July and August 1964, obeying only my intuition, since experience was lacking; I hope that the music has captured some of the freshness and gaiety of those adventurous days.'[1] Each moment incorporates a speculation about the influence of ring modulation upon instrumental sound. Some of them, 'Ruhe' ('Quiet') for instance, or 'Blech' ('Brass'), seem not to need ring modulation as a matter of form: in such cases modulation acts as an encroaching expressive coloration, like a wash on a line drawing. Others, for example 'Translation', play on modulation effects that are specifically foreseen; in these the instrumental score without modulation has little independent meaning, and modulation may be regarded as more structural than colouristic in intention.

Mixtur thus continues the trend away from static structure to the definition of continuous processes of change which we have observed in the planning and realization of *Kontakte*. But *Mixtur* is also aware of the possibilities of intermodulating instrumental sound suggested by the pioneering research in speech synthesis made by Bell Telephone laboratories in America in the fifties. Those famous examples of speech-modulated thunder, aircraft, and locomotive noise—not forgetting Jack Benny's talking violin— conjure up visions of revolutionary, automated processes of timbre synthesis which a composer of Stockhausen's training and inclinations would find hard to resist. If a voice could be made to speak with another sound, what could be more natural than a music in which, say, the rhythm of a drum could be imposed on a sustained violin note, or conversely, the onset and timbre components of violin sonority could be extracted electronically from the complex sound spectrum of a drum roll?

Though easy to conceive, it is quite another matter to put such an idea into practice. Ring modulation is not the same as a Vocoder circuit. Ring modulation generates interference between two inputs instead of subtracting one spectrum from another; instead of a 'clean' transformation, one hears a rigid, magnified chord complex, usually strong in high harmonics which give the modulated sound an iridescent sheen that obscures its resemblance to either source. On the other hand, the Vocoder process was clearly out of the question for Stockhausen's purposes. The 'voice' material to be modulated by Vocoder has to be recorded and processed in advance, and furthermore the processing involved, though satisfactory for a voice input, would degrade instrumental timbre to an unacceptable degree. Stockhausen was familiar with ring modulation; it is a simple process, and it gives immediate results. His decision to modulate instrumental sound with simple sine tones, instead of with other instruments (as he was later to do in *Mikrophonie II*), may be taken as a sensible endeavour to limit the complexity of the modulated result and thus preserve the identity of the source.

One may interpret *Mixtur*'s procedure in this sense as the analytic, negative counterpart to the positive timbre-synthesis procedure of *Studie I*. One could either build new timbres by aggregation of simple tones, he had written at the time, or extract them from dense spectra with the aid of filters. Perhaps the sine-wave generators of *Mixtur* were originally expected to act as filters of a kind (they actually behave rather like Ondes Martenot). But the suggestion of 'tuning in' on specific frequencies is also a sign of

[1] *Texte III*, 52.

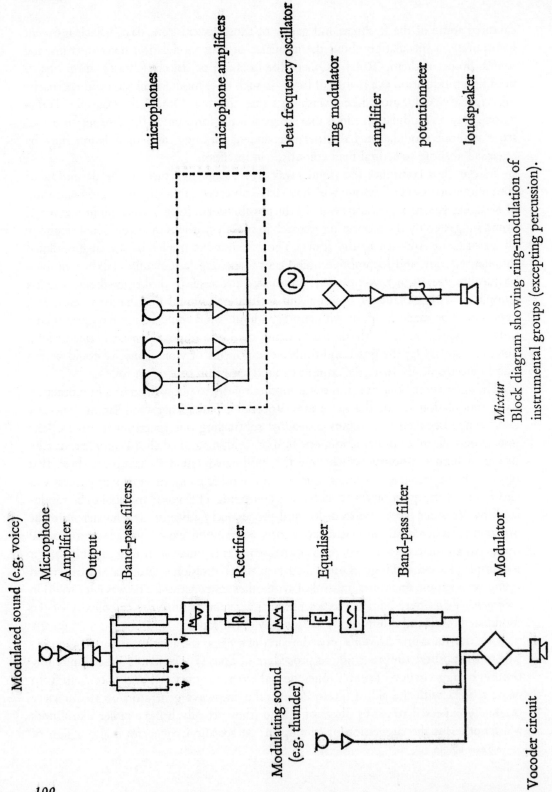

microphones

microphone amplifiers

beat frequency oscillator

ring modulator

amplifier

potentiometer

loudspeaker

Mixtur
Block diagram showing ring-modulation of instrumental groups (excepting percussion).

Modulated sound (e.g. voice)

Microphone

Amplifier

Output

Band-pass filters

Rectifier

Equaliser

Band-pass filter

Modulator

Modulating sound (e.g. thunder)

Vocoder circuit

Stockhausen's emerging preoccupation with the formal and expressive properties of radio. In its manipulation of broad surface textures *Mixtur* resembles *Punkte 52/62*. In terms of orchestral size it certainly belongs with Stockhausen's big league, although there are some omissions from *Mixtur's* orchestra to take account of the effects of ring modulation. The small percussion section (no skin, no wood, no keyboards) is unusual, its customary 'consonantal' function taken over by pizzicato strings. The role of the three suspended cymbals and three tamtams, providing a halo of *natural* resonance to which the modulated sound may be heard to refer, corresponds to the place of the tamtam in the timbre schemes of *Kontakte* and *Momente*.

Ring modulation of the four remaining groups stimulates a split-level response, first an immediate reaction to the brilliant surface effect created by the process, and secondly a critical interest in identifying the source instruments 'in depth', and in following the degrees of harmonic distortion to which the original sonorities are subjected. Modulation also restores *liaison*, linear continuity, to a position of importance from which it had lapsed in *Momente*. The oscillators function not only as colouring devices, but also as unifiers of an instrumental material that is frequently sparse and pointillistic, and which runs through a gamut of note forms from verbal and graphic to conventional, each form corresponding to a calculated degree of indeterminacy.

In his sleeve note to the recording of *Mikrophonie II* Stockhausen speaks of the need to restrict the music to extremely plain and unambiguous gestures, and the remark may be taken as a retrospective comment on the perhaps excessive riches of *Mixtur's* original scoring. The work poses many problems in performance, problems specifically of balance: of balancing the diversity and depth of 'live' instrumental sounds with the homogenizing consequences of electronic intervention; of balancing live and electronic dynamics; of relating textural detail to outline in a satisfactory manner. These difficulties seem in part conceded in Stockhausen's reduction of the score for smaller instrumental ensemble in 1967. There are a number of circumstantial reasons why Stockhausen might choose to reduce the scale of the piece. He was by 1967 more interested in working with smaller groups; he was more interested in relating *Mixtur* to the transformation processes of *Prozession* than to the large-scale, lush effects of *Punkte 52/62*; the ensemble for which the reduced version was commissioned was not very large. These extraneous considerations do not alter the fact that Stockhausen's reduction of the size of his orchestra did bring beneficial results. Because the number of instruments in each of the four modulated groups is smaller, the 'live' input may be more greatly amplified: this lessens the bland effect of numbers, allowing individual timbres to come through more strongly. By the same token, it reduces the unwanted interference caused in the modulated result by superfluous part duplication. But since the normal balance of the orchestra is completely upset, responsibility for stabilizing the relationship, both between unmodulated instrumental groups and between unmodulated and modulated sound, shifts on to the shoulders of the sound technician. *Mixtur* for reduced ensemble is an artificially-balanced, essentially studio piece.

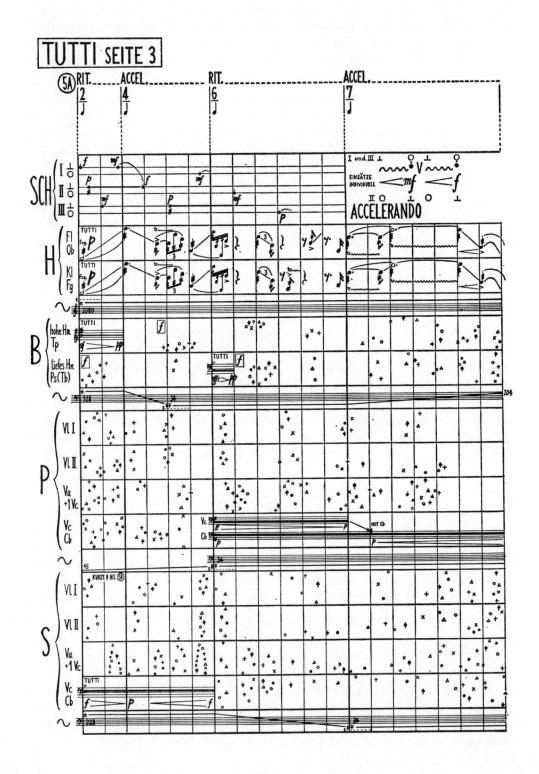

Some distension of the time scale may be observed in the new version, reflecting a change in the composer's attitude to tempo as a means of generating a sense of continuous momentum. In the fifties, ultra-fast tempi were the only conceivable way of holding pointillist music together; the ultimate is reached in *Kontakte*'s acceleration of rhythm until it becomes pitch. When material is ring modulated, however, the electronic medium itself creates a continuity strong enough to sustain attention, even through pauses of unusual length. In his original score Stockhausen recommended a basic time-unit of crotchet 50–60, but in 1971 in a letter to Boulez he advises a unit beat of crotchet 40, and adds:

Please be so kind as to check with the tape on how long I think of the ritardandi and accelerandi, and in particular the durations of the *fermate*, as being. Above all, at points like 'Translation', fig. 2, the ritardando should be so big that in the middle of the section one achieves so sparse a texture that one hears not more than one attack every two seconds. . . . In 'Tutti', the ritardandi should lead to similarly sparse passages. . . . In the moment *Ruhe* you have many opportunities for cueing the instruments freely in and out with hand signals, controlling the density yourself, and shaping the stationary sound [*sic*]. . . . You will have the greatest difficulties in the moments where the musicians have to accommodate a specified number of notes within a prescribed time-span. Generally they all play straight away at the beginning, and the rest of the time isn't filled out with sound.[2]

The conductor's role is thus changed. He is no longer expected to create and sustain momentum: this function is taken over by the electronic medium. What the conductor does have to do instead is to regulate the flow of events within a field of reference so that each change of the transformation process is clearly audible. The music passes as it were in slow-motion 'action replay', with the conductor controlling the degree of slowing down and freezing of the acoustic image. Thus too the problem of metrical coordination and control found in *Zeitmasse* and *Gruppen* gives way in *Mixtur* and subsequent works to the problem of regulating harmonic relationships.

Mixtur's spirit is exploratory, and allied to Stockhausen's electronic researches of 1952–4; the representational simplicity of his musical images is however a sign of the sixties. It marks an awakening interest in acoustic processes analogous to classical tonality, a move away from 'democratic' pointillism, in which every element has equal value, to something resembling a tonal hierarchy. It is this development which, after a long and troubled passage through the sixties, was to lead ultimately to *Mantra* and triumph.

[2] *Music and Musicians*, October 1972, p. 32.

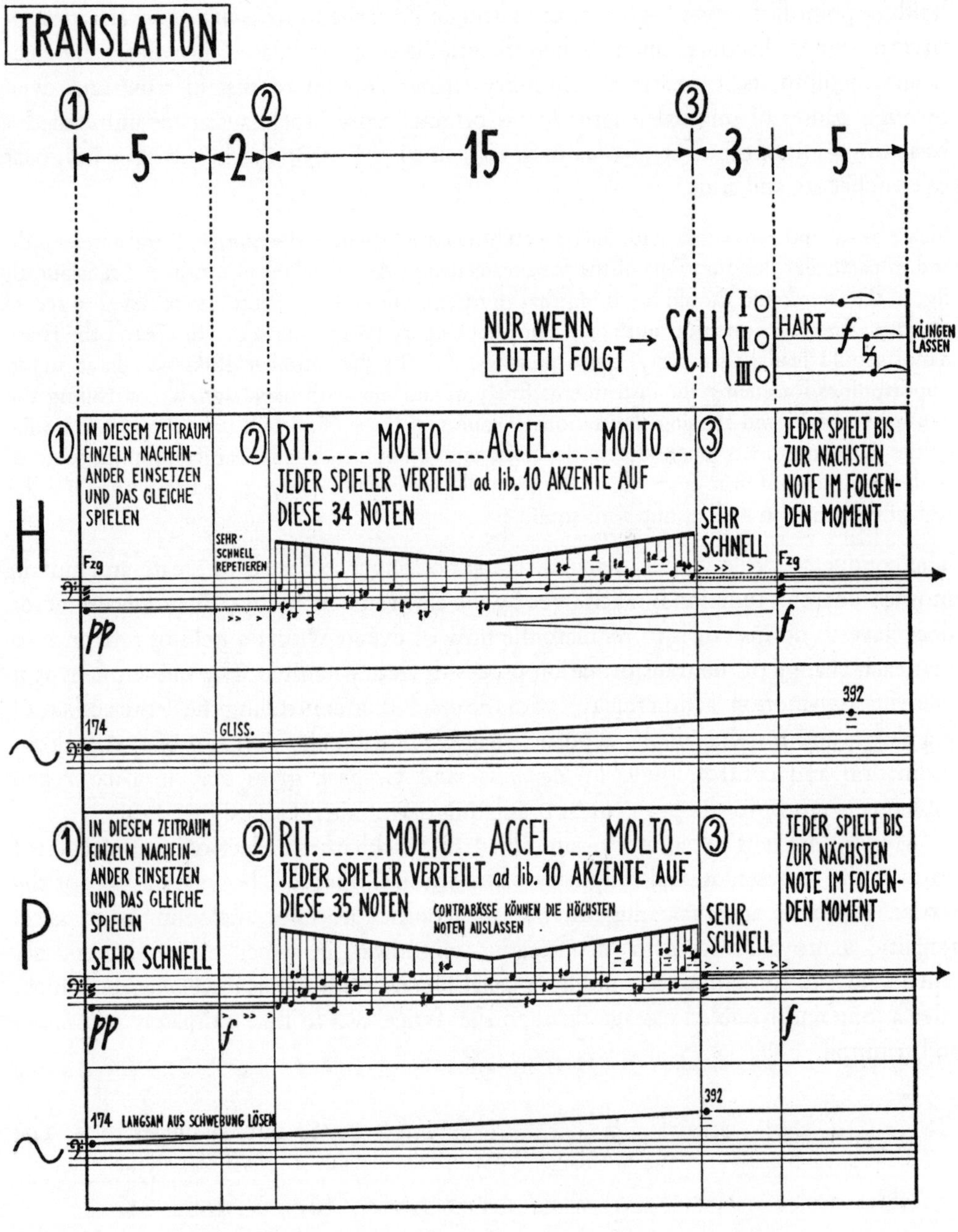
TRANSLATION
1
2
3
5
2
15
3
5
NUR WENN
TUTTI FOLGT →
SCH
I
II
III
HART
KLINGEN LASSEN
IN DIESEM ZEITRAUM EINZELN NACHEIN-ANDER EINSETZEN UND DAS GLEICHE SPIELEN
RIT. MOLTO ACCEL. MOLTO
JEDER SPIELER VERTEILT ad lib. 10 AKZENTE AUF DIESE 34 NOTEN
JEDER SPIELT BIS ZUR NÄCHSTEN NOTE IM FOLGEN-DEN MOMENT
H
Fzg
SEHR SCHNELL REPETIEREN
SEHR SCHNELL
pp
f
174
GLISS.
392
IN DIESEM ZEITRAUM EINZELN NACHEIN-ANDER EINSETZEN UND DAS GLEICHE SPIELEN
SEHR SCHNELL
RIT. MOLTO ACCEL. MOLTO
JEDER SPIELER VERTEILT ad lib. 10 AKZENTE AUF DIESE 35 NOTEN
CONTRABÄSSE KÖNNEN DIE HÖCHSTEN NOTEN AUSLASSEN
P
174 LANGSAM AUS SCHWEBUNG LÖSEN

The title of 'Translation' refers both to the movement in pitch from the low F to the G a ninth above, and (more importantly) to the change from pitch- to beat-frequency and back which accompanies the movement in pitch. This latter kind of 'translation' is heard when the signals from two sine-wave oscillators progressively diverge from the same initial frequency. One hears first a slow, then an increasingly rapid beat produced by mutual interference of the two signals. This fluctuation eventually becomes audible as a difference tone rising in the bass register. Such an interaction is suggested by differences in the notated curvature of the two sine-wave parts at fig. 1: as the P frequency rises, interference with the stable H signal produces an accelerating fluctuation of intensity becoming audible at the barline as a pitch in the region of two octaves lower than the starting F. At this point, fig. 2, both H and P generators begin an upward parallel slide leading to the G a ninth higher. P reaches its goal at fig. 3 and steadies; as H closes the gap, the difference tone—which has not significantly changed in pitch, being a function of the constant interval between H and P, not of their actual frequencies—sinks back into a pulsation which decelerates to reach nought at the moment that the two sine-wave pitches once again coincide exactly.

In the two instrumental parts the process is reversed. Initially rapid pulsations (flutter-tonguing, pizzicati tremolandi) yield first to irregularly accented, more discrete repetitions, then give way at fig. 2 to sequences of pitches which retard to a rarefied anti-climax, then reverse, accelerating gradually and always tending upward in pitch, to settle finally on the upper G. If the 'translation' of the title is to be pinned down precisely, it probably refers to the crossover points between the electronic and instrumental 'beats' which occur in the bar before fig. 2, and in reverse after fig. 3.

Mikrophonie II

1965: No. 17, UE 15140

For choir (6 sopranos, 6 basses), Hammond organ, 4 ring modulators and tape.
Duration 15 minutes.
Recorded by members of the WDR choir, Herbert Schernus, conductor; Alfons Kontarsky,
Hammond organ; Johannes G. Fritsch, timekeeper; K. Stockhausen, sound balance, on
CBS 32 11 00 44 (New York), S 77 230 (Paris), 72647 (London).

D ESPITE the name, *Mikrophonie II* is a sequel not so much to *Mikrophonie I*, the distinctive innovation of which is the *mobile* microphones, as to *Momente, Originale,*

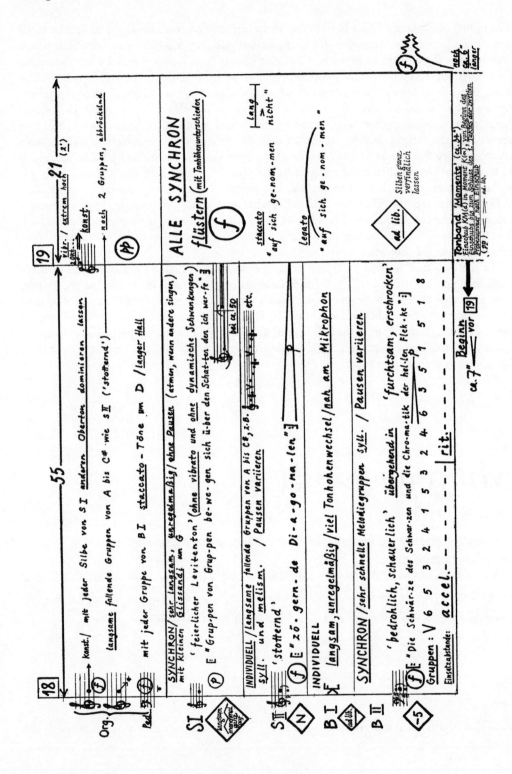

and of course, to *Mixtur*. The work is scored for twelve singers: three first and three second sopranos, three first and three second basses. The output of each of the four voice-groups is picked up by microphones and individually ring-modulated with music played on a Hammond organ; the resulting four channels of transformed sound are relayed over four loudspeakers on stage. Smaller in scale than *Mixtur*, *Mikrophonie II* is notwithstanding richer in sound potential: on both sides of the ring-modulated equation instruments of greater flexibility are employed. Instead of an orchestra operating on more or less fixed pitches, there are voices of infinite nuance; instead of *Mixtur*'s monophonic oscillators a polyphonic electric organ. The greater expressive potential on both sides combines with greater immediacy of response and more scope for self-adjustment between performers—a considerable advantage where close fusion of voices and organ is required. The work resembles *Mikrophonie I* in modulating all four groups with one and the same instrumental source: as the tamtam is acted upon by two sets of players simultaneously, so here the sound of the organ is 'agitated' by four voice-groups working independently. The organ combines the microphone and filter elements of the earlier piece in a single instrument able to vary in timbre from single pitches of almost sinusoidal purity to extremely dense complexes.

The subject-matter of *Mikrophonie II* is taken from the 'crowd scenes' of *Momente*: those episodes in which the chorus, acting the part of a sceptical German public, interrupt, cajole, and torment the solo soprano. This time there is no dialogue; the Christ-figure in this Brueghel crowd is mute. But the voices are a reflected portrait of the composer himself, and his own silence is eloquent testimony of loneliness and despair. Flashbacks to *Gesang der Jünglinge*, *Carré*, and *Momente* itself reinforce a sense of contrast between the hemmed-in, dark introspection of *Mikrophonie II*'s sound-world and the triumphant brightness of earlier times. Desolation is in the text, which uncharacteristically—as if to emphasize the unusual importance he attaches to its meaning—he has had translated into English, and which ought to be read together with the troubled programme note, 'A Self-Portrait', which he furnished for the 1965 performance of *Momente*. Alienation is a constant theme of both texts, that and despair at the powerlessness of words to move people who do not want to be moved. 'Deutschland ist wieder ein verdammtes Pflaster geworden' he writes; 'Germany has turned back into a nation of Philistines'. And in *Mikrophonie II*:

> 'Talking intersects talking and there is none none . . .
> The region in which I find myself is the region in which I find myself . . .
> The region in which I find myself is yes and no . . .
> Groupings of groupings are moving across empty surfaces . . .
> Disintegrating reflections and disintegrating midafternoons . . .'

The sentences are taken, with additions by Stockhausen himself, from *Simple Grammatical Meditations*[1] by Helmut Heisenbüttel. The image of enclosure is persistent:

---

[1] *Einfache Grammatische Meditationen*, Walter-Verlag, 1955.

'swarms of enclosures' (p. 7), 'environments and landscapes and either' (p. 6), 'to have been circumscribed' (p. 6). Dualism is another recurrent element: darkness/light, being/not being, association/disintegration, movement/fixity, arrival/departure. In his *Momente*-text he insists that these pairs should not be considered as opposing; it is not a question of either/or, but of either *and* or:

'Und und entweder und oder und und.
UND.'
('And *and* either *and* or *and* and.
AND.')[2]

Stockhausen's mood may be depressive, but it does not hamper his invention. Encouraged by the ease and speed with which his verbal indications were translated into sound in *Mikrophonie I* (e.g. 'hooting', 'rasping', etc.), he asks his singers to produce a range of voices, again vividly characterized by name rather than by method of production: 'like a typewriter', 'solemn Levite chant', 'birdlike—pigeon, parrot', 'like a Sicilian hawker, choked', 'like a confused toothless old crone, enraged'. These suggest caricatures (others refer directly to jazz), but although the resulting characterizations serve the composer's dramatic intention well enough their purpose is not merely illustrative. Each type is chosen for its special quality of timbre, rhythm, and inflection, and the musical sense in which this range of possibilities is exploited emerges for example in the composer's frequent instruction to cross over from one style of voice to another, as in the passage where basses repeat the phrase 'oder und oder oder' to begin with 'à la jazz, cool, fast—like plucked string basses', changing gradually to the style of voice of 'an affected snob'. It is interesting to note that such changes of style tend to affect the timbre of utterance rather more than the rhythm: the concentration on sonority could be a hint of *Stimmung* to come. On the dramatic plane, too, the voice-characterizations are more symbolic than actual. Stockhausen's word-setting is often extremely literal, which is another untypical feature. On page 9, for instance, the words 'hesitating diagonals' are 'stammered' in a manner suggested as follows:

On the same page, the phrase 'blacknesses of blackness and the chromatic of the bright-lit patches', chanted by basses in a manner at first 'menacing, horrifying', changing to 'timid, frightened', is dovetailed with a taped extract from *Momente*, played over a fifth loudspeaker to sound as if coming from a great distance. The effect is like seeing light at the end of a tunnel: but the light is behind. Orpheus' descent has only begun.

[2] *Texte III*, p. 32.

Stop

1965: No. 18, UE 14989

For orchestra. One orchestra is divided up by the conductor into 6 characteristic, mixed groups. The number of instruments per group should be about the same.
Duration c. 15 minutes.

1969: No. 18¹/2, 'Paris version', UE 14989

For 18 players in 6 groups:
Group I.   Oboe, piano, trombone.
Group II. Electronium,[1] trumpet, 2 cellos.
Group III. Vibraphone, bass clarinet, cello.
Group IV. Basset-horn, 2 violas, bassoon.
Group V.   Clarinet (E flat and A), violin, trombone with fourth valve.
Group VI. Flute (doubling alto flute), violin, horn.
Duration 15 minutes.
Recorded by members of the London Sinfonietta on DGG 2530 442.

LIKE *Adieu, Stop* (the title suggests 'static' as well as 'obliteration by noise') is a piece whose imagery derives from short wave. It is written for an orchestra divided into 6 sections of approximately equal weight (the composer advises equality of number, but he is clearly thinking in terms of mixed groups even though the score allows for the possibility of grouping by sonority). The music 'works' on two levels: (1) the manipulation of background noises of different textures, and (2) the emergence from background noise, either while it is stable or at points of transition, of signals or melodic fragments of varying clarity. These signals have enormous emotional power, and one senses, for example, a deep nostalgic melancholy in the muted melody just before the end of the piece:

[1] Note on the electrochord and the electronium:

'The electrochord consists of a Hungarian peasant zither with 15 strings and a VC–S synthesiser. The sound and resonance of the zither are picked up by 2 contact microphones and modulated by frequency-, amplitude-, and ring-modulation, and by filtering.'

'The electronium is a sound-generator with special combinations of filters. Its frequencies extend to the upper and lower limits of audibility. By means of a built-in keyboard one can produce fixed pitches, and with a potentiometer, glissandi. The sound is modulated by a ring-modulator and a wah-wah filter'.

(From sleeve notes to EMI box set, by Peter Eötvös)

Throughout, general dynamic indications represent overall amplitude, not degrees of emphasis. The listener must try and imagine himself listening to radio signals filtering in and out of static, and in and out of range. Like listening to short-wave radio, the ear must *search* for these events and hear them in relation to alterations in background texture ('tuning').

Although the piece is 'sequential', the effect created is one of exploration of various simultaneous and mutually exclusive layers of sound.

This is not a music that makes dramatic gestures. It is a music that expresses poetic situations through the acoustic imagery of radio communication and reception, and its emotional basis is the explorer's heightened dependence on maintaining communications links with 'the outside world'.

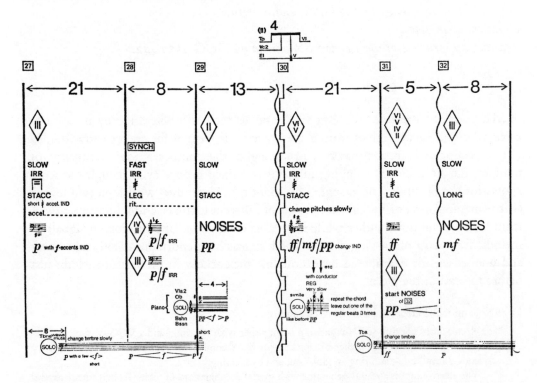

Stockhausen wrote out a version of the score in 1969 for the Parisian conductor, Diego Masson. This 'Paris version' is included with the published original score as a demonstration model.

Solo

1965-6: No. 19: UE 14789

For one melody instrument with feedback (1 player and 4 assistants).
Six versions from 6 to 10 minutes.
Recorded by Vinko Globokar, trombone, on DGG ST 137005/104 992.

'SOLO' is a piece for melody instrument and feedback (or tape-loop arrangement) allowing a single player to make polyphonic music. Written and first performed in Tokyo in early 1966, its origins reach back a number of years to the time of *Kontakte,* in particular the invention of the 'copy head', a rearrangement of erase, record, and playback heads on a tape recorder allowing the composer to build up sound complexes on a tape-loop by continuous accretion. *Solo* is his first piece to apply this tape-loop principle of cyclic repetition and transformation of material. *Zyklus* was inspired by a different sort of tape-loop; in his later plus-minus scores from *Prozession* onward Stockhausen imitates rather than reproduces the electronic process. *Solo* is thus a unique expression of the interaction of individual and mechanical influences in electronic music synthesis.

As in *Originale*, an essential ingredient of the piece is the tension one experiences in the recording studio. *Solo* is a piece of intimate theatre, the performer representing the composer, his instrument the composer's voice (i.e. a makeshift sound source, just the one which happens to be around), and his style of performance expressing the composer's excitement of investigation. It is a modest view of the performer/composer's function. The artist is no longer seen as an originator, but as an intermediary, drawing from sources around him, and transforming what he hears into something new. A miniature litany from the composer's programme note to *Momente 1965* clarifies both the message of the piece and Stockhausen's new attitude to his own position:

> 'His work and your work and my work play a TRIO, their works accompany.
> Your work and my work play a DUO, his work accompanies.
> Your work plays a SOLO, my work accompanies.
> My work plays a SOLO, your work accompanies.
> My work and I play a DUO, the second I accompanies.
> My work and I and the second I play a TRIO, the third I accompanies . . .'

'Solo' in this context sits at the centre of a vortex (call it the 'I' of a hurricane). The composer represents himself as a focus of outside influences ('their works') which he converts into expressions of himself and passes on to the listener. In a similar way the piece *Solo* provides the performer with material which he sets metaphorically spinning around him, from which he draws inspiration, and on which he builds new musical entities. One finds the image repeated in the recycling of past musical images in *Prozession*, and of radio material in *Kurzwellen*.

There are thus two sides to the piece, one represented by the performer, the other by the technical set-up. Their roles in the composition are complementary, and to some extent their respective musical processes follow similar patterns, as if to suggest a polarity between performer subjectivity and recorded objectivity. The process, or technical aspect, represents a fixed scheme of possibilities. Considered alone, it may be appreciated in the context of Stockhausen's studio work, as a commentary on the uses of feedback. The musical side of *Solo*, that is, the material put through the technical process, is by contrast highly variable. Thrown into relief by the technical process, Stockhausen's notated material and performance directions give a useful picture of the composer's concept of instrumentation and the kinds of musical expression he prefers.

Let us consider the technical setup first. A line of music is laid down by the performer on one or both tracks of a two-channel feedback circuit or tape-loop. After a predetermined lapse of time the recorded material is played back and may be re-recorded with an additional layer of music superimposed. Two factors govern the superimposition process: the number of times a given cycle repeats, and whether or not the accumulated material is re-recorded each time around. The first limitation is set by the score, the second requires the assistance of two technicians to switch the two recording microphones on or off as the score requires. With two feedback circuits it is possible to regulate the nature and density of the resulting polyphony, from the production of a continuously evolving two-part canon at the simplest level, through a hierarchy of intermediate levels (such as generating an ostinato accompaniment underneath a constantly renewing theme) to a simple pile-up of layers into a dense band of sound. Not only the shape but also the texture and character of polyphonic aggregations may be varied. A certain progressive deterioration of quality is the normal outcome of successive recopying; *Solo* also provides for the intermittent interruption of playback material by another two assistants making quick, sporadic cutbacks of the volume control on each channel. Depending on the speed of interruptions and density of the music thus punctuated, 'blocks' or 'chords' will appear to be sliced out of the recorded musical material, which is in principle fairly continuous. The shorter the segment isolated, the more its constituent 'layers' will tend to merge into a stable chord; if the transition between silence and sound is made abrupt enough an illusion of accentuation will also tend to be created.

These modifications to the tape-loop material may seem unsophisticated by comparison with those employed in the synthesis of *Kontakte*'s electronic material. The reason for this is simply that the tape cannot be stopped in *Solo* as it was in the former work, nor can the basic circuitry be altered from one moment to the next. *Kontakte* is a product of 'studio time', *Solo* an exercise in 'real time'. Nevertheless, this limited

SCHEMATIC DIAGRAM:

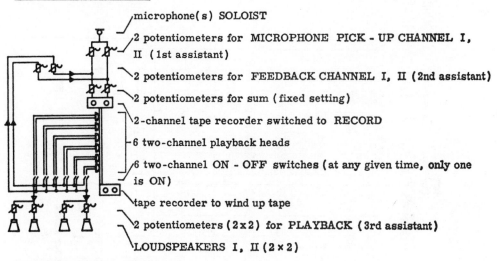

microphone(s) SOLOIST

2 potentiometers for MICROPHONE PICK - UP CHANNEL I,
II (1st assistant)

2 potentiometers for FEEDBACK CHANNEL I, II (2nd assistant)

2 potentiometers for sum (fixed setting)

2-channel tape recorder switched to RECORD

6 two-channel playback heads

6 two-channel ON - OFF switches (at any given time, **only** one
is ON)

tape recorder to wind up tape

2 potentiometers (2 x 2) for PLAYBACK (3rd assistant)

LOUDSPEAKERS I, II (2 × 2)

(Amplifiers must be added.)

The diagram shows how the sound picked up by the microphone(s) is fed back after a time delay, at the same time synchronized with new sounds, and played back over loudspeakers.

range of mechanical transformations provides the basis for the principal soloist's rules of interpretation, and it is to this aspect that we now turn.

The work has six possible form-schemes, varying in duration between 10½ minutes and 19 minutes. Each form-scheme is divided into six subsections, called 'cycles', representing successive patterns of feedback aggregation. Each cycle 'pulsates' at a given frequency, timed in seconds, and corresponding to the tape distance between record and replay heads. Six pages of music are also provided. The same six pages are used for every form scheme, with the performer choosing one page for each 'cycle'. Each stave of notes represents one layer of a cycle, so its tempo may vary with the size of the tape-loop on which it is recorded (in *Formschema II*, for instance, the frequency of cycles A, B, and C is 12, 24, and 6 seconds respectively, so that the same page of note material would be played at half the speed of A for cycle B, and double the speed of A for cycle C).

The performer is expected to select a form-scheme and feedback plan of which he and his instrument may take full advantage. Written in to the form-scheme are symbols instructing him on how to interpret the notated material for each cycle (as in *Klavierstück XI*, these instructions apply to whatever material is being played). They define the kind of vertical complex to which the soloist should steer his performance, either *polyphony*, or dense *blocks* of sound, or *chord structures*. He is also instructed to concentrate on *elements* or *parts* or complete *figures* within the notated material, or combinations of these. He may also have to vary the contrast between layers or parts of layers,

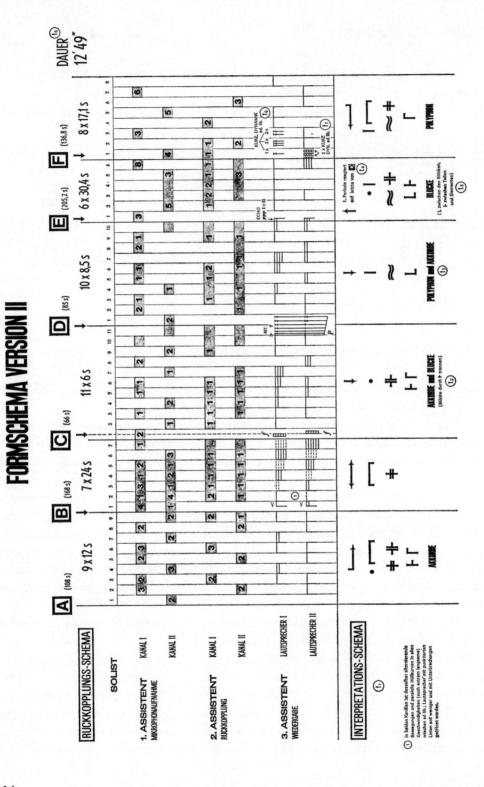

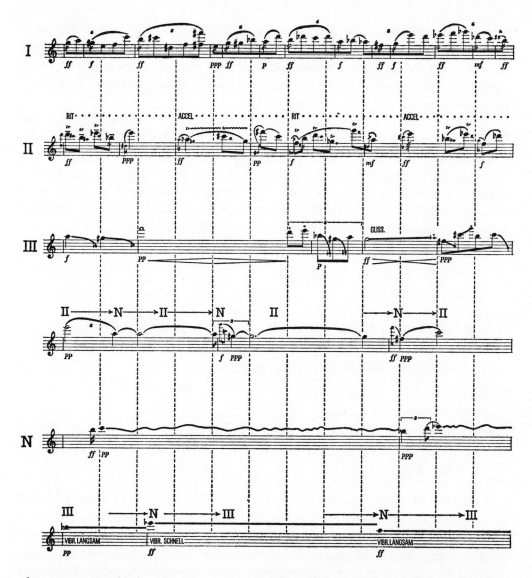

choosing material of *consistent*, *varied* or highly *contrasted* characteristics. Finally, he is expected to be able to dovetail what he is playing with material from a previous or following cycle—remembering or anticipating himself, that is, as the score may require.

What the technical process does automatically to the sound material provided, the performer imitates actively, and during the course of *Solo* a battle of wits can easily arise between the two processes, and the merits of each may be compared and evaluated. Two further instructions should not be overlooked. The performer has first to produce three alternative timbres distinct from the normal tone colour of his instrument, and secondly three degrees of 'noisiness' (somewhat noisy, noisy, and very noisy) as well as the normal tone colour. The range of timbres, presumably clean-sounding, may be imagined as corresponding to degrees of filtering of the basic tone colour. Degrees of noise, on the other hand, imitate stages in transformation of the recorded instrumental identity, or in the progressive obliteration (as in *Stop*) of audible signals. Noises, being acoustically rich, also emerge as potentially distinctive attacks—plosives or fricatives— in sequences where frequent sudden interruptions occur.

Solo is a difficult piece, not least because there is so much the performer has to know in advance about feedback and its expressive possibilities. One work which might be said to have anticipated its cyclic structure is Stravinsky's *Rite of Spring*, a work in which forward momentum is consistently generated by a systematic build-up of ostinato figurations in layers. But *Solo*'s most remarkable feature in the long run is that it revives ostinato and periodicity principles in the work of a composer who once believed, with his Darmstadt colleagues, in the total rejection of formal repetition.

Telemusik

1966: No. 20, Realization score UE 14807

Electronic music.
Duration 17 minutes 30 seconds.
NHK Tokyo realization recorded on DGG ST 643546.

'TELEMUSIK' is a purely electronic piece: small, polished, beautifully precise, standing in jewel-like contrast to the generally sombre background of the mid-sixties. It was realized in the electronic music studio of NHK Tokyo during the first quarter of 1966, a remarkably short space of time. Stockhausen was able to save time by using a special 6-track tape recorder allowing material to be laid down, edited and mixed on different tracks of the same section of tape. This efficient procedure to some extent dictated *Telemusik*'s structure. The piece is composed as a succession of 32 short sections varying in duration from 13 to 144 seconds. Each was designed to be realized during one working day. Ease and speed of production probably account also for *Telemusik*'s unusually lively character.

The Tokyo studio's 6-track tape recorder allows up to 5 tracks to be laid down independently and then re-copied on to the sixth remaining track.[1] A linear amplitude-

---

[1] Each time material is transferred from one track to another it is delayed by ca. 0·3 seconds, representing the distance between recording and playback heads. This 'time delay' ('Zeitverzögerung') crops up in later works, e.g. *Hymnen, Tunnel-Spiral*, as an expressive device.

modulator imposes the amplitude envelope of a signal A upon a second input B; the resulting output is a mix of signal A direct and the AB modulate. Conventional ring-modulators and a tape recorder of continuously-variable transmission speed contribute further to *Telemusik*'s special vocabulary of effects.

The work is a study on two major levels: an examination of attack and resonance relationships, resuming the percussion-orientated researches of *Studie II*, and a further investigation of the possibilities of ring modulation. *Telemusik* develops and refines the procedures employed in *Mixtur* and *Mikrophonie II* for generating new timbres and incorporating 'pre-formed' elements of speech and music into a serially organized form. The wider implications of combining abstract and concrete elements, namely the prospect of an all-embracing 'world music', seem to have given the composer particular satisfaction, and it is as a model of the new cosmopolitanism, rather than as an essay in sonority, that 'Tele-music' is presented to the public. It is worth remembering, however, that the 'ready-made' material that animates so much of *Telemusik* was not chosen simply for ornament. Each source illustrates an acoustic process describable in purely abstract terms, which suggests that Stockhausen's selection was originally motivated as much by scientific curiosity as by the search for an international style. Wailing temple chanting in section 22, for instance, is typically treated as vocal imitation of bell-like resonance. Again in section 9, the entry of a fragment of Hungarian folk music is geared to intermesh with an accelerating beat-interference pattern produced by the slow divergence of two ring-modulated sine-wave frequencies,[2] itself an electronic echo of the gagaku drum 'Mokugyo' (see overleaf).

The listener is able to follow the train of Stockhausen's thought with unusual clarity in *Telemusik*, for with one minor exception—track I of sections 24–5, which a footnote informs us was realized 'after section 26 was completed'—the recorded sequence follows the order of composition. The work is simply outlined: the durations of its 32 sections, like *Adieu*, are based on a Fibonacci series. Each section is introduced by the recorded sound of a Japanese ceremonial drum or gong: dry-sounding *Bokusho* or *Taku* beats for shorter sections, ringing *Rin* or *Keisu* strokes for longer, with the characteristic accelerating beat-pattern of the *Mokugyo* injecting from time to time an element of dynamic relief. Each initial stroke signals the passage of time and a change to a new process of intermodulation or style of resonance. The work may be regarded, in fact, as a series of miniature studies, united by common basic materials, recurrent similarities of procedure, and outward regularities of design.

Right at the start the written score reveals a marked debt to *Studie II*. One observes the same essentially rectangular formations, the same opposition of short and long events, and of attacks and resonances, and too the idea that attacks are simply interrupted resonances. Stockhausen's concern with the fabrication of cymbal-like electronic radiances is another feature reminiscent of *Studie II*; the score's rounded-off shapes

---

[2] Cf. *Mixtur*: 'Translation'.

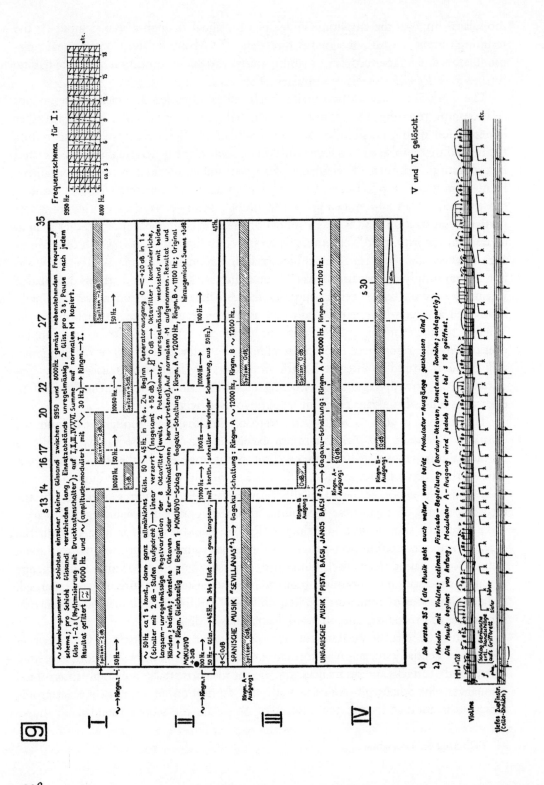

and lines, and more sophisticated technique of synthesizing harmonic chromata, showing the composer's greater interest in formal continuity and his deeper understanding of electro-acoustic processes. One is impressed from the outset as well by *Telemusik*'s cleanness of sound, its lack of unwanted interference.

On the surface, Stockhausen's use of either very high or very low sine-wave frequencies for intermodulation seems calculated to avoid generating the level of interference encountered in *Mixtur* and *Mikrophonie II*; but at a deeper level his attention to the upper and lower fringes of audibility suggests a further interest in exploring the two fundamental frequency areas of human consciousness: the hiss of the nervous system and the thump of the heart. *Telemusik*'s peculiar stratification of low-frequency beats, middle-frequency speech-patterns and high-frequency intermodulation anticipates *Hymnen*'s adventures in memory and perceptual assimilation, and gives effective expression to the composer's frequently-drawn parallel between 'stream-of-consciousness' mental processes and radio reception.

Though the score contains a substantial amount of pre-formed material, including music from the Japanese Imperial Court, from Bali, from the Amazonian Shipibos and the South Sahara, only rarely is the listener able to isolate this source material from the electronic context. A similar reticence in acknowledging 'borrowed' material may be observed in *Mixtur*, and persists in the composer's original ban in *Kurzwellen* on the use of totally unmodulated short-wave music as material. Stockhausen has relaxed this condition since, of course (and the success of *Telemusik* was undoubtedly instrumental in persuading him), so much so that *Hymnen* and *Kurzwellen mit Beethoven* rely on the listener's spontaneous recognition of such sources. Nevertheless, the fact that so much of *Telemusik*'s borrowed material is obscured makes it difficult to see the work as an overt message of cultural integration. Stockhausen probably conceived *Telemusik* more in terms of the private heart-searching of *Stop* than the heroic utterances of *Hymnen*.

'*Telemusik* is *not* a mere collage', he insists in a sleeve note to the DGG recording. To label *Telemusik* a collage is to interpret the work's claimed universality as no more than the superficial juxtaposition of music from different cultures, whereas Stockhausen's music demonstrates structural and functional affinities between widely separated forms of musical expression and certain fundamental acoustic processes. In *Telemusik* he seems to have stumbled unexpectedly upon one or two rules of musical linguistics, suddenly recognizing, in music remote from his own age and culture, intuitive models of musical processes which he had previously considered exclusively his own. Not until 1962, in his account of public reaction to the first performance of *Momente*, do his writings reveal him admitting even the possibility of spontaneous resemblances between his own music and that of other lands. So the reader may well imagine his excitement being aroused at finding a percussion instrument, the *Mokugyo*, acting the same role in ancient Gagaku music as the woodblock in his own *Kreuzspiel*. He, who had always endeavoured to rid his music of external influences, was now finding it to

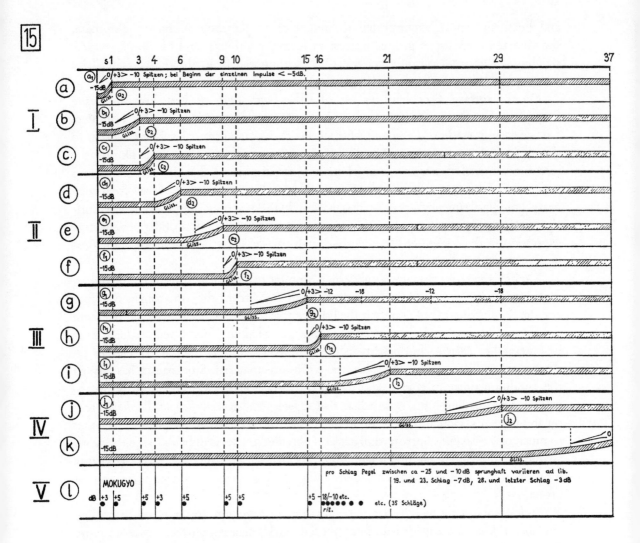

have mysterious affinities with music from the most unexpected quarters, music with which he had never before been acquainted.[3]

Telemusik resembles *Mixtur* in many ways, for instance in passages of attenuation and compression of statistical point-complexes, or the similar role assigned to percussion. The impulse-like character of much of *Telemusik*'s percussive material also bears a strong family resemblance to *Kontakte*—especially that work's famous transformation of pitch to rhythm at 17′ 0.5″ followed by the long study in reverberation at 17′ 38.5″. Parts of *Telemusik* are temperamentally very close to *Adieu*: at least, *Adieu*

[3] Detectable influences are manifest in his earlier works, of course, but the composer until the time of *Telemusik* had shown little inclination to accept them as significant. By 1966, however, he is eager to discover parallels between his own and other music (especially traditional music of oral cultures) as proof that his personal intuitions are in tune with universal forms of musical expression.

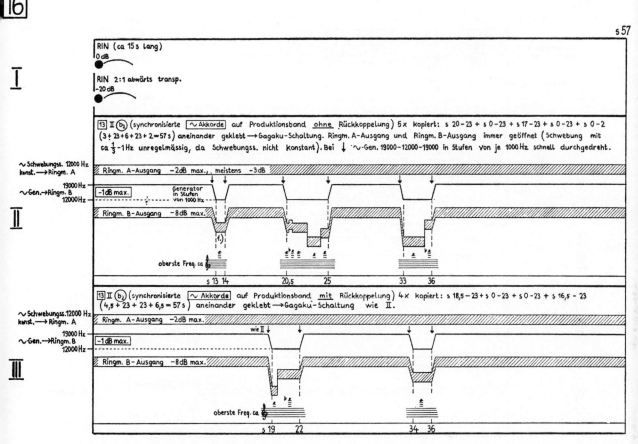

RIN (ca 15 s lang)
0 dB

RIN 2:1 abwärts transp.
-20 dB

I

13 II (b₂) (synchronisierte ⌐∿Akkorde¬ auf Produktionsband ohne Rückkoppelung) 5× kopiert: s 20-23 + s 0-23 + s 17-23 + s 0-23 + s 0-2 (3 + 23 + 6 + 23 + 2 = 57 s) aneinander geklebt →Gagaku-Schaltung. Ringm. A-Ausgang und Ringm. B-Ausgang immer geöffnet (Schwebung mit ca 1/3 -1 Hz unregelmässig, da Schwebungss. nicht konstant). Bei ↓ ∿-Gen. 19000-12000-19000 in Stufen von je 1000 Hz schnell durchgedreht.

∿ Schwebungss. 12000 Hz
konst. → Ringm. A

∿-Gen. → Ringm. B   19000 Hz ... 12000 Hz

Ringm. A-Ausgang -2dB max., meistens -3dB

-1dB max.   Generator in Stufen von 1000 Hz

Ringm. B-Ausgang -8dB max.

1.)

oberste Freq. ca

s 13 14   20,5   25   33   36

II

13 II (b₂) (synchronisierte ⌐∿Akkorde¬ auf Produktionsband mit Rückkoppelung) 4× kopiert: s 18,5 - 23 + s 0 - 23 + s 0 - 23 + s 16,5 - 23 (4,5 + 23 + 23 + 6,5 = 57 s) aneinander geklebt → Gagaku-Schaltung wie II.

∿ Schwebungss.12000 Hz
konst. → Ringm. A

∿-Gen. → Ringm. B   19000 Hz ... 12000 Hz

Ringm. A-Ausgang -2dB max.

wie II ↓

-1dB max.

Ringm. B-Ausgang -8dB max.

oberste Freq. ca

s 19   22   34 36

III

1.) an dieser und den entsprechenden Stellen in II und III sind die ∿ Akkorde mit ihren originalen Frequenzen (und mit langsam variierender Schwebung) zu hören.

IV, V, VI gelöscht.

expands on a curiously tangible sadness associated with some of *Telemusik*'s electronically ululating resonances. This strong human element is new; section 11, a study in low-frequency beats, hypnotically evokes the unstable oscillations of a heart under stress. In quite another way, recording from a tape pulled by hand past the recording head (explained in a footnote to section 12 of the score), Stockhausen contributes a powerful sense of sustained hesitancy to collections of events which might otherwise —as in comparable passages in *Mixtur*—be interpreted by the listener as simply dislocated.

Sections 15, 16 and 17 form an interesting structural episode. In section 15 twelve 'layers', superimposing material taken from sections 1, 4, 5, 6, 7, 9, and 14, soar upward one by one to merge into a hissing chroma of sound at the limit of audibility. This

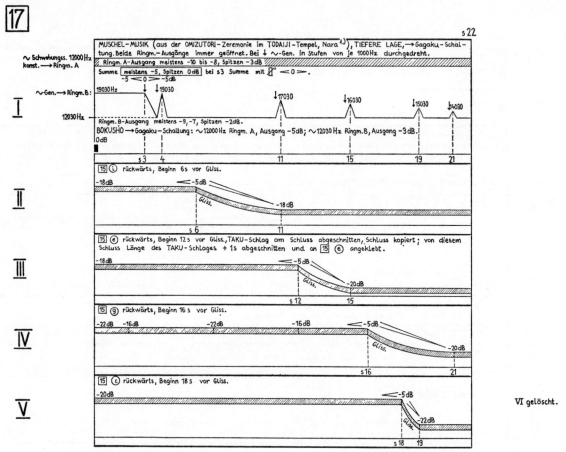

1.) *Innerhalb dieser Zeremonie blasen 5-6 Priester auf verschieden grossen Muscheln, die mit Mundstücken versehen sind. Charakteristisch sind sehr unregelmässige Glissandi, Mischungen von Tönen und lauten Blasgeräuschen (oft sprechen Muscheln kaum oder garnicht an, und man hört „zerbrechende" Töne oder nur das fauchende Geräusch); immer sind kontinuierliche und mit verschiedenen Tempi periodisch wiederholte Töne polyphon gemischt, höhere und tiefere alternieren manchmal paarweise in 2-tönigen Gruppen ⌐⌐ ⌐⌐ etc. Es gibt 2 charakteristische längere Teile, einen in TIEFERER und einen in HÖHERER LAGE, von denen jeder mehrere Minuten dauert.*

'resonance of consciousness' is sustained, with minute interior adjustments, through into section 16, an extraordinary twilight sequence in which tiny arpeggiate figures descend like flames of Pentecostal or St. Elmo's fire, then retreat again over the top of awareness. The sense of the passage is coda-like, comparable with those poignant, distant melodic fragments in *Gesang der Jünglinge* and *Kontakte*; what makes the new gesture so moving is the fact that here the impression the music gives corresponds exactly to the technical process. The sounds do actually condense out of the background resonance instead of being 'made up', reverberated and inserted at the appropriate moment. In section 17, the same material as in section 15 reappears transformed and reversed in time. The original music returns to earth, giving the three-section sequence the shape of a great arch, perhaps a prototype of the radiophonic span which supports the orchestral 'Russian Bridge' of *Third Region of Hymnen with Orchestra*.

But this sequence, though coda-like in mood, comes too soon to be a real coda. Sure enough at section 29 a regular 'instrumental' recapitulation and coda brings *Bokusho*, *Mogukyo*, *Rin*, and *Keisu* together to beat a series of measured, cadential responses. A long (144 seconds) meditation on the sound of temple bells follows, and the piece ends with a sudden rush of upward glissandi like a flock of birds taking off (cf. *Kontakte*) and the 'Yo-ho' cry, in this context distinctly triumphant, of a Noh percussionist.

Adieu

1966: No. 21, UE 14877

For wind quintet: Flute, oboe, clarinet, horn, bassoon.
Duration 11–15 minutes.
Recorded by members of the London Sinfonietta: Sebastian Bell (flute), Janet Craxton (oboe), Anthony Pay (clarinet), John Butterworth (horn), William Waterhouse (bassoon), on DGG 2530 443.

> 'I chose a number of aspects of a cadence.
> Then I made something that began to flow'.[1]

'ADIEU' was written to the memory of a young musician killed in a motor accident. Written for wind quintet—flute, oboe, clarinet, horn and bassoon—it draws on the speaking and breathing associations of these instruments. Its form is based on musical images of interrupted movement: incomplete cadences, simulated breaks in transmission, and so on, as expressing the idea of bereavement. These images relate directly to the composer's vocabulary of time images in *Originale*, and similarly derive from the ambiguous nature of recorded events, which may be 'past' or 'present', 'live' or 'dead'. *Adieu* imitates 'live' the studio manipulation of a 'dead' tape recording. The sound abruptly cuts out, is distorted, played back in slow motion, subjected to feedback.

The image of interruption is close to the surface in *Carré* and returns in *Stop*. Stockhausen's other sources of inspiration are images of various kinds of natural and

[1] Ritzel: *Musik für ein Haus*, Darmstädter Beiträge XII, 1970, p. 37.

artificial reverberation, as also found for example in the long E (at 17′ 38.5″) of *Kontakte*, in *Mikrophonie I, Telemusik,* and subsequently in *Stimmung*. One often has the impression in *Adieu* that a tape recorder has jammed; the musical continuity seems suddenly to freeze, abruptly altering the listener's perception of time. These sudden transitions, which Stockhausen compares to the right-angle intersections of Mondrian's paintings, may also have been intended to convey a sense of the suddenness of the young man's death. (A certain fatalism may be read into the fact that the interrupted fragments of music are themselves tonal cadences.)

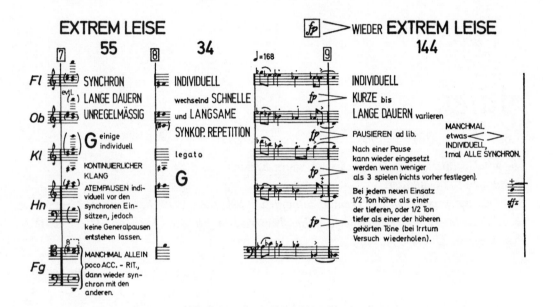

Adieu's long, drawn-out chords have been described as images of weeping. Such a degree of literalism would be unusual, but is not unknown (see *Mikrophonie II*, for instance). The work gains from being played in a spirit of sadness, but compositionally it does not reflect the emotion, playing instead on the distinction between classical performance time, based on a constant physical pulsation, and studio or electronic time, which is motionless.

Compared with *Mikrophonie II*'s mechanical ring modulation of material, in particular its use of 'expressive distortion', *Adieu*'s imagery is gentler, more restrained, and its distortions subtler. The five players are sometimes co-ordinated, but more often treated as separate 'tracks'. It would take vast equipment resources to give as great a range of feedback effects, and as clean a sound, as the five instruments can give.[2]

[2] The artificiality of Stockhausen's musical imagery is shown in his performance instructions. The predominant dynamic is *ppp* with or without individual microphone pickup; this in turn suggests a 'dead' studio acoustic, without echo or aural perspective.

Adieu is constructed very simply on a Fibonacci series of durations, falling into four principal sections 144 units in length each, separated by tonal part-cadences. The first section divides in two, the second into six, the third is unbroken and the fourth split into twenty-two measured subdivisions. Fermatas of unspecified duration regroup the smaller divisions into larger structural units:

$$144 \qquad 144 \qquad 144 \qquad\qquad 144$$

$$89:55 \qquad 55:55:34 \qquad 144 \qquad 34:13:8:34:21:34$$
$$4 \qquad\qquad\qquad\qquad\qquad\quad 8 \quad 4 \quad 4 \quad 4$$

Each division, represented by a barline, marks a change affecting the whole ensemble; thus the more frequent the changes the more uniformly articulate the quintet's music, whether or not they synchronize within the divisions.

In this way *Adieu* oscillates between large units of rhythmically unstructured polyphony, requiring intense, in-depth listening by players and audience, and generating the pathetic sensibility associated with classical slow movement, and passages whose uniform rapidity of change project an aggressive, physical energy. Closing the gap between these two extremes is the tonal material, which is both the summit of rhythmic cohesion and the imaginary continuous background from which the main action is derived.

Stockhausen's fermatas also fit into the notion of incompleteness expressed in a positive sense by the interrupted cadences. Each 'General Pause' occupies the place of the last element of a suggested symmetrical formation. At fig. 6 the structure of subdivisions is 8–13–21–13–[8]; at fig. 17 2–3–5(3–3)–(5–5)–(8–[8]); the 'sehr lang' after fig. 25 links with the following formation as [13]–8–5–8–13; while the fermata at fig. 29, together with the four pauses of varying length at the work's final cadence may be interpreted as a descending series of silence durations (8–5–3–2–1) cut into the last unit of a rising series of music durations (5–8–13–21–34).

The music looks simple enough on paper, but I found out in 1969, rehearsing it for the first time myself in Paris, how difficult the work actually is. The dynamic balance between the instruments, free glissandi around a pitch, synchronized groups and fairly frequent fast changes of playing technique, require an ensemble in complete understanding and agreement. On top of that, the musicians have to be able to experience deeply and form into notes, the sense of closeness to death that vibrates in this music.[3]

Some may hear a similarity between the repeated piccolo high B in the final section of *Adieu* and Bartók's melancholy piping around the same note, also for piccolo, in the third movement of his Concerto for Orchestra. In the context of his own work Stockhausen's more open use of 'tonal' material marks a further cautious stage in his development towards *Hymnen*, while his emphasis on subtle variations of intonation as an

[3] *Texte III*, p. 93.

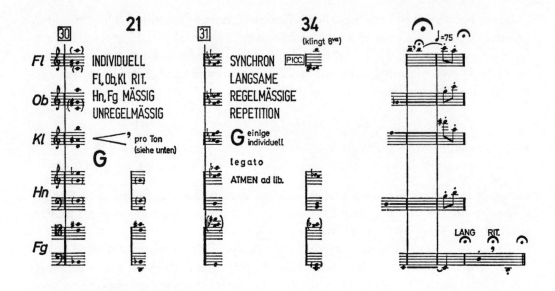

9 Pausen relativ lang.
Hn,Fg: ungefähr in der Mitte zu
den anderen Tonhöhen übergehen.

expressive device sets the scene for, without seeming yet fully conscious of, the imminent appearance of a new harmonic lyricism in *Stimmung*.

Hymnen

1966-7: No. 22, study score UE 15142

Electronic and concrete music (four-track tape).
Duration 113 minutes.
Electronic realization by WDR, Cologne; recorded on DGG 2707039/ST 139421/22
(two-record set).

Hymnen mit Solisten

1966-7: No. 22^I/2, UE 15143

Electronic and concrete music with soloists.
Duration c. 125 minutes.

Hymnen with Orchestra

1969: No. 22^2/3, UE 15145

Electronic and concrete music with orchestra.
Woodwind and brass either duple, triple or quadruple (flutes, oboes, clarinets, bassoons,
horns I, horns II, trumpets, trombones, 1 or 2 tubas), strings 10.10.10.5.5 or in equivalent
ratio to size of wind ensemble.
Duration 38 minutes.

'HYMNEN' is a vast, contradictory work, an enormous tapestry of national anthems, and Stockhausen's grandest electronic composition in scale, if not his greatest in imaginative scope. The electronic realization was achieved in 1966 and 1967 in the composer's studio at WDR Cologne, but the idea of a large-scale work involving tape, voices, and instruments, and depicting the transformation and integration of recognizable musical signals, had been turning over in his mind for many years. At present the electronic score consists of four principal regions, with a total duration of about 113 minutes. Stockhausen regards the work as unfinished, however, and further regions incorporating more and different anthems may be added at a future time (only about forty of the 137 anthems originally collected have so far been used).

Stockhausen has since composed versions of *Hymnen* for tape and orchestra, and for tape and soloists, but the version for electronic tape alone is a fully autonomous piece, evoking the limitless spaces of *Carré* and peopling them with the turbulent crowds of *Momente* in a radiophonic pageant that for all its surface animation is as profoundly withdrawn and contemplative as both these earlier works. It also relates in a formal sense to them as a further essay in the stream-of-consciousness technique suggested by *Carré* (though not, I think, intentionally) and pursued in a literal sense in *Momente*; a projection of the kind of music envisaged for continuous performance in his 'new halls for meditative listening' first proposed in the lecture 'Music in Space'[1] and eventually realized in the spherical music pavilion at Expo '70.

Each region of *Hymnen* has several centres, usually selected anthems, which act as points of reference and convergence for the transformational structure. The first region, dedicated to Boulez, has two centres, the *Internationale* and the *Marseillaise*. It begins with a Babel of short wave and gradually resolves into a rigid and orderly form. The second region, dedicated to Pousseur, has four centres: the West German anthem, a composite group of African national hymns, alternated with (influenced by?) the beginning of the Russian anthem, and fourthly, an *individual centre* which cuts through the musical continuum into a recording of a discussion between Stockhausen and his assistant, David Johnson, made at the same time as the music was being prepared in the studio. Suddenly in this peeling away of time the whole process of *Hymnen*'s synthesis is laid bare, and in Stockhausen's words, 'present, past and the ulterior past all become simultaneous' in an interplay of tenses suggested in *Originale* but never before so vividly expressed.

The third region is dedicated to Cage. Its three centres are the Russian anthem, this time standing alone, the American anthem, and the Spanish anthem. The Russian anthem is composed uniquely of electronic tones, and is heard in vastly distended form, 'the greatest harmonic and rhythmic expansion of anything I have composed to date'. In complete contrast, the American anthem attracts around itself a colourful, cosmopolitan medley of national and festive pieces, an affectionate collage of clearly descriptive character. The third centre, the Spanish anthem, is a highly edited composite subjected to progressively greater acceleration, out of which the anthem emerges as a figure emerges from a surrealist landscape by Dali, when the viewer looks at it from a greater distance.

The fourth, most mysterious region, dedicated to Berio, has two centres interconnected. One is the Swiss anthem, the other 'a hymn associated with the Utopian realm of *Hymunion in Harmondie unter Pluramon*, which is the longest and most penetrating of them all: the final chord of the Swiss anthem is shaped into a calmly pulsating bass ostinato, over which are heaped gigantic blocks, surfaces and highways, in whose clefts the calling of names, with their many echoes, is heard.'[2]

This unearthly last anthem, effectively the climax of the work as it stands at present, is characterized by a continuous downward glissando complex of extraordinary richness and radiance, sounding like the combined decelerating whine of jets of a plane newly landed and stationary. This sound eventually gives way to the sound of slow, steady breathing, with which the region ends.

The most significant innovation of *Hymnen* is precisely Stockhausen's exposure on the surface of the 'ready-made' anthems he uses as material. He had quoted from other music before: in *Mixtur*, 'Spiegel' (an earlier citation of the *Marseillaise*, in fact), and in

---

[1] *Die Reihe 5, Texte I*, p. 157.
[2] *Texte III*, p. 97. (Wörner, op. cit., p. 60.)

Telemusik. But in these words the borrowed material is generally well hidden, its identity obscured. The idea of *Hymnen* always depended on the source material being readily identifiable, but it was probably only after the success of *Telemusik* that Stockhausen felt confident enough to put the idea into practice. With *Telemusik* he had successfully identified his own abstract compositional interests with the musical forms of traditional ritual from distant lands, and this enabled him to claim, with some justice, that his role as a composer was that of a catalyst of peoples through music, an instrument of spiritual reconciliation. Certainly *Hymnen* is widely interpreted as a piece with a message of universal brotherhood.

There must unquestionably be a programme hidden here that embraces as great a vision of a pragmatic Utopia as could be conceived today. . . . The words Hymunion, Harmondie, Pluramon are chosen entirely for their hidden verbal meanings (hymns-union, *harmonia mund* —harmony of the world, pluralism-monism), so as to tell us that the work reveals the conception one very forward-looking contemporary has of the world and of life.[3] . . . What Stockhausen has in mind is a universal humanism, a single idea to span the world and to unite all peoples, the idea of what is common to us, namely our humanity.[4]

But this enthusiastic view, though perhaps not misplaced, seems naïve for several reasons, the most important being that the vision attributed to Stockhausen does not correspond to the spirit of the music itself. The idea of a truly international music acting as a force for good in the world is as old as Darmstadt: after the Second World War young composers believed that in pointillist serialism they had at last discovered a musical language that transcended national frontiers (in Europe, at least, and it is significant that the present four regions of *Hymnen* are decidedly Western in emphasis). And pointillist composers believed in their serialism with religious fervour. *Hymnen* is no more, in this sense, than a re-awakening of old idealism, and certainly no sudden flash of social conscience. The idea of synthesizing a new musical reality from 'found objects' is not new either. That very phrase, used by Stockhausen to describe his anthems, was used by the *musique concrète* composers back in the early fifties, and *Hymnen* is as much a gesture of reconciliation in their direction, after the bitter division between Paris and Cologne, as it is a general manifesto. To single out *Hymnen* for special moral endorsement is in any case to ignore the fact that all his works, whether considered as pure research or as musical metaphor, is music dedicated to the service of mankind and bearing a message of reconciliation.

'Il faut considérer le délire, et, oui, l'organiser', remarked Boulez at the conclusion of his essay 'Son et Verbe'.[5] This remark could stand as *Hymnen*'s epigraph, and it is no coincidence that Stockhausen's dedication of 'Region I' to Boulez alludes to it. The Babel to which both refer is a mental confusion: the saving organizing principle, reason—as represented by serialism. *Hymnen*'s socio-political programme is in fact a

[3] Wörner, op. cit., p. 144.
[4] Wörner, op. cit., p. 141.
[5] *Rélévés d'Apprenti*, p. 62.

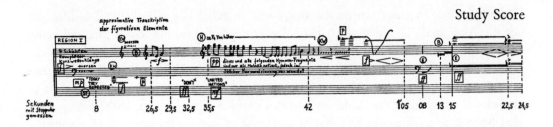

sustained metaphor for an essentially interior struggle to discover the secret of musical order, the philosopher's stone of musical alchemy.

In one of its early projected forms, *Hymnen* was conceived as a work for three pianos and electronic tape. At this stage, Stockhausen's purpose in using national anthems was primarily to furnish the instrumentalists with tangible points of reference. Since he had to consider the likelihood of his work being performed in far-off countries he could quite simply have felt obliged out of fairness to include the anthems of as many different nationalities as possible. The musical necessity for such signposting may be inferred from his earlier difficulties with *Kontakte*, which as we remember was originally conceived as a piece in which live performers were to manipulate, select from, and individually 'comment' upon predetermined electronic material. Since his musicians proved unable to cope in these ways with the electronic music of *Kontakte*, he felt they might better succeed with material they already knew.[6]

Having decided to build a piece around national anthems, it was inevitable that Stockhausen would seek to compose links between them. At this point the philosophical implications of such a programme could no longer be disregarded. But even though he acknowledges the message of univeral brotherhood popularly read into the work in its present form, *Hymnen* remains primarily a practical essay in form-building designed to introduce performers to the kind of collaborative invention later manifested in *Prozession*.

Hymnen's other dedications, to Pousseur, Cage, and Berio, likewise pay tribute to those composers' researches into musical association. By and large they are gestures of temperamental affinity rather than stylistic indebtedness: one remembers Boulez's preoccupation with Mallarmé, and Berio's with James Joyce, and in the same way Cage is identified with 'Third Region's' 'fleeting collages and pluralistic mixtures'. An exception is Pousseur, whose influence is specifically procedural as well as literary.

[6] See his letter concerning *Kontakte*, p. 144.

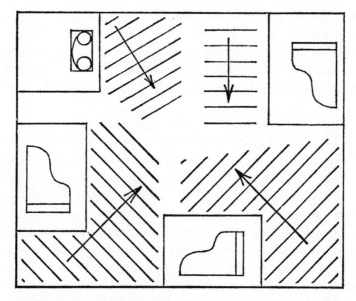

Early project for 'Hymnen' using 3 pianos and electronics.
Diagram shows staging envisaged.

Stockhausen's French-speaking croupier in *Hymnen*, a character who interrupts and seemingly controls the flow of events, inviting the audience ('Faites vos jeux, Mesdames, Messieurs') to participate in the work as in a game of chance, recalls the entrepreneur figure in Pousseur's opera *Votre Faust*, a Machiavellian type who calls on the audience to vote at critical moments on how the plot is to proceed. Again, the spoken 'Rouge, rouge' sequence beginning at 9′ 25,5″ of 'Region I' reminds one irresistibly of Pousseur's litany on the word 'Hélas' in *Electre*, and on a street name in *Trois Visages de Liège*, both electronic compositions. A precedent for Stockhausen's manner of building his anthems into a continuous melodic stream may also be discovered in Pousseur's synopsis of the history of keyboard music in the curious *Tarot d'Henri*, a piano soliloquy played by Henri, the composer hero of *Votre Faust*, at a major turning-point of the opera.

The question to which *Hymnen* addresses itself is in fact whether music may duplicate the inner resonances and processes of thought itself.[7] It is an attractive idea, foreshadowed in *Momente*'s imitation of reverie, and occasionally glimpsed in the biological rhythms of *Telemusik* (e.g. the heartbeats of section 11). On the surface, then, *Hymnen* is simulated radio, complete with morse, static, intermodulations, and tuning

[7] An instance is the curious tearing sound which punctuates 'Region I' from time to time, and which may be likened to the shock of waking out of reverie suddenly, when the ears are left tingling as if from a violent electric current passing through the cochlea. Another sign is Stockhausen's attention to extremes of pitch, which recalls Cage's often-quoted experience in an anechoic chamber, in which he heard two sounds, 'one high, one low'. The low sound, he was told, was his circulatory system; the high sound, his nervous system.

transitions. At a deeper level these snatches of radio and anthem material suggest the elusive immateriality of passing thoughts. 'The work is composed in such a way that different libretti or scenarios for films, operas, and ballets can be compiled for this music. The arrangement of the individual parts and the total duration are variable. Regions can be interchanged—depending on dramatic requirements—extended or omitted.'[8]

To perform, then, is to form: both in his use of radio imagery, and in the deliberately informal nature of his electronic material Stockhausen detaches himself from the immediate political or philosophical implications of *Hymnen*'s programmatic content, and dissociates himself from any intention to moralize. *Hymnen* is not a manifesto, not a latter-day 'Choral' Symphony. Stockhausen leaves it to the performer or listener to draw what conclusions he may from the music. Even 'Fourth Region's' vision of 'Hymunion' contains no anthem, no gesture of synthesis. Indeed, rather than lead the listener into a rousing chorus, Stockhausen heightens the impression of loneliness, drawing the music around him like a shroud until all that is left is the sound of amplified breathing, perhaps an image of man the explorer, Cortez as astronaut, silent and alone at the moment of encounter with a new world.

IV Region: 'Hymunion'

The concept of performance as spontaneous organization is one Stockhausen takes to extremes in his later plus-minus scores. The objection to this procedure is that it produces merely derivative music, and can do little more than add decoration to an already coherent form. But *Hymnen*—except possibly the 'Hymunion' sequence—is not a coherent form. The tape has direction and continuity but no shape; the musicians select, juxtapose, and manipulate elements from the continuum in a conscious effort of rationalization. In both *Hymnen with Soloists* and *Third Region of Hymnen with Orchestra* the tape functions as a kind of computer memory to the performer-programmer. The notation comprises a series of equations.

[8] *Music and Musicians*, May 1971, p. 32.

[The soloists] comment freely on what they hear on tape, using a score which contains a transcription of the tape. Actually this freedom is relative, because I've rehearsed the work quite a lot with musicians I've worked with over a number of years. So it is a matter of very precise mutual agreement. On the basis of this agreement I'm at present (1971) writing out a sort of generalised score, with instructions how soloists should react.[9]

Stockhausen's orchestral parts for 'Third Region' involve simpler transformations than he expects from his own ensemble of soloists, and relies on orchestral numbers to generate large-scale impressionistic effects. His notation is a combination of abbreviated verbal instructions and conventional signs, similar to *Stop* and *Adieu*.

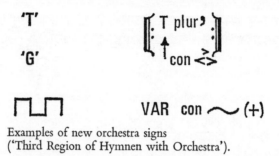

Examples of new orchestra signs
('Third Region of Hymnen with Orchestra').

On paper, the music appears designed as a succession of textures emitted at a tangent to the flow of electronic events. Sometimes the pattern consists of showers of lines or points thrown off the surface of the tape sound, like sparks flying from a grindstone; at other times the orchestral texture is denser and more continuous. The instruments act individually or in groups, may simply prolong selected notes or figures, or develop them—again independently or uniformly—in shape, pitch, or complexity. The orchestral music as a whole is a succession of contrasting episodes cut to the proportions of the electronic matrix and completely dependent upon it. Its purpose is to retard, sustain, divert, or co-ordinate the tape flow by 'feedback', sympathetic resonance, progressive deviation, or selective enhancement of electronic material.

The instrumentalists have instructions how they are to react to what they hear. Sometimes these instructions are for individual players. sometimes for a group, or for the whole orchestra. . . . They have signs, such as T, which means listen, pick out a single tone and repeat it. Then I give a sign to show how fast it should be repeated, whether the player maintains the pitch or transposes it, slowly upwards and downwards, or whether he repeats it periodically and then speeds up the repetitions or slows them down. The same applies to signs like IN—pick out an interval or GR—pick out a group of notes, and so on. You see, the musician works like a transformer, like a real 'interpreter'. . . . It's like taking an element from its context and then letting it run like a strip of sound until I stop it again. And these strips form a polyphony with the music that is already on tape.[10]

[9] Loc. cit.
[10] Op. cit.

Stockhausen's orchestra for *Third Region of Hymnen* is primarily a *resonating* medium. It consists of duple, triple, or quadruple wind (flutes doubling piccolos, oboes, clarinets, bassoons, horns I and II, trumpets and trombones), with 1 or 2 tubas and strings in the proportions 10.10.10.5.5 to balance. There are neither keyboard nor indefinite-pitch percussion instruments, in fact, no instruments of *fixed* pitch at all. All players are expected and able to adjust the tuning of their instruments to chime with frequent slight deviations from standard pitch of the taped material.

Hymnen with Orchestra

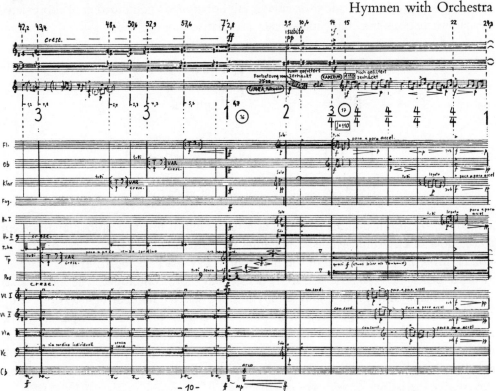

Where his instrumentalists are required to select and transform notes or note groups independently, Stockhausen's cues are clear and the transformations easy to grasp and execute. This simplicity is partly a concession to musicians unused to such a procedure, and partly intended to allow the conductor a measure of freedom to shape the resulting aggregates into sharply characterized movements and textures.

The work begins at the third centre of region II, following the pregnant pause after the spoken words 'Wir können noch eine Dimension tiefer gehen' ('We can go one dimension deeper still'). One hears at first a composite of African anthems, imitated at first discreetly, then gradually with more assertion, by the orchestra. After a little more than three minutes the immensely distended Russian anthem moves into the foreground, and is reflected by the orchestra in constantly-changing instrumental colours. Fragments of melody, harmony, and quasi-short-wave effects break surface at sporadic intervals.

After 7 minutes, at fig. 17, Stockhausen's pointillistic surface texture against a background of sustained harmonies is reminiscent of *Spiel* and *Punkte 1952*, with the difference that the 'points' are now melodic fragments which repeat over and over, gradually disintegrating into the flux.

At 7′ 39″ an upward surge in the tape sound is accompanied by a three-part glissando of string harmonics, the first of several appearances of a high radio static effect which doubles as a change-of-waveband bridge signal. It marks the end of 'Region II' and a momentary hiatus in transmission. In the version for tape alone a short intermission is prescribed at this point. After it the music re-enters with a 27-second downward surge, quite simply the reverse of the previous upward movement, with which Stockhausen 'tunes in' again to a continuation of the Russian anthem. This great interrupted arch reaching through the silence to link 'Regions II and III', is used in the version for orchestra to buttress a specially-composed insert for orchestra alone, called the 'Russian Bridge'.

This 'Russian Bridge' lasts between 4 and 5 minutes. It is composed of three main musical processes, (1) a sustained, slowly expanding chord played by muted strings, taking the pitches of the Russian anthem harmonization at the fadeout of region II as points of departure; (2) repetitions of these same pitches at irregular intervals by woodwind and brass, gradually diverging individually in pitch and repetition frequency to give a halo effect; and (3) anthem fragments, also played by woodwind and brass, sporadically inserted into the glissando texture. Like fig. 9 of *Adieu*, which it closely resembles, the passage is played at an ethereal pianissimo: even the anthem fragments are played 'just loud enough to be recognizable'.

The slow and powerful effect this passage produces is like the uncertain feeling of being in a great aircraft taking off, with its accompanying sense of hiatus between being earthbound and airborne. One consequence of the loss of tonal fixity is a change in the character of the anthem fragments. Instead of snatches of memory, they now appear like radio call-signs, signals of emotional and spatial detachment.

The string glissando 'bridge' element eventually reconverges on the parallel C–E flat minor thirds in soprano and baritone registers with which 'Region III' begins. As the anthems return the orchestra reverts to an imitative role. Simulated morse signals are imitated at pitch by piccolo in the seventh minute of 'Region III', an early warning of the entry of the U.S. anthem two minutes later. As the music on tape increases in complexity so the orchestra's music becomes increasingly diverse and perhaps intentionally Ivesian.

At the second transition, 13′ 24″, the orchestra reverts to *Adieu*-like commentary. Gunfire clusters puncturing the electronic continuum at 14′ 53″ are answered by the instruments in what is perhaps the score's most rhythmically concerted and aggressive passage. At fig. 30, high ribbons and figurations of tape 'static' are imitated by violins in a passage recalling the Bartók violin tremolandi suggested by the impulse trails of *Kontakte*. A new type of mimicry appears at fig. 101, the Spanish introduction (18′ 43″). Over strings playing *col legno battuto* in imitation of recorded guitar strumming, wind instruments pick out elements from the vocal theme, linear fragments which by free octave transpositions they render as arpeggiated vertical formations. Stockhausen's composite anthem, which appears at the third centre (19′ 15″) gives rise to another *Adieu*-like complex of overlapping responses by wind instruments playing in groups. This same collage-anthem reappears several times at greatly increased speeds and consequently elevated pitch, and is accompanied by *Mantra*-like ostinati against a background of an immense sustained chord which begins in the bass register, expands into the treble at 20′ 58″ to drop back into a low 3-voice organum in the bass. After reaching a fortissimo climax, the orchestra begins to weaken from fig. 137 (22′ 27″). Gradually the tape moves back into the foreground, while low strings sustain their open fifth chord in the bass, and high strings add harmonic colouration up to and beyond the tape fade at 23′ 40″.

Prozession

1967: No. 23, UE 14812

For tamtam, viola, electronium, piano, 2 microphones, 2 filters and potentiometers; 6 performers. An alternative instrumentation is possible, though it should correspond to the given ensemble in variety and expressive potential.
Minimum duration 30 minutes.
Recorded by Alfred Alings and Rolf Gelhaar (tamtam), Johannes G. Fritsch (viola), Harald Bojé (electronium), Aloys Kontarsky (piano), K. Stockhausen (sound balance), on Vox Candide CE 31001 (New York), STG BY 615 (London), CBS S 77230 (Paris).
A second version recorded by the above ensemble is released on Fratelli Fabbri Editori mm-1098 (Vox recording).

'P ROZESSION' for viola, tamtam, electronium and piano is a piece of meta-musical 'process planning' written in 1967 for Stockhausen's touring ensemble of musicians. A programmed structure of transformations, indeterminate in length, *Prozession* is difficult to discuss except in rather abstract procedural or historical terms. It is the first of a series of compositions (the others are *Kurzwellen*, *Spiral*, *Pole für 2*, and *Expo für 3*) in which the notion of displacement takes precedence over definition. The score, principally noted in plus, minus, and equal signs, represents a severe ration-alization of the original *Plus-Minus* concept, and the simplified notation itself is a clear improvement on his earlier code of element-relationships (see *Mikrophonie I*). The music transformed in *Prozession* is taken more or less freely from earlier Stockhausen compositions. As far back as *Klavierstück XI* one can see Stockhausen manipulating liaisons between structures independently of their material implications; again, in the form-scheme of *Momente*—or more particularly in the ramified speech-sound classifica-tion system from which *Momente*'s form-scheme appears to be derived—the possibility of composing to rules of displacement alone is clearly indicated (remembering that it too is a system based on combinations of plus and minus signs).

It was Pierre Schaeffer in 1952 who first announced the need of such a system of regulating music:

Suppose we record a sound obtained by lightly stroking a few strings of the piano with the finger. . . . What can be done with such a sound? First of all, we can make a melody in the classical sense. Our equipment enables us to play with the pitch of this *complex note*, to give it rhythm, and so on. . . . But as an alternative to evolving a more or less commonplace melody, we can also attempt to create a family of objects similar to the prototype, but playing on an aspect of its form: a progression in intensity or brevity of attacks, progressive enlargement of the internal rhythm, or alteration of the dynamic envelope. . . .

In such a way new musical processes may be discovered . . . in the alignment of a series of musical objects bearing an intrinsic relationship one with another, like the materials of architecture. For this to happen, the existence of alternatives to pitch-evolution have to be recognised; at least, pitch must relinquish its supremacy. A *series* of identical sound-objects, but varied in intensity, might be considered not as a series, but as a *dynamic melody*. . . . A complex note, [representing] not only a point in the scale, a letter in the alphabet of sounds, [but] often a whole word, or even a phrase of a new musical language, . . . heard once, twice, three times in succession, describing any desired gradient of intensity, could amount in itself to a miniature work, or at least the self-contained fragment of a work.[1]

Schaeffer's case is based on the composer's experience of recording media. This is not to say that the uses of such a technique would be limited to electronic or concrete music; indeed, the 'new musical processes' he advocates were already to some extent prefigured in works as diverse as Messiaen's *Neumes Rythmiques* and Schoenberg's 'Farben' movement from the Op. 16, *Five Pieces for Orchestra*, in the cellular construction of the former, and the *Klangfarbentechnik* of the latter. It is simply that the electronic medium already postulates alternative modes of perception. Recorded sound is subject to important technical conditions which overlay a further meaning on the original. The listener must cope with sometimes contradictory systems of reference. Film, for instance, makes visual movement observable by postulating successive 'states of motion' for what could previously only be conveniently described as continuous transition between successive states of rest. By an analogous process disc and (more effectively) tape recording have made it possible to contemplate, and therefore manipulate, noises formerly considered as unusable. But whereas the subdivision of time into 'frames' is built into the film process, tape recording merely offers the possibility of dissecting movement (tape-cutting). It does not set any standards for breaking down acoustic motion, at least no human standards. Schaeffer does not propose any either, and Stockhausen now attempts to make up the deficiency. And it is clear that, whatever freedom may be suggested by a notation system that depicts only relationships, the music describable in the terminology of *Prozession* belongs without any doubt to a special and very limited type.

It is based, first of all, on two fundamentals: (1) reiteration of material, and (2) persistence of action (continuity of transmission). Reiteration presupposes recognition of that which is reiterated as a 'self-contained fragment'. Continuity of transmission implies that the pattern of reiteration will be maintained, that there will always be something to listen for. Repetition intensifies: it arrests attention by arresting the flow of events, and this arresting quality passes to the musical phrase thus intensified. If incomplete, it assumes completeness; if originally perceived as 'leading', it becomes stable, cadential. Beethoven exploits the effect in the first few bars of his 'Pastoral' Symphony

[1] *L'Objet Musical*, pp. 69–71.

when, just as the listener is getting comfortably adjusted to the music's pattern of change, the composer suddenly intensifies and deepens the music by repeating a routine cadence at the dominant ten times:

A cadential character is also noticeable in the transformational sequences of repetitions in Varèse's *Intégrales*, which comes a great deal closer to Stockhausen. The cadential form creates a discontinuity between successive repetitions at the same time as it reinforces the interior flow of individual events, but whereas Beethoven only arrests the harmonic movement, Varèse interrupts the tempo as well, and it is this latter feature which distinguishes an effect of merely 'marking *time*' from one of regular renewal of musical material.

Varèse, unlike Beethoven, belonged to a generation familiar with the cyclic repetition effect of a cracked record, and had learned from the experience to distinguish musical time, tempo, from transmission time. It is Stockhausen's achievement in *Prozession* to have retained a sense of continuous development in a structure based on arrested continuity, without confusing the flow of events with the sense of movement within events themselves. Only an exceptionally close experience of electronic sound-transformation processes could enable the composer to preserve the distinction in composing. One recalls his efforts in *Kontakte* to formulate processes of change independently of the sound-material to be processed; but it is something more that he has succeeded in simulating, has indeed superseded the studio approach in a live instrumental context. The elegance and simplicity of *Prozession*'s notation is a sure indication of his success.

Electronic sound criteria are reflected in the instructions for interpretation. In principle the simple changes permitted by plus and minus signs are of a mechanical nature, but in practice most would be extremely difficult to achieve with currently available equipment, even using previously-recorded material. For each player there is a part with a succession of +, −, and = signs. These signs signify:

+ higher *or* louder *or* longer *or* more sections;
− lower *or* softer *or* shorter *or* less sections;
= the same pitch (register) *and* volume *and* length *and* tone-colour *and* number of sections.[2]

'Higher' and 'lower' denote exact transpositions. This is a mechanical change, and yet it requires the complicated machine invented by Dr. Springer to transpose a signal in pitch without affecting its duration or speed (density of events). 'Louder' and 'softer' do not seem out of the ordinary until one sees further down the page of instructions, that 'the term "Lautstärke" (volume) refers to the maximum volume of sound as well as to the characteristic [dynamic envelope]'.

Stockhausen's German studio equipment registers amplitude on a negative decibel scale. When the potentiometer is regulated to zero, that does not mean 'no signal' but the optimum amplitude for recording without distortion. Loudness in *Prozession* is also a mechanical, specialist concept. To play louder in Stockhausen's sense of the term does not therefore mean to play more fiercely, for that would unduly alter the timbre by distortion; one must strive to sound 'the same, only louder'—something a little more subtle.

'Longer' and 'shorter' again seem to imply ordinary tempo changes, but the performer should preserve a cool distinction between the time it takes to repeat an event and its inner tempo. Once more an analogy may be drawn with the Springer machine, which is also able to speed up or slow down *recorded* sound without changing its register. Live instrumentalists are no less able to stretch and compress material, indeed they can do it better, since the transformations are effected without loss of quality. (The same overall intensity of activity should be preserved in *Prozession*, however, by constant attention to the sharpness of initial attacks and final cut-offs. It is for this reason that the composer recommends the help of an assistant tamtam player, whose function is solely to dampen the instrument abruptly on cue. A similar acuteness of cut-off is expected of viola bowing, piano pedalling, etc.)

'More' and 'less' (fewer) sections *does* refer to tempo, not, as appears on the surface, to the expansion or contraction of an original duration:

[2] *Texte III,* p. 103.

A length can be subdivided into any desired number of sections. When relating a sign to this number, + means an increase in the number of sections (the rhythm accelerates within the constant length); = the number remains the same; — the number of sections is decreased. Furthermore, under + the rhythmic and melodic subdivisions should become more complicated, under — simpler, and under = they should remain more or less the same.

It may be easier to understand this instruction if the inclusive term 'density' is substituted for the aggregate concept 'number', likewise 'complexity' for 'rhythm'. Stockhausen customarily complicates his note-structures by introducing quasi-ornamental figurations, and it is this kind of rhythmic intensification to which he now alludes. Events under a minus sign which simplify rhythmically should phase out their extreme long or short durations first. The sign 'Per' indicates that whatever proportional sequence is in operation should be modified to comform to a perceptible regular periodicity, e.g. a sequence $11: 7: 3: 9; 5$ could become $12: 8: 4: 10: 6$ $(6: 4: 2; 5; 3)$ or $12: 7\frac{1}{2}: 3: 9: 6$ $(8: 5: 2: 6: 4)$ or more drastically still, $12: 6: 3: 9: 6$ $(4: 2: 1: 3: 2)$.

As indicated above, the musical material scrutinized in *Prozession* is drawn from earlier Stockhausen compositions, the composer recommending choices suitable to the instrument in each case. (It is interesting that *Kontakte* is recommended for viola, in view of the resemblance already noted between parts of *Kontake* and the Bartók Violin Concerto No. 2.)

Each player starts an event when he likes.[3] As soon as one player finishes an event he reacts, according to his sign, either on the event that he himself has played (immediately or after a pause), or on the event of another player which begins next and which he first hears right through before he reacts. He can wait for as long as he likes before he reacts (which gives rise to trios, duos, and solos) . . . If one applies a + or — sign to one parameter, the other parameters remain as in the reference event. A vertical combination will apply to as many parameters as there are signs above each other. . . . Should a performer react to an event he himself has just played he is at liberty to change the tone-colour (which is not conditioned by +/— changes). If he reacts to someone else's event he must imitate that player's tone-colour.

No full score of *Prozession* is issued because the four parts do not regularly coincide; all, however, are equivalent in structure and 'work-load'. Each part comprises a sequence of 250 symbols or symbol combinations, representing successive stages of transformation; the events are gathered in turn into sections of multiples of 10 symbols' duration: 18 for viola,[4] 19 for tamtam, 20 each for piano and electronium. These major subdivisions are indicated by heavy barlines, and changes in the pattern and combination of symbols. All four parts share 12 major subdivisions as follows:

---

[3] An initial plus or minus sign should not be taken as a sound greater or less in all characteristics than an imaginary middle value, needless to say. On the contrary, a sequence of minuses would tend to begin loud, etc., a sequence of pluses soft, etc.

[4] A heavy bar-line seems to be missing from the viola part following the 10 plus-symbols under the instruction 'Klavier gibt' (see illustration). If so, the number of ensemble subsections increases to 13, of viola subsections to 19, and subsection (7) in the scheme below splits into two parts of 10 and 20 elements respectively.

F

1—Introduction: 30 changes' duration
2— 10 changes (Electronium leads)
3— 10 changes (Viola leads)
4— 30 ,,
5— 10 ,,
6— 20 ,, (Tamtam leads)
7— 30 ,, (Piano leads)—see note 4
8— 10 ,,
9— 30 ,, (Tamtam leads)
10— 40 ,, (Electronium leads)
11— 20 ,, (Viola leads)
12— 10 ,, (Piano leads)

Imitation of another player implies a degree of event co-ordination (and audible *Klangfarben* transformation). Co-ordination of the whole ensemble under one player and within specific tonal limitations occurs at the cue points indicated above. At these points the leading instrument plays a distinctive call-sign, at which the others bring what they are playing into limited conformity, imitating the leader's register (R), or dynamic envelope (I), or basic duration (D) or internal rhythm (G). Occasionally two or more parameters are to be imitated at the same time; how long (for how many changes) imitation continues is shown by a number after the initial sign.

These episodes in which all the players come together act like cadences to counteract the naturally divergent tendency of *Prozession*'s distorting-mirror procedure. It lies in the capacities of the players to make such moments powerful and poetic, as they are intended to be.

Looking more closely at the score, one notices first of all a predominance of simple changes (i.e. restricted to one parameter at a time). A second feature is the rich abundance of symmetrical formations. The following type has a special 'refrain' significance:

It appears once in each part, each time in a place in the score unlikely to be interrupted by external call-signs. A five-degree rise in one parameter is coupled with a matching fall in another parameter; at the sixth change the pattern is reversed and the event reconverges, so that after another five changes it is back to an equivalent (though not necessarily identical) condition as before. Another symmetrical formation frequently encountered is the juxtaposition of two ten-unit sections of which one is exclusively composed of plus signs, the other of minuses. The following example from the tamtam part is typical:

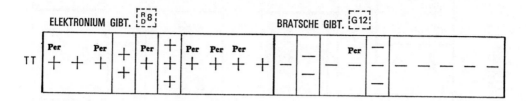

Sections 6, 7, 8, 9, and 10 of the viola part constitute a great sequence of symmetrical groups:

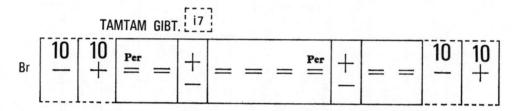

Vertical symmetries between parts are provided for, though naturally their degree of coincidence can only be approximate. In the following example can be seen two vertical combinations of all-plus and all-minus sections (viola-tamtam, tamtam-electronium). A subtle linear asymmetry may also be seen in the tamtam part alone, also a reciprocal succession between electronium and piano. But the region is altogether rich in 'direct' and 'canonic' imitation: vertically between piano and electronium, then between piano and viola (dislocated slightly in each part by the insertion of a 'wild' equal sign); delayed imitation between electronium and tamtam, and between the second half of the piano middle section (itself a mirror-symmetry) and the fourth electronium section in the example overleaf. It makes sense to recognize these correspondences and to try to bring them out in performance.

Reconstructed section of 'full score'.

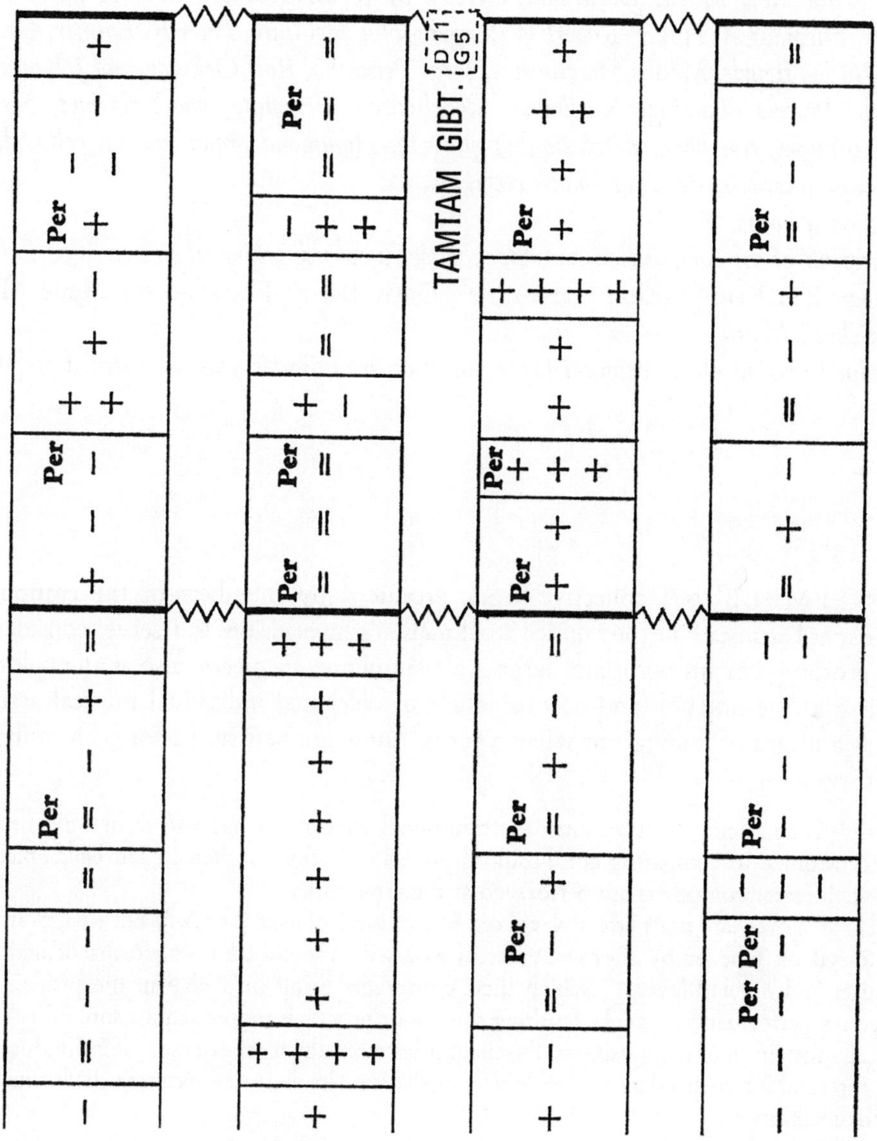
TAMTAM GIBT.
D 11
G 5
Per

Ensemble *(1967)*

Collective composition by members of the composition course, International Vacation Courses for New Music, Darmstadt, directed by K. Stockhausen: Tomás Marco, Avo Somer, Nicolaus A. Huber, Robert Wittinger, John McGuire, Peter R. Farmer, Gregory Biss, Jürgen Beurle, Mesias Maiguashca, Jorge Peixinho, Rolf Gelhaar, and Johannes G. Fritsch. Process planning: Karlheinz Stockhausen. For flute, oboe, clarinet, bassoon, horn, trumpet, trombone, percussion (1 player), Hammond organ, violin, cello, double bass, tape recorders, and short-wave receivers.

Duration 4 hours.

An account of the composition and Stockhausen's co-ordination scheme may be found in Gelhaar: Zur Komposition 'Ensemble', Darmstädter Berträge für Neue Musik, *XI (Schott, Mainz, 1968).*

An edited version of the original tapes, duration 62 minutes, has been issued on Wergo 60065.

'ENSEMBLE' is a collective work produced by members of the composition seminar at Darmstadt in 1967 under Stockhausen's supervision. It deserves consideration as a prototype of his own later large-scale simultaneous pieces, also as an exploratory exercise in the notation and co-ordination of delegated individual musical activities, and as a means of finding out what types of music are best suited for such multi-level enterprises.

Ensemble is an attempt to transform the traditional concert format into something new. We are accustomed to comparing compositions played one after another. In *Ensemble*, 'pieces' by twelve different composers are performed at the same time.

These 'pieces' are not perfectly worked out musical objects ('works') but images in sound (produced on tape or by short-wave receiver), with individual rules, forms of action and reaction and notated 'events', which their composers bring into play in the process of the collective performance. . . . The resulting four-hour process is more than the sum of its 'pieces'; it is a composition of compositions, fluctuating between the total isolation of individual events and the total interdependence of all levels, mediating also between extreme determinacy and unpredictability.[1]

Ensemble's open-plan construction, distributing the component compositions as small pockets of instrumental sound within one moderately large auditorium (an assembly hall with a flat floor), seems primarily intended to examine first the possibility, in a

[1] *Texte III, p. 212.*

236

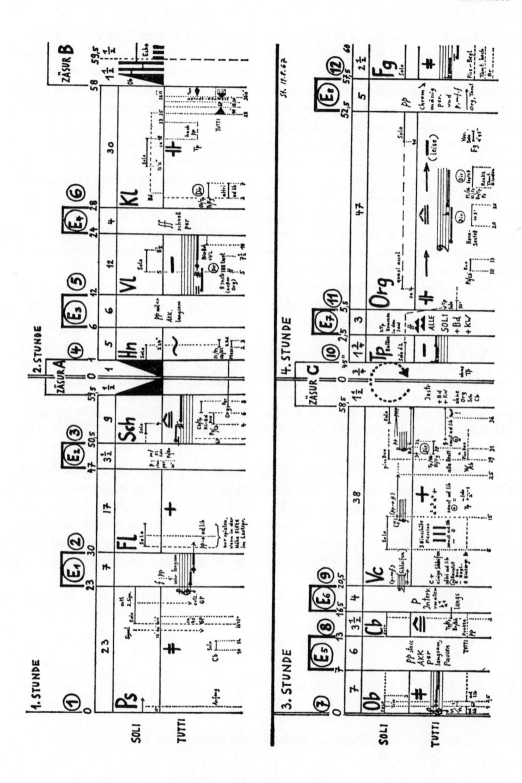

concert context, of audience mobility, and second the coexistence, short-wave radio fashion, of essentially independent musical processes. But over this Stockhausen has erected a superstructure of electronic relays which transmit modified or selective images of the live material to loudspeakers at some distance from their respective sources (as in *Mikrophonie I*). The spatial disposition of speakers and players both allows inter-group dialogue, and to some extent establishes a preferential network of communications.

Rolf Gelhaar's account[2] of the composition of *Ensemble* focuses on a number of questions which bear significantly on Stockhausen's subsequent development. In the first place, a degree of uncertainty emerges over whether the work is to be regarded essentially as a loose aggregation or as a single compartmented structure. This confusion of aim appears to have affected the composer-participants in particular, who seem by their own account understandably more concerned to make personally identifiable statements than to collaborate positively with one another, in spite of Stockhausen's coherent agenda and firm chairmanship.

Structural relationships also come under scrutiny, notably the concept of 'difference' which mediates in *Ensemble*'s terms of reference (as in *Mikrophonie I*) between 'similarity' and 'opposition' of adjacent events.

It must be emphasized that the 'difference' is a very specific relationship; not any old *different* thing, but different in *relationship* to something. An elephant, for example, is in this sense not different from a tree, but is 'something else'. To make the 'similar' relationship clear, one must show that there are only two extreme possibilities, a dualistic approach; the 'different' relationship is pluralistic and demonstrates that there are many possibilities. . . . Both 'opposite' and 'different' must display a certain 'similarity' to the structure to which they relate, in order to be perceived as relating at all.[3]

It is interesting to reflect that Stockhausen's later multi-level works explore three distinct categories of plurality. *Musik für ein Haus* expresses the concept of a simultaneous concert the musical material of which has a strongly-defined signalling character. In *Musik für die Beethovenhalle* 'active' signalling concert items (music played within the auditoriums) is offset by 'passive' reverberating complexes played in the corridors (*Fresco*). Finally *Sternklang* explores the notion of extended co-ordination among groups artificially separated in space.

[2] *Zur Komposition 'Ensemble'*, Darmstädter Beiträge XI, Schott, Mainz, 1968.
[3] Gelhaar, op. cit., p. 47.

Stimmung

1968: No. 24, UE 14805

For six vocalists, optional amplification.
2 Sopranos, alto, 2 tenors, bass.
Duration unspecified, hitherto 73 minutes.
Recorded by the Collegium Vokale Köln, director Wolfgang Fromme—Dagmar Apel
(soprano), Gaby Rodens (soprano), Helga Albrecht (mezzo-soprano), Wolfgang
Fromme (tenor), Georg Steinhoff (baritone), Hans-Alderich Billig (bass)—on DGG
ST 2543003.

No. 24¹/2, 'Paris version', UE 14805

A version of the above as performed by the Collegium Vocale Köln.
Duration 73 minutes.

'STIMMUNG' is two things: a leisurely, very 'cool' meditation for six voices, and at the same time an extremely rarefied and methodical investigation into speech as a process of harmonic modulation. Temperamentally it makes a sortie out of *Mikrophonie II*'s spiritual eclipse into the clear light of day; as research it marks a continuation of *Telemusik*'s very interesting line of development in the field of timbre synthesis.

The work has acquired a certain mystique through being composed entirely from a single aggregate of pitches corresponding to partials 2, 3, 4, 5, 6, and 7 of the B flat below the bass stave. Such harmonic invariance for a work lasting 70 minutes, combined with the mystical character of Stockhausen's text, principally a collection of names of ancient and tribal identities of the Godhead, has created a popular impression of *Stimmung* as essentially a hallucinatory ritual. But there is more to the piece than tuning in and turning on, especially if the phrase—its latter half anyway—is taken to mean dropping out of consciousness, into a warm bath of sympathetic vibration. Stockhausen could hardly have succeeded in developing the distinction between a carrier sound and the information vocally impressed upon it had he not reduced the work's pitch content to a single chord.

Stability is needed for fine tuning, and mastery of intonation and balance involves a style of singing dedicated to purity of note relationships instead of range and agility of projection: a return, in fact, to pre-operatic vocal style.

Form-scheme

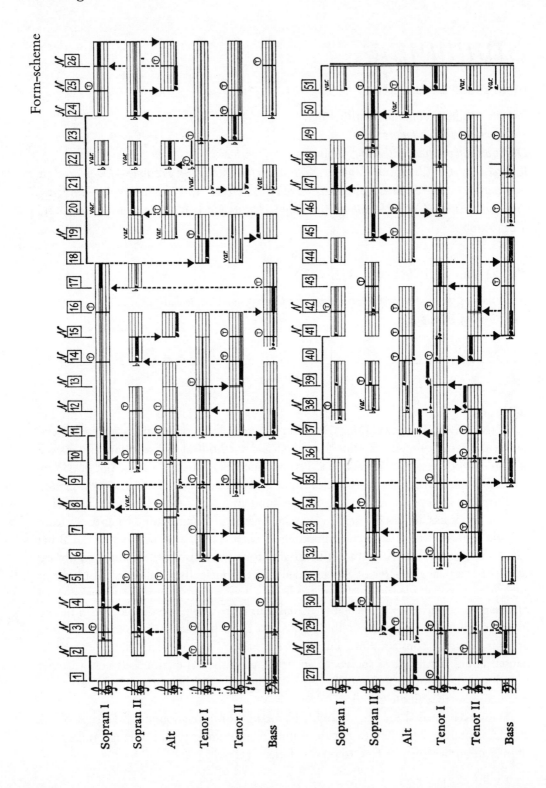

Down to the seventeenth century singers were practised by the monochord, for which Zarlino in the middle of the sixteenth century reintroduced the correct natural intonation. Singers were then practised with a degree of care of which we have at present no conception. We can even now see from the Italian music of the fifteenth and sixteenth centuries that they were calculated for most perfect intonation of the chords, and that their whole effect is destroyed as soon as this intonation is executed with insufficient precision.[1]

Stockhausen's return to harmonic simplicity corresponds to a switch from a primarily gestural form of expression—in which uncertainty of intonation, either systematic (equal temperament) or expressive (vibrato) connotes physical emphasis—to an intimate, non-rhetorical mode of utterance, more sociable in tone, in which personal deviation—individuality—is carefully adjusted to a discreet nicety. Phonetically, *Stimmung* marks a change of emphasis from inflected and consonantal fragmentation (e.g. *Mikrophonie I*) to continuity and the more affective connotations of vowel sounds.

The work is in 51 sections, a fixed order of combinations of the basic pitches, animated by 'Models'—tuning combinations of speech elements, invoked by a leader, taken up by the other singers, and assimilated into the prevailing harmonic combination. The leadership of a given section is indicated in the form-schema of pitches by a thick line after the note (which also suggests that the performer sings somewhat louder). The order of models is not fixed; the three female voices have eight each to choose from, the three male voices nine, and leaders are free to match model with chord combination as they choose.

The subordinate singers, acting as 'resonators', have three possibilities of tuning in to the leader depending on circumstance. If cued in after a silence or caesura (double bar), the singer adjusts unresistingly to match the tempo and inflection of the leading voice. If a change of leader occurs while a subordinate part is still singing, but the change is not indicated in the subordinate part by a barline, the new leading-voice tempo and pattern of inflection are ignored, even though the pitch of the subordinate part may have to change. Third, if a change of leading voice occurs while a subordinate voice is singing, and *is* indicated in the subordinate part by a barline, the 'resonator' adjusts *gradually* to the new tempo and inflection (Stockhausen suggests a linear substitution process, one by one shifts of tempo, vowel complement, and accentuation as it were along sliding scales: a diagram showing a continuous cycle of vowel transformation is provided in the score instructions).

The duration of a section is determined by the number of cycles (repetitions of the lead 'model') necessary for the group to reach and hold the desired condition of harmoniousness. The process of assimilation is sometimes held up by a voice's late entry. Planned distortion is introduced in the bracketed unison passages by the sign 'var.'. The effect required is a gradual phasing in and out of tune, in imitation of the slow interference oscillation between adjacent radio stations. Such deviations are restricted to one parameter at a time.

[1] Helmholtz, *On the Sensations of Tone*, p. 326, Dover, 1954.

Twenty-nine of the 51 sections bear the letter 'N'. In these sections, after total consonance has been reached, and before the cue to move on to the following section is given, a voice other than the leader may invoke one of a selection of 'magic names' which he holds in reserve. One by one, those already singing take up the 'magic name', blending it into the previous harmonic and rhythmic pattern. At least one 'magic name' and as many as six—contributed in rotation, the leader last—may be introduced into an 'N' section, which for this reason last considerably longer than an unmarked section. After an 'N' section the same continuation procedures already described apply, though only the last-invoked 'magic name' is affected by the transition rules.

Model page for female voice

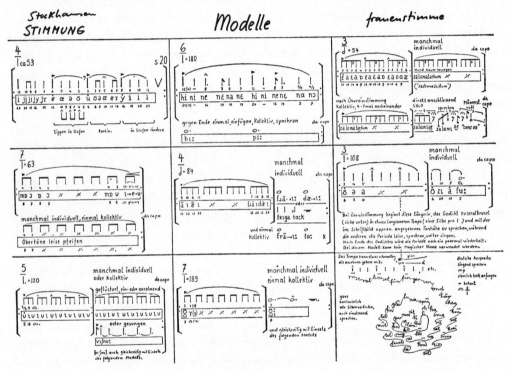

One female voice and each of the three males has a part with a poem attached as a coda to one model. The poem is inserted into the music by the voice concerned in place of a 'magic name' (he can do this as leader by simply not waiting for another voice to propose one). The poems are inflected, but not sung; like magic names, they are meant to be assimilated into the prevailing resonance, but in view of their greater complexity and length this is necessarily a piecemeal affair. 'The speaker of the poem', Stockhausen advises, 'should make pauses of varying lengths in order to follow the integration of his text'.

Finally, at a number of places singers are given empty staves; in such places they move freely among the pitches in use at that moment, introducing random deviations of intonation, rhythm, and accentuation from the prevailing model.

Stimmung's special vocal technique is not a self-conscious archaism. The mouth is employed as a flexible modulator of voiced fundamental pitches; the different 'colourings' or effective resonant envelopes for the given note, being notated as consonant-vowel combinations in phonetic script. (One's mouth behaves in a similar way when playing a jew's-harp.) The six voices not only 'tune in' among themselves as partial frequencies of a common (unstated) fundamental, but each also contributes to the composite timbre a varying harmonic spectrum associated with its own component frequency. In pipe-organ terms, the voices act as mixture stops independently modifying each pitch of a common chord.

These voices provide a model solution to the problem of synthesizing new timbres which eluded the first electronic composers of the fifties. More important, *Stimmung* provides a serial rationale for further trials and researches, which Stockhausen himself was to pursue in *Mantra* and *Sternklang*. This important breakthrough is united with two more personal interests: the prolonged, as it were microscopic, analysis of a single timbre, and the formal convergence of initially differentiated materials and musical events into a harmonious whole.

One cannot fail to be moved as well by *Stimmung*'s formal purity and radiant spiritual composure after the dark uncertainties of *Mikrophonie II*. When agitators broke up a performance in Amsterdam in 1969, Stockhausen wrote, '*Stimmung* will yet reduce even the howling wolves to silence.'

Kurzwellen

1968: No. 25, UE 14806

For piano, electronium, tamtam with microphone, viola with contact microphone, 2 filters with 4 potentiometers and loudspeakers, 4 short-wave receivers: 6 players.
An alternative instrumentation is possible, though it should correspond to the given ensemble in variety and expressive potential.
Duration 50 to 65 minutes.
Recorded by Alfred Alings and Rolf Gelhaar (tamtam), Harald Bojé (electronium), Johannes G. Fritsch (viola), Aloys Kontarsky (piano), K. Stockhausen (filters and sound balance), on DGG 139451 (two versions, two records).

Kurzwellen mit Beethoven

'Stockhoven–Beethausen Opus 1970'
1969: UE 14806

For ensemble as above, but with 4 tape recorders substituting for short-wave receivers. Each soloist listens to a special tape montage of Beethoven compositions.
Duration c. 54 minutes.
Recorded by Alfred Alings, Rolf Gelhaar (tamtam), Harald Bojé (electronium), Johannes G. Fritsch (viola), Aloys Kontarsky (piano), K. Stockhausen (filters and sound balance), on DGG 139461.

'KURZWELLEN' continues the formal investigations begun with *Prozession*, from which it differs most obviously in taking short-wave broadcasts ('Kurzwellen' means 'short-waves') as source material. An essential difference between 'group improvisation' and compositions of the *Prozession* type, is that Stockhausen's pieces offer little opportunity and show scant regard for the two principal elements of this fashionable activity, which are self-indulgent virtuosity and a search after random instrumental effects.

Free jazz is relevant in so far as it leads individual players to collaborate in a collective creative process. But what they did this year at Donaueschingen (1971) with internationally known free jazz players was just chaos. Everyone played as loud and as fast as possible, and everyone at once. There were hardly any solos, and when there were they were full of unconscious citations of idioms I would rather get rid of. But that's what always happens when people say, 'Let's be free': it produces chaos and destruction, because they have never learnt to use freedom as a means of restricting oneself, so that others can also be free. It was very interesting, for instance, that in this free music there was rarely any silence to enable one musician to play for a while.[1]

Certainly the listener to Stockhausen's recordings of *Prozession* and *Kurzwellen* cannot fail to be impressed by the solemnity and restraint of the music he hears, the outcome of a notational system by which instrumental and performing techniques are strictly subordinated to sound quality. Some concessions begin to appear in *Kurzwellen*, however. The transformational patterns composed are more complex, for a start; but on top of that his requirement that performers imitate short-wave events—i.e. consistently aim at a foreign sound quality—extends a priori the scope of both player and instrument. In identifying short-wave sound as a common goal Stockhausen emphasizes the convergent tendency latent in *Prozession*. For when all four instruments strive

[1] *Music and Musicians*, May 1971, pp. 38–9.

to sound 'short-wave-like' they will begin to be heard as quasi-electronic transformations of one another; thus to the linear process of motivic assimilation employed.in the earlier piece, is added a vertical dimension of timbre-association.

Kurzwellen has a more open form than *Prozession*, but one in which time-co-ordination of the four players is from the outset more strictly controlled. It has 136 symbol units (compared with *Prozession*'s 250), divided into sequences of 5, 20, 25, 35, and 51 units. Ensemble co-ordination at each major subdivision, indicated in the score by a heavy barline, is brought about by each player repeating the last sign of his previous sequence until all have 'arrived'. Then the designated 'host' gives a signal for all to proceed, synchronized with him for a given number of events. By placing the first such 'cadence point' after an introduction of only 5 events Stockhausen allows the players to come quickly to an awareness of their relative 'speeds' and to adjust if necessary to closer agreement. As the piece proceeds and distances between co-ordination points increases, so the paths of all four instruments will tend more and more to diverge; even so, the number and precise placing of cues for subsidiary interactions suggest a tighter limit on temporal displacement than in *Prozession*.

Stockhausen's notation of performer interaction is also tighter. The co-ordinative repeat, indicated by (W) (*Wiederhole*) is a neater sign and a more natural usage. *Prozession*'s 'Per' (periodic) sign is omitted, so are the compulsory imitations of Register, Number, and Duration. His specification of short-wave sound as a common source of reference to some extent accounts for these omissions: short-wave events are predominantly periodic in structure, and imitation of transistor radios creates a natural drift of sonority towards the high frequency region. As a result a performer is also more likely to imitate another *indirectly*, via short wave (imitating the other instrument's event with his own short-wave receiver, or imitating the other's short-wave event), than directly, instrument to instrument:

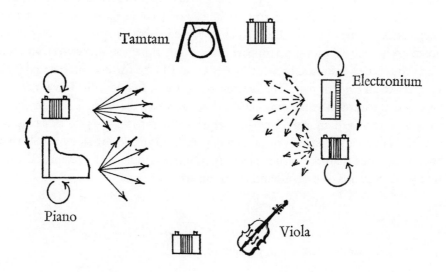

4 options of I–II imitation:
(1) Direct (2) Instrument to KW2
(3) KW1 to Instrument 2 (4) KW1 to KW2

'When and how often a player alternates between short-wave and instrumental events is left to his discretion; he should, however, aim for a balance,' reads the instruction, but the balance is, as we see, statistically weighted in favour of short wave. Clearly this will tend to bind the ensemble into an acoustic unity, and reciprocally limit the function of each instrument to that of an imperfect resonator of the radio-wave continuum.

In place of the 'tuning' co-ordinations of *Prozession*, a large number of precise polyphonic interactions are inserted into the score. So many are these in relation to *Kurzwellen*'s smaller number of constituent events, that few opportunities remain for the individual performer to go his own way. Even if he does so, the composer at the mixing console may still bring him to heel:

His group undergo lengthy rehearsals before they appear in public. He himself sits at the electronic controls and when any idea he considers inappropriate is produced, he promptly phases it out by the twist of a knob. Not surprisingly, this has sometimes caused resentment, which reached explosion point last year [1970] at Darmstadt. Several of his players parted company with him and Stockhausen confessed himself surprised and deeply hurt.[2]

The score is tighter, then, and also more complex. Its introductory section, the reader will quickly notice, features a canonic sequence of miniature symmetries in parts II, III, and IV. In contrast to *Prozession*'s opening trails of minus signs, its material remains virtually constant in all parameters (see opposite).

The principle of imitation exposed in the introduction is pursued in the first major section of 20 units (or section A, if we designate the score's five sections as Introduction, A, B, C, D). It is not difficult to spot blocks of 3 equal signs disposed at successively later stages in parts I to IV. Each block is preceded by an aggregate of 5 events composed exclusively of plus signs (in part II a 4-event sequence intervenes), and is followed by a sequence of minuses, of which parts I and III (the former interrupted by an equal sign) make an evident pair. The bracket signs, more frequent than in *Prozession*, create new and intricate internal symmetries. For instance, the basic 4 × 5 structure of the section is rendered in part I as the sequence 1–4–3–2–2–3–4–1, whereas in part II brackets create a sub-structure of 2–3–4–5–6. Symmetries of signs and between parts are less obvious than the earlier piece. A simple example is the reciprocal pair formed by the last 8 events of parts III and IV in this section:

[2] Peter Heyworth, *The Observer*, 25 April 1971.

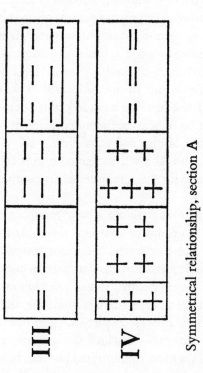

Symmetrical relationship, section A

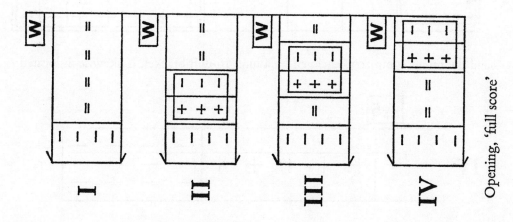

Opening, 'full score'

Section C divides into 5 distinct subsections of 5 events. Here the symmetries are more regular, and a fair degree of unanimity is found among the four parts. Part IV's opening 4 × 3 minuses followed by an equal sign are balanced by III's answering 4 × 3 plus signs and an equal; in their second 5-unit phrase parts I, II and IV present a following sequence similar to the introduction: in this case a box of triple-plus aggregates is progressively displaced in a context of double-pluses. Five-event sequences of minus signs follow in all four parts: I and III are reciprocal; a vertical combination of 4 minuses is passed back IV–III–II–I (making a grand 5 plus 5 symmetry in all four parts). The final 10 units of this section present ascending symmetries of various sizes ('ascending' because composed mainly of plus and equal signs): 1–4–4–1 for I, its last unit of 5 reciprocal with II and IV, and III a self-contained symmetry; furthermore part II's last unit of 4 events balances with the 4 minuses of its continuation in the following section.

Section C finds part I again maintaining a basic grouping in fives while II and III at the outset favour irregular groups of four and three. At first the musical balance remains fairly constant, but each part suffers one major and one minor fluctuation, the relationships between which Stockhausen has carefully manipulated. In part I, in the fourth 'bar', the pattern is: major decline, minor rise, minor decline, major rise; in part II beginning at the 12th event, the pattern is moderate decline (4 units), major rise (5), moderate decline (6), minor rise (4); in part III, from unit 16: attenuating decline, major rise, major decline, minor rise—of which the last three are symmetrical, and all are grouped in fives. In part IV a more sophisticated plan can be seen: the opening 3-unit decline balances with a 5-unit rise and subsequent 2-unit fall after a lapse of three bars:

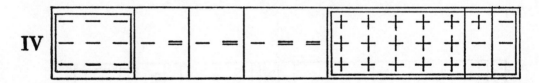

—and the minor symmetry, enclosed by a long 10-unit bracket, is likewise dislocated:

The final 5-unit group of the section is mirror-symmetrical between I and IV, and reciprocal between I and the previous 5-unit group of II.

The remaining section pursues a pattern of plus–minus symmetrical orders varied this time by the intercalation of 'wild' equal signs. Bars 2–5 of II furnish an obvious example:

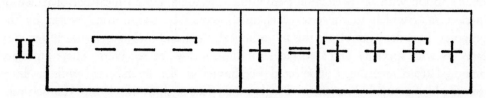

But by and large there is less obvious reciprocity between parts than previously, partly because the bar-divisions, after the first 10 units, progressively diverge from 5–unit groupings, and partly because changes on the whole are less elaborate. A degree of complementarity may, however, be observed between I and IV, and between II and III, in terms of complexity of change. This only lasts to about half way; at 17 before the end I and II are paired, and III with IV in the simple symmetrical sequence:

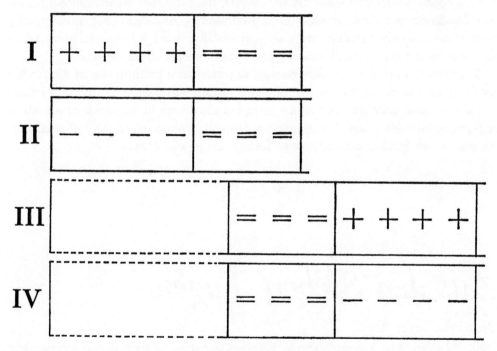

The final bars of each part reciprocate processes (or their negative images) from near the beginning. Part I's final 14 units reflect its first 14 after the introduction; part II's final 4 bars are a variant mirror-image of its section A bars 2–4; part III's last 2 bars recapitulate the last 2 bars of its section A (and mirror the first 5 events of II section A); while part IV's final minus grouping recalls the end of I section A and bars 2–5 of III section A.

Kurzwellen mit Beethoven (Opus 1970)

Invited to lecture on Beethoven as part of Dusseldorf's celebration of the bicentenary of his birth, Stockhausen resolved instead to present an evening's meditation on Beethoven's music with his performing ensemble. He imagined an ideal performance of *Kurzwellen* in which all short-wave channels would be transmitting works by the composer. In order to re-create this hypothetical situation Stockhausen substituted tape recorders with specially prepared tapes for the short-wave receivers. These tapes are composed from recordings of selected Beethoven works, interspersed with readings from the Heiligenstadt Testament. To give the effect of short-wave, Stockhausen subjected this material to a variety of electronic transformations based on processes previously used in *Hymnen* and *Telemusik*. Innovations in ring modulation he made at this time led to the development of the Modul 69B circuit and thus, eventually, to *Mantra*.

Opus 1970 is closer to the original concept of *Hymnen* than to what *Hymnen* eventually became, even *Hymnen mit Solisten*. Instead of one polyphonic tape playing continuously and 'commented upon' by the players, there are four separate mono tracks, each simulating an individual selection of programmes. And these programme tracks, though continuously running, are only sporadically heard by the audience, when players exhaust a line of transformation and opt to tune into fresh material.

That Stockhausen felt confident enough to undertake a performance of *Kurzwellen* involving meditating on 'totally unmodulated realistic short-wave events', says a great deal for the close understanding which he had reached with his ensemble of soloists in performing intuitive music. It also marks a deepening of interest in classical tonal procedures, which Stockhausen subjects to further scrutiny in *Mantra*.

Aus den Sieben Tagen

'From the Seven Days'
1968: No. 26, UE 14790, 14790e English version, 14790f French version

15 compositions: Richtige Dauern, Unbegrenzt, Verbindung, Treffpunkt, Nachtmusik, Abwärts, Aufwärts, Oben und Unten (theatre piece), Intensität, Setz die Segel zur Sonne, Kommunion, Litanei, Es, Goldstaub, Ankunft.
For ensemble (number of players unspecified).
Durations unspecified, from 4 to 60 minutes per piece.

Recorded complete as a boxed set by DGG (7 LPs: cat. no. 2720 073). Es, Aufwärts *(2561 295),* Richtige Dauern, Verbindung *(2561 297),* Unbegrenzt *(2561 298),* Kommunion, Intensität *(2561 296),* Treffpunkt, Nachtmusik *(2561 299),* Abwarts, Setz die Segel zur Sonne *(2561 300), Harald Bojé (electronium), Alfre- Alings and Rolf Gelhaar (tamtam), Aloys Kontarsky (piano), Jean-François Jennyd Clark (double bass), Johannes G. Fritsch (viola with contact microphone), Michel Portal (E flat and B flat clarinets, tenor saxophone, and taragod), Jean-Pierre Drouet (percussion), Carlos Roqué Alsina (piano), Karlheinz Stockhausen (filters and potentiometers), and an anonymous trombonist.*

Goldstaub *(2561 301), Peter Eötvös (electrochord, keisu, rin), Herbert Henck (voice, sitar, saucepan part-filled with water, 2 little bells, ship's bell), Michael Vetter (voice, hands, recorder), Karlheinz Stockhausen (voice, conch trumpet, large cowbell, keisu, 14 rin, key and jar of water, Kandy (Ceylonese) drum, jingles.*

All except Goldstaub *were recorded in 1969,* Goldstaub *in 1973. The versions of* Unbegrenzt *and* Es *are the same as those issued earlier on Shandar 10 002; the version of* Setz die Segel zur Sonne *is different from that issued on Musique Vivante MV 30795.*

Setz die Segel zur Sonne, *and* Verbindung *are recorded by Harald Bojé (electronium), Alfred Alings and Rolf Gelhaar (tamtam), Aloys Kontarsky (piano), Jean-François Jenny-Clark (double bass), Johannes G. Fritsch (viola), Michel Portal (clarinets), Jean- Pierre Drouet (percussion), K. Stockhausen (filters and sound balance), on Musique Vivante MV 30795 (*Setz die Segel *is also available separately, cat. no. HM 30899) (Harmonia mundi).*

Unbegrenzt *and* Es *are recorded by Vinko Globokar (trombone), Carlos Roqué Alsina (piano), Jean-François Jenny-Clark (double bass), Jean-Pierre Drouet (percussion), Michel Portal (saxophone, flute, clarinet), Johannes G. Fritsch (viola), K. Stockhausen (sprechstimme, siren, short-wave receiver, filters and sound balance), on 'Nuits de la Fondation Maeght' (St. Paul), Belgium (two-record set).* Unbegrenzt *is available separately on Shandar SR 10002.* Es *and* Aufwärts *are recorded by Group Stockhausen (Kontarsky, Bojé, Fritsch, Alings, Gelhaar, Stockhausen) on DGG 2530 255.* Kommunion *and* Intensität *are recorded by Fritsch, Alings, Gelhaar, Alsina, Jenny-Clark, Portal, Drouet, Stockhausen, on DGG 2530 256.*

I have called this music, which expresses the spiritual accord among musicians, channelled by means of short texts, *intuitive music.* 'Improvisation' no longer seems the right word for what we are playing, since it invariably conjures up an image of underlying structures, formulae, and peculiarities of style . . .

By *intuitive music* I mean to stress that it comes virtually unhindered from the intuition, and that as music, in the case of a group of musicians playing intuitively, it amounts to more, qualitatively speaking, than the sum total of individual 'accidents', by virtue of a process of mutual 'feedback'. The 'orientation' of musicians, which I call 'accord' (Einstimmung) is not, I would emphasise, random or merely negative—in the sense of exclusive—musical thought, but joint concentration on a written text of mine which provokes the intuitive faculty in a clearly-defined manner.[1]

THE 15 *Aus den Sieben Tagen* texts, written during five days of total withdrawal early in May 1968, represent the needle's eye of the composer's development. They mark the limit of a phase of introversion begun at the turn of the sixties and expressed in a growing sense of personal limitation, a focusing of his musical imagery on states of consciousness, and, judging from his writings, increasing alienation from his fellow-countrymen. If *Prozession* (1967) may be described as essential form, the *7 Tagen* texts are essential feeling. Each complements the other, and both, for all that they represent deliberately minimal intervention, are sharply revealing of the composer's *musical* priorities in design and expression. Yet even at this point of near-complete self-abnegation one is aware of a mind turning outward once again in a gentler, more dependent spirit of collaboration with people and events external to itself.

Stockhausen has been adversely criticized for resorting to verbal texts to express this changed consciousness, but we should remember that language has always been important to him both as a source of inspiration (in phonetics) and also as a highly efficient supplementary notation. Words and borrowed vocal conventions have tended to avoid the misunderstandings which his musical notations have often aroused. Words, not notes, enabled his musicians to reach speedy agreement on the whole range of new timbres conceived for *Mikrophonie I*, and it is, significantly, a verbal exchange in the first Region of *Hymnen*, that signals a sudden and dramatic rupture of the electronic web of sound. And Stockhausen chooses his words with great care, as the reader of Fred Ritzel's account of the composer's 1968 Darmstadt seminar cannot fail to notice.[2] Meditation was not, he assured his young students, some sort of mystical decline into a lower level of consciousness, but intense concentration on the moment, whether listening or playing. He takes care, furthermore, to limit his texts to images and events drawn from his own experience, as the following dialogue makes clear:

Stockhausen.—Have you ever before felt with absolute certainty, that you had 'all time and space at your disposal'? (referring to the text 'Unbegrenzt').
Jaroslav J. Wolf.—No!
Stockhausen.—I have. I heard it. Nothing instrumental. But I have experienced this piece! It is performable! (*ausführbar*: 'feasible', 'communicable').[3]

[1] *Texte III*, pp. 123–4.
[2] *Musik für Ein Haus*, Darmstädter Beiträge zur Neuen Musik XII, B. Schott's Söhne, Mainz, 1970.
[3] Op. cit., pp. 14–15.

The student must not only know what he is doing, but must try to extend his self-awareness as well: 'He who has experienced nothing out of the ordinary, will do nothing out of the ordinary. There is a direct relationship between the ability to respond and the ability to act'.[4]

This does not however deter Stockhausen from seeking to draw students out of their narrow framework of experience by the sheer force of his personality:

> Ahern: SOLO
>> 'Play two sounds: one very high, one very low.
>> Then play all the sounds that lie between'. (Cf. Stockhausen: 'Aufwärts')
> Stockhausen (following on):
>> —and make the high sound ever higher!
> Ahern: Why?
> Stockhausen: So as to draw the composition upwards—to raise its sights
>> —to stimulate the interpreter to a higher level of achievement![5]

Stockhausen recounts that after composing *Kurzwellen* he suffered feelings of deep depression, from which he eventually discovered solace in reading a book of Sri Aurobindo's teachings given to him by an American acquaintance some time before but hitherto unopened. Aurobindo is generally credited with having turned Stockhausen towards a philosophy of transcendentalism. This may well be true: he was certainly inspired. But it would be wrong, I think, to conclude from this either that he was thereby diverted from the creative path he had been following, or that he was altogether unprepared for the encounter. What Aurobindo does seem to have done has been to dislodge the composer out of the idea that his creative and expressive potential was limited to physically graspable events and sensations.

The sense of perceptual straining outwards in *Hymnen* and elsewhere yields, in *Aus den Sieben Tagen*, to a calmer exercise of meditative power. The liberating effect of this change of attitude takes on a different complexion when one considers how much Stockhausen's music has depended, for inspiration as well as execution, on electronic processes, to the point even of being impeded by them. For the freedom to range abroad in the imagination is also the freedom to draw unhindered from one's own imaginative resources, and if and when expression is obstructed by equipment failure or inadequacy, invention must be curtailed and frustration correspondingly high.

At another level, the texts show a reversal in Stockhausen's research method. In the fifties effort was concentrated on the synthesis of new timbres, and though that research did not bring him far in that direction at the time, the spin-off certainly gave him a good deal to work upon. Now, after a decade of applying these incidental discoveries in his compositions, Stockhausen returns to the notion of a 'pure' objective, designed to extend the mind and stimulate new practical invention. The difference between his purism of the 1950's and that of 1968 is that the composer's goal is now mental, not

[4] Op. cit., p. 37.
[5] Op. cit., pp. 27–8. See also his lively discussion with Gregory Biss, pp. 43–4.

physical, and his resources are spiritual and human instead of linguistic or technological. That is why in his texts he rarely specifies the means (instrumentation): not that the means are no longer important—quite the reverse—but that the mind must not be distracted from its meditative goal by material considerations.

These pieces are studies, as private and dedicated to spiritual excellence as Czerny's studies in the nineteenth century were committed to technical virtue. They have been translated into English, but as in orthodox poetry I believe that special store must be set by the German originals. One reason is the peculiar resonance of Stockhausen's native speech: the sense of 'directedness' as well as 'rightness' that envelops his use of *richtig* in 'Richtige Dauern' ('Just Durations') for instance. Another is Stockhausen's style of address, which is translated less well as the English imperative form 'Do', I feel, than as the invitation to 'Consider'. English performers of these texts, I have observed on several occasions, do tend to respond with enthusiastic obedience to the implied imperative, but seem to pay little attention to the meaning of what the text may actually say. German performers are more critical.

Some of our musicians, especially the most intellectual, Kontarsky, for example, said, 'I can't do anything with that instruction ("Play in the rhythm of the Universe"). What shall I do with it, the rhythm of the universe?' I said, 'Have you never had any dream experience of the rhythm of the universe, have you never been flying in between stars, have you never had a direct experience of the rotation of the planets, let's say of our own planet, or of the other planets of our solar system?'. . . . And he said, 'No, no, no, I have no experience, I'm sorry.' And then I said, 'Well, at least you have one possibility, because you're a very visual person, you read a lot, your education is visual, and your thinking is visual. What about the constellations of the stars?' He said, 'Oh, wonderful!' I said, 'Well, just one more suggestion. Think of the interval constellations of Webern's music. And then combine them with the constellations of the stars. Let's say you think of Cassiopeia or the Big Dipper.' And from that moment on that player became the most precise member of our group for performances of such intuitive music.[6]

Of the fifteen texts, one, 'Litanei', is addressed specifically to the performing attitude. The other fourteen may be classified in the following categories:

1. *Extension of the time perspective* (concentration—endurance)
   Richtige Dauern
   Unbegrenzt
   Intensität

2. *Extension of frequency perspective* (pitch—rhythm)
   Verbindung
   Nachtmusik
   Abwärts
   Aufwärts
   Kommunion

[6] Jonathan Cott, *Rolling Stone*, 8 July 1971, p. 33.

3. *Translation from one focus of awareness to another*
   Nachtmusik
   Abwärts
   Aufwärts
   Kommunion

4. *Reconciliation of opposites*
   Abwärts—Aufwärts (considered as a pair)
   Intensität—Setz die Segel zur Sonne (likewise)
   Oben und Unten

5. *Convergence—Divergence*
   Treffpunkt
   Oben und Unten
   Setz die Segel zur Sonne

6. *Extension of Influence*
   Intensität
   Setz die Segel zur Sonne
   Kommunion

7. *Freedom from External Influence*
   Richtige Dauern
   Es
   Goldstaub
   Ankunft

Many will be recognized as quintessential statements of a composing philosophy Stockhausen has maintained for the whole of his life. 'You must strive for the faith to be able to do these things,' he tells the performer in 'Litanei'. 'I have had that faith from the beginning.' Three texts, 'Litanei', 'Goldstaub', and the theatre piece 'Oben und Unten' are of particular autobiographical interest. 'Goldstaub' in fact summing up the effects of his self-imposed seclusion:

GOLD DUST

Live completely alone for four days
      without food
in complete silence, without much movement.
Sleep as little as necessary,
think as little as possible.

After four days, late at night,
without conversation beforehand
      play single sounds.

WITHOUT THINKING what you are playing
      close your eyes,
      just listen.

29

10. Mai 1968 ©

für kleines Ensemble

GOLDSTAUB

Lebe vier Tage ganz allein
ohne Speise
In größter Stille ohne viel Bewegung
Schlafe so wenig wie nötig
Denke so wenig wie möglich

Spiele nach vier Tagen spät abends ohne Gespräch vorher
einzelne Töne

OHNE ZU DENKEN welche Du spielst

Schließe die Augen
Horche nur

Musik für ein Haus (1968)

Collective composition by members of the composition course, Darmstadt International Vacation Courses for New Music, directed by K. Stockhausen: Jorge Peixinho, Clare Franco, Rolf Gelhaar, Thomas Wells, Fred van der Kooy, Boudewijn Buckinx, Jaroslav J. Wolf, John McGuire, David Ahern, Mesias Maiguashca, Gregory Biss, Costin Miereanu, Junsang Bahk, Jens-Peter Ostendorf, Satoshi Nozaki. Process planning: Karlheinz Stockhausen.

Flute, flute in G, oboe, bass clarinet, bassoon, horn, trumpet, trombone, electronium, piano/celesta, viola, cello, double bass: microphones, tape recorders, short-wave receivers, 5 mixing consoles. Performed in 5 separate rooms, on three levels, of the Georg-Meller-Haus, Darmstadt, Sunday, 1 September 1968.

Duration c. 4 hours.

An account of the composition, with circuit diagrams and Stockhausen's co-ordination scheme may be found in Ritzel: Musik für ein Haus, *Darmstädter Beiträge zur Neuen Musik, XII (Schott, Mainz, 1970).*

'MUSIK FÜR EIN HAUS', Stockhausen's 1968 Darmstadt composition project, pursues the idea of simultaneous presentation of several compositions attempted in *Ensemble* the previous year. This time, as might be expected, the compositions are notated verbally; some further limitation of scope is implied by Stockhausen's advance allocation of instrumentalists to the participating composers.

Ideal conditions for the 'House Music' are provided by a cluster of rooms of various sizes on two floors, connected and acoustically isolated by a network of passages. Each listener comes and goes in his own time and is able to change his listening perspective within the House at will.

What the instrumentalists play is picked up by microphones in each room and relayed at varying amplification over loudspeakers. Each of the four rooms is linked by loudspeaker with the three others. The players not only react to one another, but also to the music emanating from the other rooms. In a fifth room ('Klangbox') may be heard a continuous relay of the music from all four rooms over four separate speakers.[1]

Stockhausen himself took charge of overall co-ordination and distribution of individual compositions throughout the evening's four-hour programme. Fourteen instrumentalists in all took part, in groups of up to seven at once.

[1] *Texte III,* p. 216.

'The texts direct each performer to concentrate exclusively on *inward and outward hearing*'. Quite clearly, what Stockhausen had in mind was the creation of a miniature communications network in which instrumentalists might converse with one another as though over great distances, identifying themselves by musical call-signs and com-

ZEITPLAN

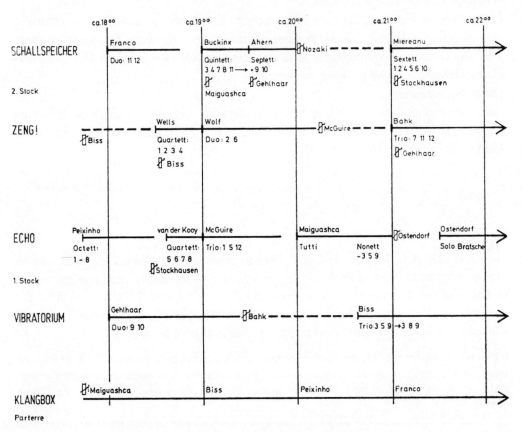

Die Zahlen 1-12 bei den verschiedenen Ensembles korrespondieren mit der Aufzählung der Instrumentalisten (siehe vorn).

posed limitations of gesture. Just how essential his co-ordination scheme was to the success of the project seems to have escaped the notice of the student participants; to judge by their reactions to the course (as reported in Ritzel) most seem to have interpreted Stockhausen's schema simply as idiosyncratic stage management of their pieces.

But the function of his external controls, and the communications emphasis thereby laid on their individual text materials, enable us to infer how the *Aus den Sieben Tagen* pieces are meant to act: as models to put performers in the right frame of mind for discovering new species of musical interaction.

Für kommende Zeiten

'For times to come'
1968-70: No. 33

17 texts for intuitive music: Übereinstimmung, Verlängerung, Verkürzung, Über die Grenze, Kommunikation, Ausserhalb, Innerhalb, Anhalt, Schwingung, Spektren, Wellen, Zugvogele, Vorahnung, Japan, Wach, Ceylan, Intervall.
For ensemble, instruments unspecified.
Durations unspecified.
Available in German or English translation from the composer.
Japan *recorded by Harald Bojé (electronium[1] and Japanese temple block), Christoph Caskel (percussion), and Peter Eötvös (electrochord, Japanese bamboo flute, and Japanese temple block).*
Wach *recorded by Harald Bojé (electronium), Christoph Caskel (percussion), Peter Eötvös (electrochord, antique cymbal, short-wave receiver). EMI Electrola C 165–12 313–14 (Germany) (2-record set).*

STOCKHAUSEN wrote several more texts at the time of the Darmstadt seminar in August 1968, and these, together with others written at various times between then and July 1970, have been gathered into a further collection of seventeen under the title 'Für kommende Zeiten' ('For times to come'), By and large these texts display little of the emotional tension so palpable in the earlier sequence. True to form, as his apparent self-confidence returns, so the pathetic tone diminishes, and his thoughts take on a more practical turn. An exception is 'Über die Grenze' ('Across the Boundary'), a piece of amused detachment that might almost be translated as 'Over the edge' or 'Beyond the Fringe':

[1] See note on page 199.

> Imagine you are a HIGHER being
> which comes from another star
> discovers the possibilities of your instrument
> and proves to your co-players
> that in its homeland
> it is a 'Humorous Master-Interpreter'
> The shorter pieces in its repertoire
> Last roughly one earth-hour.[1]

An inherent problem in the realization of intuitive music, I became aware after watching a supposedly expert ensemble struggle unsuccessfully with this text for several hours, is that a concern to produce aesthetically pleasing sounds may prevent performers from coming to terms with what the text asks them to do, in this case using their instruments in more lively and imaginative fashion. A kind of inarticulate aestheticism results from too much regard being paid to sound quality, and too little to action. The problem is aggravated by performers confusing these pieces with others like *Prozession* and *Kurzwellen*, in which the performer's personal initiative is limited by external signals, which have to be waited for patiently. Such difficulties ought not to arise in 'Über die Grenze', however. Paraphrased, Stockhausen's instructions are 'Play humorously, with a lively instinct for the sound-potential of the instrument': i.e. not to be self-conscious, not to waste time checking sound quality ('Master performers' by definition should be beyond such things). The players are invited to outbid one another in inventiveness; the mood is conversational, relaxed, the emphasis on performer action. One may not feel able to will oneself into a higher state of being, but it should be easy enough for good performers to let themselves go.

The other 'For times to come' texts range from expressionist studies in the 'Aus den Sieben Tagen' manner, to pieces whose formal and instrumental specifications are spelled out in some detail, and at the other extreme, verse miniatures in which the musical element is not immediately obvious:

WELLEN	WAVES
Überhole die anderen	Overtake the others
Halte die Spitze	Hold the lead
lasse Dich überholen	Allow yourself to be overtaken
Seltener	Less often

The notion of pausing between two movements is new,[2] as is the expressed or implied ostinato movement also to be found in 'Schwingung' and 'Zugvogele'. Reciprocal

---

[1] Reproduced in Ritzel, op. cit., p. 40, under the title 'Music Fiction'.

[2] At least, this is how I interpret the wave motion implied by the title. A wave, moving faster on the surface than the supporting current, builds to a peak or point ('Spitze'), remains motionless for an instant, then falls back as the current overtakes it again. But every wave motion involves changes in the direction of motion, and thus points of suspense between movements.

pairs of texts are here also; 'Verlängerung' and 'Verkürzung' for example, the one addressed to eternity in the moment, the other to the momentariness of excessively long durations. Both relate very closely to the text 'Übereinstimmung' in which long, quiet sounds are to be reconciled with short, loud sounds. The idea is to bring the two ('resonance' and 'attack'?) into synchronization, but the adjustment suggests more than conjunction in time, implying also a perceivable consistency of relationship between note intensity and note duration: the 'justness' of timing prescribed for 'Richtige Dauern', in fact. 'Übereinstimmung' seems also to have inspired 'Intervall' for piano and two players of 1969, in which the coming together of musical extremes is given an added dimension of personality conflict and resolution.

Hinab-Hinauf (1968)

Environment in sound and image: project for spherical music auditorium, Expo '70, Osaka.
For small ensemble, electronic and concrete music, film and light projection.
Duration 13 minutes 31 seconds.
Score and explanation reproduced in Stockhausen: Texte Band III, *pp. 155–65.*

STOCKHAUSEN had long nourished the idea of a spherical auditorium when in 1968 an official invitation to submit a project for a German auditorium at Expo '70 in Osaka gave him an opportunity to realize this ambition. After a long period of uncertainty his original plan was drastically curtailed by the committee of music representatives appointed to advise on the matter. The principal casualty of this intervention was *Hinab-Hinauf* (roughly equals 'To the depths, to the heights'), a 13½-minute, Schopenhauerian meditation in sound, light, and space originally intended to repeat continuously throughout the exposition.

For the 1970 World Exposition in Osaka Stockhausen will compose the project *Hinab-Hinauf*. It is a model of musical, visual and sculptural-environmental *(raumplastisch)* integration. . . . The work lasts 13 minutes, 31 seconds. The title 'Hinab-Hinauf' signifies a dynamic movement passing continuously through 8 levels of consciousness of appearance and experience. Beginning with bright, exalted, nameless happenings, a first phase of concerted light, sound and spatial movement leads through a panorama of abstract forms, then technical-objective images, then living-organic forms, then surreal and dreamlike, then fauna and flora, then mineral and inorganic images through to the unimaginable level of the atoms. In subsequent phases, sound, light, and spatial movements diverge more or less from one another, passing independently through the various levels, meeting again from time to time and ultimately coming together in a long, contrapuntal upward movement out of the deepest sphere of dead and lifeless things, finally reaching the highest attainable level, a region of calm, pure, lasting brightness of sound and light. . . .

Spontaneous play within the set pattern is an absolutely essential and profitable aspect of the work, guaranteeing—within determined limits—that the music will vary over a period of months in a vital process of development, and not fossilize into a static object. . . .

It will be evident that the visual composition—like the music—combines a *determined* sequential framework, in strictly synchronized, polyphonic, and contrapuntal relationship with the music, with *variable* and constantly regenerating elements of play: tape and film running to programme in uninterrupted synchronization, and the chosen interpreters at musical and visual instruments playing within the programmed sequence, influencing, transforming, and remodelling it from one moment to the next.[1]

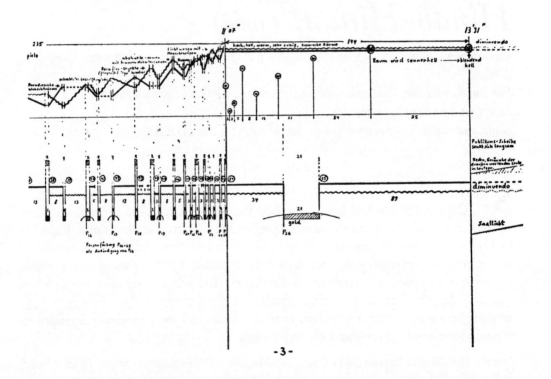

('Flying carpets—ha ha!')

p. 3 from sketch score

[1] *Texte III*, pp. 155–8.

The sketch score, reproduced in full in *Texte III*, was completed in the month after the above text was written. Its scant three pages are notated in a manner resembling *Mikrophonie I*, and the score is separated into 'image-production' and 'image-projection' systems in a similar way. The whole work is simply proportioned to a Fibonacci duration-series, and is effectively based on a multiple conjunction of opposites—dark-light, low-high, silence-sound—drawn together and given immediacy by a continuum of recorded images expressing the spectrum of human perceptions. This sort of integration of sound, light, and feeling, though latent in many of his earlier works—the polished, spotlighted sun-tamtam of *Kontakte* or *Momente*, for instance, or the dark verbal imagery of *Mikrophonie II*—emerges strongly in the *Aus den Sieben Tagen* texts, but in *Hinab-Hinauf* is co-ordinated for the first time in a regular musical structure. There is obviously enormous scope for further adventure in this largely uncharted territory, even if the ideal apparatus envisaged for Expo '70 is unlikely to be readily available outside a television studio. A reminder of the work's audo-visual synthesis may be found in the violet scenario of *Trans*; but by the time of *Alphabet für Liège* Stockhausen seems to have discarded the idea of an intellectual conjunction of visual and musical *images* in favour of studying their interaction as substance.

Spiral

1968: No. 27, UE 14957

For a soloist with short-wave receiver.
Duration indeterminate.
Recorded by Michael Vetter (amplified recorder) on Wergo 325/HÖR ZU SHZW 903 BL. Michael Vetter (amplified recorder): another version, also Harald Bojé (electronium): 'Nuits de la Fondation Maeght' (St. Paul)—France (two versions), and by Heinz Holliger (oboe) on DGG 2561109. Peter Eötvös (electrochord, Japanese bamboo flute, and short-wave receiver); Harald Bojé (electronium and short-wave receiver): both versions on EMI Electrola IC 165–02 313/14 (Germany) (2-record set).

THE composition of *Spiral* arose from a request from a young American guitarist, which accounts for the nice distinction in subtitling between *Solo*, 'for a melody instrument', and *Spiral*'s 'for one performer' (later emended to 'for a soloist'). Provision for a harmonic instrument is a special feature of *Spiral*, but the change of emphasis from instrument to person is even more interesting, and may be explained in the first instance as an effect of Stockhausen's meditative texts.

Spiral brings to the plain arithmetical notation of *Prozession* and *Kurzwellen* a supplementary vocabulary of performer-orientated signs, and a flamboyance of style both of which create new expressive ambiguities (and tautologies) in the notation—and in consequence allow a greater subtlety of interplay between performer and music than the two previous pieces. Indeed the piece is much more improvisatory, and more reflective, than either them or *Solo*.

The supplementary signs, some restored from *Prozession*, others derived from *Solo*, fall generally into groups of four, and may be categorized as follows:

1. *Intensification of material* (non-development)

OR . .	(ornament)	intensifying duration	D
POLY .	(polyphonic)	intensifying register	R
PER . .	(periodic) . . .	intensifying inner structure	G
E . .	(echo) . . .	highlighting intensity—loudness	I(L)

2. *Non-linear transformations* (performer-centred)

    'Expand' in all dimensions;   linear equivalent $+$
    'Contract' in all dimensions; . . . equivalent $-$
    'Repeat' an element from the previous event; alternate it from time to time with another element . . . . . . equivalent $=$
    ('Spiral-sign') Repeat the previous event several times, each time transposing it in all dimensions, transcending the previous limits of your skill and the known capabilities of your instrument/voice . . . . . equivalent $\pm$ [1]

3. *Diffusion of material* (partial development)

    . . . Repeat previous event as often as indicated, retrospective applying the given sign each time.
    . . . Recollection of previous event.
    . . . Projection of following event.[2]
    anticipatory

PERM-POLY   . . Transform a permutation of the previous sequence into polyphonic continuity (quasi feedback overlay).

To these three groups of signs may be added a final group of two:

4. *'Freeze' signs* (semi-automatic)
  (AKK)   vertical 'fix':

[1] The combination $\pm$ may be applied simultaneously to *one* parameter.

[2] Until the sign is reached it cannot be acted upon, so the anticipation must be effected in terms of previously determined material.

> 'Make the previous note-succession into an arpeggio or chord played in the rhythm of the previous event.

(BAND)   horizontal 'fix':

> 'Play parts of the previous event singly, then in a chosen sequence, so fast that they blur into a band of sound'[3]

From time to time special emphasis is laid on particular types of event. Here too a selection of four signs is available: P (points), Gr (groups), M (mass texture), and a mixture ('Mix') of two or all three of the other categories.

Of all the signs in this new array, the most provocative is certainly the 'spiral sign' inviting the performer to go beyond the limits set by the piece. This has widely been misread as symptomatic of a supposed conversion to Indian mysticism: an injunction to 'do the impossible'. But Stockhausen's Indian phase simply represents a change of outward profile and mode of communication; his patterns of thought—including both his expressive and procedural objectives, and also his desire to establish a co-operative relationship with his interpreters—remain much the same as before.[4] From the outset, remembering his frustrated efforts at synthesizing a 'Klangatom' with inadequate equipment in Paris in 1952, his music has been consistently informed by a sense of the limits imposed by technical and compositional procedure. Now, as then, it is the self-mortification of the serial composer that speaks, not the frustration of impotence. What the sign says in effect, is 'break out of your hitherto forced dependence on short-wave material. Until now you and your instrument have been acting as servants of external signals over which you have no control and which you cannot anticipate. Now you are free to draw on the store of experience and inspiration you have accumulated through adhering strictly to the rules of the piece.' It is most important to see the 'transcendental' invocations in context; they do not refer to the performer's technique in isolation. Such moments are not therefore opportunities to 'drop out' or 'freak out', but restore the balance between technique and expression.

In an unusually detailed introduction to the piece, Stockhausen explains with examples how the first 8 symbol-units may be interpreted. He lays great stress on the close relationship of instrumental and short-wave sound. The radio source must be 'played' like the tamtam of *Mikrophonie I*: the voice or instrument is to be considered as like a violin bow or drumstick, i.e. as a means of selecting from this store of rever-beration, rather than as an imitating or competing source. In view of the severity of such a condition, the transcendental element appears as a release, not as an added pressure.

The work's new richness of vocabulary permits a range of reciprocal formulations of a more subtle order than ever before. Not only are plus- and minus-complexes juxtaposed in familiar fashion:

---

[3] The interpretations given above offer only a broad picture, and the reader is advised to consult the score for precise specifications.

[4] The spiral sign could as easily be interpreted as the cue for a 'break' in the spirit of jazz.

—but reciprocal pairs may also be formed from different types of sign:

Paired elements or groups are frequently separated by intruding elements:

The scale of *Spiral*, as suggested by the unusual complexity of notated transformations
—a preponderance of three- and four-sign aggregates—is monumental: this is certainly one work to be played

> . . . 'mit der Gewissheit
> dass Du beliebig viel Zeit und Raum hast' *(Unbegrenzt)*

Two features of the score in particular testify to its grandeur of concept and a com-
pulsive forward urge that goes beyond the retrospective, point-to-point movement of
the earlier pieces. One is the exponential group, which may be expressed either vertically
or horizontally:[5]

Three 'exponential groups'.

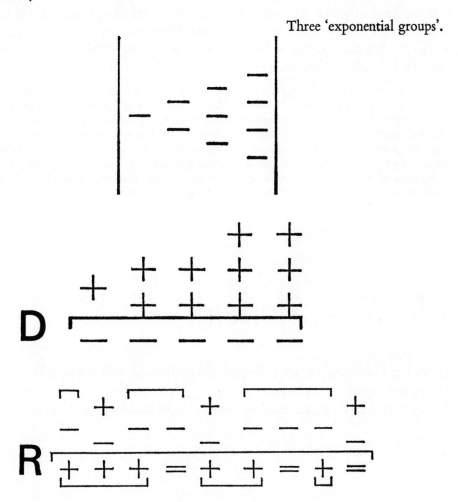

[5] The 'D-minus' succession progressively shortens the duration, i.e. concentrates and intensifies
increases in the other dimensions.

267

The other is also exponential in effect, but cyclic rather than linear; a most striking example being the following 'super-symmetry':

It is this kind of group that really deserves the 'spiral' designation. *Spiral* is Stockhausen's most closely reasoned work of the *Prozession* sequence, and exposes that intensity of will characteristic of his solo works, here given added edge by his encounter with the writings of Aurobindo.[6]

[6] An early sketch of *Spiral* is reproduced in *Texte III*, p. 138. Apart from corrections visible in the MS. itself, all the 'Mix' indications are subsequent additions. Double minus signs are added to the first of three plus signs marked 'OR' in the third system of the final score, and again after PERM→POLY at the beginning of the sixth system. The penultimate 'spiral sign' is now inverted; it is one of several evidently inserted later into the fabric of the score, confirming the composer's habit of variation by interpolation already deduced. In 1971 Stockhausen made a further tiny alteration, substituting the initial I (intensity) for L (loudness) in the bracketed group, second system. To distinguish this version from the earlier he altered the subtitle 'für einen Spieler' to 'für einen Solisten'.

Dr. K. – Sextett

1969: No. 28
For sextet: Flute, bass clarinet, piano, vibraphone/tubular bells, viola, cello.
Duration 3 minutes 28 seconds.
Commissioned by Universal Edition, London. Score held by the publishers.

IN January 1969 the London office of Universal Edition requested a number of the firm's 'house composers' to contribute a short chamber piece[1] to a birthday concert

[1] Pieces were to be playable by the Fires of London ensemble.

for the director Dr. Alfred Kalmus. *Dr. K.,* Stockhausen's contribution, is a tiny masterpiece of beguiling simplicity and subtlety: a slow-motion study of a wave, in 26 eight-second 'frames'. The piece's image of a shock wave emitted and reflected back through itself is caught in words in Stockhausen's text 'Waves' (from the collection *Für Kommende Zeiten*), though the piece antedates the poem by some 18 months.

Dr. K. is a structure of eights: eight voices, eight dynamics, eight divisions of the fundamental pulsation. The bar is treated as a fixed time-point module scanned at regular intervals at a constant speed, like the periodically renewed image on an oscilloscope screen. This basic duration is subdivided graphically into units forming a logarithmic series, corresponding at first to a notated ritardando; its structured beat-inequality guaranteeing unity within each *ictus*-group as well as expressing the outward expansion of a wave.

Usually the surge of a wave is represented musically by the rise and fall in combined pitch and intensity of a surface melody. In this work Stockhausen has tipped the convention on its side: instead of a vertical pitch-intensity undulation relative to a horizontal pitch-plane, the wave motion of *Dr. K.* is expressed as a series of lateral displacements in time and intensity with reference to a vertical pitch-plane.

The work is written for flute, bass clarinet; vibraphone, tubular bells; viola, cello; and piano (two hands). Each part is assigned one note of an initial semitonal cluster:

Starting pitches.

o Bright tone (high register)
● Dark tone (low register)
∧ Tonal displacement upwards
∨ Tonal displacement downwards

One first hears the cluster played fortissimo, then pianissimo eight seconds later, also 'on the beat'. The strong attack signifies the wave-making shock, the weaker a state of rest, and the interval between defines the fundamental periodicity. After this brief exposition the wavelike motion becomes gradually audible as a progressive warping of the vertical surface of the original cluster. One by one, like a string of corks bobbing on the surface, the notes played by bell, vibraphone, viola, cello, piano (R.H.), bass clarinet, piano (L.H.) and flute, move away in that order from successive downbeats, bending the cluster in an arpeggio curve. This reaches its greatest degree of attenuation in the ninth bar, after which the leader bends back towards its original down-beat position, 'passing' the others still on the outward journey. Bouncing back, however, the outward time-point structure is reversed, as if reflected from the barrier of the following downbeat, and this produces an audible interference pattern between the emitted ritardando and the reflected quasi-accelerando:

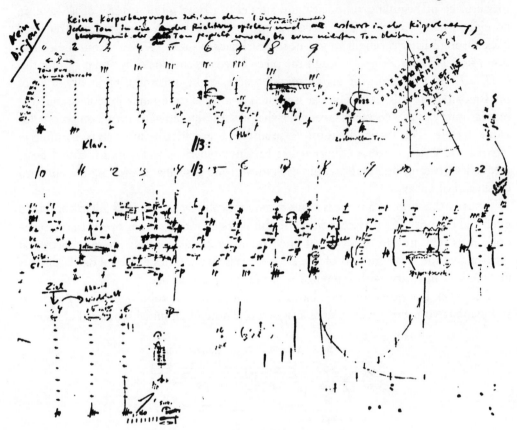

As each voice returns to its first position its intensity changes abruptly to fortissimo. By the 24th bar all eight have regrouped at the downbeat; the chord is repeated once, tenuto, as a vertical surface, then in the final, 26th bar the piece seems to go suddenly into 'fast rewind': its eight-second periodicity switching to MM=160, and the newly expanded chord shrinking and fading telescopically to a pianissimo aggregation of major and minor thirds.

Though the forward-reverse motion might appear to suggest a pendulum action, Stockhausen's pitch organization indicates a consistent non-reversible process. As each note of the original cluster is displaced in time, it shifts in pitch in a constant direction, and this upward or downward evolution persists through the return half of the cycle, just as a reflected ripple continues to expand. In this connection Stockhausen's instrumentation of the original chord shows masterly subtlety. With the exception of the two middle-register piano parts, each pair of related sonorities (flute-bass clarinet, viola-cello, vibraphone-tubular bells) comprises a treble instrument playing in its bass register and a bass instrument playing in its treble register. This means, when dynamics

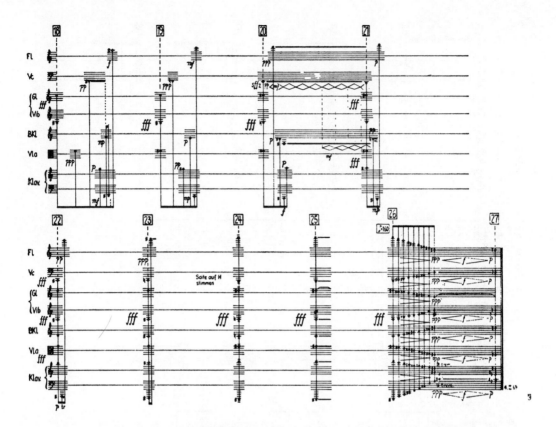

are balanced out, that those playing relatively high will tend to sound brighter than those playing relatively low, which suggests in turn that the initial cluster is in a state of compression—presumably as a result of the opening fortissimo impact—and that its subsequent dispersal is no arbitrary motion but a natural redeployment of pitches to mid-register equilibrium.

By way of adding interest to the piece's simple outline, Stockhausen has introduced a few 'deviations'. Certain pitches are unexpectedly prolonged, some repeated, others agitated by trill or tremolando. In a few cases a deliberate performance 'mistake' is built into the dynamic or time-point structure: the original sketch-plan identifies three such 'Fehler', in the seventh, eleventh, and eighteenth bars. The reader must also take his performing instructions into account, in particular the following:

> Notes short, but not staccato.
> No body movement between notes. Play each note facing in a different
> direction and hold the body rigid in the same attitude until the
> following note. The performance should *not* be conducted.

Performer-rigidity emphasizes the discontinuous structure of *Dr. K.* and helps the listener to grasp the direction of flow within each 'frame' of time and from player to player. Considerations of this sort, relating the stage behaviour of performers to the music being played, begin to appear in his music after *Telemusik* and may be attributed to his experience of the ritual formality of Japanese musical performance. Structurally, the piece itself is descended from 'Pizzicati' *(Mixtur)*, while the suggestion of sounds radiating outward conveyed in Stockhausen's performance instructions anticipates *Ylem*'s depiction of an emission process in terms of actual physical movement on the part of performers.

Fresco

1969: No. 29, UE 15147

'Wall sounds' for meditation, for four orchestra groups. One orchestra is divided by the conductor in four characteristic, mixed groups. A principal conductor and three co-conductors are required. Fresco should if possible be performed in four foyers or four different rooms of the same building.
Duration 5 hours 4 minutes.

'F RESCO' arose out of an offer to Stockhausen from the principal conductor of the Bonn Symphony Orchestra, that he take over the recently-opened Beethovenhalle for an evening of music. Funds and rehearsal time were limited, but apart from that (and a discreet hint that an event resembling *Ensemble* and *Musik für Ein Haus* would be welcome) the offer was unconditional. After composer and conductor had met and seen over the hall, which comprises a large symphony concert auditorium, two smaller salons for rehearsing (or recording) and chamber music respectively, service rooms, and inter-connecting passages allowing a reasonably fluid movement between them,

I agreed at once, and the same evening drew up a plan for four-hour non-stop performances in each of the three rooms of the Beethovenhalle (the plan remained unaltered), already hearing in my imagination orchestra musicians playing quiet 'wall sounds'—starting at the entrance, through the cloakrooms, along the lengthy foyers, from the cross-bridges leading to the balconies, right through to the entrance to the most distant studio. . . . The idea of 'wall sounds' intends no irony. What I had in mind was that for once, instead of the usual concert story the whole area from cloakroom to seat in the auditorium could be made an experience in sound, so that the listener could begin listening, if he wanted, from the moment of entry, making his own selection from a timetable placed at the entrance giving details of the three programmes to take place simultaneously in the three auditoria.[1]

This idea of enlivening the acoustic of a concert hall brings together a number of related musical images from the composer's past. The first is an image of cathedral resonance, the way in which distantly heard music draws a listener into the fold of a great church and induces a contemplative frame of mind: in this sense *Fresco*'s 'wall sounds' are designed to counteract the precise and insular tuning of a modern concert hall which focuses attention deliberately on particular areas and encourages a consciously selective mode of listening. The second is an image of transport: the feeling of excited anticipation aroused when one enters an aeroplane at hearing the hiss and hum of distant power, in the sound of air conditioning, as resonance of the machine's metal skin, and as vibration of the floor, seat; and windows: this is the emotional territory of *Carré* and *Kontakte*. A third is the image of exploration, of perceiving music dimly in an acoustic haze and then seeking it out: this is the short-wave experience of *Hymnen* and *Stop*. A fourth motive is to restore to the listener an individual sense of wonder at the concertgoing experience itself. 'Let us not only "hanker after the past"', Stockhausen remarked in his programme note, 'but let us also be on the lookout for what is to come'.

Fresco is written for four instrumental groups taken from a large symphony orchestra. Each group is directed by a conductor who may also be an instrumentalist. Since the groups are completely cut off from one another, cues are regulated in the score by clock time. The instruments of each group are not seated in conventional fashion but distributed in single file along a wall or in the angle of a corner. The constitution of each group for the first performance reflected the timbre of its leading instrument. Thus Group I, with an oboist in charge, consisted of woodwind, brass, and tuned percussion (two pedal timpani, marimba, and vibraphone) reflecting the wind and finger-action sound vocabulary of the oboe. Groups II and IV, led by harmonium and accordion (alternatively chromatic mouth organ) respectively, consisted entirely of strings, suitable for sustained complex resonance effects. Group III, originally in the charge of Aloys Kontarsky on the piano, comprised wind and string instruments but no other percussion. Each group is arranged in linear order of tessitura from low to high.

The 'wall sounds', which began before the concerts started within the auditoria, and continued after they finished—starting at 7.10 in the evening, that is, and continuing, with intermissions, until 12.40 the following morning—consist of slow, alternately rising and falling glissandi complexes in which every instrument joins, range permitting, producing an effect of movement both vast and slow, like a great

---

[1] *Texte III*, 143–4.

Form scheme

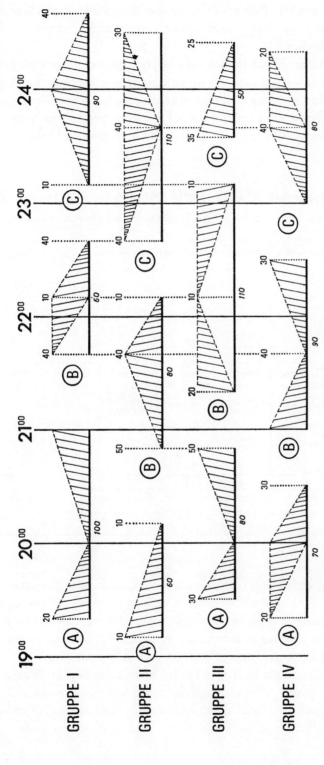

Die Musiker jeder Gruppe sitzen in einer Reihe nebeneinander an einer Foyer—Wand, auf einer Emporenbrücke oder in besonders konstruierten musikalischen Meditationsräumen (siehe Entwürfe auf dem Umschlag), der Dirigent jeder Gruppe sitzt so nah wie möglich vor den Musikern. Am besten hat jeder Musiker ein Pult. Die Dirigenten können auch zeitweilig mitspielen mit einem Instrument freier Wahl (siehe Vorschläge).

Vorschlag
für die
Aufteilung
des Orch.
und für die
Sitzordnung

I   1 Tuba – 2 Pos. – 2 Fg. – 3 Hn. – 1 Schlagz. (2 Pedalpauken, Marimba) – Dirigent (Oboe) – 2 Ob. – 2 Tp. – 2 Klar. – 2 Fl. – Vibraphon (weiche Schlegel)

II   2 Cb. – 3 Vc. – 4 Br. – Dirigent (Harmonium) – 5 Vl.II – 6 Vl.I

III   Dirigent (Klavier) – 1 Pos. – 2 Cb. – 1 Fg. – 2 Vc. – 2 Hn. – 2 Br. – 1 Ob. – 1 Tp. – 2 Vl.II – 1 Klar. – 2 Vl.I – 1 Fl. (sitzen im rechten Winkel

IV   2 Cb. – 3 Vc. – 3 Br. – Dirigent (Akkordeon oder chromatische Mundharmonika) – 4 Vl.II – 7 Vl.I

lava flow. The height or breadth of the resulting band of frequencies expands or contracts upward or downward over long periods towards one or other extreme of pitch. The basic dynamic is pianissimo.

On to this shining acoustic surface (which may be compared in effect with Stockhausen's monumental downward-sliding 'Hymunion' complex in *Hymnen*, 'Region IV') the composer has etched a variety of surface textures comparable with the various 'noises' of *Stop*. These changes are carefully graded, occur at periodic intervals, and articulate each major expansion or contraction—usually a symmetrical formation of

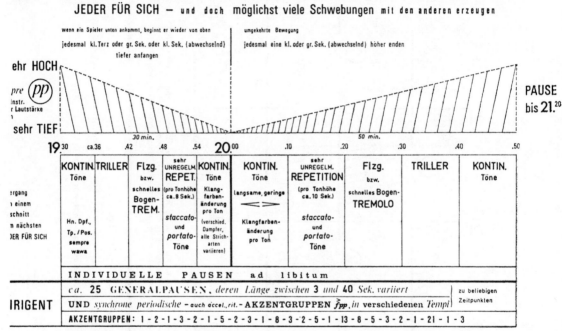

both—as a cycle of rising and falling textural complexity, peaking in the centre and fading away at either end. The pattern of textural activity so produced corresponds to the sympathetic vibration caused by the approach and retreat of a mysterious presence: like a rattling of shutters at the passing of a heavy truck, but in this case brought on by a suggested presence infinitely larger and slower-moving.

Stockhausen's outwardly simple basic material has advantages beyond being easily learned. It is unobtrusive (easily assimilated and dismissed from surface consciousness by a listener), is not difficult to sustain over long periods (an unchanging complex might eventually cause discomfort to performers), readily combines group with group and group with interior 'auditorium' performance to create perspectives of resonance and movement, and finally, as an image of 'taking off' (upward glissandi) and 'landing' (downward), it may have been calculated to arouse powerful subconscious associations.

Comparison of *Fresco*'s glissandi with the 'Hymunion' passage suggests that Stockhausen was inspired by tape-loop formations, and it is perhaps not surprising that in another respect his treatment of *Fresco*'s glissando material recalls *Solo*, another exercise in the progressive disintegration of continuous tape-loop complexes. This 'other respect' is his introduction of 'negative music' in the form of ad lib. pauses for individual players, general pauses (affecting a whole group) ever 2–4 minutes, and as frequent 'accent groups' in which the group sonority is briefly amplified as it were by the turn of a volume control. These ensemble fluctuations of amplitude sometimes recur periodically as if the total sound were being modulated by a vast carrier frequency, and reinforce the ultimate illusion of the building as a great ear: the walls acting as eardrum, and the players as a living cochlea, sensitive to sounds of unimaginable vastness and depth.[2]

Tunnel-Spiral (1969)

For sound tunnel. Project for reader, Japanese temple bells, and short-wave receiver, using a special feedback relay designed for the Los Angeles Department of Municipal Arts Junior Arts Center Sound Tunnel.
Duration unspecified.
Circuit described in outline, with sketch, in Stockhausen: Texte III, pp. 188–93.

AN INVITATION from John Mizelle of the Los Angeles Junior Arts Center, to contribute a piece for the centre's 'sound tunnel' project, led to the composition of *Tunnel-Spiral* in November 1969.

[2] Stockhausen's arrangement of instruments according to tessitura re-creates the movement in space corresponding to pitch associated with the relationship of pitch to nerve stimulation in the inner ear.

TUNNEL SPIRAL — page 3 —

The movement of sound shall be <u>spirally</u>

Jf Altec I is on the floor (Altec II as well), speaker 1 should be at the place of speaker 7, and all the numbers rotate correspondingly.

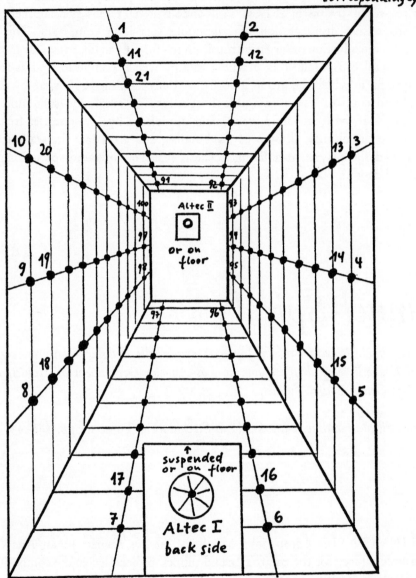

9. XI. 69   Stockhausen

It is not clear from Stockhausen's account[1] whether the 'tunnel', a rather cramped, virtually anechoic corridor (40′ × 6′ 6″ × 3′ 6″) lined with speakers, was designed for audience occupation or, as seems more likely, as a kind of acoustic shooting gallery. *Tunnel–Spiral* in any case appears to have treated the space as a telephonic aperture for speaking or listening into rather than inside; in effect, as a speaking or ear trumpet.

Stockhausen designed a fixed relay of 100 speakers to reproduce a given signal in apparent spiral rotation (the speakers are actually arranged in perpendicular ranks), at progressively increasing time-intervals. Successive delays of 1/12 sec. between speakers 1–12, increase to lapses of 1/3 sec. between speakers 90–100. To the listener standing near Speaker 1 this spiralling movement will indeed appear to expand outward like a trumpet shape, since the increasing delay appears to slow down the speed of rotation progressively and reduces the apparent amplitude of the signal.

Since he could not be at hand to test such an arrangement personally, Stockhausen kept his specifications for the sound-material simple: (1) a reading (by a deep male voice) from Sri Aurobindo's *The Synthesis of Yoga*, punctuated from time to time (2) by strokes on the *rin* (the clear, fragile-sounding Japanese temple instrument heard in *Telemusik*, three of which are specified here, tuned at semitonal intervals), (3) by sporadic short-wave signals, briefly faded up and down ('scarcely comprehensible speech') from a continuous background murmur, and (4) very occasionally by single handclaps.

To a great extent the spiral relay itself imposes a characteristic pattern on vocal delivery; experiments have shown that a speaker who hears his own voice back over earphones at a constant delay soon adopts a speaking tempo geared to the prevailing time-lapse. We may therefore assume that the excessively resonant tunnel would lead Stockhausen's speaker to adopt an incantatory style of utterance, stable in pitch and rhythm, like plainchant. Such a style is best adapted for signal penetration in a resonant environment, enabling the speaker to focus on what he is saying without becoming confused by the reflected sound of his own voice. Stockhausen adds a few specifications for the manner of delivery, aimed at giving the performance a slightly 'electronic' air:

At intervals, break off reading (this also means breaking off in the middle of a word as well), repeat individual syllables, words, [or] groups of words; occasionally sink into a rapid pro-tracted murmuring undertone (reading at speed without regard for comprehensibility, slowing down only once in a while, or bringing out isolated words).[2]

Tunnel–Spiral clearly profits from Stockhausen's experience in making *Telemusik*, and may be taken as a commentary on the time-delay effect *(Zeitverzögerung)* which was a feature of the Japanese six-track tape recorder at which most of that work was composed. He also builds on the idea of using live ritual incantation as a means of illus-trating a mechanical sound-transformation process, in this case directing the listener's attention back and forth from the sense of the spoken word to an imaginative awareness

[1] *Texte III*, pp. 190–3.
[2] *Texte III*, p. 190.

of its flow. The work also coincides, however, with Stockhausen's increasing attention to the interaction of his music with an external environment—his remarkable series of concerts in the Jeita caves of Lebanon took place a matter of weeks after this work was composed—and anticipates to some extent the gyrations of sound planned for the spherical pavilion of Expo '70, for which Stockhausen had designed his hand-cranked 'sound wheels' the previous year.

Pole für 2

1969-70: No. 30

For two soloists, optional amplification (the score includes a part for the sound distribution)
Instruments unspecified.
Duration indeterminate.
Score available from the composer.
Recorded by Harald Bojé (electronium, bokusho (Japanese temple block), and short-wave receiver); Peter Eötvös (electrochord,[1] antique cymbal, and short-wave receiver): EMI Electrola 1C 165–02 313/14 (Germany) (2-record set).

'POLE FÜR 2' and *Expo für 3* were composed at short notice to supplement Stockhausen's programmes for the German Pavilion at Expo '70 in Osaka, after the failure of his initial *Hinab-Hinauf* project to materialize. To the reader acquainted with *Spiral* the freshness and simplicity of both scores may come as a pleasant surprise. As its title suggests, *Pole* ('Poles') revives an early and favoured idea of the composer's, that of the reconciliation of opposing tendencies,[2] but two features link it more directly with *Spiral*. One is the idea that a vertical plus-minus combination may be applied simultaneously to a single parameter; the other is the notion of one-directional expansion also encountered for the first time in the working instructions to the earlier work. Exponential sequences also figure prominently in *Pole*, but in contrast to *Spiral* symmetry of evolution is tightly maintained:

[1] See note on page 199.
[2] Cf. his prescription of the relationship of the two principal structures in *Schlagtrio*, 'als Pole aufeinander begozen' (*Texte II*, p. 13).

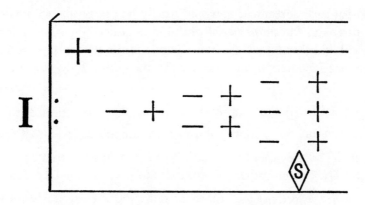

The larger plus and minus signs are an innovation, and they signify that the associated parameters are to be held at *maximum* intensity: thus the transformations indicated in smaller signs are given an unusual negative significance.

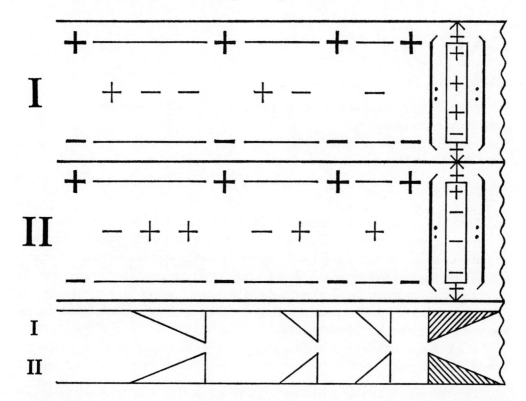

The two instrumental parts are either stabilized vertically, as shown in the second example above, or linked in a continuous horizontal array, the material oscillating from positive to negative as it passes from one part to the other. This dialogue construction presupposes a higher than usual degree of co-ordination of approach and timing. Without such agreement it would hardly be practicable to notate the sound technician's part with the symmetrical precision indicated (the supplementary system indicates spatial distribution of the two outputs over the speaker complex at the German pavilion; its notation must not be confused with *Mikrophonie I*'s filter indications).

Of interest is the peripheral, even ornamental, role assigned to *Spiral*-type symbols for expansion ⟨↔⟩, contraction →⤓←, and permutation ✳ of material. The 'Spiral-sign' itself, on the other hand, to judge by its frequent proximity to the end of a section (wavy line), seems rather paradoxically to have assumed a cadential function, to which the newer reflective signs (E) (echo) and ◇S◇ take on clearly ancillary status.[3]

Expo für 3

1969-70: No. 31

For three soloists, optional amplification: 4 players. Instruments unspecified.
Duration indeterminate.
Score available from the composer.

CLOSELY synchronized gestures and canonic imitation feature prominently in *Expo für 3*, an altogether more relaxed piece in which the relation between synchronized ensemble episodes and individual 'leads' suggests an almost jazz-like intimacy of understanding among the three players. The single page so far composed terminates with the wavy line that signifies a 'possible' ending, but the score begins with a repeat sign, and this and the relatively uncomplicated structure of the page suggest that a further extension of the piece is not out of the question.

A combination of factors give *Expo* its agreeably cheerful appearance. One is the hybrid sign language used, in which conventional verbal indications and notated

---

[3] The score of *Pole für 2* is also reproduced in *Texte III* (on page 230). At the end of 1971 a few slight modifications were made. In part II, first system, immediately following the second ◇ sign, two plus signs have been superimposed on the two-minus aggregation. A short distance further on, following part I's first 'Spiral-sign', the number of equal signs in both parts is increased to three, the third in part I remaining ornamented (OR). A final detail is the addition of a trill/tremolo superscription to the minus sign just before the second spiral sign in the second system of part II.

rhythms, accents, and dynamics appear along with plus-minus signs for the first time. Another factor is the simplicity of the arithmetically-notated successions, which revert from the complexities of *Spiral* to mainly one- and two-sign aggregates. Yet another feature is the unusually individual characterization of each of the three parts, which suggests they were composed with particular performers in mind.[1] Of the three, player III emerges as clear leader, moreover one with a sense of humour. His rhythmic leads into the piece's two radio 'inserts' read like scarcely-veiled quotes from *Kreuzspiel*:

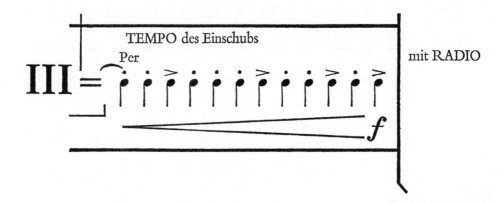

—while in an extraordinary sequence later on there is a distinct suggestion of self-parody:

Just how a player sustains quadruple minuses for such a length of time, while remaining principal voice, is bound to lead to amused perplexity. Here and elsewhere, opportunities to 'comment' upon one another's material, and in imitative and exponential sequences, to 'agree' or 'disagree' with the musical ideas in circulation, give the score a lively wit. The present ending, with all three players playing individually as fast as possible, then abruptly synchronizing for a seven-times-repeated in-tempo 'cadence' followed by a throwaway gesture from player II, suggests an exuberance and mock-heroic finality reminiscent of Satie:

[1] Which of course they were.

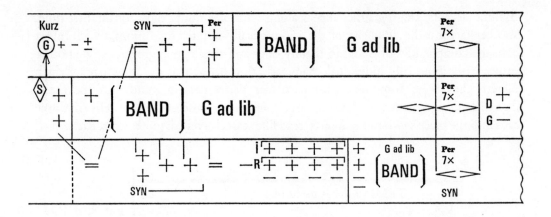

Mantra

1970: No. 32

For 2 pianists, short-wave radio or tape of short-wave sounds, ring-modulators, woodblocks and antique cymbals: 1 assistant for sound projection.
Duration 65 minutes.
Recorded by Alfons and Aloys Kontarsky, on DGG 2530 208.

'MANTRA' is a masterpiece. It defines Stockhausen's musical aims in the seventies as surely as *Mikrophonie I*, another superbly focused work, sums up his preoccupations of the previous decade. In *Mikrophonie I* Stockhausen addressed himself to the tactile associations of sound, and to the achievement of exactly defined musical aims by flexible means: a line of approach common to works as diverse as *Stop*, *Kurzwellen*, and *Aus den Sieben Tagen*. With *Mantra* for two pianos, modulators, and incidental percussion, this order of priorities is abruptly reversed. It still seeks to represent a vision of harmony embracing diversity, but its method and terms of reference are far removed from those of the work for tamtam. *Mikrophonie I* is sensual, passive, and analytic; as its instrumentation suggests, *Mantra* is objective, active, and synthetic.

It is not concerned as much with feeling as with articulation. There is a coolness and reserve in the composer's return to the neutral sonority of the piano, to the world of equal temperament and to a rigorously conventional notation, using verbal, not metronomic tempo indications, including grace notes but no 'irrational' note values (i.e. triplet, quintolet, etc.).

Structurally, the work returns to the crystalline ideal of the fifties, according to which every aspect of a work's form, from the smallest detail to the overall shape, ought to be derivable from one basic serial configuration. On a more technical level, *Mantra* takes up again the continuity problem also tackled in *Mikrophonie I*: the problem of making successive episodes in electronic or mixed works flow into one another more naturally, so as not to have to rely on the artificial convention of added reverberation. Whereas *Mikrophonie I* is held together by continuity of gesture and timbre, *Mantra* considers the deeper issue of establishing a viable continuity between instrumental and electronic sound.

Formidable as these prescriptions appear, *Mantra* is fresh and immediately appealing as music. Its very simplicity is hard to adjust to. Where else, other than in the new opening measures of *Momente 1972* (moment i(k), dating from the same period as *Mantra*) do we find Stockhausen's beat so even, his rhythms so regular, his manner so relaxed and conversational? It is in these most obvious features, the way the piece flows, and the way the piano timbre swings back and forth between steely clarity and a kaleidoscope of novel tone colours and sonorities, that the work's true originality resides.

The music follows no programme, but may reasonably be described as a trip into an expanded world of sound, systematically exploring a cycle of harmonic spectra through which the piano timbre is electronically refracted. The mantra, or basic formula, is a pattern of notes, inflections, and intensities by which this exploration process is regulated; it is also the sole form of musical utterance by which the resulting harmonies are constantly invoked.

After a certain level of consciousness it is no longer ideas that one sees and tries to translate. *One hears.* There are literally vibrations or waves, rhythms which lay hold of the seeker, invade him, then clothe themselves with words and ideas or with music, colours, in their descent. But the word or the idea, the music, the colour, is the result, a secondary effect; they just give a body to that first terribly imperious vibration. And if the poet, the true one, corrects and recorrects, it is not to improve upon the form, as one says, or to express himself better, but to catch that vibrating thing—and if the true vibration is not there, all his magic crumbles, as that of the Vedic priest who has badly pronounced the mantra of the sacrifice.[1]

One hears. This is the point, a lesson (one might say) of *Stimmung*'s composure and *Aus den Sieben Tagen*'s concentrated meditation: no more a sense of striving for the unknown, instead a striving for precision, 'right saying'.

At the outset, one hears the mantra compressed into a brief fanfare of four chords.

[1] Programme note, English Bach Festival, 1971.

After a pause, it is restated in full by the first piano, the right hand playing the mantra, the left hand an inverted form. The whole work grows from this kernel of rhythm and interval, of image and reflection. The flourishes on antique cymbals marking successive statements of the mantra follow the original sequence of pitches (A–B–G sharp—E . . .), for instance; so do the repeated-note ostinati passed from one piano to the other throughout a long passage immediately following the introduction. Transformations of the mantra always begin and end on the note A. Consistency and explicitness of invention are sustained throughout, making *Mantra* both a reassuring piece to listen to, and also enabling the listener to recognize Stockhausen's terms of reference easily, and follow the piece's argument without too much difficulty.

These transformations of the mantra involve not only extension and compression of the original proportions in time, but also magnification of its intervallic dimensions. The original mantra compresses the pitch series into the smallest possible compass of a major seventh interval. A series of expansions enlarges the mantra progressively until at maximum magnification it occupies half of the piano keyboard (leaving the lower half free for its corresponding inversion). A Stravinskian passage in dotted rhythms heard early in the piece represents a modestly expanded form. It is followed soon after by an example at maximum expansion, which sounds very like the Boulez of *Structures*, Book I, No. Ia. *Mantra* is rich in such unintended allusion. There is a distinctly Schoenbergian sound to the original unadorned mantra itself, which at first hearing sent this listener scrambling for his copy of Schoenberg's piano piece Op. 11, No. 2:

Less fortuitous, perhaps, is the superficial resemblance of *Mantra*'s palette of piano timbres to the curious sounds of John Cage's prepared piano, about which Stockhausen had expressed guarded approval long before in 1957:

More than anything else Cage astonishes his listeners in that he—the pupil of Schoenberg—has combined the development of a personal musical language with the reconstruction of sound material, instruments, and musical performance. Thus he invented the 'prepared piano'; whereby various materials such as rubber, wood, and metal screws are fixed between the piano strings. . . . The result of such preparation is that the piano sound changes significantly (certain overtones suppressed, others enhanced, the attack sounding muffled or metallic, etc.). It is significant that a composer should undertake himself preparation of the sounds for a composition, to some extent composing the timbres along with the music, as far as that may be achieved with instruments already in existence.[2]

Though deeply impressed by Cage's idea, Stockhausen was unimpressed by his method of synthesizing timbres, and the Modul 69B modulator circuit he devised for *Mantra* cannot fairly be said to derive from Cage's rustic invention. For one thing, Stockhausen's circuit gives altogether superior results: it is more flexible, better controlled, and free of the dynamic inconsistencies which debilitate the prepared piano sound. For another, the specialized nature of Stockhausen's invention, and its evolution out of ten years of research with ring-modulated instrumental sound, entitle it to be recognized as an original discovery. Indeed, the characteristic harmonic polarization of live instrumental sound, which is the circuit's outstanding feature, is already indicated in the scores of *Mixtur* and *Mikrophonie II*, long before the Modul 69B was invented. In 'Spiegel' of *Mixtur*, and on page 1 of *Mikrophonie II*, 'live' instrument or voice parts move in and out of consonance with the electronic modulating pitches in such a way as to suggest that the moments of true consonance were expected to sound louder and clearer by mutual reinforcement. But because the 'live' sound is unsteady, and the circuit primitive, the desired effect is obliterated in these pieces by a dazzle of sum and difference tones. *Mantra*'s cleaner sound results from Stockhausen's addition of a compressor and a filter to the ring-modulating circuit, suppressing the rogue 2nd and 3rd harmonics of the modulated consonance, and filtering out the high frequency halo generated by the piano.

In each of the 13 large cycles of the work, each pianist introduces a sine tone, corresponding each time to the central note around which all the mantra-transformations are centred. The first pianist presents the upper 13 notes of the mantra in succession, and the second pianist the lower 13 notes, that is, the mantra-mirror.

Each first and thirteenth note of each recurrence of the mantra are thus identical to the mirroring sine tone; hence they sound completely consonant, and thus completely 'natural'—like piano notes; and depending on the intervallic remoteness of the remaining mantra notes from the mirror note of the ring modulation, the modulated sound sounds more or less unlike the piano (minor seconds, and similarly minor ninths and major sevenths, produce the most 'dissonant' modulator sounds, octaves and fifths the most 'consonant'). Hence one perceives a continual 'respiration' from consonant to dissonant to consonant modulator-sounds.[3]

By using two pianists Stockhausen is able to balance exposition (increasing differentiation) and reconciliation (harmonization), analysis and synthesis, static and dynamic elements simultaneously. The familiar conjunction of opposites is expressed not only in the reciprocal relationship of the two piano parts, but also in the relationship of each piano part with its electronic transformation. This latter symmetry is beautifully expressed at fig. 110, where a slow descent in the piano II part is followed by a slow rise in the piano I part, each accompanied by its electronic mirror-image.

[2] *Texte II*, p. 147.
[3] Sleeve note, DGG recording.

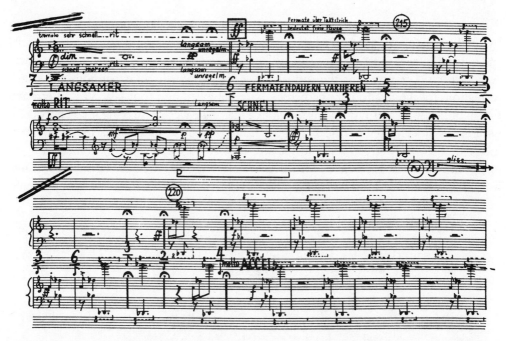

Stockhausen has described working on *Mantra* as 'the happiest composition time I have ever spent in my life'. Time and again the composer's high spirits bubble to the surface: in the Zen-like target practice at fig. 212, for instance, which comes back again at the end of the piece, climaxing with the 'Yo-ho!' shout in imitation of Noh percussionists; or fig. 329, where he mimics the sound of a studio-manipulated tape-loop, with a woodblock acting as off-on switch.

There is high exultation at fig. 421, a passage of gigantic chords, scanned back and forth by spotlight sine-waves, from which highlighted tones, marking points where artificial and natural pitches meet, leap out of the sustained piano resonance as if freshly struck. A concentrated reprise near the end of the work, in which 'all expansions and trans-formations (of the mantra) are gathered, extremely fast, into four layers', is interesting first in obliterating all rhythmic distinctions other than accents (making it an equivalent, in terms of Stockhausen's article '. . . how time passes . . .', to a 'subharmonic' mirror-image of the major structure), and second, in that the expression 'extremely fast' no longer means 'as fast as possible'. Effortlessly the passage lifts itself above measured time, its two halves interlocking and closing like a zip fastener around the work's perimeter.

Both *Mantra* and *Telemusik* were composed in Japan (*Mantra* was completed in Kürten) and it is tempting to draw a connection between the elation of both works and the exhilarating effect of the Japanese environment. We may be sure, in any case, that the spiritual associations of *Mantra*, like the 'world view' of the earlier work, arise from the composer's identification of the alien convention as a mystical formula-tion of his personal composing experience. In *Mantra* the point of contact is formal rather than aural: the mantra may be identified as a transcendental expression of Stockhausen's tape-loop, itself the image of a musical seed, a complete work com-pressed into a single cycle (cf. 'The Concept of Unity in Musical Time'). The mantra is more distantly prefigured in the Schoenbergian note series; a prayer itself, it retro-spectively endows a prayerful disposition on those extremely abstract serial composi-tions of the early fifties in whose company *Mantra* belongs.

As a study in musical temperament and harmonic relationships *Mantra* could also be classified, with *Stimmung* and *Sternklang*, as a work of Stockhausen's 'Helmholtz' phase. It may be objected that Stockhausen's system of electronically tempering the piano corresponds to a return to the hierarchical principal of classical tonality. That *Mantra* offers a new perspective on tonality and tonal modulation cannot be denied, but it would be rash to conclude that the work marks a turning away from serialism: it is, after all, a serial composition. However, *Mantra* certainly extends Stockhausen's sphere of influence back into the past, strengthening the links between his music and similar researches into the mathematics of sound vibration as practised in the eighteenth century and as far back as the Renaissance. But this greater range is a consequence, let us remember, not simply of higher illumination but also of the higher polish and superior technology of the work itself.

Sternklang

1971: No. 34

Park music for 5 groups, each of 4 players (instruments and/or singers) and a percussionist, with optional amplification. Instrumentation unspecified.
Duration at least 3 hours.
Recorded by D.G.G. Polydor (Hamburg).

That expression which modern music endeavours to attain by various discords and an abundant introduction of dominant sevenths, was obtained in the school of Palestrina by the much more delicate shading of various inversions and positions of consonant chords. This explains the harmoniousness of these compositions, which are nevertheless full of deep and tender expression, and sound like the songs of angels with hearts affected but undarkened by human grief in their heavenly joy. Of course such pieces of music require fine ears both in singer and hearer, to let the delicate gradation of expression receive its due, now that modern music has accustomed us to modes of expression so much more violent and drastic.

Hermann Helmholtz.

'STERNKLANG' is a vision of celestial harmony, translating the peaceful inner resonances of *Stimmung* into a park setting 'during the warm summer weather, under a clear starry sky, preferably at a time of full moon'. Five groups of players, who may be voices or instruments in any balanced combination, are distributed in planetary fashion around a central percussionist—a formation reminiscent of *Momente* (which Stockhausen was also completing at the time). Since 1968 (1967 if one includes *Ensemble*) his interest in multiple-group performance 'environments' had noticeably revived, giving practical expression to the signalling potential encoded with increasing refinement throughout the early and mid-sixties. With *Stimmung* and *Aus den Sieben Tagen* in 1968, however, one detects a meditative, more outwardly receptive style emerging: the musical persona becomes a listener rather than a signaller, and it is at this point that Stockhausen begins to move his musical performances beyond the physical confines of the concert hall and into the open. Late 1969 marks an important period for this line of development, starting with an evening-long performance of *Unbegrenzt* in the open in St. Paul de Vence in July, during which three versions of *Spiral* were performed. This was followed by the first performance of *Fresco* as part of the simultaneous Beethovenhalle concert in mid-November, and the series of open-air concerts scarcely a fortnight later in the massive Jeita caves in Lebanon, which included performances of *Spiral*, *Kurzwellen*, *Stimmung*, *Intensität*, *Setz die Segel zur Sonne*, *Telemusik*, and *Hymnen mit Solisten*.

The translation of works as concentrated in feeling as these into the open has the effect of altering their original focal length, and with it their function, from the production of individual and sharply focused images to the generation of a larger collective response, attuned not only to the object of contemplation but also to the resonant character of the environment. The music springs out of a collectively sensed intuition and mediates between the participants and their immediate setting in place and time. Superimposed on the common resonance, which may be *Stimmung*'s harmonic spectrum, or *Fresco*'s ensemble glissandi, or *Unbegrenzt*'s common expressive tendency—one is able to discern individual modulations which, like the disturbances of *Refrain*, reveal the individual as a more or less independently articulate particle.

The composition of *Sternklang* in 1971 as Stockhausen's first work specifically designed for out-of-doors performance, thus followed a period of thorough practical research and experimentation. A park planted with trees (the first performance took place in the English Gardens of the Berliner Tiergarten) is acoustically absorbent, ruling out a music completely dependent on environmental resonance and group-to-group signals. Stockhausen combines two principles from *Stimmung* and *Fresco* in a plan for isolated pools of resonance distributed around the park, related by tuning, orientation, and activity as in *Stimmung*, and also by a gradual elevation of harmonic focus, a dynamic ingredient adapted from *Fresco*. In general each of the five satellite groups harmonizes independently on a given pitch-combination in a manner similar to *Stimmung* (greater sound-penetration assured by the provision of alternate pitches for siren-type oscillations). Using the note material prescribed, performers take turns in leading their groups in intoning the names and vowel constituents of zodiacal constellations. Instruments imitate the notated voice modulations by analogous variations in timbre—a procedure shown by the trombonist Vinko Globokar to be feasible for brass instruments at least. The 'constellation names' take the place of *Stimmung*'s 'magic names'. As in the earlier work, when a group reaches satisfactory cohesion the leader gives a sign to move on to the next notated name and note-combination. This freedom of timing creates problems for inter-group co-ordination which cannot be solved, as in *Fresco*, by reference to clock-time. Co-ordination in *Sternklang* is achieved in three ways, (1) by group-to-group signalling followed by a general pause (like the follow-my-leader signalling in *Prozession*), (2) by reference to the central percussionist, who from time to time articulates a beat-frequency which can be heard by all (again derived from *Prozession*), and (3), by selected participants *running* the circuit from group to group, bearing new pitch and text material. This last device has considerable charm: 'I am the postman who is bringing the mail without knowing what is in the letters,' says the composer,[1] and indeed the spectacle of torch-bearing runners wearing *Sternklang* T-shirts singing as they wend through darkened groves does strike a nostalgic chord of remembered youthful idealism. But sentiment should not obscure the fact that the runners also serve a useful musical purpose, given the peculiar demands of the work, first as a means of regulating the tuning between groups, and second as a means of rotating events somewhat in the manner of *Carré*. Fig. 35, in which runners from all five groups rotate all five basic harmonies simultaneously, is a splendid example of the latter effect.

    Sternklang's use of five harmonic spectra, tuned to a common e′ − 330, is an innovation perhaps suggested by *Mantra*'s technique of harmonic polarization. As in *Stimmung* (as also, if one looks further into the past, in Schoenberg's 'Farben', Op. 16, No. 3), the music lays great stress on accurate intonation, and this in turn implies a choice of style and instrumentation both sensitive and adaptable to microtonal adjustments of pitch. As may be seen from the diagram, *Sternklang*'s pitches diverge frequently from ordinary equal temperament:

Some idea of the refinement of intonation required for individual notes may be gauged from a comparison of the appropriate frequencies with their nearest equal-tempered equivalents:

[1] Interview, Tony Palmer, *Sunday Times* colour supplement, 11 March 1973, p. 50.

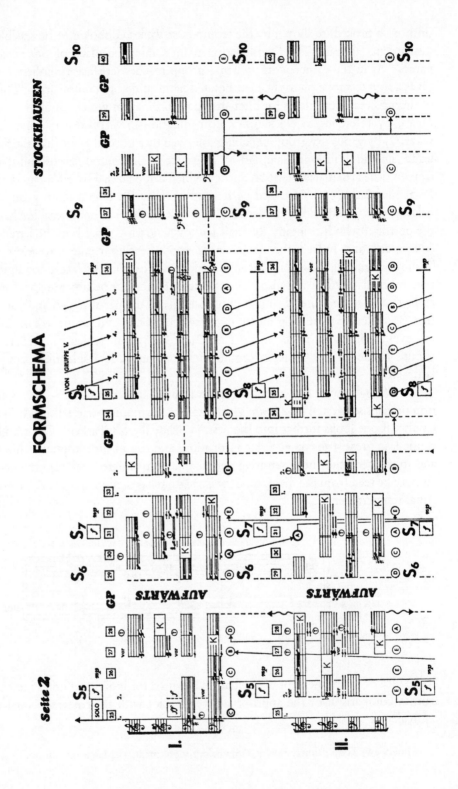

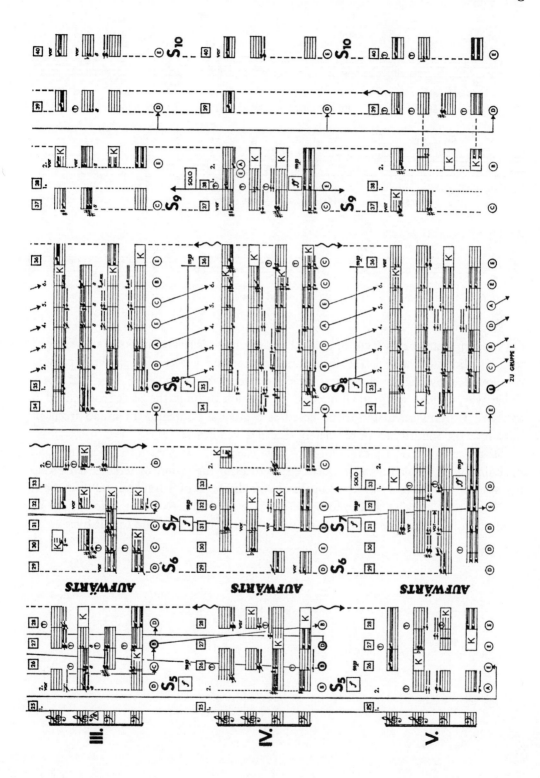

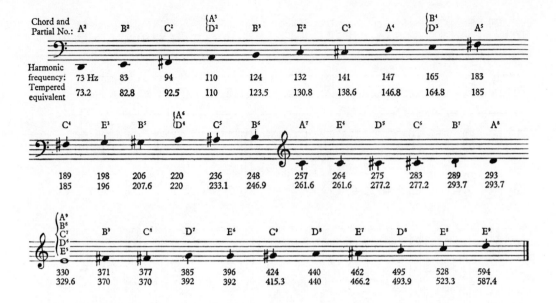

On modern instruments favouring equal temperament 'sharper' intonations will tend to sound brighter, and 'flatter' intonations darker and less certain, qualities perhaps compounded by the psychological effects of 'forcing' or 'holding back' the tone. Either way, *Sternklang*'s gradual upward progression through the piece from chord A to chord E seems calculated to be heard as a gradual lightening of mood from an initially 'dark' sonority to an ultimately elevated 'brightness'.

Stockhausen's model incantations for *Sternklang* are also structured to correspond in timing with the harmonic frequency structures of the sound material. Each group has a set of six 'models' representing harmonic divisions of a fundamental pulsation: MM=16, 18, *c.* 20.6, 24, and 29 for groups I–V respectively. As with the note material, a common frequency, here MM=144, serves as tempo-co-ordinate for all five:

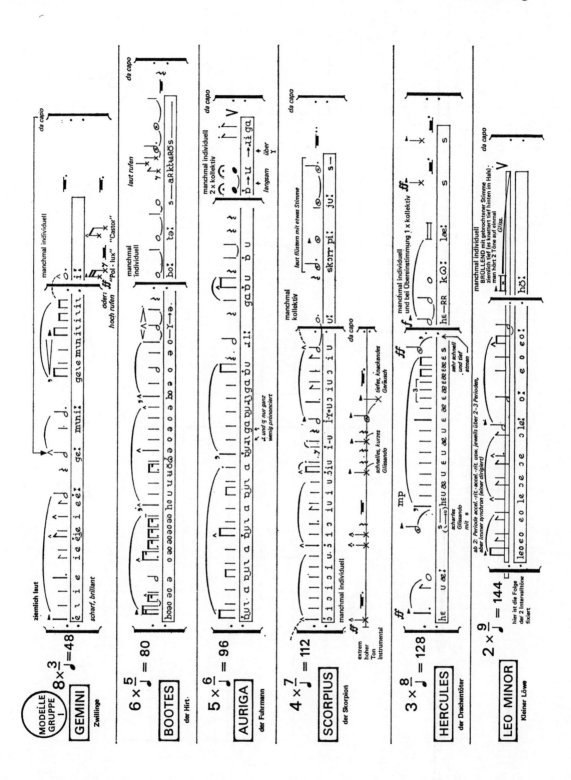

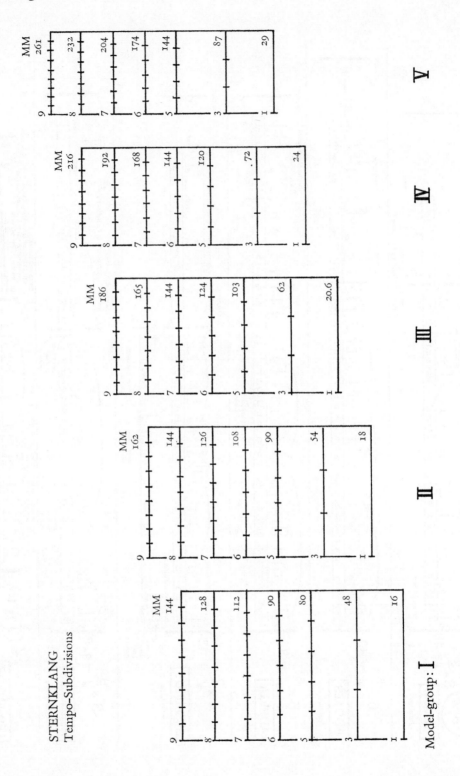

STERNKLANG
Tempo-Subdivisions

Model-group: I

Each fundamental tempo unit in turn, by cyclic repetition, is also revealed as an harmonic partial of an overall fundamental frequency, a cycle of 60 seconds' duration:

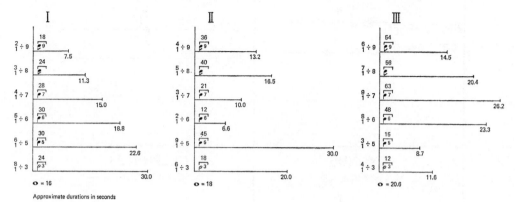

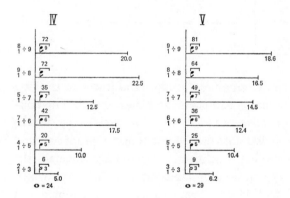

Sternklang's harmonic structure can thus be seen as an exceedingly subtle and far-reaching network of proportional relationships affecting both pitch and duration values. With present-day metronomic devices tempo-refinements of this order are perfectly feasible.

At sections marked 'K' in the score performers leave intoning the *names* of constellations and sing or play their *shapes* in the heavens as drawn by the composer, *Zyklus*-fashion, on a separate page:

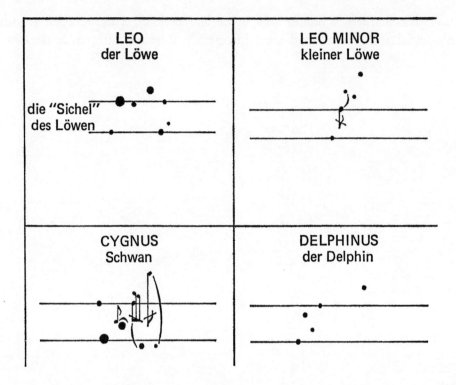

The two-line 'stave' on which each is drawn signifies the upper and lower of the two pitches being played or sung when the constellation-image is introduced. The constellation Leo, Stockhausen's birth-sign, appears twice: once as seen facing northwards, the other from a south-facing viewpoint. Leo Minor is also reproduced, and in its name-invocation (as a Group I model) Stockhausen ingeniously dovetails the final syllable of 'Leo' with the Noh-percussionist's climactic 'Yo-ho!' cry, which having already appeared in *Telemusik* and *Mantra*, seems to have been adopted as a kind of musical signature.

Trans

1971: No. 35

For orchestra. The orchestra is divided into four wind/percussion groups, and strings with organ.
Group I.   4 Flutes, bass clarinet; celesta; 5 small cymbals (1 player).
Group II. 4 Oboes; trombone with fourth valve; vibraphone, cow-bell, 2 cymbals, one Turkish (1 percussionist).
Group III. 4 Clarinets (B flat); bassoon, double bassoon; tubular bells and 2 Chinese gongs (1 player).
Group IV. 4 Trumpets (B flat); tuba; 3 tomtoms, 1 tenor drum, tamtam, military side-drum (1 percussionist). Strings 22.8.6.4; 1 electronic organ.
Duration c. 25 minutes
Score available from the composer.

'MANTRA' began with a dream, and ends with a symbolic awakening (to an alarum of small cymbals). But Stockhausen is dreaming again in *Trans*, a twenty-five-minute work for four orchestral groups, strings, and electronic organ, which translates a vision of the mysterious violet luminosity of approaching dawn[1] into a Debussyan panorama of transparent, shifting sonorities, suggesting auroral patterns against a background of starlight, through which small signals of awakening life can be heard.

It is a work which almost asks to be performed in a planetarium: indeed, its audio-visual style belongs under the same dome as *Hinab-Hinauf*. But for a more conventional setting Stockhausen has devised a scenario of the kind popularly associated with television entertainment. Behind a sheer curtain drawn across the proscenium, and bathed in violet light, sit the string players in two tiers: violins in the centre supported on either side by the lower instruments. The arrangement may be likened to that of a salon orchestra, to which it also corresponds in balance (22.8.6.4) and distribution. It is a formation calculated for the production of homogeneous background textures; here its function is to provide a transparent acoustic screen, and a visual barrier, between the audience and the four wind and percussion groups stationed behind. Stockhausen is concerned to make his music sound ethereal, and indeed very little performing action is directly visible. The string players, whose music consists entirely of greatly attenuated, intangible chromatic aggregations, hardly move; to help them to keep still in the first performance violins and violas were in fact provided with left arm supports.

[1] His account (in conversation with Jonathan Cott) of the colour as 'warm, reddish-violet' also suggests a memory of ante-natal existence (presumably in a spherical auditorium).

Each of the four instrumental groups concealed behind the strings is likewise composed as a single timbre, and consists of three 'formants': four of a high wind instrument representing the upper partials or 'chroma', a solo bass wind as 'fundamental', and a small middle-register percussion group for colouring and consonantal articulation. Group I, four flutes, bass clarinet, celesta, and five small cymbals—is tuned high and 'impalpable' (to use Messiaen's adjective); Group II (oboes, trombone, vibraphone, cowbell, and two large cymbals, one Turkish) is more penetrating and slightly lower in tessitura; Group III (B flat clarinets, bassoon *and* contrabassoon, tubular bells, and two Chinese gongs) is a hollower combination sound, lower still in register, while Group IV (B flat trumpets, tuba, three tomtoms, military side-drum, and two tamtams, one very large) transposes the ensemble timbre down to the lower limit of audibility. The effective tessitura of each group is indicated by both the range and harmonic richness of wind, and by the pitch and definition of percussion sounds, which descend from Group I's crystalline pitches and hiss resonances, to Group IV's soft labial thuds and indefinite hummings.

Stockhausen's instrumentation is very similar to *Spiel für Orchester* in its delineation and occupation of registral spaces, but stylistically the music of *Trans* pursues the path indicated by *Stimmung* and *Sternklang* towards a reconciliation of sonority—a new refinement of collective intonation—with the active delineation of form. Like *Mantra*, the piece is concerned with certainties rather than probabilities, and its return to classical notation and mensuration, in eliminating a major source of performer apprehension both creates an atmosphere of emotional detachment and emphasizes his expressive preoccupation with states of awareness rather than physical activity. In this respect *Trans* differs from a work such as *Third Region of Hymnen with Orchestra*, the more subjective notation of which is suited to a primarily vocal–tactile mode of expression (instrumental 'commentary' on the taped sounds and the production of statistical textures).

Perhaps the most interesting aspect of the work, however, and a pointer to future development, is its evident suitability for balletic interpretation, which may be inferred not only from the scenic character of Stockhausen's music, but also from his mounting interest, associated with a new relaxed sociability of manner, in combining sound and choreographed gesture. *Trans* already provides some narrative interest in the characters of a reveille trumpeter and a viola player (the latter casting one's memory back to the poignant 'arme Saitenmann' of the *Chöre Für Doris*); as such it may be identified with the new expressive outlook of *Dr. K., Sternklang, Momente 1972,* and *Ylem*. As ballet, *Trans* could easily become one of Stockhausen's more widely accessible works.

Alphabet für Liège

1972: No. 36

'Visible music' for singer, other soloists, and natural resonators.
For performance in separate rooms of the same building, e.g. an art gallery.
Female voice, other soloists and media unspecified.
Duration unspecified but long, at least 3 hours.
A colour film, Alphabet for Liège, *duration 1 hour, is available for hire from Belgian Radio, RTB Liège.*

Am Himmel Wandre Ich

'In the sky I am walking', No. 36¹/2

12 songs based on American Indian poems, for 1, possibly 2, male and female unaccompanied voices.
Duration approx. 50 minutes.
Score available from the composer.

THE nature of *Alphabet für Liège*—a kind of exhibition, occupying many rooms, of various manifestations of the responses of animate and inanimate matter to the stimulus of musical vibrations—makes one regard the work at first as a 'one-off' affair in the same category as *Ensemble* or *Musik für ein Haus*: a work, that is, adapted to its time and circumstances to the point of being virtually unrepeatable. But in giving the work an opus number Stockhausen gives notice of the importance he attaches to investigation of this new musical territory, and thus of his intention to pursue the possibilities raised in *Alphabet*'s preliminary survey. In any case, thanks to television, 'one-off' events can no longer be classed as ephemeral.[1]

Alphabet is a new *Originale*: its title signifies 'the rudiments of a new musical language', and in it Stockhausen returns again with enthusiasm to the spirit of research which animates the earlier work and, before it, the first electronic studies. *Originale* was a study in alternative notations: the effects of indirect stimulus—scripted or situational—upon activities of potentially musical significance. *Alphabet*, reflecting the composer's new directness of approach, studies the immediate physical responses of matter to

[1] The work was in fact restaged in La Rochelle in 1973.

sound: ripples produced in water, patterns assumed by powder on a vibrating surface, the gill movements of fish synchronizing with fluctuations of a musical signal, even the effects upon a living yeast mixture of specifically chosen frequencies.

Chladni Plate patterns

Demonstrations of a non-organic kind—sand patterns formed on a Chladni plate, for instance, or in a Kundt tube—form a routine part of elementary acoustics. During the past twenty years, however, primarily as a result of the development of the tape recorder, it has become possible to measure the long-term effects of exposure to various categories of sound upon living creatures, particularly man. In recent times attention has been focused upon the strange and hazardous consequences of high-amplitude infrasound upon the human central nervous system. Much fundamental research remains to be done: indeed, research into the sensory (as distinct from the merely communicative) correlates of sound vibration has barely begun, and in *Alphabet für Liège* Stockhausen is asserting the duty of the composer to take part, and his right to be taken seriously by the scientific community.

But there is another side to this study, and that is the beauty it reveals, the harmony it makes visible. His delight at the visible proof of music's power to bring man into sympathetic vibration with his environment links Stockhausen with the mediaeval philosopher, for whom music was the highest expression of spiritual order, and the key to all understanding.

Am Himmel Wandre leh

Sounds can do anything. They can kill. The whole Indian mantric tradition knows that with sounds you can concentrate on any part of the body and calm it down, excite it, even hurt it in the extreme. There are also special mantras, naturally, that can lift the spirit of a person up into supernatural regions so that he leaves his body.

This information must be taught in schools . . . We must know what the waves do to us—all the waves, most of the waves have no names, cosmic rays constantly bombarding and penetrating our bodies . . . People should use sounds for very particular things: to heal, to stir up certain abilities which are asleep.[2]

[2] Cott, *Stockhausen: Conversations*, pp. 81–2. Stockhausen several times refers in these conversations to the influence of sound or other environmental programming on animal behaviour. See p. 127, where he describes an encounter with factory-farm chickens, 'clucking along with Johann Strauss and laying eggs furiously'; with experiments at the University of Pennsylvania to test the threshold of pain in rats, using a colour-coded piano; 'Some rats even go beyond the red' (the killing threshold) (p. 133); and his own interest in 'parametric transformation' of fish: 'Let's say you have a fish that's a certain size, length and form: if you place it in water that has a higher electrical charge or more warmth for a longer time or put certain chemicals into it, you'll then see the fish blow up vertically and become a completely different species' (p. 102).

Ylem

1972: No. 37

For ensemble (19 or more players/singers): 4 Electric instruments (e.g. electronium, amplified cello with pedal filter, keyboard synthesizer, amplified saxophone and bassoon connected to VCS 3 synthesizer), placed at rear of stage; tamtam, vibraphone (1 player); electronic organ, harp, cello placed at front edge of stage, piano in centre stage; 10 or more players of portable instruments (e.g. flute, oboe, cor anglais, clarinet, bass clarinet, bassoon, horn, trumpet, trombone, violin).
Instrumentation variable; however tamtam very difficult to replace.
Duration c. 22 minutes.
Performance instructions available from the composer.
Recorded by the London Sinfonietta on DGG 2530 442.

'YLEM', 'for 19 or more players/singers', takes a fresh look at a recurrent Stockhausen image: the attenuation and compression, over an unusually long span of time, of a constellation of musical 'points'. The idea first appears in *Spiel für Orchester* of 1952; it is also found in *Mixtur* ('Translation'), in *Adieu*, at fig. 9, and most recently in the 'Russian Bridge' sequence of *Third Region of Hymnen with Orchestra*. In *Ylem* (Stockhausen says that the name means 'period of oscillation of the Universe', or alternatively, 'the mixture of free neutrons, protons, and electrons' from which the elements, planets, and ultimately life congealed) the cyclic image is stated with medieval directness. The piece begins with most of the players grouped in a circle around the piano at centre stage.

At an initial 'big bang' on the tamtam, the circle of players jerk their heads up and begin to play, pouring out a stream of repeated notes, each choosing either an E flat or A in the middle register. Almost immediately players and notes begin to disperse, in pitch, time, intensity, and space. The performers of portable instruments leave their places around the tamtam and move gradually out into the auditorium, taking up positions, with eyes closed, facing inwards, against the auditorium walls.

As the pitches become more and more spaced out during 11 minutes of general ritardando, they begin to take on a life of their own, making small, more or less complicated but mainly continuous variations in pitch, intensity, and/or timbre around a note, sometimes brief staccato flourishes, like miniature *Sternklang* constellations. 'In this *animation* of the individual notes,' Stockhausen suggests, 'the musicians can think

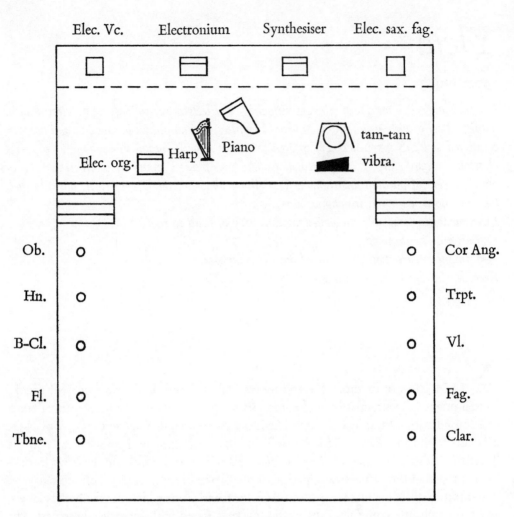

Ylem—diagram of staging. Instrumentation refers to
London Sinfonietta premiere 1973

of the diversity of quite differently animated planets in the universe.' Larger 'constellations' and 'clusters' between instrumentalists may also occur, but the composer insists that these should not be pre-planned, but arise spontaneously.

Four players of electric instruments (in the first performance an electronium, a synthesizer, and an amplified cello and saxophone/bassoon combination) remain on stage, and make little 'interstellar voyages' between chosen 'free-floating' pitches and timbres. Each of the four also has a short-wave receiver, which is switched on once during the expansion, and once during the contracting cycle. The player connects a pitch from the radio signal to an instrumental pitch in the same way.

After 11 minutes of expansion, by which time the repetition rate should have slowed to one attack every 90 seconds, one of the four 'connection players' calls out the syllable 'Hu!' and is answered by the other players (the cry 'Hu, Hu' also occurs in *Telemusik*, taken from a Suyai Indian chant). From this point the movement reverses, players and pitches gradually and symmetrically reconverging on the original tritone and their positions around the tamtam. At the second stroke, however, the tritone interval leaps a tone higher and the cycle begins again, only this time the players expand out into another dimension, as it were, moving out of the auditorium, continuing to play as long as they may be heard from inside.

Ylem compares in this respect with *Intervall* for two pianists, though it gives a complete oscillation where the earlier work confines itself to the converging part of the cycle. In both works (as in *Momente 1972*) the element of movement to and away from the stage puts a fresh interpretation on 'performance' and illustrates in poetic fashion Stockhausen's notion of the musical experience as a momentary glimpse of universal order.

Inori

1973-4: No. 38

Adorations for a soloist and orchestra.
The orchestra is divided into two principal groups:
Group I: 4 Flutes (2nd also piccolo), 4 oboes, 4 B flat clarinets (2nd also E flat), 4 trumpets, violins 14.12, antique cymbals, vibraphone, glockenspiel, rin (Japanese temple bells).
Group II: 8 Horns (4 high, 4 low), 3 bassoons, double bassoon, 2 trombones, bass trombone, tuba, piano, bell plates, 10 violas, 8 cellos, 8 double basses.
Duration: c. 67 minutes.

Vortrag über HU

'Lecture on HU'
1974: No. 38^{1}/2
for a singer.

'INORI' is a meditative work in a long line of such pieces. It is like an opera with only one character and no singing, only thoughts visible as gesture and audible as reciprocally modulated sound.

The work is composed around a series of 13 attitudes of prayer taken from various religions and cultures throughout the world. Each attitude is assigned a pitch, a vowel sound, a tempo and dynamic level, and the soloist's part in the score, referred to as the *Beter*—'one who prays', is notated simply as a melodic line. The music for the orchestra swells and dies, thickens and attenuates harmonically, pulsates and moves as if in direct response to the soloist's actions. Each basic pitch is associated with a specific harmonic spectrum, and each incantatory vowel with a certain distribution of instruments and registers. Dynamic levels (there are 60 of them) are modulated according to the amplitude of the soloist's gesture, arms outstretched for loud, folded inward for soft sounds; tessitura is modulated according to the position of the hands relative to the stage floor (actually a platform perilously raised over the oboes and double basses), higher meaning higher pitches, lower deeper.

The most important pitch of all is the note G above middle C, which occupies a central position in both pitch and dynamic ranges, and is also associated with the tempo MM: 71, as near as may be to the *tempo giusto* or heartbeat frequency of medieval theory, with the hands positioned over the heart, and with the syllable HU, representing the Divine Name, which has already figured in the musical fabric of *Telemusik* and *Ylem*.

Like *Mantra*, *Inori* is derived from an *Urgestalt* or musical germ in five parts distinguished by respective emphasis on rhythm, dynamic, melody, harmony, and polyphony—a sequence, as the reader will see, leading directly from the concrete to the transcendental. The whole work's structure represents a projection of this basic form on to a duration of about an hour. Technically, then, *Inori* is a continuation and expansion of the hermetic formal processes so brilliantly expounded in the earlier work for two pianists, and of the neo-classical sobriety of notation and expression associated with the form.

The listener is impressed straight away by the piece's full and rich orchestral sonorities, splendidly regulated and distributed (treble to the right, bass instruments to the left), and clearly pointed by a variety of metal percussion instruments, so creating an impression of a vast, enveloping but essentially transparent sound mass. Particularly surprising is the music's uninhibited allusion to classical tonality, or polytonal procedures of earlier this century (e.g. Stravinsky, Debussy, or Messiaen at half speed). Unisons and octaves feature prominently, also triadic combinations in up to seven parts, sometimes static, at other times moving in parallel. Rhythmically, too, *Inori* pursues the trend towards greater simplicity and explicitness in notation that makes *Mantra* so easy to come to grips with. Each phrase or harmonic combination gently pulsates in a given frequency corresponding to a fundamental pitch, and the inner regularity this device

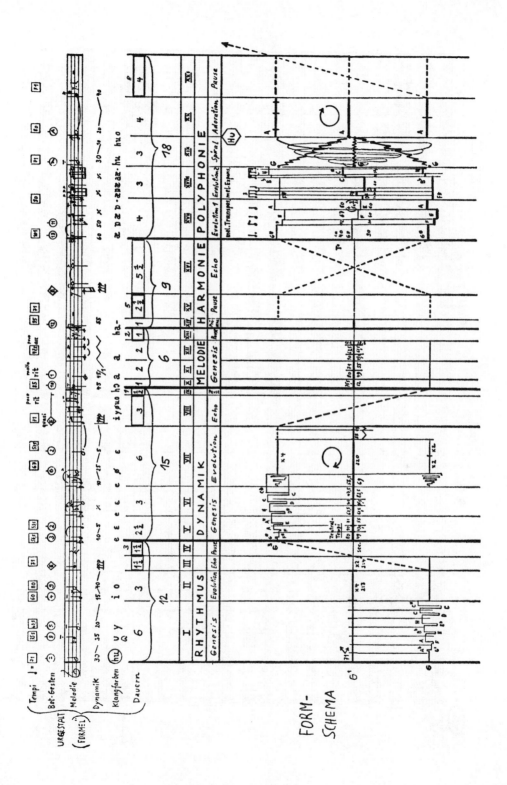

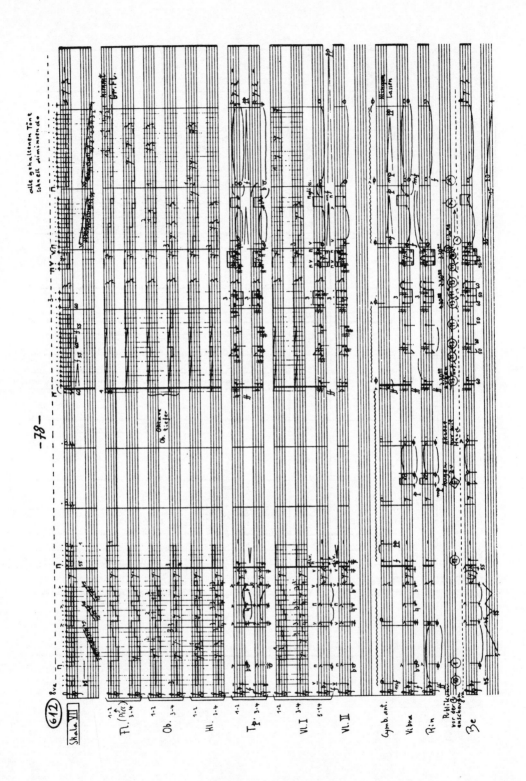

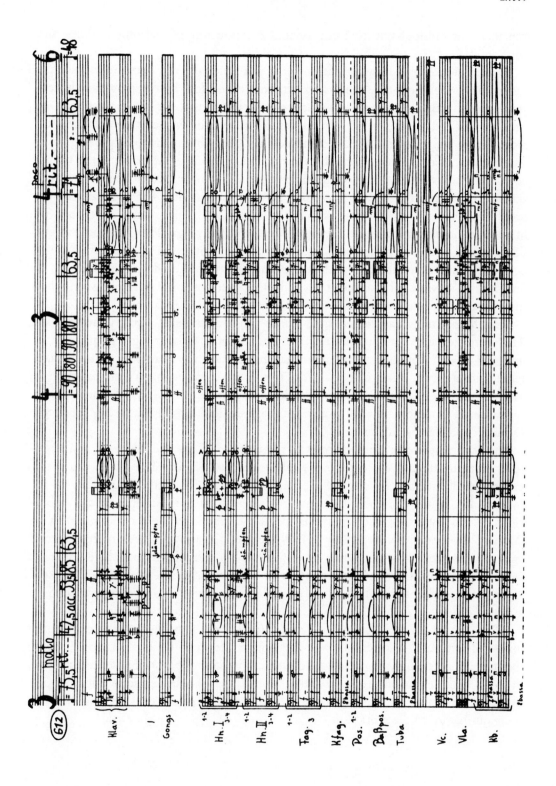

imparts to the music shows itself in playing and conducting of welcome freshness and elan.

Commissioned by a Japanese patron, *Inori* was originally rumoured to involve the conductor himself adopting the prayer attitudes called for. In assigning the choreographic conducting to a mime (though a solo instrumentalist or vocalist may be employed instead, a mute mime would seem to convey Stockhausen's essential meaning most clearly and eloquently), the composer has been able to introduce a degree of dramatic interplay between himself (as conductor) and his other persona (the mime) not otherwise available. On occasions, for instance, the mime's intricately beautiful actions are interrupted by the bass tuba (a rude fellow, this, harking back to the orchestrated cat-calls of *Momente*) who has to be silenced by her stamping her foot. At other times, in movements both personally and religiously significant, she looks to one side, cupping a hand to her ear as if attentive to distant sonorities beyond her influence or at the limits of audibility. In all, the mime's gestures are effective stylizations of Stockhausen's own clearly articulated conducting gestures; only once or twice, when she points dramatically upward, does the pose seem a little theatrical.

For all its systematization of design, *Inori* is rich in allusions of a purely musical sort. The protracted initial meditation on the symbolic note G is strongly reminiscent of liturgical chant over shifting organum-like harmonies, for example; some passages recall Mussorgsky's 'Death of Boris' scene from *Boris Godunov*, others, in less liturgical vein, sound more like Gershwin (Stockhausen's indebtedness to the anonymous specialism of American salon orchestration is as remarkable as his duty to Schoenberg, Debussy, and Bartók in this sense).

Spiritually, however, *Inori* belongs to the world of *Carré* and *Momente*, as a large-scale dramatization of the composer's relationship to his art. The mime is a literal expression of Stockhausen's concept of the soloist as a conductor figure, and in the longer view, of the composer as a vessel for receiving and transmitting cosmic vibrations. In this respect the mute mime is an exact antipode to the cheerful garrulity of *Momente*'s solo soprano. Temperamentally the music relates to *Carré*'s more reflective moods; it is more flowing, subtly and continuously modulated, and there are times when a note sustained by flutes, trumpets or horns detaches itself from the orchestral bas-relief to wander stereophonically around the auditorium in a discreet reference to the earlier score.

The 'lecture on HU', given by a singer (preferably female) serves to explain the principal structural features of *Inori*. Explanatory lectures by the composer having become an increasingly important (and publicly welcome) part of his concert routine, it seems both helpful and reasonable that Stockhausen should decide to publish a performing version of his explanatory text, one also perhaps more in keeping with the religious nature of the work.

'Atmen gibt das Leben . . .'

1974: No. 39

For unaccompanied mixed choir.
Duration: 5-7 minutes.

T HE composition of *Atmen gibt das Leben* arose from a request by the president of a German national federation of amateur choirs, for a piece singable by amateurs which might go beyond the traditional narrow limits of sentiment and style. This request Stockhausen conveyed to his private students as a compositional exercise to be done in place of the scheduled lesson, and he himself set to with the energy and secrecy of a schoolboy examination candidate, to satisfy the commission. His students were less enthusiastic at the idea, offended on the one hand at the idea of writing for amateurs, and unsure on the other hand of the level of skill for which they should write. Other than that, Stockhausen specified only that the music should be suitable for more than one text, and that the text itself should be neither Christian nor political.

Refusing to divulge his own efforts, Stockhausen gave his students until the following week to complete the pieces they had begun. Few did. After looking over their manuscripts, he produced his own, to a text by himself modelled on an apothegm by the Sufi philosopher Hazrat Inayat Khan.

The work is almost a miniature cantata, and falls into three defined sections. The first, *sehr langsam*, is quietly meditative something in the manner of *Adieu*, and is chiefly remarkable for making singers hum and keen while breathing in as well as while breathing out, as a way of musically illustrating the motion of breathing. The whole section is cued by vocal signs, one or two male voices force-breathing through pursed lips (as in the last minutes of *Hymnen*) in and out, with pauses between, as a kind of audible down-and-up beat, and with down-beat accents provided by sopranos one by one making a sharp percussive 'hic'. (Both the singing while breathing out and the hiccuping are hazardous to trained singers, perhaps less so to amateurs: one remembers the opposition Stockhausen encountered when he tried to introduce heavy breathing-in noises into the choral effects of *Momente*. One suspects that the use of microphones would be advisable, both to ease the strain on the voices concerned, and to make the musical purpose of the breathing sounds more immediately apparent.)

The second section, which introduces the 'singing' part of the text, is constructed as a little dramatic oratorio-like exchange between a tenor solo and the rest of the chorus, one which reminds me of the brief scene from Stravinsky's *Sermon, Narrative*

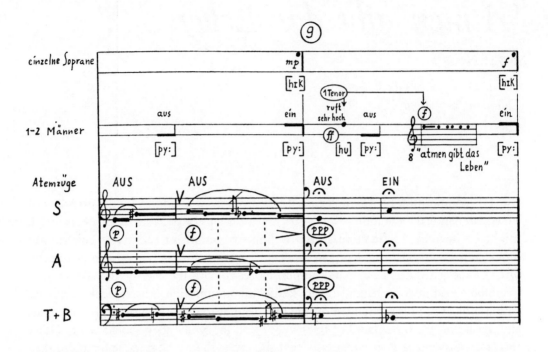

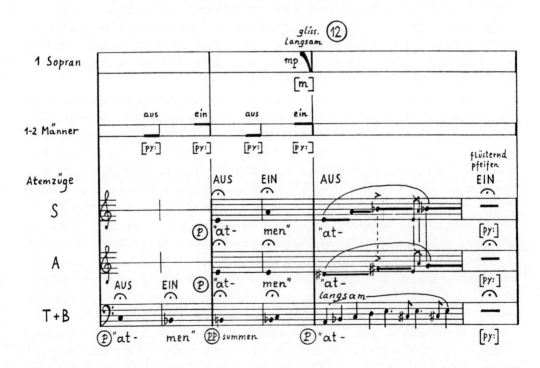

and Prayer where St Stephen confronts the Elders ('Ye do always resist . . .') It is interesting to see illustrated once again the idea of an individual emerging prophet-like from the masses to point the way ahead, interrupt the action, or even merely to react to a general mood as an individual (remember the 'deviant' players in *Trans*, for instance), and who is greeted by stony amazement on the part of his fellow musicians. Here too, 'all gaze in astonishment' while the tenor sings his piece: 'Doch erst, doch erst das Singen gibt die Gestalt', and react first by drawing back, then in a disquieted murmuration.

The third section, naturally, is sung. A chorale with obbligato soprano (*ossia* trumpet), it consists of the refrain heralded by the tenor sung in four parts and repeated three times, beginning very softly and slowly and gradually getting louder and faster to the end. At each repeat of the text the chorale appears to transpose upward, though the harmonies do not remain exactly the same. Besides building to a conventional climax, the process of gradually increasing tempo is one perhaps designed for ease of coordination in the absence of a conductor, another feature of the piece.

There is something strangely old-fashioned in Stockhausen's overall scenario, which has the choir initially standing or squatting fairly randomly on a dimly lit stage, raising the illumination as the tenor sings his message, and having the assembled chorus rise and face the audience to sing the closing chorale. The feeling is visual, in the symbolism of dark and light, and in the formalized double-take reactions and fixed expressions of the players, which seem to refer to expressionist films of the thirties as much as to gagaku musicians or puppets; and it is also, perhaps by virtue of this, old-fashioned in the sense a spectator has of the presence of an unseen régisseur—a much more potent presence, possibly, than that of the composer himself as conductor of a piece like *Originale*. Stockhausen is still very conscious of imagery reflecting the relationship of the individual and society, and of the boundary between the musician and his audience, and his music, however formulated, continues to work on a didactic level.

This sense of tradition is also reflected to a remarkable degree in the music of *Atmen*, which reaches back to those early pieces for choir a cappella which he wrote as a student. There is the same freedom in the solo part, the same 'floating' quality over a stolid choral foundation. As in *Choral*, we find a tendency to move in small intervals, and a harmonic construction stabilized by recurrent perfect fourth and fifth intervals. In the *Drei Chöre*, too, we noticed a reliance on textual cues for musical expression, the flexibility of the solo part, and a Lutheran density of choral writing. More than that, the division of the choir into dramatis personae, as in 'Armer junger Hirt', reappears in *Atmen*. Where there is a difference is in the greater ease of movement up and down by comparison with the earlier works, which tend to fall in pitch with more control than they leap upward. Like the early works, *Atmen gibt das Leben* . . . is dedicated to Doris Stockhausen, on this occasion as a birthday present. An alternative text from Hazrat Inayat Khan may be sung to the music, in which case the title becomes *Schlafen ist erquickend* ('sleeping is reviving').

Herbstmusik

1974: No. 40

Autumn actions for four players:
1. *'Nailing a roof' (Duo with Accompaniment).*
2. *'Breaking wood' (Quartet).*
3. *'Threshing' (Trio).*
4. *'Fallen leaves and falling Rain' (Duo).*
The stage set comprises an uncompleted box-frame shed, rear centre-stage, a square plastic paddling pool covered over with and containing leaves, front centre-stage, a pile of unthreshed seed grass stage left, four chairs with bundles of sticks stage right. The instrumentation comprises claw-hammers, nails, planks of wood, threshing flails, water sprinklers. Players 3 and 4 play viola and B flat clarinet respectively.
Duration: c. 70 minutes.

Laub und Regen

1974: No. 40^{I}/2

Final duet from 'Herbstmusik' for clarinet and viola.

'HERBSTMUSIK' may be described as a radio play of few words and many sounds. The music of Autumn, to Stockhausen living out in the country, in a house looking out on a hill slope planted with young trees, belongs to the sounds and rhythms of harvesting and building. Autumn, like the luminous pre-dawn of *Trans*, is a mysterious time, a time of stillness, when sounds carry, hovering between an end and a beginning. The activities of Autumn are rites both of consummation (gathering in the harvest), and of preparation for winter (providing storage and shelter). The original idea for the work was simple and straightforward. Having written about the desirability of recording endangered oral traditions of music, Stockhausen thought of doing something practical to preserve some of the sounds and customs of his own locality which appeared to be on the verge of extinction. Threshing, for instance: 'Nobody threshes by hand any more, the people have forgotten how.'

The work is in four sections or scenes, which follow on without breaks. The first, 'Nailing a roof', consists largely of a two-part polyphony of hammering nails. The pattern of rhythmic relationship between the two hammerers is richly varied from totally synchronized to totally independent blows, and is ordered and described in detail. Both hammers and nails are exactly prescribed: the hammers having claws of unequal length, the nails comprising a series of five different lengths and thicknesses (for musical variety).

Hammering produces the same type of sound as Stockhausen's beloved impulses. The sound of two diverging trains of hammering is most vividly evoked in the composer's earlier music in *Telemusik* (the *Taku* beats at 19). What distinguished these from pure electronic impulses was their origin as physical percussion sounds; this fact was important to Stockhausen at the time, as we have seen, and now the subtler nuances, and more flexible patterning available to live performers bring this a stage further. Hammering solo had also formed part of the musical material of the recorded version of 'Intensität', in the sleeve note to which the composer remarks:

First I cleaned the timber with periodic [i.e. rhythmically regular] sandpapering and rasping. I then knocked in long nails one after another: at first individual ones completely, then groups of nails to different depths,and finally deeper until they were right in (big differences in pitch). . . . The 'intensity' of my playing conveyed itself directly to the other players. . . . The 'intensity' which I first interpreted as the purely physical one of hammering and sweating, turned suddenly into an extremely spiritual one, into a wealth of rhythmic polyphony.

In the second scene, the four players break twigs in front of microphones. Their actions are stylized in much the same way as the hammering of the previous action. They draw their stick material from separate bundles. These have been specially organized, so that the thickest of them, more branches than sticks, lie at the top. Beneath them, sticks of more modest thickness, and right at the bottom the thinnest twigs. The combined sound over the duration of this episode is devised therefore to shift gradually from a generally low, sharp, loud crackling to a delicate, almost inaudible (save with amplification) splintering. 'All resulting tones and noises from every individual player must be deliberately formed, varied, and carried through.'

'Threshing', the third scene, 'should create a very detached overall impression, with elegant, wonderfully far-out threshing movements, also the manner of pacing about. Not the slightest impression must be given that this is difficult or especially hard physical labour', instructs the composer. The sound vocabulary of this episode includes the swish of the flail through the air, the shock of it hitting the straw, and the occasional thud as a stroke connects with the stage through the straw. The sense of the movement is primarily one of rhythmic unity, though there is considerable variation in speed. Perhaps it corresponds to the sine wave as the first movement corresponds to the impulse.

The fourth and last episode, 'Fallen Leaves and Falling Rain', resembles nothing quite so much as an after-hours rough-and-tumble in freshly raked leaves. Unlike the third scene, this is intensely physical in impact, and since most of the action involves hurling the body (the player's own, or his (her) opposite number's) on to and around the stage cushioned by leaves, the sound material is predictably low and muffled in frequency, like numerous greatly magnified low-frequency passages in the composer's

Abbildung 2: Aufstellung des Instrumentariums und Verteilung der
Mikrophone und Lautsprecher mit technischer Schaltung.

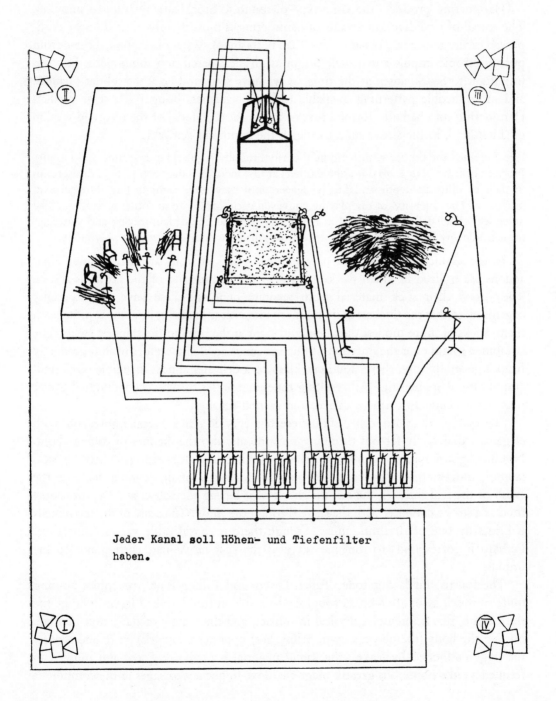

Jeder Kanal soll Höhen- und Tiefenfilter
haben.

electronic work, for instance *Kontakte*. These thumping sounds, greatly amplified, are offset by the sharp, rapid, measured tread and heel-click of Player 1, who from time to time encroaches on the main action with the ritual timing and step of a palace guard.

The sprinklers begin to sprinkle 'rain' on the two in the leaves. The sound of rain is like white noise without the lower frequencies. In electronic music such white noise can be superimposed on low frequency interference tones, but in real life the two types can actually be heard to interact. Gradually the pile of leaves is compacted by damp; gradually the actions of the players acquire clearer acoustic contours and richer overtone spectra. As they get more and more soaked, the protagonists' movements become increasingly stylized, finally assuming the rhythm of an eventual 'closing duet' played after the rain has stopped, on viola and clarinet.

Musik im Bauch

'Music in the breast'

1975: No. 41

Musical fable for six percussionists and music boxes.
A life-size mannequin, stuffed, with the face of an eagle, suspended by a wire attached to the crown of the head; 2 crotala boards (2 players); glockenspiel (1 player); another, smaller glockenspiel played at different times by the 3 foregoing players; marimbaphone (2 players); bell plates and tubular bell in G sharp (1 player).[1] Also 3 of a range of 12 music boxes.
Duration: c. 45 minutes.

Tierkreis

'Zodiac'

1975: No. 41$^{1}/_{2}$

12 melodies for music boxes from 'Musik im Bauch'.
I Aquarius; II Pisces; III Aries; IV Taurus; V Gemini; VI Cancer; VII Leo; VIII Virgo; IX Libra; X Scorpio; XI Sagittarius; XII Capricornus.

[1] Bell plates are tuned rectangular duralumin plates, suspended on a frame and played with special disc-head mallets of various diameters, constructed in a fashion analogous to piano hammers.

THIS is a fairy tale for children, related in dumbshow, somewhat in the spirit of Noh entertainment but with the important difference that music is central as well as incidental to the narrative. It may be interpreted as a variation on the traditional theme of a mystical quest, involving sacrifice and ensuing revelation. There are four characters, three of them like the three brothers so frequently encountered in mythology, and a mysterious figure like the good giant of olden tales, represented in this case by a stuffed mannequin with the head of an eagle. The brothers are played by the glockenspiel player and 2 crotala board players. The story, as in all good fables, is simple. It falls into three parts. In the first part the three brothers are discovered practising their own themes (i.e. 'doing their own respective things') against a measured background of tolling bells and marimbaphone strokes. The music for both bells and marimbaphone is the same music, though at a much slower rate, as that the brothers are playing. The brothers' playing is decorative but undifferentiated and essentially aimless and lacking in purposeful coordination. (Their instruments do not allow for dynamic variation and all three occupy the same pitch area.) The bell plates and marimbaphone could be said to represent opposite principles of organization. The former instruments are played with considerable drive and a great deal of contrast in dynamics and articulation; the latter by two players whose actions are completely stereotyped in the manner of mechanical dolls, and whose music, when it happens at all, interrupting interminable cycles of slowly rising and descending arms, is lifeless and unvarying.

In the second part the brothers abandon their instruments and take up thin rods which they swish through the air a bit like practising samurai but wearing the intense facial expressions of characters out of a Fritz Lang silent film. When the swishing is done, each player to his own rhythm, and we have heard what purposeful action sounds like, the three approach the silent mannequin suspended in the centre and a little nearer the front of stage. For the first London performance the dummy was dressed in the composer's distinctive uniform of frilly white shirt and Ivy League jeans, and festooned with myriad strings of small Indian bells. Cautiously they pat the figure with their wands. The bells tinkle. They pat faster, as if trying to keep as many bells in motion as possible. The sound here is reminiscent of *Kontakte*. Then, putting order into their actions, the three players form into a druid circle and pace slowly, then faster round the mannequin, their strokes, always sharp and abrupt, falling gradually harder to produce a thudding accompaniment to the shimmer of jingles. On a signal from the tubular bell they stop. Followed by the fixed stares of his companions one of the brother characters runs offstage, to return bearing a pair of shears as big as those of the scissor-man in *Struwwelpeter*. Deftly inserting the blades between the buttons of the mannequin's shirt, he makes one or two quick snips and then reaches into the cavity and removes a small wooden box. This he opens and places reverently on a low table front of stage right, in front of a microphone. The box begins to play the same music, heard over a speaker in a corresponding position, that he was playing at the start. Kneeling

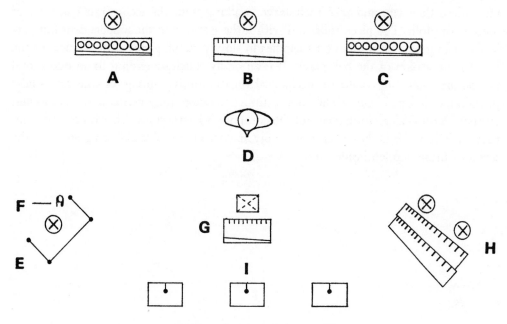

A, C: Crotala boards
B: Glockenspiel (played with sticks)
D: Suspended mannequin
E: Bell-plates
F: Tubular bell in G sharp
G: Small glockenspiel and cushion
H: Marimbaphone
I: 3 small low tables with individual microphones

Note: The positions of loudspeakers are not indicated.

at the other small glockenspiel which is placed centre stage in front of the mannequin, the first brother plays along with the music box when it begins the melody a second time. He is interrupted by a loud bang from a bell-plate and runs off stage.

The second brother repeats the action of extracting a music box, which he places on a table at centre stage after closing the first box, and whose music he follows on the small glockenspiel. Before he leaves the stage he sets both boxes playing. The third brother also finds a music box in the dummy after a good deal of jingling about, which he places on a table stage left and starts after closing the first two boxes. He imitates its melody, again at pitch, on the small glockenspiel, then, having wound up the first box with a flourish and restarted all three, he salutes the mannequin with an elegant bow and departs, leaving the boxes to run down. After a while the marimbaphone players reach the end of their run and take their leave, walking with the exaggerated stiffness of mechanical dolls. The piece ends, and with it the story, with the independent but perfectly distinguishable music box melodies in slowly running-down opposition to the last defiant strokes of the bell plates. It is an oddly touching ending to an odd moral tale on the conflicting values of mechanical versus intuitive timing, of true versus false precision, of independence versus cooperation, of a questioning versus an unquestioning attitude to musical performance and the composer's instructions. That is how an adult may see it. To a child, however, it is simply an enchanting fable about a giant with the secret of music hidden inside him.

Epilogue

LOOKING back over twenty-five years of Stockhausen's composing life, one sees a cyclic pattern emerging. His music in the fifties is characterized by extreme surface differentiation made audibly coherent by progressively more refined techniques of performer inflection. During this period he appears to view music as the expression in sound of fundamentally intellectual models; even though his ideas of organization relate ever more closely to acoustical processes, their manner of reconstruction remains essentially abstract, i.e. based on classification and permutation of a range of sound categories. This first stage reaches a peak and turning-point with *Kontakte*, and is succeeded in the sixties by a development in the opposite direction, in which his attention is focused on the sensual and allusive properties of sounds themselves, and his music is designed to demonstrate that sounds we ordinarily classify as different are acoustically related. This stage of his development reaches its extreme with *Stimmung* and the *Aus den Sieben Tagen* texts of 1968. A new period of synthesis is signalled with *Mantra*, which combines the formal objectivity of the fifties with the continuity of movement and sound-relationship characteristic of his music in the sixties. The sense of evolving in a circle and beginning again becomes increasingly clear during the latter years of the sixties, from hints like *Spiral*'s distant reference to Schaeffer's 'dynamic melody' theory, or *Sternklang*'s revival of the earlier 'star sound' ideal, or *Mantra*'s allusion to Cage's prepared piano, to such obvious signs as the 1972 Stockhausen retrospective in Paris, including first public performances of the earliest pieces, and the composer's 1973 restoration of *Spiel*.

All Stockhausen's music is serially orientated, even his most 'minimal' scores. At a very early stage he rejected the numerical organization of *materials* characteristic of conventional serialism, in favour of a system based on *interval*, i.e. degrees of differentiation. Alone among present-day composers Stockhausen has refined and extended our awareness of audible change, particularly in complex sounds. His attraction to rich, fluid textures derives to a great extent from a practical involvement with recording media. Stockhausen's ears are attuned to radio, and his imagery and manipulation of sound material frequently draw on the profounder implications of quite familiar radio and tape effects, for example static, tuning in or out of a broadcasting frequency, or mutual interference of adjacent stations on radio, and variable playback speeds, feedback, and 'hard cutting' in tape recording.

He is fascinated by pair-symmetries and the reconciliation of opposites. Two-part writing predominates in all his piano pieces, and double formations representing reciprocal tendencies are a consistent feature of his style, in *Schlagtrio*, *Kontakte*, *Mikrophonie I*, *Solo*, *Pole*, and *Mantra*. In works combining live and electronic elements they too function reciprocally.

Despite outward appearances of calculated impersonality, it will now be apparent that Stockhausen's music is greatly influenced by his emotional condition, to the extent that one may even say that the music is a biography of the man. Temperamentally he oscillates between periods of buoyant self-reliance and periods of extreme dependence upon other people; one can gauge his mood at the time of composing a particular piece to some extent by whether and how much he imposes either on technique or on the emotional sympathy of his performers. How he feels may also be indicated by the instruments and notational style he chooses. The piano, for instance, is typically associated with a rational determination of form: from the piano's imposition of order on the material of *Kontra-Punkte* to the stabilizing rationality attributed to the pianist Aloys Kontarsky in the Stockhausen ensemble's performances of intuitive music. The tamtam repeatedly appears as an image of generation, in *Kontakte*, *Momente*, *Mixtur*, *Ylem*: an image probably derived from his studies in *musique concrète*. Wind instruments, woodwind especially, serve as emotional complement to the intellectual piano. When Stockhausen wants to make his feelings public he uses voices—solo to express himself, choral groups to express how he feels about the society in which he finds himself (the more intelligible his text, the more confident he feels, as a rule). Unpitched percussion instruments generally signify division and change, by articulation of formal divisions (by analogy with consonantal action in speech), as in *Kreuzspiel*, *Mixtur*, *Telemusik*, and *Mantra*, or alternatively to show that the prevailing mode of organization is gestural, as in *Spiel*, *Punkte 1952*, *Kontakte*, and naturally *Zyklus*. Apart from his early Sonatine, Stockhausen has shown little interest in string instruments except as an orchestral sonority. A sentimental association is suggested by the early song 'Der Arme Saitenmann', however, and allusions to the string style of Bartók are frequent in his later works.

Of course strings play only a minor role in the jazz big-band sound which has exerted such a powerful influence on Stockhausen's style of expression and instrumentation, in its opposition of solo and block sonorities, its delineation of structure by changes of timbre and density, and its characteristically 'sprung' rhythms. An awareness of jazz timing, and of its intuitive discipline, peculiar instrumental combinations, and exceptional blend of sonorities, all are constant features of Stockhausen's approach to music from the Sonatine to *Trans*.

Predictions are unreliable, but it is clear that with *Mantra* Stockhausen has entered a new phase of emotional detachment and technical restraint. He seems to have discovered a sympathy with neo-classical artificiality at a time when many of his most pressing problems of the sixties have at last been overcome. These include the longstanding technical difficulties of intermodulation, resolved in his invention of the

'Modul 69B', his successful training of performers to realize intuitive and process scores, and not least his having finally won public acceptance and interest in these most demanding works.

His latest compositions, including *Alphabet* and *Ylem*, rely much less on emotional preconditioning. Instead we are presented with concrete situations—sometimes theatrical, sometimes simply procedural—out of which the music arises and to which it constantly refers. We may compare this development with the changeover from sound assemblage to sound processing in the synthesis of material for *Kontakte* in 1959.

Another important development indicated in *Mantra* is the composer's surprisingly late conversion to contrapuntal thinking. This has interesting implications for the future of live electronic music. We may expect a change from *Mixtur* and *Mikrophonie II*, in which ring modulation functions as a source of harmonic tension ('dissonance' in classical tonality), or *Mantra*, in which timbre-transformation corresponds more closely to classical key-modulation, to a new kind of intermodulation in which selected characteristics of one instrumental 'layer' may be imposed directly upon another live or pre-recorded music, the novelty being that both modulating and carrier signals may be equally flexible. Such a development is clearly within Stockhausen's reach.

He is also likely to continue using and refining the transformational notation developed for the orchestra of *Third Region of Hymnen with Orchestra*; on the evidence of *Fresco* and *Alphabet* there is also a strong likelihood that he will pay increasing attention to techniques of sound reproduction. There is much to be found out concerning large-scale loudspeakers, and the operation of infrasound on audience perceptions. In contrast to the static, enclosed spaces of *Carré*, *Kontakte*, *Hymnen*, and the Expo '70 auditorium, we may see the production of static, three-dimensional sound sculpture, experienceable only by the audience's own movement, and more sound mobiles of the kind first envisaged for *Carré* and *Kontakte* but not achieved then. These two works, and perhaps *Momente* as well, may ultimately be revised to bring out their latent spatial movement.

But enough. These are only the idle speculations of a prejudiced observer. Stockhausen's work of exploration continues. It is up to us to follow.

Appendix:

Compositions unfinished or for other reasons unpublished[1]

1. 'Study on one sound'. Musique concrète. December 1952.
   Produced a few days before the *Konkrete Etüde*, subsequently discarded. Sketches survive. The work to which Stockhausen presumably refers in his letter to Eimert (see p. 39).

2. *Nr. 5* for 10 Instruments. (1952). Original version of what became *Kontra-Punkte* (note change of numbering). Form-scheme the same, though serially much 'purer' than *Kontra-Punkte*; however the pitches are different, and the rhythms much more complicated, than the later version.

3. Piano Piece '5½'.

4. Piano Piece '6½'.
   Both pieces date from 1954, and relate to Pieces V and VI respectively. They were first performed 18 January 1974 by Aloys Kontarsky, at a seminar in the Musikhochschule, Cologne.

5. *Monophonie* (1960–). Unfinished work for orchestra. Wind and percussion instruments, including two pianos and guitar, are distributed in front of and over a multi-level stage with side and rear curtains. Behind the rear curtain, unseen, play the strings under a second conductor, making a 'wall of sound' as an acoustic backdrop (a situation like *Trans*, but in reverse). Complicated hand signals were devised to cue in the players at their various stage levels. Only one page of music was sketched before contractual difficulties forced Stockhausen to abandon the composition for the time being.

6. *Projektion für Orchester* (1967–). Unfinished work for orchestra divided in 9 mixed groups of 8–10 players. Of *c.* 25 minutes' duration, *Projektion* is largely sketched in short score, though a few pages have been fully orchestrated. One of these densely-written pages invites comparison with the last (1966) revision of *Punkte*, though the orchestral division and parallel harmonic writing also suggests the style of *Trans*. It was Stockhausen's original idea to have the work performed against a film back projection of the same orchestra playing the piece, thus giving the performance a simultaneous 'present' and two layers of 'past' tense. The two filmed performances would presumably be intended to be relayed over separate loudspeaker

[1] For this information I am particularly indebted to Richard Toop.

systems. The musical material of *Projektion* is designed in part to allow 'filtering out' of various layers of music at different times, and also performance at different tempi.

7. *Vision* for two pianos (1969–). Unfinished and set aside for the composition of *Mantra*, *Vision* was to have been a piece based on actions not normally associated with piano playing (e.g. typewriting). Five pages of sketch score were written, using a mixture of *Pole/Expo* sign language and written exhortations in the manner of *Aus den Sieben Tagen*. Stockhausen discusses the work briefly in Cott: *Stockhausen: Conversations*.

8. *Singreadfeel* (1970). For singer and special 'Instrument Case' containing 'touch objects', note stand, 2 pages of text and music, 1 rin (Japanese temple bell) with cushion and beater, and a pair of asbestos gloves. Also required are a short-wave radio, 5 tumblers containing different drinks, a tuning fork if needed, a hand basin containing perfumed water, and a hand towel.

The performer opens the instrument case, the lid of which forms the note stand, grasps the 'touch object' in both hands and chants selected text fragments from *On Yoga I* by Sri Aurobindo. Singing is to be as continuous as possible, ideally each fragment being performed in a single breath. The 'touch object' consists of two identical aluminium castings of mildly erotic nature (different editions for 'Gentlemen' and 'Ladies' are prescribed), one of which is heated, the other cooled electrically. Current is switched on at the start of a performance, which ends abruptly when either object becomes too hot or cold to handle.

A joke piece, it may be compared with Hugh Davies' 'shozyg' invention, a kind of Harlequinade doctor's kit containing all manner of curious and commonplace sound-producing objects.

Bibliography

Part 1 *Books, including periodicals in book format devoted to a single topic*

BOEHMER Konrad, *Zur Theorie der offenen Form in der Neuen Musik.* Tonos, Darmstadt, 1967. *(Piano Piece XI.)*

BOULEZ Pierre, *Boulez on music today.* Faber, London, 1971.
  Rélévés d'Apprenti. Editions du Seuil, Paris, 1966.

CAGE John, *Silence.* Wesleyan University Press, Connecticut, 1961.

CLOUGH Francis F. and CUMING Geoffrey J., *The World's Encyclopaedia of Recorded Music.* Sidgwick and Jackson, London, 1952.
  ibid. Second supplement 1951–2. Sidgwick and Jackson, London, 1953.
  ibid. Third supplement 1953–5. Sidgwick and Jackson, London, 1957.

COTT Jonathan, *Stockhausen: Conversations with the composer.* Robson, London, 1974. (Especially valuable on *Mantra, Trans.*)

GELHAAR Rolf, *Zur Komposition 'Ensemble'.* Darmstädter Beiträge zur Neue Musik, Heft XI, Schott, Mainz, 1968.

GOLÉA Antoine, *Rencontres avec Pierre Boulez.* Julliard, Paris, 1958. (Boulez on *Piece XI.*)

HÄUSLER Josef, *Musik im 20. Jahrhundert.* Schünemann, Bremen, 1969.

HEISENBÜTTEL Helmut, *Einfache grammatische Meditationen.* Walter, Breisgau, 1955. (*Mikrophonie II* text.)

HELMHOLTZ Hermann, *On the sensations of tone.* 4th edition, 1874, Dover, New York, 1954.

HERZFELD Friedrich, *Musica nova.* Ullstein, Berlin, 1954.

HERZOGENRATH Wulf (ed.), *Selbstdarstellung: Künstler über sich.* Droste, Dusseldorf, 1973. (Includes Stockhausen: Four criteria of electronic music) *(Kontakte).*

LE CORBUSIER, *The Modulor.* Faber, London, 1954. (Influential concept of form.)

MILLER Glenn, *Glenn Miller's method for orchestral arranging.* Chappell, London, 1943. (Sample influence on orchestration, sonority.)

MOLES Abraham, *Les musiques experimentales.* Cercle d'Art Contemporain, Paris, 1960.

MOOSER R.-Aloys, *Panorama de la musique contemporaine.* René Kister, Geneva, 1953. (Reviews of *Spiel, Kontra-Punkte.*)
  Visage de la musique contemporaine 1957–61. Julliard, Paris, 1962. (Reviews of *Gruppen, Kontakte.*)

PRIEBERG Fred K., *Musica ex machina.* Ullstein, Berlin, 1960.

RITZEL Fred, *Musik für ein Haus.* Darmstädter Beiträge zur Neue Musik, Heft XII, Schott, Mainz, 1970. *(From the Seven Days.)*

SAMUEL Claude, *Panorama de l'art musical contemporain.* Gallimard, Paris, 1958.

SCHAEFFER Pierre, *A la recherche d'une musique concrète.* Editions du Seuil, Paris, 1952.
  La musique concrète. Presses Universitaires de France, Paris, 1967.

SCHILLINGER Joseph, *The Schillinger system of musical composition* (2 vols.). 4th ed., Carl Fischer, New York, 1946.

SCHOENBERG Arnold, *Letters*. Faber, London, 1964.

STEINECKE Wolfgang (ed.), *Darmstädter Beiträge zur Neuen Musik 1958*. Schott, Mainz, 1958. (Résumé of Darmstadt Courses and concerts 1946–58.)

STEPHAN Rudolf, *Neue Musik*. Vandenhoek und Ruprecht, Göttingen, 1958.

STOCKHAUSEN Karlheinz, *Texte Band I: zur elektronischen und instrumentalen musik*. DuMont Schauberg, Köln, 1963.

    Texte Band II: zu eigenen Werken; zur Kunst anderer. DuMont Schauberg, Köln, 1964.

    Texte Band III: zur Musik 1963–70. DuMont Schauberg, Köln, 1971.

    Vier Kriterien der elektronischen Musik. See Herzogenrath, W. (ed.).

STRAVINSKY Igor and CRAFT Robert, *Themes and episodes*. Knopf, New York, 1966. *(Carré.)*

WDR KÖLN, *Zwanzig Jahre Musik im Westdeutschen Rundfunk: eine Dokumentation der Hauptabteilung Musik 1948–1968*. Westdeutchen Rundfunk Köln, 1969. (Résumé of Musik der Zeit concerts, Eimert's evening lecture programme on new music, etc.).

WINCKEL Fritz, *Music, sound and sensation*. Dover, New York, 1967.

WÖRNER Karl H., *Karlheinz Stockhausen, Werk und Wollen 1950–1962*. Tonger, Rodenkirchen, 1963. (Includes contemporary press reviews omitted in translated later edition.)

    Stockhausen: Life and work. Faber, London, 1973. (Revised and updated.)

Part 2 *Periodical essays, articles, interviews*

BABBITT Milton, 'Twelve-tone rhythmic structure and the electronic medium', *Perspectives of New Music* I/1, Princeton, 1962 (U.S. criticism of post-war European developments).

BEYER Robert, 'Elektronische Musik', *Melos* 1954/2, Mainz. (Optimistic predictions for electronic timbre synthesis by a pioneer researcher.)

BOCKELMANN Peter, 'Karlheinz Stockhausen antwortet', *Melos* 1971/10, Mainz.

BOULEZ Pierre, 'At the ends of fruitful land . . .', *Die Reihe* 1, UE/Presser, Pennsylvania, 1958. (Indirect criticism of Piano Piece I.)

    'Eventuellement . . .' *La Revue Musicale* 212 (L'Œuvre du Vingtième Siècle'), Richard-Masse, Paris, April 1952.

    'Music and Invention', *The Listener*, London, 22 January 1970.

    'Schönberg is dead', *The Score* 6, London, May 1952.

BURT Francis, 'An antithesis: the aesthetic aspect', *The Score* 19, London, March 1957. *(Studie I, II.)*

CARDEW Cornelius, 'Notation—interpretation, etc.', *Tempo* 58, London, 1961.

    'Report on Stockhausen's "Carré" ' (in 2 parts). *Musical Times*, London, October–November, 1961.

CONNOLLY Ray, 'So you think you have an ear for music?' *Evening Standard*, London, 16 September 1971.

COTT Jonathan, 'Being in Sound', *American Review* 16, February 1973, Bantam, New York.

    'Talking (Whew!) to Karlheinz Stockhausen', *The Rolling Stone*, 8 July 1971, Straight Arrow Publishers, New York. (Both the above are incorporated in Cott: *Stockhausen* listed above.)

CRAFT Robert, 'Boulez and Stockhausen', *The Score* 24, London, November 1958. *(Zeitmasze.)*

DAVIES Hugh, 'Working with Stockhausen', *Composer* 27, London, 1968. *(Mikrophonie I.)*

EIMERT Herbert, 'Der Sinus-Ton', *Melos* 1954/6, Mainz.

'So begann der elektronische Musik', *Melos* 1972/1, Mainz.

'How electronic music began', *Musical Times*, London, April 1972. (Abridged translation of above.)

GOEYVAERTS Karel, 'The sound material of electronic music', *Die Reihe* 1, UE/Presser, Pennsylvania, 1958.

'Was aus Wörten wird', *Melos* 1972/3, Mainz.

HELM Everett, 'Current Chronicle: Germany', *Musical Quarterly* 37/4, Fischer, New York, 1951. (The politics of music in post-war Germany, by a co-founder of the Darmstadt New Music Courses.)

HEYWORTH Peter, 'Composer-prophet', *The Observer*, London, 25 April 1971.

'Spiritual dimensions', *Music and Musicians,* London, May 1971. (Essential reading, this wide-ranging interview forms the basis of *The Observer* profile above. Comments on *Third Region of Hymnen with Orchestra.)*

KELLER Max Eugen, 'Gehörte und komponierte Struktur in Stockhausen's "Kreuzspiel" ', *Melos* 1972/1–2, Mainz.

KIRCHMEYER Helmut, 'Zur Entstehungs- und Problemgeschichte der "Kontakte" von Karlheinz Stockhausen', essay enclosed with disc Wergo 60009.

KONTARSKY Aloys, 'Notation for piano', *Perspectives of New Music* X/2, Princeton, 1972.

MACONIE Robin, ' "Momente" in London', *Tempo* 104, London, 1973.

'Stockhausen's "Mantra" ', *The Listener*, 30 August 1973, London.

MARTIN Frank, 'Schönberg and Ourselves', *The Score* 6, May 1952, London.

MEYER-EPPLER Werner, 'Statistic and psychologic problems of sound', *Die Reihe* 1, UE/Presser, Pennsylvania, 1958.

OAKES Meredith, 'Stockhausen explains?', *Music and Musicians,* London, April 1972.

ORGA Ates, 'Stockhausen's "Momente" ', BBC Programme note, 15 January 1973. (Includes libretto of 1972 'Europa' version.)

PALMER Tony, 'Sound of mind, wind and limb', *Sunday Times* magazine, 11 March 1973, London.

POUSSEUR Henri, 'Formal elements in a new compositional material', *Die Reihe* I, UE/Presser, Pennsylvania, 1958. (Difficulties facing early electronic composers.)

SCHAEFFER Pierre, 'Introduction à la musique concrète', *Polyphonie* No. 6, 'La Musique Mecanisée', Richard-Masse, Paris, 1950.

'L'objet musical', *La Revue Musicale* 212 (L'Œuvre du Vingtième Siècle'), Richard-Masse, Paris, April 1952.

STADLEN Peter, 'Serialism Reconsidered', *The Score* 22, London, February 1958.

STEIN Leonard, 'The performer's point of view', *Perspectives of New Music* I/2, Princeton, 1963. *(Piano Piece* I).

STOCKHAUSEN Karlheinz

   1. *Articles in English*

     'Actualia' *Die Reihe* 1, UE/Presser, Pennsylvania, 1958. *(Gesang der Jünglinge.)*

     'The concept of unity in musical time'. *Perspectives of New Music,* I/1, Princeton, 1962. *(Kontakte.)*

     'Electronic and instrumental music', *Die Reihe* 5, UE/Presser, Pennsylvania, 1961.

'. . . how time passes . . .', *Die Reihe* 3, UE/Presser, Pennsylvania, 1959. *(Zeitmasze, Gruppen,* Pieces V–XI.)

'Music in space', *Die Reihe* 5, UE/Presser, Pennsylvania, 1961.

'The origins of electronic music', *Music and Musicians*, London, July 1971. (Prompted Eimert to reply with 'How electronic music began'—see above.)

'Speech and music', *Die Reihe* 6, UE/Presser, Pennsylvania, 1964.

'Structure and experiential time', *Die Reihe* 2, UE/Presser, Pennsylvania, 1958.

'A Stockhausen Miscellany', *Music and Musicians*, London, October 1972. (On the vocal tradition in Europe, letters to DGG, Boulez) *(Mixtur.)*

2. *Interviews in English*

see Cott, *Rolling Stone*, 8 July 1971.

see Connolly, *Evening Standard,* 16 September 1971.

see Heyworth, *Music and Musicians*, May 1971.

'Notes and Commentaries', *New Yorker,* New York, 18 January 1964. *(Momente.)*

see Palmer, *Sunday Times* magazine, 11 March 1973.

3. *Programme notes in English*

Programme, English Bach Festival, London, 27 April–7 May 1971. *(Expo für 3, Hymnen, Mantra,* Piece IX, *Pole für 2, Prozession.)*

English translations of Stockhausen's notes are published on the sleeves of the following composer-supervised recordings in addition to those by DGG:

Kontakte with instruments (Vox), *Mikrophonie I* and *II* (CBS), *Momente 1965* (Nonesuch), Complete Piano Music (CBS), *Prozession* (Vox), *Refrain* (Time Series 2000/Mainstream), *Refrain* 1968 (Vox), *Zyklus* (Time Series 2000/Mainstream).

TIMES LITERARY SUPPLEMENT, 'Musical vibes and cosmic vibes', *Times Literary Supplement,* London, 2 March 1973.

TUDOR David, 'From piano to electronics', *Music and Musicians*, London, August 1972. (Collaboration with Stockhausen on Piano Pieces V–VIII. Comments often refer to early, unpublished versions.)

WÖRNER Karl, 'Current Chronicle', *Musical Quarterly* 45/1, Fischer, New York, 1954. (A perspective on the current European musical scene.)

Index

I. Compositions and Projects

Index

II. General Index

Index